Scientific and Technical Libraries

by

D.S. Thakur

Ess Ess Publications

4837/24, Ansari Road, Darya Ganj,
New Delhi-110 002
Tel: 011-23260807, 41563444
Fax: 011-41563334
E-mail: info@essessreference.com
www.essessreference.com

First Published **2006**

ISBN: 81-7000-497-7

Rs.1200/-

Published by:
Ess Ess Publications
4837/24, Ansari Road, Darya Ganj, New Delhi-110 002
Tel: 011-23260807, 41563444 Fax: 011-41563334
E-mail: info@essessreference.com
url: www.essessreference.com

Printed in India at:
Printline, New Delhi

Dedicated to :

ALL MEMBERS OF MY FAMILY

ACKNOWLEDGEMENTS

First and foremost I express my heartiest and profound gratitude to my supervisor Dr. K. G. Tyagi under whose guidance and inspiration I have accomplished my research work. I am grateful to all librarians, scientists and research scholars of the CSIR laboratories for their cooperation and help. I am very thankful to the library staff of the CSIR Headquarters and NISCAIR (formerly INSDOC).

I express my special thanks to Late Prof. (Dr.) S.M. Tripathi, former University Librarian and Head of School of Studies in Library and Information Science, Jiwaji University, Gwalior, for his help and constant support in the completion of my research work. I owe my special thanks to Prof. (Dr.) J. N. Gautam, Head, School of the Studies in Library and Information Science, Jiwaji University, Gwalior (MP), who inspired me to carry out Ph.D. work and supported me during the course of this study.

I owe my special thanks to Dr. Dev Raj Singh, former Sr. Library and Information Officer of NIPFP, New Delhi, who has discussed the issues involved in the study and has helped in its accomplishment. His indepth knowledge of the subject has helped me to a great extent to complete this study.

I sincerely thank faculty and staff members of the National Institute of Educational Planning and Administration (NIEPA), New Delhi, for their cooperation and encouragement. I wish to record my special thanks to Prof. Ved Prakash, Director, NIEPA for his support, guidance and valuable comments. I am thankful to Sh. P.R.R. Nair, Registrar, NIEPA for his encouragement and support. I am thankful to Prof. Marmar Mukhopadhyay, former Joint Director NIEPA for his inspiration and encouragement. I would like to express my gratitude to Dr. Arun C. Mehta, Senior Fellow, NIEPA for his suggestions.

I am also thankful to Dr. Shailendra Kumar, Head, Department of Library and Information Science, Delhi University,

Delhi for his help and support during the conduct of study and investigation. I am grateful to Dr. S. D. Khan, Librarian NIFM, Faridabad, for his kind support and encouragement. I am thankful to Dr. Sanjaya Mishra, Reader, IGNOU, New Delhi for his help and support. My thanks are also due to Dr. Jayashree Roy, Associate Fellow, NIEPA for advice and encouragement to publish this work. My special thanks are due to my colleagues at NIEPA for their encouragement and support. I am grateful to the professionals who inspired and encouraged me to devote my knowledge and energies towards this profession.

My parents and brother Shri K. S. Thakur have always encouraged and supported in my endeavours in life. Without their blessings, this work would not have accomplished. Last but not the least, I am grateful to my wife Smt. Anjana Thakur and my sons Master Vipul and Master Abhinav for their encouragement and many lost hours during which they would have been enjoying with me.

New Delhi **D. S. Thakur**

March 2006

PREFACE

Libraries are recognized as an integral part of education, research and society. They are endowed with the rich resources to meet the requirements of their users. "Libraries are not mere store houses, they are springs of knowledge, which flow out to irrigate the wide fields of education and culture". Quality of teaching, learning and research of any organisation largely depends upon the potential of the library to meet the expectations and requirements of its users. Special libraries came into existence at the dawn of the 20th century. Explosion in the growth of scientific and technical literature and paradigm shift in the access and use of information and communication technology (ICT) have posed a serious challenge to the scientific and technical libraries of different organisations such as ICAR, ICMR, DRDO, DAE, DST, DSIR in terms of their collection, management, services and application of ICT to deliver effective and efficient services. With the advent and use of ICT, the very nature of library and reference services has undergone a change. Hence, it is imperative that the development of the library and its services must be evaluated from time to time in order to bring continuous improvement and qualitative change in the overall functioning of the libraries.

The present book is an outcome of a research work based on a Ph.D. thesis in Library and Information Science on "Effectiveness and Use of Library and Information Services of the Laboratories of Council of Scientific and Industrial Research in India", awarded by Jiwāji University, Gwalior in 1997. Council of Scientific and Industrial Research (CSIR) is a premier autonomous scientific industrial research and development organisation established in 1942. Later, a chain of national laboratories and institutes were set up under its umbrella. Its multidisciplinary and multi-location network of 38 laboratories and 39 regional centres has significant roles in the socio-economic development and strategic growth of the country. These 38 laboratories belong to five groups, namely Physical and Earth Sciences Group (PESG) (5); Chemical Sciences Group (CSG) (7); Biological Sciences Group (BSG) (11); Engineering Sciences Group (ESG) (13); and Information Science Group (ISG) (2). These laboratories are engaged in research and development (R&D) in diverse fields, such as agriculture, food, chemicals, environment, healthcare, aerospace, electronics, leather, energy, housing, etc. CSIR has a team of around 8000 highly qualified scientists and engineers and 10,000 technical support personnel to deliver science-based services.

This book consists of nine chapters. Chapter one deals with the importance, functions, development and role of scientific and technical libraries. Chapter two brings out an overview of literature; third one deals with the organisational structure of CSIR. Chapter four is on the pure and applied research in India. It focuses on the role of universities in higher education and research, agricultural research, medical research, defence research, atomic research, electronics and information technology, oceanographic research, space research, Department of Science and Technology, Department of Scientific and Industrial Research and Department of Biotechnology. Chapter five presents application of information and communication technology (ICT) in scientific and technical libraries and discusses the issues pertaining to impact of information technology on library service, use of specific technologies in scientific and technical libraries, communication and information networks and future of electronic resources and web-enabled services. In the sixth chapter, national information centres established under the National Information System for Science and Technology (NISSAT) programme of Department of Scientific and Industrial Research (DSIR), Government of India have been discussed in terms of their objectives, functions, resources, services and publications. These centres are engaged to deliver excellent standard of services to the scientists and engineers working in the CSIR Laboratories and other research organisations of the country.

Chapter seven throws light on the assessment of the 34 libraries of CSIR Laboratories in terms of their budget allocation, library collections, document delivery and reference services and application of ICT to deliver effective and efficient services to the scientists, engineers and technologists of their respective organizations. In chapter eighth, efforts have been made to present the perceptions of library users mainly scientists and research scholars about the library collections, services and application of ICT in the libraries of CSIR Laboratories. A questionnaire was prepared to ascertain the users' perception about library services and a total of 500 questionnaires were distributed to the scientists and research scholars working in CSIR Laboratories on diverse fields. Based on their responses, the chapter discusses (the survey of 380 scientists and research scholars) issues pertaining to library collection, reference services, computerised services, organisation of reading material, reading room facilities, etc. The last chapter brings out main findings and makes suggestions for the improvement of library collection, services in library and to strengthen the use of ICT to deliver high caliber services in the libraries.

During the last decade, many developments have taken place in the information and communication technology sector. The book comprises broadly an application of new information technology in S&T libraries. I am confident that the book will definitely be a source of reference to develop libraries in a systematic and well-planned manner. It will consider the efforts in this research work and publication worthwhile, if the researchers and information professionals find the book valuable and useful source for understanding the needs of customers in special libraries and for acquisition of resources and extension of services and facilities in the libraries of scientific and technical organisations in India.

New Delhi — **D. S. Thakur**

March 2006

CONTENTS

List of Tables

1
Special Libraries: An Introduction

1.0 GENERAL

The establishment of the scientific, technical and research institutes, and such other organisations laid down the foundation for the genesis of special libraries. Earlier, these libraries were considered as entity and integral part of the parent body but later on these came to be called as special, research, scientific or technical libraries. These libraries came into existence as a phenomenon of the last part of the nineteenth century which marked the beginning of the new era of industrial revolution and development of scientific and technical researches. This period also witnessed the formation of academic societies and research institutions. Such institutions took major initiatives to establish their own libraries with a greater emphasis on specific information and documentation access. The research and technical libraries of the early industrial and business organisations at the time of the Industrial Revolution are thus the ancestors of the special libraries of the modern time. It is therefore rightly described that a "Special library is a product of the twentieth century. It is directly related to scientific and technological research and industrial development. Although in some loose sense of the term, it had existed since antiquity as made out by library historians, having limited subject collections and serving some special groups".[1]

Democratisation and industrialisation leading to the rapid growth of scientific inventions in the recent past, have made considerable impact on the development of the human mind and its means of communication. The immense growth of scientific literature from day to day researches and innovations had increased the necessity for a cogent entity for accumulation, organisation and effective use of all the recorded information at all levels. This was possible only with the growth and development of specialised information centres for the preservation, organisation and dissemination of materials related to their respective specialised fields. Thus enormous growth of subjects and the deluge of scientific publications created the necessity for specialised information centres. These scientific and technical libraries accumulate and retrieve information at the right time in order to meet the specialised needs of their readers.[2]

The emergence of scientific and technical libraries has been largely influenced by the following factors:

i) Exponential growth in the scientific and technical literatures, both print and electronic.

ii) Preservation, organisation, maintenance and dissemination of specific information.

iii) Active participation in the resource sharing activities.

iv) Exact and precise demand for specific information.

v) Speedy and easy access to the vast and ever increasing quantities of published information to scientists, research scholars and technologists.

vi) Utilising the research results for further growth of research areas.

vii) Use of new technological developments and information technologies, i.e., automation, networking, electronic communications, etc.

viii) Need for conducive environment to attract users by providing individual study carrels, adequate lighting, emergency light, air-conditioning, quiet environment, attractive furnishings and interiors.

The basic function of such libraries is to provide information service in accordance with the requirements of the researchers, scientists and engineers and objectives of the parent organisations.

1.1 IMPORTANCE OF SCIENTIFIC AND TECHNICAL LIBRARIES

Scientific and technical libraries are an imperative part of scientists and researchers without the use of which and without whose resources the scientific community of users cannot make the most efficient and effective use of their valuable time and talent. Stressing upon the importance of libraries, Paul Buck in his book entitled 'Libraries and Universities' remarked that "In truth and effect, the quality of teaching and research work in any institution is dependent upon the potential of the library to respond".[3] The well equipped and well organised research library is the basis of modern research and development of the organisation as well as the nation. The scientific research and information enhances the development of the nation and makes the country prosperous. The development of any country is based upon the foundation of quality research, which brings the nation at par with developed countries. The strength of a research system is largely dependent upon its capacity to create, organise, and use information. The effectiveness of research and development is dependent upon the information services discharged by the library and information centres of scientific and technical organisations.

The libraries have been repository of knowledge and information. The exponential growth of published literature in science and technology has enhanced the role and importance of libraries in acquiring, organizing and communicating the relevant, accurate and precise information to the scientists and researchers to achieve the organisational goals.

After the Indian independence, a large number of scientific and technical organisations came into existence. Their libraries and information centres offer multifarious functions and cater to the needs of a wide range of clientele having divergent interests and complex demands. Earlier these libraries were vested with the responsibility of preserving the literature for future, but today with the gradual growth of published literature, they are now endowed with rather more important functions of acquiring, organizing, preserving, analysing, interpreting, filtering and communicating information in a meaningful way to the clientele with a variety of needs. These scientific and technical libraries play a significant role in supporting research and development at scientific organisations by acquiring and maintaining the library resources and by rendering effective and a wide range of library and information services to their users. Their main objective is to maximize their utility by expanding the size of library collection and services through the use of information and communication technology (ICT). Top most students, talented scientists and scholars join reputed organisations that have well equipped infrastructure such as modern library facilities, labs and other academic facilities for the survival of research in the organisations.

1.2 OBJECTIVES OF THE SCIENTIFIC AND TECHNICAL LIBRARIES

The scientific and technical libraries exist to implement and to promote the interests and policies of institutions and organisations or parent bodies with which they are attached. The specialists of scientific and technical libraries make use of the specialised resources thereof in pursuit of their objectives and for furthering interest of the parent body. The objectives of the scientific and technical libraries are to provide the up-to-date information and the latest report about the research and developments within and outside the country to researchers, scientists, experts and managers who are involved in promoting the interests of the organisation. The clienteles of scientific and technical libraries require exact, up-to-date, accurate and timely information for their serious research work and programmes. Without exact up-to-date and timely information, the research work and programmes of the organisation may not progress in the manner expected. No organisation can bear losses not merely in terms of finance, but of time, energy and prestige of the organisation and parent body. In fact, no scientific research can be carried out in the absence of accurate, up-to-date and timely information. The library acts as a crucial resource and learning centre of the organisation to meet the information needs of its users for the growth and overall development of the organisation. The main objective of a scientific and technical library is to meet the information needs of its users for the growth and overall prosperity of the organisation.[4]

Users of these libraries make use of the resources for their research and project works. The objective of the library is to provide the latest information to the scientists and research scholars who visit the institute in various training programmes. The library acts as a crucial resource and learning centre of the Institute to meet the information needs of its clientele for the growth and overall development of the organisation. Scientists, research scholars, technical personnel and decision makers rely on accurate, relevant, timely and easily accessible information that may assist them in the research and development of the organisation. Value of information and information services to organisations depends to the extent the information provided meets the expectations and requirements of their users. Information can be from any source. It could be from electronic databases, books, journals, reports, proceedings and reference services provided by the library professionals. The value of information is determined by its relevance and importance to the scientists, scholars and researchers for the end result of their research and decision being made. Today users need information that should not only be accurate, timely and relevant but also presented, interpreted and filtered in a meaningful way. Collection and dissemination of data and information and the creation and sharing of knowledge are crucial to the success of an organisation in the age of global competitiveness.[5]

1.3 FUNCTIONS OF SCIENTIFIC AND TECHNICAL LIBRARIES

The primary functions of scientific and technical library are to provide timely, exact and up-to-date information to the scientists, research workers and technologists in their areas of specialisation. In addition, these libraries are required to keep their users abreast of current research and development (R&D) programmes of national and international importance. Some significant functions of scientific and technical libraries are as under:

1. Development of resource centre containing books, periodicals, research/ project reports, grey literature and others and non-book material, such as microfilms/ microfiches, slides, audio video cassettes, CD-ROMs and online databases.
2. Online list of new additions, journals subscribed and discontinued in the library from time to time and routing of periodicals and current contents of periodicals.
3. Generate the online documentation activities like library bulletins, newspaper clippings on latest research and developments, list of theses, dissertations and research project reports, bibliographical references and OPAC (Online Public Access Catalogue) and to specify the current and new services of the library.
4. Render online reference services, such as list of new additions, list of journals subscribed/discontinued, current contents of periodicals (CCP), bibliographical references and OPAC (Online Public Access Catalogue) and to specify the current and new services of the library through intranet across the organisation.
5. Develop and provide Current Awareness Service (CAS) on demand and in anticipation of the interest of organisation.
6. Indexing of journal articles, reports and their abstracting.
7. SDI service - Provide pinpointed and precise information to satisfy the profile of users.
8. Computerise the library activities of the organisation, including acquisition, cataloguing, circulation, serials control, document delivery, interlibrary loan, resource sharing, etc.
9. Systematic organisation and management of reading material for easy access.
10. Translation of foreign language scientific literature.
11. Develop the scholarly publications from scientists, research scholars and technical personnel and enable them to be accessible through intranet and extranet.

12. Develop the Knowledge Management System of the organisation by integrating the online and in-house databases and capture the expertise and technical knowledge from the scientists, technical people and intellectuals.

1.4 SCIENTIFIC AND TECHNICAL LIBRARIES: INDIAN SCENARIO

Scientific and technical libraries emerged when the country became independent from the British regime. But it was World War II which brought a phenomenal growth of special libraries, stimulated by the tremendous increase in the establishment of a number of scientific, technical, business, and industrial research and development organisations. The flood of scientific and technological materials produced and the need for transfer of information and technology for an immediate utilitarian value gave rise to such type of libraries.

The establishment of these research organisations, can be said to be a pertinent cause behind formation of associations and societies of librarians. Such associations and societies, specifically of information officers/specialists/librarians, are a 20th century phenomenon. Before this, however, information officers/specialists/librarians appear to have been members of general library associations. With increase in their number and growing specialisations, they realised that their objectives were not being fulfilled by those associations adequately. Since the existing associations had greater representation of public and academic libraries, the concerns of those associations were obviously on the issues pertaining to these types of libraries. Hence the need for the associations of scientific and technical libraries for having proper platform dedicated to their problems was realised. These professional associations and societies conduct conferences, seminars, workshops and meetings to share and exchange the ideas and experiences and to contribute to the growth of their profession.

Research associations and institutions blossomed in the 20th century. However, some of them came into existence much earlier. Of the earliest research organisations, mention could be made of Indian Research Association (1876), Indian Veterinary Research Institute (1895). Governmental scientific organisations also have their libraries with specialised collections. The Geological Survey of India Library founded in 1851 has rich collection of volumes, besides reports, pamphlets, maps, etc. The Zoological Survey (1916), and the Anthropological Survey (1946) also possess good collections pertaining to their specific subjects.

The Indian Institute of Science, Bangalore (1909), is a distinguished organisation. It was founded by Tata for carrying out original investigation which might be of help to industries. The Indian Statistical Institute (1932), Indian Institutes of Technology (1951) are of similar pattern. They have developed rich libraries which maintain good collection in the areas of science and technology.

In 1942 the Council of Scientific and Industrial Research (CSIR) was constituted by the then Legislative Assembly as an autonomous body registered under the Societies Act of 1867. The CSIR has 38 laboratories and 39 regional centres under its control. These are spread all over the country. Excepting for the National Physical Laboratory and the National Chemical Laboratory where research on fundamental sciences is carried out, other laboratories are generally concerned with problems of interests to particular industries, like agriculture, food, drugs, leather, electronics, glass, ceramics, etc. All these laboratories have libraries catering to their research requirements.

Rapid growth of scientific and technical libraries is a phenomenon of the twentieth century, which in fact commenced with the attainment of independence in 1947. Thereafter, a large number of medical, engineering and technological colleges, and the research laboratories and scientific institutions were established under the Council of Scientific and Industrial Research, Defence Research and Development Organisation (DRDO), Department of Atomic Energy (DAE), Department of Electronics (DOE), Department of Space (DOS), Indian Council of Agricultural Research (ICAR) and Indian Council of Medical Research (ICMR). At present all these research institutions have their own specialised libraries. Besides, special libraries have been set up by various agencies, governmental and non-governmental as well as public and private sectors. In many cases, universities have also come up with libraries having special collections.[6]

It is relevant to mention some of the scientific and technical libraries which have the largest collections, good organisation and offer high quality services. These are: Bhabha Atomic Research Centre, Bombay; Tata Institute of Fundamental Research, Bombay; Geological Survey of India, Kolkata; Indian Statistical Institute, Kolkata; Indian Institute of Science, Bangalore; DESIDOC, New Delhi; National Science Library of INSDOC, New Delhi; National Medical Library, New Delhi; Indian Agricultural Research Institute, New Delhi; SIET Institute, Hyderabad; and the seven Indian Institutes of Technology.

1.5 SCIENTIFIC AND TECHNICAL LIBRARIES: A PROFILE OF THEIR COLLECTION, SERVICES, STAFF, USERS, BUDGET AND PHYSICAL FACILITIES

1.5.1 Collection Building: Its Nature and Process

The scientific and technical libraries play an important role in accomplishing the missions and goals of organisations. They acquire, organize and maintain informative materials related to the research areas of the organisation which are useful to the researchers and scholars. They have strong emphasis on the development of research collection. Their resources also meet both current and anticipated requirements of their users. The demand of collection in scientific and technical libraries goes on changing from time to time because of new services, new products, developments, new approaches of marketing, etc. adapted by their organisations and agencies. Hayes and Borko (1983) investigated the relationship between the size of academic research libraries' collections and faculty research productivity as measured by faculty publications. They found a significant relationship between the contribution of library collections and faculty research productivity.[7] It is quite plausible that well equipped organisations attract the talented and well-known researchers and learners that leads to higher level of prestige to the organisation. The library collection depends upon the nature of the organisation and its objectives. It generally contains diverse collection such as books, journals, online databases, pamphlets, translations, theses, dissertations, periodicals, newspapers, press releases, transactions, reports, archival materials, yearbooks, directories, research and laboratory notebooks, patents, trademark specifications, and standards, audiovisual materials, recordings, manuscripts, clippings, abstracts, maps, blueprints, punched cards, magnetic tapes, tables, photocopies, microforms, and computer hardware and software. The size of the collection is determined by the purposes of the library and the availability of materials in the special areas; it may contain works of permanent or historical value or literature which is only currently useful.[8] These libraries expand and maintain their collection of books, journals, online databases and other library material to support the teaching and research activities of the organisation. It has been observed that best students and talented scholars join those reputed organisations that have good infrastructure, such as well equipped libraries, labs and other research facilities.

Ronald F. Dow, Salvatore Meringolo and Gloriana St. Clair (1995) stated that "Library collections have been viewed as the soul of the academic disciplines, the repository of all the research and scholarly effort that has gone before. For that reason the size of the library's collections in each of the disciplines in some way is seen as a reflection of the institution's commitment to learning within an academic discipline. For as a college or university invests in collections, it vests the academic discipline on campus with local value and prestige too. As the library collections support research and study in an area of knowledge, the institution will be able to attract the best scholars and students of that discipline, enhancing faculty reputation, the value of the degree earned by students, and institutional image".[9]

The resources of scientific and technical libraries, such as books, journals, reports, conference proceedings, tapes, slides, videos, etc. must be acquired in small number and it should be dynamic and useful to the research community. To keep the collection development up-to-date, it is essential to discard the materials which are not used for a long time. However, at times discarded items may be equal to the new items added in the collection. To provide a place for the new acquired materials, the less or out-of-circulation materials must be weeded out with the assistance and consultation of the patrons and the administrators of the organisations.

The collection of the library should be built with the materials frequently used. Rest can be borrowed from other research libraries through interlibrary loan and resource sharing to avoid duplication of material and to fully use the financial resources. The librarians of these libraries must keep good liaison with their counterparts to augment the reciprocal borrowing and service arrangements.

The ascertaining factor in the organisation of the collection of a scientific and technical library is a need for quick, efficient and effective access. Such libraries stress on the access of latest and up-to-date materials which is relevant to meet the research fields and pertinent to the work of organisation. Space constraints is one of the problems faced by the scientific and technical libraries today. The librarians of these libraries should stress more and more on the collection of microforms, microfilms, CD-ROM databases, bibliographical databases, online full-text databases in place of less used materials. In scientific and technical libraries, books are used less than the periodicals, technical and research reports, indexes and abstracts, specifications and standards and non book materials.

Now the efforts may be made to devise an entirely new and effective system of bibliographic access, including a new classification scheme, printed checklists, indexes, computer printout catalogues and electronic data-processing equipment which can enhance the usefulness and effectiveness of the scientific and technical libraries.

1.5.2 Services

The scientific and technical library serves the specific and specialised requirements of the specialists and researchers related to their research fields by examining all new literature which comes into the library, "evaluating it, and making certain that it reaches the right persons; providing quick reference service, using photocopies as needed; making literature searches and providing bibliographies, abstracts, summaries, and translations if necessary; using interlibrary loan to provide additionally needed materials; providing selective dissemination of information (SDI) and document delivery service; maintaining company archives; encouraging the use of the library through displays, lists of new materials, and liberal loan policies; and developing programmes to retrieve information through the use of computers".[10] The scientific and technical library arranges regular and systematic information services to meet the current and anticipatory needs of the users of research organisation.

Scientific and technical libraries join the cooperative activities, i.e., storage of certain materials, including microfilms, microfiches, or optical discs; interlibrary loans; directories; cooperative cataloguing and acquisition; duplicates exchange; union lists; and shared resources. Scientific and technical libraries participate in national and international networks or other bibliographical networks. Besides computer, many scientific and technical libraries exploit CD-ROM technology, telefacsimile transmission of documents, telecommunications, and other electronic technologies.

In order to provide effective and better information services to the readers of research organisations, the information scientists and other library staff must have the knowledge and specialisation of the specific subject as well as background of library and information science. Specialised information scientists can secure, assemble and present information in a usable form to the concerned scientists and technologists pertaining to specific R&D. A feature of special library is identified by Henkle as "it involves participation by the librarian in the seeking and organising of information for specific purposes."[11] But the tremendous growth in the publication of scientific and technical literature needs an improvement over the conventional methods of operations in providing services in these libraries. Latest sophisticated information technologies, such as computerised information services, CD-ROMs, online access to national and international databases may be executed to provide better services.

1.5.3 Staff

The development of scientific and technical libraries is not only restricted to the co-operative acquisition of specialised materials, their preservation and dissemination, but it also pertains to organising them efficiently and responsibly. The responsibility of the librarian of the special library is not only the location of the reference material but also its interpretation. Hence, the librarian of a scientific and technical library must have a background in the field of specialisation as well as good knowledge of library techniques.[12] The librarian must be subject specialist with a solid background of library education and new information technologies as it is one of the necessity of our scientific and technical libraries. But most of information officers, information specialists and librarians working in business, industrial, scientific and technical libraries, are not experts in the fields they serve.

The librarian of a scientific and technical library is given non-traditional designation like 'Documentation Officer', 'Information Specialist', 'Scientific Officer', 'Information Scientist', 'Information Manager' and so on. To accomplish the goals of a special library, it is imperative that "the information specialist must have an understanding of the structure and policy of the organisation; knowledge of the subject specialty of the library, the supporting literature, and the techniques of reference and information service; a familiarity with the entire collection and the particular interests of the clientele, and the ability to match literature and client; an understanding of the basic principles of classification in order to adapt or devise systems to meet the needs of the diverse materials and forms of materials; an acquaintance with outside sources useful in locating needed information; ability to perform such special services as indexing, editing, abstracting, translating and database searching, or knowing where these services can be procured quickly. The information specialist must be able to work well with people and within an organisation".[13]

The staff of the typical scientific and technical library is small. However, some scientific and technical libraries have a number of specialists on the staff, such as translator, abstracter, indexer, or information systems specialist.

1.5.4 Users

The clienteles of scientific and technical libraries are scientists, researchers, research scholars, engineers, experts, technical personnel, trainees, etc. who need correct, accurate, comprehensive, up-to-date and timely information on new research and development programmes in their respective domains. Knowledge of information needs of these users form an essential factor for the efficient and effective library service. The satisfaction of the readers of such libraries is of paramount importance as these factors form the basis to measure the efficiency and effectiveness of a library and its services.

1.5.5 Budget

Adequate budget to procure the resources of the library whether in print or online, is necessary to offer effective information services to users. Most of the budget of the library is spent on the subscription of the periodicals, since periodicals are the latest and current source to inform the researchers and scientists about the recent developments in their respected areas. As White (1988) has stated that "Budgeting for a library is rather like budgeting for a yacht. It is not a question of how much is needed, but of how much is available. There is no limit to the amount that can be spent; usually there is not enough".[14]

Budget constraints are a problem to all types of libraries. This has badly affected the R&D in scientific and technical organisations and university research system. It is impossible to maximize and retain both quality and quantity of the collection and services with these constraints. If the funds are limited, the library has to make a choice to give priority to the journals instead of books, particularly online databases of full text journals which are cheap than printed journals.

1.5.6 Physical Facilities

Making physical facilities available to the clienteles of scientific and technical libraries is essential to help the users make effective use of library resources and its services. These facilities are integral part of the library services. The users of scientific and technical libraries should be provided comfortable place for reading, peaceful and conducive environment, individual study carrels, good lighting, emergency light (generator system facility), air-conditioning and heating facility, drinking water and toilets. These facilities are necessary for effective use of library resources. Moreover, attractive furnishings are also essential as these encourage the library use. Cubicles must be made for the researchers and scientists for their serious research and project works. These cubicles should made available to the users who are engaged in research and project work.

The library must provide a variety of learning and research environments that involves audio-visual equipment, Internet and access to other electronic as well as online resources. The Online Public Access Catalogue (OPAC), electronic databases and access to Internet provide library users with a wide variety of information resources. These services are augmented with traditional as well as modern electronic reference sources and services to meet the needs of users.

The information specialists, information officers or librarians of the scientific and technical libraries must walk into the library from time to time, (looking at it through the eyes of the patron) to see personally the library activities of staff and the reactions of the users in terms of resources and services. "What do they see when they enter? How easy is it to find out what's available? How do they go about getting it? How do they learn about the library's resources and services? Even more basic is the location of the library."[15] Library should be centrally located in an organisation or parent body. Scientific and technical libraries of national importance should be located at a central place of the city during any reorganisation, shifting of laboratories, offices and institutions for the convenience of all the serious readers. The special libraries of national importance should be located at the heart of the city.

1.5.7 Organisation of Reading Material

Maximum utilisation of the resources does not depend only on good number of books and other resources but also on their proper arrangement in order to provide easy access and satisfaction to the users, that is more important and essential. Proper organisation of reading material helps the users to locate their desired items without wasting much time. This helps to make easy search and access of document. Organisation of reading material in these libraries must be excellent and help the users to explore the resources quickly. It is inevitable that all print material, i.e. books, reference books, bound volumes of journals, etc. should be classified, catalogued and arranged systematically so that users should not waste their valuable time in locating the desired material. Back volumes of periodicals should also be arranged separately in alphabetical or classified order. Moreover, there should be a separate section for the non-book material and audio-visual system.[16]

1.6 ROLES OF SCIENTIFIC AND TECHNICAL LIBRARIES IN PURE AND APPLIED RESEARCH

Scientific and technical libraries serve the purpose of important and effective information centres for research and development (R&D) programmes of their parent bodies. Specialised library and information centres have their place in research, scientific and technical, agricultural, business and information centres.

The origin of scientific and technical libraries may be linked with the growth of scientific and technological research in India. These libraries came into existence in the eighteenth century with the establishment of the Asiatic Society of Bengal in Calcutta by Sir William Jones in 1784. The Asiatic Society of Bengal Library has a collection of ancient coins and medals as well as archaeological, technological and geological materials. Growth of such libraries had been gradual with the development of technical research in India. These have developed more or less haphazardly without any concerted co-operative effort.[17] There is not much available information about research libraries prior to 19th century. The only remnant with its faded glory is Tanjore Saraswati Mahal Library, established by the Maratha Kings.[18]

The collections built up by universities, special and national libraries are most important resources of the nation. In the modern world no productive activity can be executed successfully without adequate information and knowledge being made available to specialists and research workers. Without the support of such information, no fruitful research work for economic and social development can be accomplished. Many developing countries, although they have devoted much of their attention towards the development of infrastructure, still lack such effective institutions. These libraries are facing the problems of inadequate financial resources, infrastructure and support of the management or institutional heads.

During the 19th century, a number of scientific institutions and organisations were established to foster to scientific researches in various pure and applied disciplines, such as physics, chemistry, meteorology, geology, zoology, botany, anthropology, mathematics, medical sciences, etc. All these scientific institutions and organisations of various disciplines have their own specialised libraries which have rich collections in their respective fields. These scientific and technical libraries were set up to meet the requirements of the limited number of scientists, researchers and experts. The organisation, management, collection, functions and services of these libraries may be said to be different from other libraries. The main objective behind the establishment of these libraries was to disseminate the information without any loss of time. There are about 2981 scientific institutions in India at present which have been set up in almost all the States and Union Territories to coordinate and promote S & T in their respective domains.[19]

"Science remained for centuries the private pursuit of

the amateur, and the earliest special scientific collections were assembled by individuals. It was only in the nineteenth century, when science was seen to have great practical importance, that the state began to make special provision for special science libraries".[20]

After independence, interest and awareness was created towards nation building activities and the first step towards this direction was "systematic and planned attempt to apply science and technology to the growth and development of India's national industries".[21] Scientific research in India did not receive any patronage and attention of the British rulers as it should have, until the setting up of the Board of Scientific and Industrial Research (BSIR) in April 1940 on the lines of the Department of Scientific and Industrial Research (DSIR) in the United Kingdom which was founded in 1916. This Board guided the government on the lines on which industrial research in India should be conducted and it thought of new avenues to serve the object of ensuring the coordinated development of Indian industries.[22]

It was in fact after independence only, that the roles of scientific and industrial research were recognized for the economic and social development of the country. Industrial research is the most important branch of the applied research. Indian Industrial Research Bureau came into existence in 1934. It was the World War II which brought a sharp change in the industrial research with the establishment of the Council of Scientific and Industrial Research.[23] CSIR is the chief vehicle of Government's policy for the promotion and coordination of scientific & industrial research in India.[24] In 1950, several laboratories of CSIR were established for applied research. On the eve of the opening ceremony of the Central Road Research Institute on July 16, 1952, our first Prime Minister, Pandit Jawahar Lal Nehru remarked, "Our laboratories are a symbol of new India and the foundation of our progress and prosperity".[25] With the establishment of these laboratories and institutes, several scientific and technical libraries in India came into existence to assist and expedite R&D programmes of these laboratories. As Ray rightly remarked, "No organisation or institute can conduct research unless equipped with up-to-date laboratories and good libraries".[26] 1950 is marked as the golden year in the history of Special Libraries in India.

With the passage of time the scientific and technical libraries have come to occupy a position of being indispensable source of scientific information for R&D work of any scientific institution and organisation. These libraries are the life blood of any research institution and organisation and their role in the transfer of scientific information is now recognised as significant in the modern industrialised society. The scientific library traditionally acts as the focus for acquisition, organisation, storage and dissemination of published or unpublished scientific literature but now the focus of the entire library system has shifted to Information Technology (IT) and Computerised Library System. Scientific and technical libraries are recognised by their specialised type of resources and specific information services.

Emphasizing the importance of libraries in the context of scientific laboratories, an English scientist Ziman has written: "A scientific laboratory without a library is like a decorated cat: the motor activities continue to function, but lacks coordination of memory and purpose".[27]

In the recent times, communication of scientific and technical information is an integral part of research and development. The use of new technologies, such as the computer, audio and video cassettes, CD-ROM, online searching of national and international databases, participation in national and international networks and various forms of electronic technologies and telecommunications are the significant tools for the communication of information at national and international levels. These developments have in fact impacted the working of scientific and technical libraries to a great extent.

1.7 ESTABLISHMENT OF SCIENTIFIC AND TECHNICAL LIBRARIES IN INDIA

The following libraries in India may be categorised as special types of libraries established by respective institutions with the objective of providing effective information services to the members. This also shows the chronological growth of special libraries during the pre-independence period in India.

Library of Asiatic Society of Bengal, Calcutta (1784);

Library of Trigonometrical Survey (1800);

Library of the Asiatic Society, Bombay (1804);

Library of the Medical College, Calcutta (1835);

Madras Medical College Library (1835);

Library of the Geological Survey of India, Calcutta (1851);

Library of the Government Law College, Bombay (1855);

Library of Archaeological Department (1862);

Library of Indian Museum (1866);

Library of Indian Coastal Survey (1875);

Library of Indian Meteorological Department (1875);

Library of Indian Research Association (1876);

Library of Indian Association for the Cultivation of Science (1876);

Library of the Grant Medical College, Bombay (1885);

Library of Victoria Jubilee Technical Institute, Bombay (1887);

Research Centre and Library of the Theosophical Society, Madras (1888);

Library of Botanical Survey of India (1890);

Library of the Indian Veterinary Research Institute, Izatnagar (1883);

Library of the Indian Institute of Astrophysics, Kodaikanal (1898);

Library of Haffkine Institute, Bombay (1899);

Library of King Institute of Preventive Medicine, Madras (1899).

The dawn of the twentieth century witnessed a rapid growth of scientific and technical libraries in different spheres of the country, some of which are :

Library of the King Institute of Preventive Medicine, Madras (1903);

Library of Imperial Agricultural Research Institute in Pusa, Bihar (1905);

Library of Central Research Institute for Medical Research, Kasauli (1905);

Library of Forest Research Institute, Dehra Dun (1906);

Library of Pasteur Institute, Coonoor (1907);

Library of Indian Research Fund Association (1911) which later became Indian Council of Medical Research;

Library of Toklai Experimental Station in Assam for Research on Tea (1911);

Library of Indian Science Congress (1914);

Library of Zoological Survey of India, Calcutta (1916);

Library of Bose Institute, Calcutta (1917);

Library of Dairy Research Institute, Bangalore (1923);

Library of Cotton Technological Research Laboratory, Bombay (1924);

Library of the Institute of Plant Industry, Indore (1924);

Library of Indian Lac Research Institute, Ranchi (1925);

Library of Imperial (now Indian) Council of Agricultural Research (1929).

A number of libraries of scientific societies were also established during this period, such as:

Library of Institution of Engineers, Calcutta (1920);

Library of Anthropological Society, Calcutta (1920);

Library of Indian Botanical Society, Madras (1921);

Library of Indian Chemical Society, Calcutta (1924);

Library of Geological, Mining and Metallurgical Society of India, Calcutta (1924);

Library of National Academy of Sciences, Allahabad (1930);

Library of the United Provinces Academy of Sciences, Allahabad (1930) which later became the National Academy of Sciences;

Library of Indian Academy of Sciences, Bangalore (1934);

Library of National Institute of Sciences of India, Calcutta

(1935). Its headquarter was shifted to Delhi in 1947 and it was renamed as the Indian National Science Academy in 1970.

Library of the Indian Institute of Science, Bangalore (1909);

Library of Indian Statistical Institute (1932);

Library of Anthropological Survey (1946); and

Libraries of seven Indian Institutes of Technology, Bombay, Madras, Kanpur, Kharagpur and Delhi between (1951-1961) and IIT Guwahati and Roorkee.

In 1947, a large number of medical, engineering and technology colleges, and research laboratories and various scientific and technical institutions and organisations under the Council of Scientific and Industrial Research, (1942), Department of Atomic Energy (DAE), Defence Research and Development Organisation (DRDO), Department of Electronics (DOE), Department of Space (DOS), Indian Council of Agricultural Research (ICAR), and Indian Council of Medical Research (ICMR), were established for the development and prosperity of Indian economy. These institutions and organisations have organised their scientific and technical libraries which are serving the needs of their parent bodies. The other important libraries of such institutions and organisations are listed below :

Library of Department of Scientific Research (1948);

Library of National Planning Commission (1950);

Library of Ministry of Scientific Research and National Resources (1951);

Library of Department of Atomic Energy (1954);

Library of Ministry of Education and Scientific Research, (1957);

Library of Ministry of Scientific Research and Cultural Affairs (1958);

Library of Department of Electronics (1970);

Library of Department of Science and Technology (DST), New Delhi (1971);

Library of Department of Space (1972);

Library of Department of Environment (1980);

Library of Department of Ocean Development (1981);

Library of Department of Non-Conventional Energy Sources (1982);

Library of Department of Scientific and Industrial Research (DSIR), New Delhi (1984);

Library of Ministry of Science & Technology with only three Scientific Departments: DST, DSIR and DBT, 1985;

Library of Department of Biotechnology (DBT) (1986);

Library of Technology, Information, Forecasting and Assessment Council (1987).

In fact, in the world of information and research explosion, every scientific and technical organisation has a need to keep in touch with the current R&D programmes in its domain and the researches which has been done in the past. Therefore, to keep the records of such events effectively the need of scientific and technical libraries is being felt as a necessary entity. It is an accepted fact that the role of these scientific and technical libraries in promoting the scientific researches cannot be ignored. These libraries are integral part of any discovery.

1.8 CSIR LIBRARIES AND THEIR STATUS

An in-depth study of different services is being offered by the libraries and information centres of CSIR laboratories to ascertain efficiency and weaknesses in their services. The use of information technology in the libraries is being debated at different levels. In the event of fast technological developments, the application of Information Technology (IT) in libraries is proving to be a necessity, precisely because application of information technology will improve the services and bring about qualitative change in overall operation of library and information centres. Though the development has been a bit faster in scientific libraries, yet it is not fully known as to what extent the libraries of CSIR laboratories have started utilising information technology. In addition to this, there are a number of issues, such as infrastructure facilities, manpower and availability of resources, that need to be examined thoroughly. Through this study attempts to ascertain the present status of the libraries of CSIR laboratories and the obtaining state of affairs so that suggestions could be advanced indicating what need to be done now to improve situation.

1.8.1 Objectives of the Study

The objectives of the study are:

i) to investigate and analyse the various library and information services provided by the libraries and information centres of the CSIR laboratories;

ii) to study the information needs and use pattern of Indian scientists, especially in relation to the existing library and information systems of the CSIR laboratories;

iii) to evaluate their existing resources and services;

iv) to assess the effectiveness of the libraries and information services;

v) to ascertain the levels of computerisation of activities and services in the libraries for providing effective services;

vi) to identify gaps and suggest measures for effective functioning of the libraries in CSIR laboratories.

1.8.2 Nature and Scope of the Study

The present study being exploratory in nature was conducted to analyse working patterns and effectiveness of the libraries of the Council of Scientific and Industrial Research laboratories in terms of their services, resources and facilities. The study also aimed to present an analytical picture of information needs and use patterns of libraries, level of users' satisfaction with services, holdings, organisation of library material and various other facilities extended by these libraries for fostering research activities. It also aimed to examine the extent to which information technology has been brought into use in these libraries.

The study is based on data received from the scientists,

research scholars and librarians working in the libraries and information centres of 40 laboratories of CSIR situated in different parts of the country. The study includes only those scientists and research scholars of the laboratories who were reported to have published research articles/papers in journals during the last five years and those scientists who were identified to be making maximum use of the libraries of the CSIR laboratories.

1.8.3 Sampling Design

In order to examine the nature of relationship between scientists' requirements, library services and their effectiveness/ evaluation, a field investigation of the scientists and librarians currently working in CSIR laboratories and its libraries was undertaken using the method of Simple Random Sampling (SRS). The following points were considered before drawing up the sample of scientists working in CSIR laboratories for the present study and investigation:

a) Scientists engaged in paper publication were selected for the survey. Information with regard to papers published by scientists working in CSIR laboratories was obtained from "CSIR RESEARCH OUTPUT 1991: A BIBLIOMETRIC ANALYSIS" which is an authentic document in this respect.

b) In addition to this, request was made to the librarians for supply of a list of scientists who are making maximum use of the library resources and its services.

In order to make the sample totally representative, it was decided to draw up samples of 500 working scientists having the maximum number of publications and those who were making maximum use of library services. It was planned to base the present study on the sample of 500 scientists and research scholars belonging to the five categories of CSIR laboratories. The five major categories are:

1. Physical and Earth Sciences Group (PESG);
2. Chemical Sciences Group (CSG);
3. Biological Sciences Group (BSG);

4. Engineering Sciences Group (ESG); and
5. Information Sciences Group (ISG).

Respondents included in the study were grouped in four categories:

1. Senior Scientists (Scientists F, G, E-II & E-I);
2. Scientists C;
3. Scientists A&B; and
4. Research Scholars.

In the selection of scientists working in various CSIR laboratories, first of all a list of 40 laboratories of CSIR situated in different parts of the country was prepared. Out of 40 laboratories of CSIR, 500 scientists were selected by simple random sampling procedure. Again, out of 500 selected scientists, two lists of scientists working in CSIR laboratories were prepared. In the first list, the names of scientists who had published papers listed in CSIR RESEARCH OUTPUT 1991: A BIBLIOMETRIC ANALYSIS, were included, whereas the second list comprised all those scientists who were making maximum use of the libraries of CSIR laboratories. Information with regard to use of libraries was obtained through the librarians of CSIR laboratories. Now the sample of 500 scientists of CSIR laboratories was selected on the basis of the circular systematic sampling procedure to give an equal representation to each of 500 selected scientists. Therefore, a systematic circular sampling scheme was adopted to select 500 scientists of 40 laboratories from the above two lists of scientists.

In-short sampling scheme adopted for the present study had a two-stage sampling procedure where in the first stage the 40 laboratories of CSIR were selected, and at the second stage, a sample of 500 scientists from each of the five categories was drawn up.

1.8.4 Construction of Questionnaire

In order to collect the relevant data for the purpose of the study and investigation, a questionnaires and its complete schedules were developed and constructed and the same was circulated among the libraries of CSIR laboratories and also amongst the scientists.

1.8.4.1 Development of the Scale

Three point Likert scale was used to estimate the importance and to evaluate the use of library and information services and their effectiveness.

For the purpose of recording scientists' reactions, three-point scale was developed, corresponding to Excellent, Good and Poor. The respondents were required to indicate their reaction to a particular statement by putting a tick mark (✓) on an appropriate word on the scale. For statistical calculations, each respondent was given a score weightage of 3, 2 and 1 for ticking Excellent, Good and Poor respectively on the scale. Score weightages as assigned by the respondents to each factor, were further used to derive mean values for ranking the factors.

1.8.4.2 Pre-testing and Organisation of the Questionnaire

A tentative questionnaire was pre-tested on a group of 42 scientists/research scholars working in the laboratories of CSIR in Delhi. Similarly, 7 questionnaires on librarians of CSIR laboratories were also examined on pre-testing basis. The selection of the scientists/research scholars for pre-testing of the questionnaire, was also based on the same criterion as applied for the selection of the sample of the study. Personal interviews were also held with 25 scientists. Some of these participants made extremely useful suggestions which were incorporated in the final questionnaire.

Finally, the questionnaire (APPENDIX - 1) was printed, covering 11 pages. Questions included in the questionnaire were divided into five parts: (i) Background information, (ii) library collection, (iii) library services, (iv) organisation of reading material and reading room facilities, and (v) suggestions for the improvement of library and information services of the CSIR laboratories.

The first part concerning background information was designed to gather data from the users about their position, level of qualification, areas of specialisation, institution/ organisation with which he/she is working, membership of local, state, national and international professional association/

society, number of conferences attended during the last five years and number of articles/papers published during the last five years, purpose of using the library, frequency of library visits, average time spent in library at different stages of research.

The second part relates to the library collections of the CSIR laboratories, including questions on availability of different kinds of documents and users' satisfaction as regards their information needs.

The third part contains questions regarding users' reaction on the library services. Their responses have been solicited in regard to the following types of services: It includes questions on lending of books/journals, interlibrary loan facility, procuring of specific material from other countries on request of the users, help in searching locating material, guidance regarding using the library, provision of specific information when required, etc. Satisfaction of users is also rated and suggestions about these services are also mentioned.

The traditional and modern services included in this part are CAS and SDI services, translation service, reprographic service, and computerised services, i.e., literature search, indexing services, compilation of bibliography and online searching of national and international databases and name of services/databases on which online searching is being provided to its users.

The fourth part contains questions relating to the organisation of reading materials and reading room facilities. The questions included in this part are arrangement of books/journals on shelves and suggestions for better arrangement of books/journals/research/project reports, etc. reading room facilities like individual study carrels, comfortable place for reading/study, adequate lighting, emergency light during light failure, conference/seminar room, etc.

Another questionnaire (APPENDIX - II) was also prepared for the Librarian/Information-in-Charge/Library Officer of the libraries of CSIR laboratories covering 11 pages. The questions related to the library activities were included in this questionnaire. The questionnaire of librarians was also mailed to the libraries of CSIR laboratories in 1993-94 with request to return the same with appropriate and definite replies as early as possible.

The questionnaire of the librarians (APPENDIX - II) was divided into seven parts: (i) Background information, (ii) library finances, (iii) library collections, (iv) technical processing and circulation activities, (v) library services and facilities, (vi) computer application, and (vii) suggestions for the improvement of library and information services of CSIR laboratories.

The first part of the questionnaire covers the background data about librarian and the library. Information about librarian's designation, sex, age, educational qualification, year of establishment of institution and the library, working hours, categories of the users, and the library staff working in the library.

Second part of the questionnaire pertains to the library finances, budget of institution and the library for the last two years, break-up of library budget into books and periodicals, adequacy of budget, and percentage of increase on the total budget of the library.

Third part relates to the availability of number of volumes of books and reference books, bound volumes of periodicals, non-book materials and grey literature. Beside this, questions relating to number of Indian and foreign journals being subscribed, their rating and availability of non-book materials were also included in the questionnaire.

The fourth part relates to the technical processing and circulation activities of the books, periodicals and non-book materials and facilities of book reservation and inter library loan.

Fifth part describes about resource sharing, arrangement to procure material from other countries on request, library services and facilities, i.e., CAS and SDI services, translation service, reprographic service and air conditioned facilities.

Sixth part deals with the application of computer and other information technologies in CSIR libraries and its activities, software being used by libraries, and the impact of computer on the library services and facilities. In addition to this, it also relates to the number of computer databases available in the library, online searching to national and international databases, electronic facilities, i.e., telex, fax and e-mail, participation of libraries in national information network and international information network.

Seventh part relates to the suggestions for the improvement of library and information services to provide better and quality services to the scientists and research scholars.

1.8.5 Administration of the Questionnaire

Since the libraries of CSIR laboratories were situated and scattered in different parts of the country, it was thought appropriate to mail questionnaire to the scientists and the librarians for the collection of data. The survey began in December, 1993 and it was treated as 'reference date' for recording the vital events which took place before this date in the libraries of CSIR laboratories. The data collection work continued till March, 1995. The list of scientists as supplied by the librarians was taken as basis for mailing. In the first round, 500 questionnaires were mailed out, out of which 234 were received back. In order to expedite the process, reminders along with another questionnaire were sent again.

1.8.6 Field Operation Work

After having seen the rate of response, it was decided to visit concerned institutions. The lists of scientists/research scholars along with their relevant background information were obtained much before the field investigation commenced. During the visit, these lists were scrutinised in consultation with the Librarians/Library Officers or In-charge of the libraries of CSIR laboratories so as to select population/scientists in accordance with the fixed criterion. Only those scientists were selected for administering the questionnaires who fulfilled the criterion set for the study.

Prior to administering the questionnaires, informal

discussions were held with the respondents in which significance of the study was explained to them so as to establish credibility with them. The questionnaires were delivered to the respondents in person. As it was not expected or possible to contact all the respondents of a particular library under visit, questionnaires were handed over to those who were found to be available during the days of visits and for those who could not be contacted personally, the questionnaires along with duly stamped and self addressed envelopes were left with the librarians or in-charge of the library who were requested to persuade them to send their responses through post. In case some questions were left unanswered, the respondents were asked to answer such questions after necessary clarifications. Out of 500 questionnaires distributed, 380 filled in questionnaires were received. Details of the responses received from users and librarians are given in Table 1.1. Thus the response rate was 76 per cent which formed the basis for statistical analysis. In spite of the personal approach made to the respondents, some of the users refused to fill the questionnaire on the ground that they were quite dissatisfied with the services of library and information centres of the laboratories. There were some users who returned blank questionnaires with the plea that they were over burdened with the work. Therefore they did not find time for filling up the questionnaires.

1.8.7 Data Processing

Immediately after the completion of the field survey, the processing of data was carried out. First, a manual for coding was prepared on the basis of the answers of the closed and the open ended questions included in the schedule. The manual was utilized for transferring each of the information collected in the survey on PC. Later, the data entered on PC was validated through 'bound' as well as 'consistency' checks. Finally, the tables for the present analysis were prepared with the help of the computer special programmes Statistical Packages for Social Science (SPSS) in the Council for Social Development, New Delhi. The use of SPSS helped in frequency counts and cross tabs, etc.

On the basis of the data thus collected and received, the analytic position has been dealt with the appropriate point of view in relevant chapters to reveal the actual state of affairs.

Table 1.1 : Distribution of the Questionnaires to the Users and the Librarians of CSIR Laboratories

Sl. No.	*Name of the Laboratory*	*Distribution and Receipt of Questionnaires*	
		Users	*Librarian*
A.	PHYSICAL AND EARTH SCIENCES GROUP (PESG)		
1.	Central Electronics Engineering Research Institute, Pilani	15 (14)	1
2.	Central Scientific Instruments Organisation, Chandigarh	10 (6)	1
3.	National Geophysical Research Institute, Hyderabad	10 (7)	1
4.	National Institute of Oceanography, Goa	15 (11)	1
5.	National Physical Laboratory, New Delhi	15 (15)	1
B.	CHEMICAL SCIENCES GROUP (CSG)		
6.	Central Electrochemical Research Institute, Karaikudi	10 (8)	1
7.	Central Leather Research Institute, Madras	10 (6)	1
8.	Central Salt and Marine Chemicals Research Institute, Bhavnagar	10 (7)	1
9.	Indian Institute of Chemical Technology, Hyderabad	10 (8)	1
10.	Indian Institute of Petroleum, Dehradun	15 (14)	1
11.	National Chemical Laboratory, Pune	10 (6)	1

12.	Regional Research Laboratory, Jorhat	10 (8)	1
C.	BIOLOGICAL SCIENCES GROUP (BSG)		
13.	Central Drug Research Institute, Lucknow	20 (20)	1
14.	Central Food Technological Research Institute, Mysore	10 (8)	1
15.	Central Institute of Medicinal and Aromatic Plants, Lucknow	10 (9)	1
16.	Centre for Biochemical Technology, Delhi	15 (15)	1
17.	Centre for Cellular and Molecular Biology, Hyderabad	10 (8)	1
18.	CSIR Complex, Palampur	15 (15)	1
19.	Indian Institute of Chemical Biology, Kolkata	10	-
20.	Industrial Toxicology Research Centre, Lucknow	20 (20)	1
21.	Institute of Microbial Technology, Chandigarh	10	1
22.	National Botanical Research Institute, Lucknow	20 (18)	1
23.	Regional Research Laboratory, Jammu	20 (18)	1
D.	ENGINEERING SCIENCES GROUP (ESG)		
24.	Central Building Research Institute, Roorkee	15 (13)	1
25.	Central Fuel Research Institute, Jealgora	10 (3)	-
26.	Central Glass and Ceramic Research Institute, Kolkata	10 (7)	1
27.	Central Mechanical Engineering Research Institute, Durgapur	10	-
28.	Central Mining Research Institute, Dhanbad	10 (7)	1

29. Central Road Research Institute, New Delhi	15 (12)	1
30. National Aeronautical Laboratory, Bangalore	10 (5)	1
31. National Environmental Engineering Research Institute, Nagpur	10 (8)	1
32. National Metallurgical Laboratory, Jamshedpur	10 (6)	1
33. Regional Research Laboratory, Bhopal	10 (7)	-
34. Regional Research Laboratory, Bhubaneswar	10 (7)	-
35. Regional Research Laboratory, Thiruvananthapuram	10 (4)	-
36. Structural Engineering Research Centre, Ghaziabad	10 (9)	1
37. Structural Engineering Research Centre, Madras	10 (6)	1
E. INFORMATION SCIENCE GROUP (ISG)		
38. Indian National Scientific Documentation Centre, New Delhi	15 (13)	1
39. National Institute of Science, Technology, and Development Studies, New Delhi	15 (13)	1
40. Publication and Information Directorate, New Delhi	20 (19)	1
Total	500 (380)	40 (34)

Note: Figures in parenthesis indicate the number of questionnaires received back.

CONCLUSION

Libraries are the integral part of any organisation. Special libraries came into existence with the beginning of new era of industrial revolution and scientific and technical researches. These libraries have a special type of collection, services, staff, users and offer a wide range of specialized services to the users to accomplish the mission and goals of the organisations. These libraries maximize the utility of their collection and services through the efficient use of information technology and expertise of the library staff. Liu (2003) summarized that "Library volume and serials collections accounted for a significant amount of contribution to prestige of universities, particularly when considering their supporting role in research and teaching at universities".[28] There is fairly strong association between library volumes and serials collections and prestige of universities. He further asserted that when whole library collection, such as books, journals, documents, reports, patents, etc. are digitized and stored in machine readable form and computers, scholars would lose browsing opportunities. Lack of browsing opportunities may lead to decreases in research productivity.

Moreover, the problems of escalating cost of the journals, reference sources, budgetary constraints of academic and research libraries, and space problems have been solved to some extent through the networking of the libraries. It is quite plausible that online full text journals are easy to access, retrieve, use and browse in comparison to print journals. They are indexed and abstracted and the bibliographical references indicate the full text article. During research, user has to visit in the library several times to consult the documents while he/she is doing the work at the desktop. If the information is available at desktop, there is no need to visit the library. Electronic resources have made easy to access, browse and use the information as compared to print publications. Moreover, other reference sources, such as encyclopedias, directories, indexes, statistics, databases and other online reference sources or CD-ROMs are easy to retrieve, use and being portable can be carried and handled with ease.

REFERENCES

1. Mukherjee, A. K. Fundamentals of special librarianship and documentation. Calcutta: IASLIC, 1969. P.11.
2. Sharma, C. D. Use of libraries: A guide to better use of libraries and their resources. New Delhi: Metropolitan Book, 1978. P.47-53.

3. Buck, Paul. Libraries and universities: Addresses and reports. Boston: Harvard University Press, 1969. 191p.
4. Sohan Lal and Singh, Prem. Growth and development of Agricultural University Libraries in India: A case study of Haryana Agricultural University Library. *Library Science with a slant to Documentation,* 32(1), 1995, 41-55.
5. Thakur, D. S. Value of information and on-line information resources. In: *Emerging Digital Library Initiatives and Future of Business and Management Information in India: Proceeding.* 5th National MANLIBNET Convention, XLRI, Jamshedpur, March 6-8, 2003, 303-310.
6 Bannerjee, B. N. Rise of science-technology libraries in India. In: Sen, N. B., (ed.). *Development of Libraries in New India.* New Delhi: New Book Society of India, 1965, 205-14.
7. Hayes, R. M. and Borko, H. Mathematical model of information system use. *Information Processing and Management,* 19(3), 1983, 173-186.
8. Gates, Jean Key. Introduction to librarianship. 3rd ed. New York: Neal-Schuman Publishers, 1990. 198p.
9. Dow, R. F., Meringolo, S., and St. Clair, G. Academic collections in a changing environment. In: McCable, G. B. and Person, R. J. (eds.). *Academic Libraries: Their Rationale and Role in American Higher Education.* Westport, CT: Greenwood Press, 1995. 103p.
10. Gates, *op. cit.,* 199p.
11. Henkle, H. W. Introduction: What is special? *Library Trends,* 1, 1952, 169-172.
12. Krueger, Ruth. Special libraries in the United States. *IASLIC Bulletin,* 3(1), 1958, 17.
13. Gates, *op. cit.,* p.199.
14. White, Virginia P. Handbook of research laboratory management. Philadelphia: ISI Press, 1988. 240p.
15. Bolef, Doris. The special library. In: Katz, Bill (ed.). *The How-to-do-it Manual for Small Libraries.* New York: Neal-Schuman Publishers, 1988, 54-63.

16. Thakur, D. S. Growth and development of the library at National Institute of Financial Management - A case study. *Annals of Library and Information Studies,* 50(4), 2003, 163-174.

17. Misra, Jogesh. History of libraries and librarianship in modern India since 1850. Delhi: Atma Ram & Sons, 1993. P.55.

18. Ranganathan, S. R. Research libraries in Madras. *Modern Librarian,* 12(2), 1942, 77.

19. Research and Development Statistics at a Glance 2004-05. New Delhi: Department of Science and Technology, 2005. 14p.

20. Chandler, G. Libraries in the modern world. Oxford: Pergamon Press, 1965. P.119.

21. Rangachar, H. N. Nucleus of special libraries in renascent India: Council of Scientific and Industrial Research and its national laboratories. *Indian Librarian,* 10(4), 1956, 147.

22. *Ibid.,* p.148.

23. Rangachar, H. N. India and its special libraries. *Indian Librarian,* 7(3), 1952, 72.

24. Ray, Amulya Chandra. Special library in aid of research. *Indian Librarian,* 17(3), 1962, 151.

25. Mookerjee, S. Special libraries, our problems. *IASLIC Bulletin,* 4(1), 1959, 118.

26. Ray, *op. cit.,* p.151.

27. Ziman, John M. Public knowledge: An essay concerning the social dimension of science. Cambridge: Cambridge University Press, 1968. P.102.

28. Liu, Lewis G. The economic behavior of academic research libraries: Toward a theory. *Library Trends,* 51(3), Winter 2003, 277-292.

2
Use and Effectiveness of Libraries

The chapter aims at reviewing briefly the previous studies and investigations carried out on special libraries particularly scientific and technical libraries in India and abroad. An attempt has been made to present an overview of the literature related to effectiveness and use of library and information services of the special libraries. Review includes studies on effectiveness and use of library and information services as offered in India and elsewhere.

There are several techniques and factors to measure the effectiveness of library services. These include the availability of financial resources, the effective utilisation of available resources, library services, computerised activities and services of the library and reading facilities, etc. In fact these factors are some of the most important parameters which indicate the effectiveness and usefulness of any library in general and special library in particular. A review of relevant studies has been given in succeeding pages in chronological order.

Bernal (1948) made a survey of the use of scientific information. This survey was carried out over 56 years ago, but the relevance of its results and conclusions have not receded even in today's context. Bernal's findings indicated that pure and applied scientists had different needs, and that work activity (i.e. title, status) was also a factor that could affect use of libraries and other sources of information.

Bradford (1948), one-time librarian of the Science Museum in London, surveyed the scientific journal literature and showed that how a relatively small proportion of the world's journal titles generated a high proportion of useful material. The libraries of national and international importance should subscribe to more than a carefully selected titles in any subject area. The effective library and information centre may be developed whenever its selection policy is explicitly linked with its own users' predicted core requirements. The author emphasised on the selection policy of the library material by saying that library might be developed by paying more attention towards the users' interest in their area of specialisation and of organisation.

Rao (1961) in his article "Library development in India" has focused on means to achieve effective library services. He emphasised that an effective library service can be provided only when the service units are sufficiently large to afford an extensive book collection and qualified and competent staff as well as efficient communication and transportation systems.

Wessel (1967) and his co-workers attempted to develop criteria for evaluating a number of technical libraries attached to the United States Army. They succeeded in developing a number of evaluating techniques. Among them SCORE is the important one. SCORE (Service Components Reliability Efficiency) is a method of ascertaining the cost and success of different functions of the library. The technique is based on the analysis of each type of demand and the library's efficiency is measured by a time prescription. After collecting the data as set out in the technique, forecast regarding the probable future success can be made. This method of evaluation revolves around the economic efficiency of the system. Thus this method of measurement of the effectiveness is based on the cost of the services of the library, i.e., the total money spent and the amount and effective services made available.

The study of Hawgood and Morley (1969) on performance evaluation of the libraries is based on the assumption that the library spends its funds in the most effective way and on the pattern of most desired activities. The blend of activities that a library is arranging is compared with various alternative blends that can be produced. Each blend of activities signifies a certain pattern of weightage. The policy makers are presented with alternative weights, and if they prefer to review their weights, it means that a change in the activities is needed. It rather attempts a maximisation of resource allocation on a definite pattern. The emphasis is on the input, but nothing is related to the output. They remarked that it is also difficult to measure every activity of the library in terms of cost where each activity involves several resources and each research makes uses of several activities.

Orne (1969) in his paper "The placement of the library in the evaluation of graduate work" distinguished between the materials-centred and the client-centered approaches to measuring the library effectiveness. He classified that the basic difference between evaluation of the usefulness of the library for graduate education and for the under-graduate programme described in a few words as the difference between serving materials and serving people. Better evaluation of the library as an apt agency for serving graduate programmes might be achieved by examining closely how well its staff is organised to serve the users of the library, rather than to serve materials.

Wolfe (1970) and his co-workers conducted studies at Edinburgh with the purpose of developing a general methodology of evaluating non-profit organisations. They confined the study to the provision of information from the abstracts and journals. The services included title listing, selective dissemination of information, etc. They tried to establish a relation between information input and research output. They termed the information system effective, if it contributed to the increased research output. The data were collected through structured interviews from a sample of research scholars, librarians and budget allocators. The basic limitation of the study is that only a part of the system, i.e. information system is taken. The evaluation technique is based on certain assumptions that may not be true.

Joffe (1971) conducted a study on the effectiveness of the use made of the industrial and management engineering library. This is the first study of its kind to be conducted at the Technion and an attempt was made to determine the effectiveness of the use made of the Industrial and Management Engineering library by exploring, analysing and describing key aspects in the provision and use of services rendered by the library at the Technion-Israel Institute of Technology.

He remarked that development of academic libraries is being greatly influenced by the enormous growth in the quantity of published literature and by the expansion of higher education. In order to provide efficient services and ensure user's satisfaction, it becomes necessary at the outset to examine the effectiveness and use made of existing services. He studied the vast increase in the number of students attending undergraduate and graduate courses, the constant increase of staff and researchers, and the rising flow of new literature, i.e. the information explosion. All these cause numerous organisational and administrative difficulties which call for a re-examination of the nature, purpose and management of academic libraries. The study included the population of undergraduate students, graduate students and staff, including assistants. 201 copies of the questionnaires were sent, of which 126 were received back.

Reader's attitude regarding scope of the library collection, services and available facilities offering some remedial action should be adopted for improving services and encouraging library use. The results indicated that overall satisfaction rate was more than fairly high, except for the undergraduate group. Hence, a concentrated effort was suggested to be made towards improving facilities and resources. In addition, larger quantities of assigned texts must be provided as well as photocopying services improved. Furthermore, instructions on library use as part of the formal educational programme should be incorporated. The study enlightened both library staff and administrators regarding what methods to adopt for measuring effectiveness of library use as well as guide future decision-making and library planning.

Gothberg (1974) made a study to explore the effects that librarian's verbal and non-verbal communication had on the satisfaction level of the library users. The study revealed that the manner in which individuals communicate with one another was significant in a service-type setting and rendering services to users.

The study conducted by Adeyemi (1975) had three main objectives: (1) to determine the factors present in the current state of library co-operation in Nigeria; (2) to establish the availability of facilities necessary to establish resource sharing; and (3) to establish a model for co-operation among libraries in Nigeria which could be used in other developing countries. The study is based on various methods used in data collection. Questionnaires were sent to selected libraries and also to selected representatives of the Nigerian Library Association. Document analysis was also used to establish the availability of facilities required to effect co-operative activities in a network environment. Two operational systems were visited to obtain information on systems development to cultivate the culture of co-operative activities among the libraries in Nigeria.

The study revealed that library co-operation in Nigeria was on ad hoc basis. Federal and state funding were necessary to support resource sharing. Legislation was needed to give the Nigerian Library Association an active role in library development. Nigerian librarians were willing to further their co-operative efforts, yet they remained skeptical regarding certain aspects of resource sharing.

Faibisoff (1975) attempted to determine the efficiency and effectiveness of the New York State Reference and Research Resources (3R) programme. The regions surveyed demonstrated that they had developed viable interlibrary loan networks consistent with their particular characteristics and resources. Regional and statewide networks were supplying 85% of the users' information needs. Librarians were shown to be supportive of the established programme. The 3R programme was found to be reaching its intended audience.

The 3R regional interlibrary loan networks have been effective in making library resources accessible to those in need of them.

Wallace (1975) undertook the study to assess the usefulness and effectiveness of academic library consortia in the Southeast, with particular attention paid to consortia objectives, similarities, achievements, differences, problems, costs, successes, failures, and benefits. Questionnaires were sent to 110 academic library consortia in Alabama, Florida, Georgia, Kentucky, Mississippi, North Carolina, South Carolina, Tennessee, Virginia, and West Virginia. The response rate was 72 percent.

Lancaster (1977) while evaluating a library system gives importance to user's needs and judges its efficiency in terms of its value to the users. In order to have a more objective tools of evaluation, he developed the concept of 'Document Delivery System' against which the performance of a library can be judged. In his opinion, lists can be compiled from some standard sources of most commonly drawn citations and the capacity of the library to deliver the documents can be judged against it. Alternatively, actual needs of the users may be identified first by way of a survey, and then its capacity be judged against it.

A difficulty in applying this approach, in practice, may be that the users after knowing the strength and weakness of a library, may often turn to alternative sources for documents, rather than make their needs known to the library staff. Lancaster points out that when the scheme is attempted on a large library system, the scanning system will become very cumbersome. The approach concentrates only on measurement of effectiveness.

Ray (1978) undertook survey of 67 regional resource centers of the United Methodist Church in terms of services, materials available, facilities and personnel. Data were gathered using a questionnaire mailed to these resource centers. Ray recommended that regional centers should have much larger collections of materials available for circulation, be more active in training their patrons in the use of equipment, involving more people in selection and in weeding materials, maintain better records. There should be at least one full-time resource person at each center.

Oldman (1978) conducted a study on Cranefield Institute of Technology, and Loughbrough University of Technology. The study measured the performance of the libraries in terms of user's perception. Initial expectations of the users, before they had actually used the library, were first recorded and compared with their altered level of satisfaction after the use. The derived value of satisfaction was obtained by the formula given below:

$$\text{Derived Value} = \frac{\text{Perceived Actualisation}}{\text{Expectation}}$$

Burke (1979) in this paper assessed the effectiveness of the Massachusetts Science Resource Network in order to make recommendations about future communicative applications. Questionnaires were sent to a sample of 140 randomly selected legislators in Massachusetts. Achievement Test and Attitude Scale instruments were given to 42 legislators, randomly assigned to three treatment groups of 14 members each, and then analysed using a single-factor analysis of variance.

The study revealed that nearly all of the questionnaire respondents found the Network "useful" or "very useful," believed that the Network influenced their opinions, and thought that videotapes would help their understanding of technical issues. The Achievement Test results showed that videotapes combined with text were more effective than either media alone in raising legislators' comprehension of scientific or technological material. Similar perceptions were recorded on the Attitude Scale.

Joshi (1979) in his paper 'Management Information System' highlighted the need and importance of MIS. He wrote that MIS is a prerequisite not only for control action but also for managerial decisions of short-term as well as long-term nature. He further stated that, "Information pervades almost all aspects of a business organisation. As a country's economy develops in size and complexity, the need for accelerated expansion in information becomes more critical. Information is management information only to the extent to which the manager needs or wants it".

According to this paper, a good information system must enable evaluation of the manager's area of responsibility in relation to the organisation's goals. Information should flow from the level of authority to the level where decisions are being made and also the other way round. The systematic collection of information should be followed by disseminating it in a form which facilitates decision-making of all kinds.

Myers (1979) used unobtrusive techniques to measure the effectiveness of reference and information services in academic libraries in nine Southeastern States of USA. The three instruments were used to collect information from a disproportionate stratified random sample of 40 libraries and alternatives (drawn from a population of 361 academic libraries): observations on fact-type queries asked via telephone, the Library General Information Survey data from 1975, and a questionnaire (response rate 94.9%).

The study showed that librarians gave correct responses to 12 performance test questions only half the time. Performance was poorest on queries that could not be easily answered using basic tools. Even when libraries owned the tool that could have been used to answer the question, librarians did not consult it, or did not know how to use it, or misinterpreted the information given in the source. Rarely did staff members voluntarily indicate the sources for their responses. Performance did not vary by type of control (public or private) of the surveyed academic libraries but did vary by type of institution (two-year college library staff averaged fewer correct answers than did university library staff). The independent variables that explained the greatest variation in the number of correct responses were volumes held and scheduled hours of operation.

Turner (1979) conducted an experimental study to determine the effectiveness of overdue notices in medium-sized public libraries. Reminders were sent to one-half of the borrowers who had overdue items; the other half did not receive notices. The rate of return of these overdue materials was traced during the study period.

It was found that while more of the reminder items were returned than the "no-notice" items during the first 12 days after the notification date, the rate of return was basically the same after that period regardless of whether a notice was sent. The same pattern was followed at a public library which had earlier given up its overdue reminder service. No correlation between weather data and rate of returns was discovered.

Doustdar's (1980) study focused on the development of a method to improve the effectiveness of Iranian academic libraries through co-operation. Data were collected through questionnaires and personal interviews. It was found that the library collections growing rapidly were inadequate to support the full-scale research. Libraries were found to be slow and inefficient. Professional staff of these libraries was inadequate. Co-operation among academic institutions was lacking and hampered the fulfilment of research objectives.

The study suggested that there should be a co-operative acquisition programme, including such features as a copyright system, a national book depository, a national bibliography, and a register of copyrights. Also, there should be shared cataloguing, an expansion of library services through a co-operative centre for Joint Bibliographic Services. Beside this, there should be co-operative programmes in in-service training, workshops, seminars and curriculum reform, to bring qualitative change in the delivery of services.

Cheweh (1981) conducted a study on "User criteria for evaluation of library service". The purpose of the study was (1) to identify the important aspects of library service that the service-recipients, i.e. library users perceive, and (2) to develop a measurement model for evaluation of library service. The data were collected by interviewing over 200 individual library users. The interview resulted in identification of 50 important items as criteria for judging a `good' library. The top 10 items were : (1) availability of books; (2) availability of periodicals; (3) quality reference service; (4) good reference collection; (5) quietness for study; (6) integrity of catalogue; (7) friendly service; (8) copying facilities; (9) availability of non-book materials; and (10) helpful librarians. Based on the findings, a mathematical model as well as a model questionnaire for measuring library service have been developed.

DuMont and DuMont (1981) in their study discussed numerous diverse approaches for assessing and measuring library effectiveness. They showed that most adopt very limited and narrow perspectives and depend upon limited performance criteria. They suggested a way of integrating alternative viewpoints in constructing a goal typology and a systems model of library effectiveness.

DuMont and DuMont (1981) in their article "A goal typology and systems model of library effectiveness" again have recommended numerous and diverse approaches for measuring a library's effectiveness. However, most approaches adopt very limited perspectives and depend upon only narrowly defined performance criteria. They suggested a framework to integrate alternative viewpoints in constructing a goal model of library effectiveness.

Sell (1981) undertook a study to develop a general open system model for effective management and research of the academic library. The intent of this study was to develop and test longitudinally a general open system model for academic librarians by which the effectiveness of a library's performance could be determined and improved.

A tri-level conceptual model was developed on criteria generated by general system methodology. To provide feedback data, a generic straightforward domain-referenced instrument was developed along with the model. The model was pilot-tested in one academic setting, with three annual iterations of the instrument for each of two strata of users. The validity of the instrument, along with the validity and operational utility of the model, appeared to be good. The model appeared to be a valid prototype model for effective management of academic libraries.

Varnado (1981) conducted a study to evaluate the efforts of the University of the District of Columbia (UDC) in meeting the needs of its clientele and in achieving its goals. A survey instrument was used to gather data and was distributed to 262 students, 80 faculty members and 75 administrators.

Faculty members were the least pleased with the library and in general it was found that the library's existing services were not sufficiently responsive to its clientele. Faculty members believed that the library was not sufficiently supportive of the curriculum. Many of the students, faculty and administrators were found to be unaware of the services available from the library.

McGill, Brown and Siegel (1983) in their paper "The Chemical Substances Information Network: its evaluation and evolution" highlighted that The Chemical Substances Information Network (CSIN) was a unique information system which gave its users access to databases and other information systems. In order to test the viability of the CSIN design, a sampling of groups from various types of user organisations were given access to the prototype version of CSIN at an early stage in the development process. A comprehensive plan was developed for the evaluation of the system by these users with particular emphasis on the efficiency, effectiveness and utility of CSIN. The paper highlights the results of this evaluation and draws some preliminary conclusions for the design of systems.

McClure and Reifsnyder (1984) in their paper "Performance measures for corporate information centers" reviewed the current use of library performance measures. Based on performance measures that have been developed for public libraries, the paper provides examples of measures that can be applied in a corporate information centers. The importance of using performance measures as an ongoing evaluation technique, a method for justifying and improving the quality of corporate information services and encouraging the development of an ongoing planning process are stressed.

Tandon (1984) highlighted in his paper "Measuring library effectiveness" the quantitative measurement and dynamic library service. He discussed and differentiated between the terms 'evaluation' and 'measurement' and maintained that while evaluation denotes appraisal, effectiveness refers to the degree of goal achievement. He discussed types, levels, objectives and limitations of library effectiveness and suggested that it was finally related to user satisfaction. He asserted that since evaluation was a management problem, the application of management techniques such as operations research, utility theory and simulations, was indispensable. He outlines the need to alert librarians to new methods of evaluation.

Carter and Zweizig (1985) in their paper "Are we there yet? evaluating library collections, reference services, programme, and personnel" is Part 1 of a 5 lesson continuing education course in evaluation of library collections, reference, library service programmes and personnel. It discusses the terms of evaluation, the planning process and the evaluation process.

Ifidon (1986) in his article "The evaluation of performances" highlights library as a service organisation that is functionally structured for the rendering of information service, for communication and the accomplishment of the library goals. Author briefly examines the objectives of libraries and considers in detail the most important criteria by which a library's performance may be measured: resources, staff, user satisfaction, financial support/cost. Author stresses the need for an established yardsticks for measuring library performances.

Inder Vir (1986) made a study of 146 important scientific and technical libraries (national laboratories, a few agricultural universities and IITs) scattered in different parts of the country. The study dealt with the educational qualifications, placement, salary scales and problems of professional and supporting staff of these libraries. The survey covered 721 publishing scientists from various institutions about their communication patterns, problems and awareness of resources, etc. The major objectives of the study were:

1. To assess the existing resources and services of scientific and technical libraries in India.
2. To study the communication patterns and information needs, problems and awareness of Indian scientists, especially in relation to the existing library systems.
3. To formulate some plans and methods by which the existing information services of scientific and technical libraries and documentation and information centres can be improved.

In this study, 130 libraries were taken into consideration which possess 2 million books and 1.3 million bound volumes of periodicals. However, a point worth noting is that only 15 percent of the libraries possess half of these books and two-third of the bound volumes of periodicals. Similar is the position with regard to finance and other resources. These libraries mainly comprise of books and back volumes of periodicals. With a few exceptions, collections like conference proceedings, dissertations, microforms, etc. are poor in these scientific and technical libraries. With the exception of a few libraries, all libraries are facing hurdles concerning collection, staff, building, computerisation, technical processing. The documentation activities of these institutions are not regular - they start, stop publication for some time and then start again. There is not proportionate increase in library budget, while number of scientists and the cost of reading material is increasing. There is lack of co-ordination and co-operation for the development of library resources. Poor response to document supply requests indicates that co-operation among these libraries is very poor. To enhance the utility of various libraries, co-ordination and co-operation among them must be developed. Some scientific and technical libraries are providing excellent reference services like SDI and CAS while others are not at all service-oriented. The number of inquiries is disproportionately low. Even the National Science Library is not receiving a good number of reference inquiries. The number of requests for the supply of documents that are met by INSDOC in a year, is handled by the BLLD (UK) in a single day. Only development of resources and improvement of bibliographic tools is not sufficient. The document supply system should also be improved and streamlined. Resource sharing among these libraries must be developed. There is an urgent need of computer network to create an effective information network for science and technology, improve science communication facilities as well as the traditional methods of handling information.

Effective communication of scientific information requires co-operation of several individuals, agencies, institutions, etc. The problems of scientific communication in India are not only limited to irregularity of publications, lack of resources, paucity of competent staff, inadequate documentation services, and poor management of libraries but extend much beyond them. Unhelpful attitude, lack of accountability for failures, non-realisation of the value of time, cultural and behavioural problems are some other inhibiting factors. Total dedication to work, morality, spirit of co-operation, utmost sincerity and unquenchable thirst for knowledge are some of the qualities that should be cultivated in scientists if the existing methods and patterns of exchange of information are to be improved.

Certain improvements can be made in the field of information communication, like at least one copy of every doctoral dissertation submitted in the country should be accessible at a designated central place. To improve the documentation supply facilities and to meet fully the country's scientific information requirements, a centre like NISTI must be set up. Other institutions should support the centre like NISTI. Integrated information policy should be made to keeping in view such factors as scientific publications, role of mass media, etc.

Mansbridge (1986) in the paper "Availability studies in libraries" highlighted that availability studies have been used in libraries for the past 50 years to evaluate a library's effectiveness. Over 40 availability studies are examined and their individual features compared with one another. The median sample size in these studies is found to be 437 items and the average availability rate 61%.

White (1986) in the paper "Evaluating library services and programmes" defined the evaluation of library services' effectiveness in terms of providing objective information to library policy makers and programme managers on the effectiveness and cost of alternative as well as existing programmes and services. The elements of evaluation are discussed and the need to view evaluation as a continuous process is emphasised. Library administrators are urged to make a strong commitment to support evaluation efforts within their own libraries in order to improve the availability of information for library decision-making.

Hannabus (1987) in his paper on "The importance of performance measures" discussed the value of performance measures in managing an efficient and cost-effective library. The types of data and criteria which need to be applied to performance measurement are considered.

Miller and Doyle (1987) in their paper 'Measuring the Effectiveness of Computer-based Information Systems in the Financial Services Sector' evaluated the effectiveness of the overall information systems' effort in 21 firms in the financial sector using an instrument based on their previous work. The reliability and construct validity of this instrument were examined using factor analysis and measures of overall effectiveness were related to the particular factors derived.

The research findings revealed that there was no difference in ratings between age groups or levels of management. A slightly significant function discriminated between the responses of DP managers versus user managers and the four sub-sectors in financial services proved to be different, with commercial banks and life assurance firms perceiving themselves more poorly than the other sub-sectors. It has been suggested that information system and user management should adopt survey instruments so that a quick and reliable assessment of their information system function could be made and management may be in a position to focus its efforts on the most crucial areas for success.

Powell (1988) in his studies reviewed the literature on two major approaches for evaluating the effectiveness of library services: user studies and performance measures. He suggested that one of the most meaningful ways to judge the quality and effectiveness of a library's services was to measure how well it was meeting the information needs of the users. He gave suggestions for increasing the potential benefits of both approaches by combining the two techniques.

Kanwal (1990) studied 118 social science research libraries (Central Government, State Government, autonomous and private). He remarked that information is the significant and indispensable factor for the social and economic development of a society. There is a rapid change in the information concepts and its techniques and these changes are not only in scientific and technical libraries but also in social science research libraries.

He emphasised the role of social science information and its influence on policy making and national development in relation to legislation, policy formulation, crisis management, litigation, social inequalities, industrial backwardness and host of other activities. He focussed on the existence of a strong infrastructure of social science research institutions, their libraries and information centres in order to meet the potential information needs of researchers, planners and decision-makers of the country to carry out the vast changes in the social, economic and cultural life of the people through democratic means. He stressed the quantitative growth and qualitative development of social science research institutions, their libraries and information centres.

Gupta (1991) studied the organisation, functions, clientele, resources, services and publications of 80 Government of India (GOI) libraries in Delhi. An attempt was made to describe different issues related to organisational study. These included: (i) historical, (ii) administrative, and (iii) institution as an organisation by identifying its purpose or need, resources and utility or output. She stressed on the access to information on wide spectrum of subjects for meeting the complex activities of planning, decision-making and administration. It is imperative to understand the problems and their solutions to meet the socio-economic and environmental consequences of decision-makers in public administration. The study concludes that government libraries have not gained the proper concentrated attention of the decision-makers. Libraries have been established generally without statutory provision and prior planning. Each department has established its own library which has grown in course of time with response to the demands made upon it. There is no evidence of any co-ordinated effort, norms or standards for proper functioning of these libraries. The perception of the library, its need and service requirement vary considerably from institution to institution. The study traces the historical growth, development and services of GOI libraries, identifies major problematic areas non-conducive to development and suggests some practical solutions to overcome these problems.

A large number of GOI libraries got established due to the exigency of the administration. Individual departments of

GOI establish their own libraries without clear objectivity, policy or statutory provisions.

Sirkin (1991) introduced a paper on "Marketing planning for maximum effectiveness" in the context of special libraries. Author focused on the ways marketing planning process can help special library and information centres to identify the needs of their users and to organise their resources to provide maximum benefits to the users. Author stresses the importance of gaining a better understanding of the needs of the current users and nonusers that the library and information centre seeks to serve. The proper use of marketing planning provides a tool to focus limited staff, time and money for maximum effectiveness. In the case of a library, marketing is the utilisation of the library and its ability to help the user locate information. What you are trying to achieve is not the greatest profit, but the identified mission of the organisation. Marketing planning provides a process through which the organisation can examine whether specific needs can be met within the organisation's overall budget constraints. If all the needs cannot be satisfied, marketing planning provides a methodology for selecting among them to achieve maximum effectiveness. The process helps coordinate and focus staff efforts in a systematic manner.

Kaniki (1992) highlighted on the usefulness of information in a paper 'Meeting the needs of agricultural researchers in Africa: the role of unpublished reports'. Kaniki indicates that the use of information providers varies from person to person or groups of persons, and from place to place. One of the more crucial factors in the use and non-use of information providers, and their perceived usefulness is the orientation of the user to a given type or types of information providers. In other words, the orientation and experience of a person has had with and his or her competence in the use of an information provider, often determines that person's frequency of use and the perceived usefulness of such an information provider in meeting an information need. This means that a person, depending on his or her orientation, may or may not use the most appropriate information provider for a given information need. To correct this situation, therefore, requires a qualified person such as an agricultural information specialist (librarian or documentalist) to assist such an information seeker in the use of most appropriate information providers for specific information needs. In brief, if the information needs of the researcher are fulfilled then he can conduct quality research and generate utilisable information. The use of such information can enhance the production and development of a country. Information professionals or specialists can help to bridge the gap between the information contained in documents and the information needs of the researchers.

Swaroop Rani (1992) in her article 'College library effectiveness' identified the problems faced by college librarians for effective functioning of libraries and gave some suggestions to improve the effectiveness of the college libraries. Author expressed that quality of education was linked with the libraries. To derive minimum benefit from the library resources and its services, the librarians and teachers should share their experiences and convince the students that the use of library was a necessary and meaningful part of education. Author indicated some barriers to academic library effectiveness, such as financial constraints, inadequate space, large number of unprocessed books, and closed library access, lack of knowledge about rules and regulations of library, referring a catalogue, using various reference sources, ignorance about the various services which the library offers, non co-operation by teachers and administrators, lack of interest by librarians, absence of user education (orientation) programmes, system of access, library and learning and system defects. Therefore, the maximum number of books and journals, particularly in academic libraries of India continue lying idle and unused on which several lakhs of rupees have been spent because of the lack of institutes of librarians.

Author indicated that assessment of college library effectiveness can be measured through survey. The academic and research institutions are user oriented and surveys covering library and information centres of these institutions are very useful to measure the effectiveness and justify the existence of the institutions in view of their providing the maximum quantum of information services to their users.

Author suggests that enough staff is required to offer effective services to the users, specially to monitor the incoming and outgoing of books from the shelves, interaction between the 'Trio' - students, teachers, and books. Communication of current information need for the quality of education and researches must be recognised.

To increase the effectiveness of an academic library at the college level, the following programmes would be very helpful: (1) Orientation programmes, (2) library hours, (3) display of books in the classroom in connection with topics taken-up in the lecture class, (4) assignments to be given by teachers that require referring concerned library books, (5) group discussion in classroom involving assignment work, (6) allotment of certain internal mark for assignment and discussion, (7) involving students in the library extension activities like conducting book exhibition, adult education, etc.

The above methods will improve the overall standard of the education by giving a wider exposure of information stored in the library for its users.

Wesley (1992) highlighted in his article 'Human resources for information development in Sudan', that in the age of shrinking resources, it is imperative to increase the effectiveness of available resources through creating opportunities for training manpower resources and taking measures to retain such resources. The level of development of any society is directly correlated with the level of development of its human resources. Human resource development must support the long-range goals of the organisation as well as those of the individual; the aim is to increase the effectiveness and efficiency of the organisation through developing its human resources.

The trained manpower resources of library and information centre are capable to change the societal needs and to increase the effectiveness and efficiency of the organisation. The human resource development process encompasses planning, education, training, and human resource management. Evidence has shown that in-house formal group sessions on job-centred topics have optimum effectiveness. While the costs and benefits of training and the long term value to the institution must be kept in mind, the aim should be to help the individual to further his or her career aspirations within an organisational context.

Goyal (1994) evaluated the effectiveness of Management Information Systems (MIS) and explained that success of any organisation in achieving its predetermined goals and objectives lay in timeliness and quality, that is to say, effectiveness of its MIS. In the present complex world of business as well as management, every organisation must have an efficient and effective MIS to survive and grow to compete with other organisations. He indicated that an effective MIS provides accurate, up-to-date, relevant and timely information to the management of an organisation whereas a poorly designed, developed, implemented or maintained MIS, may be called ineffective, inefficient, defective or poor. Such as MIS may provide inaccurate, irrelevant and obsolete information to the management and decision-makers of the organisation which may prove too costly and even fatal for the organisation.

He further debates that an effective MIS is essential for rational policy decisions by a manager of an organisation. The quality of decision taken by a manager is directly related to the effectiveness of the MIS and the effectiveness of MIS depends upon the quality of information provided by it.

Janak Raj (1994) in his paper 'Effective and efficient library usage under present financial limitations' highlighted the effectiveness and efficiency of library and its usage. He explained that effective and efficient usage of a library to a great extent in the face of financial constraints depends upon effective and efficient functioning of a system.

He points out that "effectiveness relates to outputs and overall criterion of effectiveness is the proportion of user demands that are satisfied. It can be measured in terms of numbers of successes and failures in meeting the demands of the users posed to a system. He explains that effective and efficient usage of library depends upon the improved staff quality, reduced cost of each operation, i.e. cost-effectiveness of an operation, resource sharing and increased demand. In his words, efficient, trained and productive library staff can enhance the effectiveness of any library, by improving the cost-effectiveness of each operation. Resource sharing among libraries can improve the cost-effectiveness, avoid duplication of resources and assist in overcoming financial constraints, concentrating on public relations and bring more awareness among library users and develop library culture among users to make effective use of the library and its resources.

He presents some techniques to study the effectiveness of library usage, and for evaluation of major facets of library operations or library service, such as catalogue use, reference service, literature searching and information retrieval, collection, document delivery capabilities, technical services, computerised activities of the library. The evaluation of one is not dependent on the other. So each library operation and service has to be studied separately to present a composite picture of library effectiveness. Many steps can be taken to improve the effectiveness of a library by increasing accessibility and exposure.

Sasikala (1994) conducted a study to examine the status and picture of 21 industrial libraries in Andhra Pradesh (AP) and their managerial users. In this survey, she covered the origin of industrial library, its organisational structure, number of users, collection and their various aspects, including their kinds, size and arrangement, budget allocation, library staff and types of services provided. She also made a user survey and information seeking behaviour at senior, middle and junior managerial levels. She covered aspects, like the use made of the library, and its resources and services, actual information needs of users and their opinions about physical facilities and various other aspects relating to these libraries.

She found that most of the industrial libraries provide Current Awareness Service (CAS), interlibrary loan service and reprographic service, but Selective Dissemination of Information (SDI) and translation services are being provided by some libraries only. The CAS such as bulletins, routing of periodicals, circulation of copies of contents of periodicals, are all usual services provided by the libraries. These libraries scan a large number of subscribed journals for the CAS and SDI. Application of computer services in these industrial libraries were seen absent except two libraries. Retrospective bibliographies are not prepared as a regular service; these are prepared on the demand of users. Translation service is provided only in German, French, Russian and Japanese languages. Because of the non-availability of equipment in some libraries to provide services, these libraries use the equipment of other departments. Very few libraries conduct the training and user education/orientation programmes for their users.

The study finds out that none of the libraries offered Data Service in its true sense by offering all related data on a specific topic. News clipping service was offered by public relations departments in most of the companies surveyed. On-line literature search was offered by very few libraries. Specialised services, exclusively for top management, were offered only by few libraries, that too occasionally. Most of the surveyed libraries provided the interlibrary loan service mainly on local basis.

Singh (1994) conducted a study on "Indian Institutes of Technology libraries in India: An evaluative study of their growth, development and services". She studied the purpose of visit to the library, the availability of different types of collection, use of different categories of documents, library services, facilities and also ability of IIT libraries to fulfil information needs of research scholars and faculty. She also provides a descriptive analysis of technical and engineering education in India and further compares this system with UK, USA, FRG and USSR. All IITs libraries existing in India were included in this study. This study was also based on a survey.

Bryson (1996) in his book 'Effective library and information centre management' has studied the 'Programme review and performance measures'. He indicated that most common means of measuring a library or information centre performance and value has been through its outputs. Outputs provide a neat, measurable focal point. They can be compared with inputs to measure efficiency and with the corporate goals to measure effectiveness. Output also becomes outcomes when an attempt is made to measure the impact of the outputs on the environment. Outputs, therefore, allow management to measure the effectiveness and efficiency of the library and information centre systems, policies, procedures, leadership, resources and so on, in meeting the needs of the defined target markets. He further emphasises that user's ability to utilise the library's services to create further output is a measure of the library's performance in the form of an outcome. In order to measure performance, information needs to be collected and analysed about the library and information centre performances. The library or information centre manager must determine what pieces of information are needed to evaluate or measure the library's performance. These are called performance indicators.

Brophy and Coulling (1997) studied 'Effectiveness in library and information services' in his book 'Quality management for information and library services'. The study highlights that effectiveness has provided an important building-block on which advances in library quality management can be based. Effectiveness is, of course, concerned with the effect a library has on its users. They studied library effectiveness by prescription of inputs, effectiveness by internal processes, effectiveness by direction or contract fulfilment, effectiveness by professional approach, effectiveness by tradition, effectiveness by systems approach, the organic approach to effectiveness and the coalition approach to effectiveness. The authors suggest that studies of library and information service effectiveness based on systems model and its variants have provided a solid basis to study the future advances in quality management. Effectiveness and quality are closely linked. The combination of library effectiveness and quality management thus provides a greater opportunity to make advances in service provision.

After reviewing seriously the previous literature pertaining to determination of the effectiveness of special libraries besides some other libraries, it is revealed that the effectiveness of the libraries depends upon several factors, equally important from their own points of view. These factors are interwoven. And it is also a proved fact that the end product, i.e. service, is contingent upon availability of relevant and right types of resources and their organisation. Interestingly, enough even availability of best resources and their systematic organisation supported by good infrastructure services, may still prove ineffective in the absence of committed library professionals. In libraries, thus the library staff act as crucial partners in research activities of the organisations by way of extending necessary input.

Financial resources are equally important for enhancing the effectiveness of the library. Of course, the effectiveness can be measured in the light of the fact that what amount of expenditure has incurred on the maintenance and acquisition of informative materials and the amount of services rendered in accordance with the information needs and satisfaction of the users. Therefore, there is always need to examine every aspect of the library for determining its effectiveness.

From the foregoing description, it is clear that there have been stray attempts by individuals to investigate the area extensively. Thus, the area offers scope for research. The present study with its wide coverage would be able to look into the issues systematically.

REFERENCES

1. Bernal, J. D. Preliminary analysis of pilot questionnaire on the use of scientific information. (Royal Society Information Conference, 1948). P.589-637.
2. Bradford, S. C. Documentation. London: Crosby Lockwood, 1948.
3. Rao, K. Ramakrishna. Library development in India. *The Library Quarterly,* 31(2), 1961, 135-153.
4. Wessel, C. J., et al. Criteria for evaluating the effectiveness of library and services. John Thompson, 1967.

5. Hawgood, J. and Morley, R. Project for evaluating the benefits from university libraries. Durham University OSTI. Report 5056, 1969.
6. Orne, Jerrold. The place of the library in the evaluation of graduate work. *College & Research Libraries,* January 1969, 28.
7. Wolfe, J. N., et al. Economics of technical information system. Preager Publishers, 1970.
8. Joffe, Ruth. Determining the effectiveness of the use made of the Industrial and Management Engineering library. Technion-Israel Institute of Technology, 1971.
9. Gothberg, Helen M. User satisfaction with a librarian's immediate and non-immediate verbal-nonverbal communication. Ph. D. Thesis. University of Denver, 1974. 132p.
10. Adeyemi, Nathaniel Motunbade. Co-operation among libraries in Nigeria: A pilot study. Ph. D. Thesis. University of Pittsburgh, 1975. 163p.
11. Faibisoff, Sylvia G. Descriptive case studies of selected New York State Regional Interlibrary Lending Networks as an approach to measuring the effectiveness of the New York State Reference and Research Resources Program (3R) in meeting the information needs of the serious research user. Ph. D. Thesis. Case Western Reserve University, 1975. 414p.
12. Wallace, Burma Morgan. Analysis, usefulness and effectiveness of academic library consortia in the Southeastern States. Ph. D. Thesis. University of Alabama, 1975. 83p.
13. Lancaster, F. W. The measurement and evaluation of library services. Washington, DC: Information Resources Press, 1977.
14. Ray, Morgan Roy. A survey and analysis of United Methodist Regional Resource Centers with suggestions for improved services. Ed. D. Indiana University, 1978. 166p.
15. Oldman, Christine M. The value of academic libraries: A

methodological investigation. Ph. D. Thesis. Cranefield Institute of Technology, 1978.

16. Burke, Anthony Joseph. An evaluation of a communication support system for the dissemination of scientific and technical information in the development of public policy within the Massachusetts State Legislature and recommendations for future communications applications. Ed. D. Boston University, 1979. 232p.

17. Joshi, Navin Chandra. Management information system. *Lok Udyog*, 13(9), 1979, 53-55.

18. Myers, Marcia Jean. The effectiveness of telephone reference/information services in academic libraries in the Southeast. Ph. D. Thesis. Florida State University, 1979. 393p.

19. Turner, Anne M. Overdue reminder notices: A study of their effectiveness in medium-sized public libraries. D.A. Simmons College, 1979.

20. Doustdar, Yahya. A design for co-operation and networking among academic libraries of Iran. Ph. D. Thesis. Case Western Reserve University, 1980. 419p.

21. Cheweh, Steven Seokho. User criteria for evaluation of library service. *Journal of Library Administration*, 2(1), 1981, 35-46.

22. DuMont, Paul F. and DuMont, Rosemary Ruhig. A goal typology and systems model of library effectiveness. *Journal of Library Administration*, 2(1), 1981, 13-23.

23. DuMont, Rosemary Ruhig, DuMont, Paul F. Assessing the effectiveness of library service. Urbana: Illinois University, Graduate School of Library and Information Science, 1981. 24p. (Occasional Paper No. 152).

24. Sell, Betty Marie. Toward a general open system model for effective management and research of the academic library in its setting. Ph. D. Thesis. Florida State University, 1981.

25. Varnado, Kay Lorrell Ford. An analysis of library services at the University of the District of Columbia as perceived

by administrators, faculty members and students. Ed. D. George Washington University, 1981. 229p.

26. McGill, Michael J., Brown, Gerhard E. and Siegel, Sidney. Chemical substances information network. National online meeting 1983: Proceedings of the Fourth National Online Meeting, New York, April 12-14, 1983. Edited by Martha E. Williams and Thomas H. Hogan. Medford, New Jersey: Learned Information, 1983, 367-376.
27. McClure, Charles R. and Reifsnyder, Betsy. Performance measures for corporate information centers. *Special Libraries,* 75(3), 1984, 193-204.
28. Tandon, J. C. Measuring library effectiveness. *Lucknow Librarian,* 16(2), 1984, 65-75.
29. Carter, Jane Robbins and Zweizig, Douglas L. Are we there yet? Evaluating library collections, reference services, programs, and personnel. *American Libraries,* 16(9), 1985, 624-627.
30. Ifidon, Sam E. The evaluation of performance. *Libri,* 36(3), 1986, 224-239.
31. Inder Vir. Science communication: Problems and prospects with special reference to scientific and technical libraries in India. Ph. D. Thesis. Chandigarh: Punjab University, 1986.
32. Mansbridge, John. Availability studies in libraries. *Library and Information Science Research,* 8(4). 1986, 299-314.
33. White, Robert L. Evaluating library services and programs. *Journal of Educational Media and Library Sciences,* 24(1), 1986, 53-65.
34. Hannabus, Stuart. The importance of performance measures. *Library Review,* 36(4), 1987, 248-253.
35. Miller, J. and Doyle, B. A. Measuring the effectiveness of computer-based information systems in the financial service sector. *MIS Quarterly,* March 1987, 107-124.
36. Powell, Ronald R. The relationship of library user studies to performance measures: A review of the literature. Champaign, Illinois: University of Illinois Graduate School of Library and Information Science, 1988. 41p.

37. Kanwal, D. R. Growth and development of social science research libraries. Ph. D. Thesis. Delhi: Delhi University, 1990.

38. Gupta, Anuradha. Growth and development of Government of India libraries in Delhi. Ph. D. Thesis. Delhi: Delhi University, 1991.

39. Sirkin, Arlene Farber. Marketing planning for maximum effectiveness. *Special Libraries,* 82(1), 1991, 1-6.

40. Kaniki, Andrew M. Meeting the needs of agricultural researchers in Africa: The role of unpublished reports. *Information Development,* 8(2), 1992, 83-89.

41. Swaroop Rani, B. S. College library effectiveness. In: Nair, R. Raman and Rajasekharan, K. (eds.). *Academic Library Effectiveness.* New Delhi: Ess Ess Publication, 1992, 82-87.

42. Wesley, Cecile. Human resources for information development in Sudan. *Information Development,* 8(3), 1992, 159-163.

43. Goyal, D. P. Management information system: Concept and application. New Delhi: Deep & Deep Publications, 1994. 203p.

44. Raj, Janak. Effectiveness and efficient library usage under present financial limitations. In: Vashishth, C. P. et al. *New Horizons in Library and Information Science: Dr. Velaga Venkatappaiah Festschrif.* Madras: T. R. Publications, 1994, 449-458.

45. Sasikala, C. Industrial library systems. New Delhi: Reliance Publishing House, 1994. 278p.

46. Singh, S. P. Impact of library services of the Indian Institute of Technology. Ph. D. Thesis. Delhi: Delhi University, 1994.

47. Bryson, Jo. Effective library and information centre management. Bombay: Jaico Publishing House, 1996. P.365-73.

48. Brophy, Peter and Coulling, Hate. Quality management for information and library managers. Mumbai: Jaico Publishing House, 1997. P.133-43.

3

Council of Scientific and Industrial Research: An Introduction

3.0 GENERAL

The history of Council of Scientific and Industrial Research (CSIR) can be traced back to April 1940 when the Board of Scientific and Industrial Research (BSIR) was established with the mandate to co-ordinate the work of the existing scientific organisations. The Board consisted of eminent scientists and industrialists.

CSIR was set up on September 26, 1942 by a resolution of the then Central Legislative Assembly. It is a multi-disciplinary and multi-dimensional organisation and is an autonomous body registered under the Registration of Societies Act XXI of 1860. Sir A. Ramaswami Mudaliar, the then member of the Viceroy's Executive Council, became the founder-President of the Council. The Council of Scientific and Industrial Research is the single largest multi-disciplinary R&D organisation created by the Government of India for promoting research activities within its own laboratories and supported by it in the university system, covers a wide spectrum of scientific and industrial organisations.[1] The Department of Scientific and Industrial Research (DSIR) under the Ministry of Science and Technology provides the administrative link between CSIR and the Government of India.

The functions assigned to the CSIR are :

1. Promotion, guidance and co-ordination of scientific and industrial research in India, including the institution and financing of specific researches;

2. Establishment or development of and assistance to special institutions or departments of existing institutions for scientific study of problems affecting particular industries and trades;
3. Establishment and award of research scholarship and fellowships;
4. Utilisation of the results of the researches conducted under the auspices of the Council towards the development of industries in the country;
5. Establishment, maintenance and management of laboratories, workshops, institutes and organisations to further scientific and industrial research and to utilise and exploit for purposes of experiment or otherwise any discovery or invention likely to be of use to Indian industries;
6. Collection and dissemination of information in regard not only to research but also to industrial matters generally;
7. Publication of scientific papers and journals; and
8. Any other activity or activities to promote generally the objects of the resolution.[2]

3.1 COMPOSITION OF CSIR

After the independence of India, the first Prime Minister Jawaharlal Nehru took over as the President of CSIR. The Society of the Council of Scientific and Industrial Research is the "apex decision-making body" consisting of the following members:

1. The Prime Minister of India as the *ex-officio* President;
2. The Minister-in-Charge of the Ministry or the Department dealing with the Council of Scientific and Industrial Research as the *ex-officio* Vice-President;
3. Ministers-in-Charge of Finance and Industry *(ex-officio) members*;
4. Members of the Governing Body; and
5. Chairman, Advisory Board.

The Governing Body of the Society includes the President of the Society, the Vice President of the Society, the Director General of the CSIR, and such other members that the Governing Body may decide upon. The Director General, Council of Scientific and Industrial Research, is the *ex-officio* Secretary and the Principal Executive Officer of the Society. The CSIR being autonomous has inherent powers of an autonomous society. It reviews the progress and performance of CSIR, gives policy directions to the Governing Body of CSIR and approves the annual accounts and reports of CSIR.

The organisational structure as modified to provide CSIR the best scientific and technical advise, is given below.

CSIR ORGANISATIONAL STRUCTURE

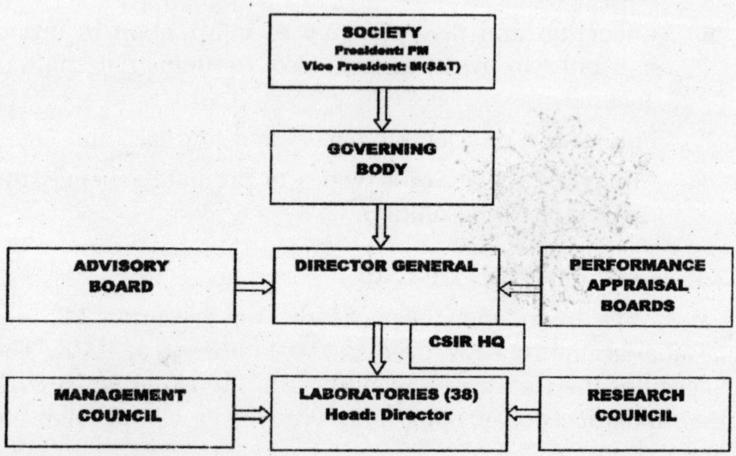

Source: CSIR Profile 2005.

3.2 COMPOSITION OF THE GOVERNING BODY

The Governing Body of the Society as per provision of ACT XXI of 1860 consists of the following members:

(1) the Director General, Council of Scientific and Industrial Research, *ex-officio* Chairman of the Governing Body; (2) Member Finance (Secretary to the Government of India for

financial matters concerning CSIR); (3) Chairmen of two Technical Advisory Boards (TABs); (4) Directors of two CSIR laboratories; (5) Two eminent industrialists, with one from the public sector; (6) Three eminent scientists, with one from academia; (7) Heads of two scientific departments/agencies of the Government of India. The Prime Minister of India who happens to be the President of the society nominates individuals who have excelled in their field for the Governing Body for a period of three years. The Governing Body being highest decision-making body provides over all directions, frames by-laws, etc.

3.3 ADVISORY BOARD OF CSIR

The Governing Body receives academic, scientific and technological inputs from its Advisory Board (AB) which is constituted with external experts from scientific, technical, social science and industrial fields. It also overviews the R&D programmes of CSIR to suggest relative priorities and resource allocations and organises periodic reviews of specific R&D areas and laboratories of CSIR.

The Advisory Board is chaired by an eminent scientist/ technologist from outside the CSIR system and its membership includes: (1) Director General, CSIR, (2) Chairmen of Technical Advisory Boards, (3) Three scientists/technologists/ industrialists, (4) An eminent social scientist, and (5) Four representatives of scientific departments/agencies of the Government of India, as members. Nominations to the Advisory Board are made by the President of the Society.

3.4 TECHNICAL ADVISORY BOARDS OF CSIR

Technical Advisory Boards (TAB) provide a forum for involving government departments, agencies and users in research planning and programme identification in broad areas of CSIR R&D programmes. The TABs are entrusted with the task of identifying newer and thrust R&D areas and evolving long term perspective plans for research priorities. TABs have been established in five broad R&D areas of CSIR which include: Chemical Sciences and Technology; Biological Sciences and Technology; Physical, Earth and Marine Sciences (including

Environment); Engineering Sciences including Electronics and Computers; and Material Sciences and Technology.

A TAB is headed by an eminent scientist/technologist from outside the CSIR system as its Chairman and has a scientist from CSIR as Convener. The other members of TAB include: (1) Laboratory Directors/Project Coordinators concerned with R&D programmes in the area, (2) Eminent Scientist/Technologist in the area from outside CSIR, (3) Representatives of concerned government agencies, departments and users, and (4) Special nominee of the DG, CSIR.

Each TAB undertakes or commissions technological forecasting and chalks out long term perspective plans for research priorities and strategies for CSIR and evolves new areas of R&D, identifies, formulates and monitors the progress of specific major R&D programmes, thrust area and mission projects and suggests networking of laboratories in implementing the programmes identified.

3.5 RESEARCH COUNCIL OF CSIR

The Research Council (RC), operational at the laboratory level, is a body of distinguished professionals in the area of specialisation of the laboratory. RC provides thrust, suggests new areas of research and orients R&D programmes in the desired direction, apart from serving as a professional vehicle for monitoring of resource allocations and utilisation in each laboratory. The Director of the laboratory is accountable to RC on matters relating to R&D activities.[3]

The Director General, Council of Scientific and Industrial Research, is also Secretary to the Department of Scientific and Industrial Research (DSIR), Ministry of Science and Technology. He is assisted in his work by a Secretariat consisting of Technical and Administrative Divisions and Units, namely Planning, S&T Personnel, Technology Utilisation, Extramural Research, International Collaboration, Information and Public Relations, Administration and Finance. His responsibilities include coordinating and exercising general supervision on over all scientific and industrial researches and other activities of CSIR.[4]

3.6 PLANNING DIVISION OF CSIR

The Planning Division is basically responsible for plan formulation, i.e. Five Year and Annual Plans, and for monitoring their implementation. The Technology Utilisation Division is concerned with promotion of the marketing and utilisation of CSIR's knowledge-base, expertise and facilities, and seeking protection of CSIR know-how vis-a-vis import of technology. It participates in inter-ministerial meetings concerned with industrial approvals, namely Licensing Committee, Technical Evaluation Committee, Foreign Investment Board, and Special Approval Committee for Non-Resident Indians. Nine Polytechnology Transfer Centres in different states have been set up to assist the local industrial units in identification and solving of their scientific and technological problems these function under this Division. A Patent Unit secures intellectual property rights for CSIR's R&D output, through obtaining Indian and foreign patents, registration of designs, and guards against infringement of the rights secured.

The Division of S&T personnel is entrusted with the responsibility of operation and maintenance of the Indian Trained Abroad Register, Operation of Scientists, Pool Scheme, running of the TOKTEN (Transfer of Knowledge/Know-how Through Expatriate Nationals) project and compilation, analysis and publication of manpower data. The Extramural Research Division supports extramural research in Universities and other Institutions of Higher Learning, primarily by providing grants for research schemes and by providing Fellowships and Associateships to bright young researchers.

The task of the popularisation of science through regional languages is being carried out by CSIR by providing financial support for publication of journals in regional languages. The Shanti Swarup Bhatnagar prises are the most prestigious scientific awards of the country. At least five prizes, each of Rs.50,000 are awarded annually in physical, chemical, biological, engineering, medical, mathematical and earth sciences.

CSIR identified and prioritised eighteen thrust areas for

conducting R&D work in all its laboratories. The areas are: development of special materials; optical systems for space and defence industrial electronics; resources and parameters mapping of EEZ of Indian seas; development of catalysts; corrosion; modernisation of the leather industry; petroleum and petrochemicals; safety in chemical reaction; software development; polymer science and technology; control of parasitic diseases; vaccines and targeted drugs; fertility regulation; agrotechnologies for aromatic, medicinal and other economic plants; low cost alternative building materials and components; mineral process engineering and mines; metals; and habitat.[5]

3.7 ACTIVITIES OF CSIR

The activities of the CSIR are directed towards providing S&T inputs for effective utilisation of India's resources, development of new products, processes and technologies, strengthening the S&T base in the country, and improving the quality of life of our people at large.

CSIR's expertise and experience is embodied in about 8000 active and highly qualified scientists and engineers supported by over 10,000 technical support personnel, working with an impressive infrastructure built over the years. CSIR is a network of 38 national laboratories/institutes and 39 field stations which are spread throughout the country, dealing with major disciplines in science or specializing in research bearing on major fields of industry. This system has also a pool of talented scientists and technologists who are dedicated to the task of tackling R&D problems of various kinds for the benefit of society. Research programmes in these laboratories range from projects of interest to industry, commerce and agriculture in areas like chemicals, food, housing, leather, mining, metallurgy, paper and transportation, to high technology areas such as aeronautics, cryogenics, electronics, environment, instrumentation, oceanography and special materials.[6]

CSIR, with its chain of laboratories in various fields is the largest organisation for public research in India. It maintains close cooperation and interaction with the Universities and

Institutes of Higher Technology and with the Indian Council of Agricultural Research, the Indian Council of Medical Research, the Atomic Energy Commission, the Railway Research and Designs Organisation, the Defence Research and Development Organisation, and with the Bureau of Indian Standards as well as with technical departments under different ministries. CSIR is now playing a very important role in the planning and formulation of science policy in India.

The focus of CSIR efforts has always been on the development of indigenous technologies and optimum utilisation of indigenous resources. CSIR laboratories today target to actively participate in the industrial growth of our country. CSIR is trying to become a major player in enhancing country's industrial growth and to improve the quality of life of its people.[7]

CSIR Laboratories and Establishments

The following are the laboratories and establishments of CSIR:

1. Central Building Research Institute (CBRI), Roorkee - 247667
2. Central Drug Research Institute (CDRI), Lucknow - 226001
3. Central Electrochemical Research Institute (CECRI), Karaikudi - 630006
4. Central Electronics Engineering Research Institute (CEERI), Pilani - 333031
5. Central Food Technological Research Institute (CFTRI), Mysore - 570013
6. Central Fuel Research Institute (CFRI), Dhanbad - 828108
7. Central Glass and Ceramic Research Institute (CGCRI), Kolkata - 700032
8. Central Institute of Medicinal and Aromatic Plants (CIMAP), Lucknow – 226015
9. Central Leather Research Institute (CLRI), Chennai - 600020

10. Central Mechanical Engineering Research Institute (CMERI), Durgapur - 713209
11. Central Mining Research Institute (CMRI), Dhanbad - 826001
12. Central Road Research Institute (CRRI), New Delhi - 110020
13. Central Salt and Marine Chemicals Research Institute (CSMCRI), Bhavnagar - 364002
14. Central Scientific Instruments Organisation (CSIO), Chandigarh - 160030
15. Centre for Cellular and Molecular Biology (CCMB), Hyderabad - 500007
16. Indian Institute of Chemical Biology (IICB), Kolkata - 700032
17. Indian Institute of Chemical Technology (IICT), Hyderabad - 500007
18. Indian Institute of Petroleum (IIP), Dehradun - 248005
19. Industrial Toxicology Research Centre (ITRC), Lucknow - 226001
20. Institute of Genomics and Integrative Biology, Delhi – 110007 (erstwhile CBT)
21. Institute of Himalayan Bioresource Technology, Palampur - 176001
22. Institute of Microbial Technology (IMT), Chandigarh - 160036
23. National Aerospace Laboratories (NAL), Bangalore - 560017
24. National Botanical Research Institute (NBRI), Lucknow - 226001
25. National Chemical Laboratory (NCL), Pune - 411008
26. National Environmental Engineering Research Institute (NEERI), Nagpur - 440020
27. National Geophysical Research Institute (NGRI), Hyderabad - 500007

28. National Institute of Oceanography (NIO), Goa - 403004
29.* National Institute of Science Communication and Information Resources, New Delhi - 110012 (After merger of erstwhile NISCOM and INSDOC)
30. National Institute of Science Technology and Development Studies (NISTADS), New Delhi - 110012
31. National Metallurgical Laboratory (NML), Jamshedpur - 831007
32. National Physical Laboratory (NPL), New Delhi - 110012
33. Regional Research Laboratory (RRL), Bhopal - 462026
34. Regional Research Laboratory (RRL), Bhubaneswar - 751013
35. Regional Research Laboratory (RRL), Jammu Tawi - 180001
36. Regional Research Laboratory (RRL), Jorhat - 785006
37. Regional Research Laboratory (RRL), Thiruvananthapuram - 695019
38. Structural Engineering Research Centre (SERC), Chennai - 600113

* NISCAIR was formed by merging the National Institute of Science Communication (NISCOM) and the Indian National Scientific Documentation Centre (INSDOC) on 30 September 2002.

REFERENCES

1. Valluri, S. R. CSIR and technological self-reliance. *Economic and Political Weekly*, 28 (14), April 3, 1993, 565.
2. Kashyap, B. C., et al., comp. and eds. CSIR handbook. New Delhi: Council of Scientific and Industrial Research, 1989. P.1.
3. Suresh, N. Fifty years of CSIR: In service of the nation. *The Hindustan Times*, September 26, 1991. P.14.
4. Rahman, Abdur, ed. Science and technology in India, Pakistan, Bangladesh and Sri Lanka. Essex: Longman, 1990. P.38.
5. *Ibid.*, p.35-36.

6. CSIR profile 2005. New Delhi: Council of Scientific and Industrial Research, 2005. 332p.
7. CSIR handbook 1995. New Delhi: Council of Scientific and Industrial Research, 1995.

4

Pure and Applied Research in India

4.0 GENERAL

In ancient India, significant advances were made in mathematics, astronomy, chemistry, medicine, and certain branches of biology. Since the third century BC close contacts with Greeks and during the eighth and the ninth century AD with the Arabs, resulted in much exchange of scientific ideas and knowledge with the Middle East and Europe. The study of science and medicine continued to the end of the 12th century. This was followed by a period of general stagnation and scientific activities had practically ceased at the time of the rise of the European nations in the 17th and 18th centuries.[1]

Research in all fields of human activities means continued search for knowledge, understanding and developing of new ideas, and expanding the horizons and frontiers of the existing knowledge. This had been a continuous process in the universe of knowledge. The process of research is inherent in all disciplines of knowledge, of course, under different names such as scientific research, social science research and research in humanities, with equally different approaches and different techniques and tools of research. The question of research arises because the traditional beliefs and dogmatic interpretations are quiet inadequate to satisfy the inquisitive mind of the modern man. The inadequacy of the beliefs and old interpretations gave rise to the problem of researches. Quest for solutions to emerging problems necessitates an enquiry which ultimately leads to research. The research alone has got an important bearing on development of knowledge. A continuous thinking process goes into the activity of search and also into the creation of new things. In this quest for knowledge, man had been engaged with all his resources for the satisfaction of his needs. Since ancient times, these types of problems or these types of researches have occupied the attention and resources of the growing number of people in the world. In the history of man's quest for knowledge, research has taken either of the two courses; sometimes the emphasis has been more on fundamental research followed by applied research, where man's endeavour is to produce new things for a better life, and this is again followed by fundamental research. However there has been definite shift in modern times. And a balance between the two is being maintained.[2] Laying stress on research, P. C. Mahalanobis said, "Improvements in science teaching and research can be brought about only through vigorous and untiring efforts of scientists themselves".[3]

In modern world, it has been established beyond doubt that the knowledge and development in science and industry are the roads for national prosperity. The richness and resourcefulness of western world today is basically due to the development of science and industry. The people in underdeveloped countries, therefore, have every reason to feel that by the development of research in sciences, and their application in technology and production, that they could be at par with the developed countries. The gap between the underdeveloped and the developed countries is not due to the gap in the intellectual standards but more because of the lack of scientific and technological development. As Homi J. Bhabha rightly said, "... the problem of establishing science as a live and vital force in society is an inseparable part of the problem of transforming an industrially underdeveloped to a developed country".[4]

India's contributions in the field of science during the earlier periods of history are well known and well recorded. However, its failure to apply its inventions and theories for production purposes has caused wide gaps. The history of science is full of landmarks created by Aryabhatta, Susruta, Varahamihira, and Bhaskara. Several historical factors caused a sudden break in scientific achievements after the twelfth century; still in certain areas, such as astronomy, the tradition continued and resulted in the setting up of observatories in Jaipur and Delhi.

The emergence of scientific research in modern India began with the establishment of the Asiatic Society of Bengal in Calcutta by Sir William Jones on January 15, 1784. It was an attempt to preserve and study the science and literature of ancient India and Asia. The Society during the first century of its existence provided an effective plank supported by a library, and a collection of ancient coins and medals as well as archaeological, technological and geological collections. In order to publicise views and results of research work, the Society started publication of the **Journal of the Royal Asiatic Society of Bengal** in 1832. The journal published papers on zoology, botany and anthropometry, with some papers in physics, meteorology, chemistry, geology and medical sciences. It thus played stimulating and most important roles in the advancement of sciences in India.

During the nineteenth century of British regime, a number of organisations were set up for promoting and encouraging scientific research activities in various disciplines of pure and applied sciences, such as anthropology, botany, mathematics, physics, chemistry, meteorology, geology, medical science, zoology, etc. The Trigonometrical Survey (1800), the Geological Survey (1851), the Archaeological Department (1862), the Indian Museum (1866), the Indian Coastal Survey (1875), Indian Meteorological Department (1875), the Indian Research Association (1876), Indian Association for the Cultivation of Science (1876), the Botanical Survey (1890) and the other periodical surveys opened up vast and previously almost untouched fields for investigation. Medical colleges were started in Madras and Calcutta in 1835, and in Bombay in 1845. Scientific activities and researches were also carried out by medical men, engineers and civilians working in defence establishments in their spare time. A number of basic monographs on various scientific subjects were published.[5]

The beginning for organised research in medical sciences was made in 1869 when Dr. Lewis and Dr. Cunningham initiated a systematic research on Cholera, Malaria, Beri-beri and Kala-azar. The Haffkine Institute which was initially started in 1899 as the Plague Research Laboratory, gradually expanded its activities to include Antirabic, Pharmacological and Biochemical research.

Research activities in Agriculture and Veterinary Science were mostly done in various Provincial Departments of Agriculture. Agricultural Departments were set up in Bombay (1885), Madras (1889), Shillong (1894), Allahabad and Nagpur (1895), and Bengal (1896). The Imperial Bacteriological Laboratory was established in Poona in 1889 for Veterinary Research and was moved to Mukteswar in 1893, where it later became the Indian Veterinary Research Institute (1895). The Indian Association for the Cultivation of Science was the first research centre to have established through private munificence. It was founded in 1876 by Dr. Mahendra Lal Sircar for the propagation of science through public lectures, and later became an important centre for physical research, culminating in the discovery of the Raman Effect.[6]

Government of India established a number of important research institutes in the early twentieth century. The Imperial Agricultural Research Institute (1905) in Pusa, Bihar, the Central Research Institute for Medical Research (1905) in Kasauli, the Forest Research Institute (1906) in Dehradun, the King Institute of Preventive Medicine (1903) in Madras, and the Pasteur Institute (1907) in Coonoor, were some of the important institutes established for carrying out applied research in diverse fields. For the prosecution and assistance of research relating to the causes and prevention of diseases, the Government of India established the Indian Research Fund Association (1911) which later became the Indian Council of Medical Research. Indian Science Congress (1914) and Zoological Survey of India (1916) were also established one by one. Bose Institute (1917) in Calcutta was founded by Sir Jagdish Chandra Bose which is famous for its pioneering work in biophysical researches.

Other applied research institutes were established during this period, in which the Toklai Experimental Station in Assam for Research on Tea (1911), the Dairy Research Institute (1923) at Bangalore, the Cotton Technological Research Laboratory (1924) in Bombay, the Institute of Plant Industry (1924) in Indore, the Indian Lac Research Institute (1925) in Ranchi, the Imperial Council of Agricultural Research (1929) which later became the Indian Council of Agricultural Research are very famous in the fields of applied sciences.

A number of scientific societies were also established during this decade, including the Institution of Engineers (1920) in Calcutta; Anthropological Society (1920) in Calcutta; the Indian Botanical Society (1921) in Madras, the Indian Chemical Society (1924) in Calcutta; the Geological, Mining and Metallurgical Society of India (1924) in Calcutta; and the National Academy of Sciences (1930) in Allahabad.

These activities in scientific research and education also were continued at the beginning of 1930s. During this period new Universities, Research Institutions and Scientific Societies came into existence. This led to greater involvement of scientists and professionals in such activities. The first Academy of Sciences, then known as the United Provinces Academy of Sciences, was set up at Allahabad in 1930. It was later renamed as the National Academy of Sciences. The Indian Academy of Sciences was established at Bangalore in 1934. National Institute of Sciences of India was inaugurated in Calcutta in 1935. In 1945, the Government of India declared the National Institute of Sciences to be the premier scientific society in the country, and in 1947 the headquarter was shifted to Delhi. It was renamed as the Indian National Science Academy (INSA) in February 1970.

In order to have organised system of technological training and research at the postgraduate level, five Indian Institutes of Technology were set up during 1950-61 at Kharagpur (1950), Bombay (1958), Madras (1959), Kanpur (1960), and Delhi (1961) and later two more Indian Institutes of Technology were introduced in the chain of IITs at Guhawati and Roorkee Engineering College was renamed as IIT. In the words of the late Prime Minister Jawaharlal Nehru, the IITs were expected 'to provide scientists and technologists of the highest caliber who would engage in research, design and development to build the nation towards self-reliance in her technological needs'.[7] In addition, there are 18 National Institutes of Technology (formerly known as Regional Engineering Colleges) (RECs). Later four Indian Institute of Information Technology (IIIT) were established to promote the information technology and its application in diverse fields in the country.

No doubt, science has made a significant contribution in the social and economic development of the society. Discussing the social importance of science, Jawaharlal Nehru once said: "It is science alone that can solve the problems of hunger and poverty, of insanitation and illiteracy, of superstition and the deadening custom and tradition, of vast resources running to waste, of a rich country inhabited by starving people.... Who, indeed, could afford to ignore science today? At every turn, we have to seek its aid.... The future belongs to science and to those who make friends with science."[8]

4.1 THE ROLES OF UNIVERSITIES IN HIGHER EDUCATION AND RESEARCH IN INDIA

India has developed a very large system of higher education in the last five decades. The tremendous surge in the number of young students seeking higher education in science has led to the emergence of new universities, colleges, national laboratories and private research facilities. The number of university level institutions has increased from 20 in 1947 to 320 in the year 2003-2004, the enrolment of students has increased from 2,28,804 in 1947 to 99,53,506 in 2003-2004, the number of colleges has increased from 591 in 1947 to 16,885 (university colleges and affiliated college) in 2003-2004. The number of teaching faculty in universities and colleges has increased from 15000 in 1950 to 4,56,742 in 2003-2004.[9] Indian higher education system is the second largest in the world after the USA which is imparting education in different disciplines. Its coverage is only 7 per cent of the population between the age group 17-23 years which is very low when compared with those attained by other developing countries like Indonesia (11%), Brazil (12%), Mexico (14%) and Thailand (19%). The levels of participation of developed countries are: France (50%), UK (52%), USA (81%), Canada (100%).[10]

The role of universities in nation building is, indeed, most crucial. Pandit Jawaharlal Nehru, in his convocation address to the University of Allahabad in 1947, emphasised the objectives of the University and its role in national life. In his words, 'A University stands for humanism, for tolerance, for reason, for the adventure of ideas and for the search of truth. It stands for the onward march of the human race towards ever higher objectives. If the Universities discharge their duties adequately, then it is well with the nation and the people'.[11]

Sir S. S. Bhatnagar in the Seventh Convocation of University of Rajputana, Jaipur, on November 20, 1954 said, "University education is dynamic in character."[12] Ancient India had well-known Universities at Nalanda, Taxila and Vallabhi, which attracted famous scholars and students from all over the country and from abroad. Modern higher education system in India is 148 years old. Modern universities in India were set up under the British regime in 1857 at Bombay, Calcutta and Madras, as institutions patterned on London University. They started purely as examining bodies and continued to be so until the beginning of the twentieth century. Later, two more universities, one at Lahore in 1882 and the other at Allahabad in 1887 were established. C. V. Raman, M. N. Saha, S. N. Bose, D. N. Wadia, P. C. Mahalanobis, S. R. Kashyap, Birbal Sahni, S. Ramanujan, and S. Chandrashekhar carried out globally competitive scientific research. Many of these scientists were trained in India and carried out their research in various disciplines in Indian universities.[13]

The appointment of the Indian Universities Commission in 1902 and the enactment of Indian Universities Act in 1904 are the two important landmark in the history of higher education in India. Higher education was given further boost by the Government of India's Resolution on Educational Policy (1913) which recommended the need for separate university for each of the leading provinces and establishment of residential universities within each Province to impart higher education. Such measures gave birth to six new universities between 1913 and 1921; namely; Banaras and Mysore (1916), Patna (1917), Osmania (1918), Aligarh (1920) and Lucknow (1921). Lucknow University was established as a residential University. The transfer of educational control from Britain to Indians in 1921, brought about faster development of universities in India. During the next 26 years, nine more universities were established between 1921 and 1947 with teaching and research facilities.

The entire field of university education was reviewed soon after Independence (1947), by an Education Commission headed by Dr. S. Radhakrishnan. It is known as Radhakrishnan Commission. Its recommendations, which have since been implemented, had considerable impact on the growth of the universities. Later on, the Education Commission (1964-66), appointed by the Government of India in July 1964 under the chairmanship of Dr. D. S. Kothari, submitted its report on June 29, 1966, which has provided the basis for widespread discussion at all levels, regarding the educational reconstruction of the country.[14]

As stated by the Education Commission in its report, the first and foremost function of an Indian University should be that it must "strive to serve as the `conscience of the nation', as assessor of the national way of life".[15]

Post-independent India saw some major changes and systematic efforts for the advancement of higher education. The University Grants Commission (UGC) was set up in 1953 on the lines of the United Kingdom University Grants Committee, with the basic objectives to promote and co-ordinate university education and to determine and maintain standards of teaching, examination and research in universities. It also advises the Government on the establishment of new universities and other matters pertaining to higher education. The Commission is generally responsible for the co-ordination and maintenance of standards in higher education.

The Commission in order to provide and promote advance level of research has started a number of "Centres of Advanced Study" in Indian universities, in special fields of Astronomy, Botany, Chemistry, Geology, Mathematics, Physics,

Zoology, etc. These Centres of Advanced Study in Science are intended to encourage the "pursuit of excellence" and to raise standards at the postgraduate and research levels, function on all India basis and provide conditions and facilities attractive to scientists of outstanding ability and qualifications.[16]

The education system should change according to the changing environment of the society. As C. D. Deshmukh said, "There is probably no country in the world which is not concerned with the progress of its educational institutions and the resolution of the problems that arise from time to time so that the educational system may be fully adapted to the modern environment." [17]

The Education Commission (1964-66) commenting upon the system of higher education in India referred to the general feeling in India, "that the situation in higher education is unsatisfactory and even alarming in some ways, that the average standards have been falling and that rapid expansion has resulted in lowering quality." Mentioning the difficulties of precise measurement of standards of higher education, the Commission pointed out that ".....over a large area of education, the content and quality are inadequate for our present needs and future requirements and compare unfavourably with the average standards in other educationally advanced countries. What is worse, the large gap between the standards in our country and those in advanced countries is widening rapidly. Many of our educationists and public men, however, have not fully realised how serious are the actual conditions, academic and physical, that obtain in the colleges and universities...." [18]

It is strange that the situation has not changed materially even after the lapse of twenty years since the Education Commission reported. As it can be gauged by the observations made in the National Policy on Education (1986) which referred to the unprecedented explosion of knowledge and the need for higher education becoming "dynamic as never before, constantly entering uncharted areas."[19]

In May 1986, the new National Policy on Education (NPE) was adopted by the Government of India due to the non-implementation of 1968 Education Policy. It laid down the emphasis on the elimination of disparities in the educational system. It says, "steps will be taken to facilitate inter-regional mobility by providing equal access to every Indian of requisite merit, regardless of his origin". Besides this the emphasis was laid on the establishment of network arrangements between different institutions in the country to pool their resources and participate in the projects of national importance. The policy focused upon enhancing support to research in the universities for ensuring high quality. On 7th May1990, the Government of India appointed a Ramamurti Committee (1990) to review the National Policy on Education, 1986. The committee emphasised that the quality of higher and technical education is to be improved in real terms not only to make it relevant to the society but also to cater to the needs of competitive industry.[20]

The Nobel Laureate Amartya Sen delivered his keynote address in South Asian Conference on Education on November 14, 1999 at New Delhi. He said, "University education in India is in a state of crisis, it is not a crisis of lack of resources. It is deterioration of quality". He argued that when it comes to higher education, there is no escape from seeking the highest quality we can get. Quality would vary from one university to another. However the minimum level of quality should be ensured. The conditions in most of the universities in India are critical due to the lack of resources and facilities to researchers. The laboratories are obsolete and depleted, the infrastructure is non-existent and faculty is indifferent, incompetent. Even financial crisis has affected the libraries, laboratories and other facilities to academics and research scholars. Lack of infrastructure has badly affected the higher educational organisations and quality of education that results unable to attract or retain the talented and high quality students and high quality faculty members. Prof. C. N. Rao of Jawaharlal Nehru Centre for Advanced Scientific Research, Bangalore, has rightly said, "What I see around me is not encouraging. The universities which are the fountains of knowledge and sources of manpower are decaying fast and there are very few of them where good quality work can be done because of the poor infrastructure and a varieties of the other factors, including unhealthy practices and interferences. The absorptive capacity of most of our universities has decreased to an extent that even if large research grants were to be provided, they would not be in a position to pursue worthwhile programmes. The situation is rather precarious and unless remedial measures are taken on war footing, we may lose these institutions entirely. It will be difficult to create them again."[21]

4.2 AGRICULTURAL RESEARCH

The commercial compulsions led the British to think about Indian agriculture in scientific terms. The Department of Revenue, Agriculture and Commerce was started in 1871. In 1880s the Colleges of Agriculture at Coimbatore and Poona were established to impart higher education in agriculture. But the Famine Commission's work, in which the Department of Agriculture was fully involved, prevented it from carrying out its main task. Around 1889, Dr. J. A. Voeloker, an Agricultural Chemist, was sent to India to advise on the application of Agricultural Chemistry to improve Indian agriculture. Veterinary research was encouraged to take care of the health of military animals, particularly horses. In this way, the Imperial Bacteriological Laboratory came up in 1889 at Poona, and the Imperial Veterinary Research Institute (presently Indian Veterinary Research Institute (IVRI) at Izatnagar in 1898. The establishment of the Imperial Agricultural Research Institute at Pusa (Bihar), and new Colleges of Agriculture in the provinces, viz at Kanpur, Nagpur, Lyallpur (now in Pakistan) was the first step in 1905. Irrigation and Famine Commissions' recommendations further directed attention to agriculture, including forestry. The Indian Central Cotton Committee set up in 1921 and the Imperial Institute of Animal Husbandry and Dairying (the forbearer of the National Dairy Research Institute at Karnal and at Bangalore) in 1923 gave a new orientation to crop research and animal sciences respectively. In spite of these, agricultural economy remained under extortive land tenures and was marked by low productivity.[22]

The beginning of the 20th century witnessed some dynamic effort towards establishment of Agricultural Research

Institutes. During this period, it was contemplated that radical improvement in agricultural practices can be brought about through establishment of experimental farms and agricultural colleges.

Constitutional changes were brought about in 1919, whereby responsibility for agricultural research and development was transferred to the State Governments in 1921. Previously, the administration and co-ordination of agricultural development work and the Government policy relating to it had been the responsibility of the Central Government. The need for a central agency to co-ordinate agricultural research was considered by the Royal Commission on Agriculture (1928) under the chairmanship of Lord Linlithgow.[23] The Commission submitted its report and proposed the setting up of Imperial Council of Agricultural Research. As a consequence, Imperial Council of Agricultural Research as a Society was set up in 1929 to promote and encourage scientific studies in the field of agriculture and veterinary sciences. The Council was renamed as the Indian Council of Agricultural Research (ICAR) on June 10, 1947.

ICAR was reorganised into a fully autonomous organisation in 1965. It was given fresh mandate for undertaking, promoting and coordinating research in the broad field of agriculture. In addition to this, the Council was entrusted with the responsibility of imparting higher education in agriculture. As a sequel, all research institutes were placed under its control.

In 1948, the Education Commission under the Chairmanship of Dr. S. Radhakrishnan recommended the establishment of Rural Universities in the country. Subsequently, several committees established by the Government of India recommended the establishment of Agricultural Universities on the Land Grant Pattern of the USA.[24] Agricultural education scaled a new height in early 1960s. During this period, a chain of Agricultural Universities was established in all provinces of India on the pattern of Land Grant Colleges of United States. It was carried out in three phases. First phase saw the establishment of agricultural universities. This phase covers the period between 1960 to 1965. During this period, seven Agricultural Universities were set up. These were (i) Govind Ballabh Pant University of Agriculture and Technology, Pantnagar (1960), (ii) University of Udaipur, Udaipur (1962) (this university was set up as a general university with an agricultural component on certain local reasons and certain grounds of policy. This University is also known as Rajasthan Agricultural University), (iii) Orissa University of Agriculture and Technology, Bhubaneswar (1962), (iv) Punjab Agricultural University, Ludhiana (1963) (from which after reorganisation of state, Haryana Agricultural University emerged), (v) Jawaharlal Nehru Krishi Vishwa Vidyalaya, Jabalpur (1965), (vi) Andhra Pradesh Agricultural University, Hyderabad (1965) and (vii) University of Agricultural Sciences, Bangalore (1965). Pantnagar pioneered in production of improved wheat seeds for the large areas and other Universities, e.g. Ludhiana recorded success in many other fields and ushered in the Green Revolution. Success of the universities and degree of agricultural progress in its area have generally gone together.

In the second phase i.e. between 1969 to 1971, eight Agricultural Universities were established, namely - (i) Mahatma Phule Krishi Vidyapeeth, Rahuri (1969), (ii) Punjab Rao Krishi Vidyapeeth, Akola (1969), (iii) Marathwada Agricultural University, Parbhani (1972), (iv) Konan Krishi Vidyapeeth, Dapoli (1972), (v) Assam Agricultural University, Jorhat (1969), (vi) Haryana Agricultural University, Hissar (1970) (Separated from Punjab), (vii) Tamil Nadu Agricultural University, Coimbatore (1971), (viii) Rajendra Agricultural University, Patna (1971).

In the third phase of establishment of Agricultural Universities, which started from 1972 to 1978, the new universities were: (i) Kerala Agricultural University, Mannathy (1972), (ii) Gujarat Agricultural University, Dante Wada (1972), (iii) Bidhan Chandra Krishi Vishwa Vidyalaya, Haringhatta, District Nadia (1974) (iv) Chandra Shekhar Azad University of Agriculture and Technology, Faizabad (1976) (v) Himachal Pradesh Krishi Vishwa Vidyalaya, Palampur, (1978). In later years two more universities were established, the latest one being Agricultural University of Jammu and Kashmir at Shalimar (Srinagar). These Agricultural Universities are engaged in pursuit of triple functions of agricultural education, research and extension education in respect of the areas assigned to them by the State Governments.

Indian Council of Agricultural Research is a vast network of Research Institutes, Bureaus, National Research Centres and Project Directorates in the country. There are 47 Agricultural Research Institutes, 37 Agricultural Universities, 5 deemed-to-be-universities and one central agricultural university, 5 National Bureaux, 32 National Research Centres, 12 Project Directorates, 93 All India Coordinated Research Projects and 415 Krishi Vigyan Kendras (KVKs) in rural districts of the country and eight trainers training centres engaged in the promotion of agricultural development in the country.[25] The ICAR is an apex organisation for all agricultural and animal husbandry research and education in the country.

4.3 MEDICAL RESEARCH

As a result of the recommendations made by the Indian Medical Congress in 1894, a series of Central and Provincial Laboratories were established by the Government, with adequate facilities for research. The Haffkine Institute was followed by the first Pasteur Institute established in Kasauli in 1900, and a second Pasteur Institute was started in Coonoor in 1907. All these institutes had adequate facilities for research work.[26]

The Government of India established the Indian Research Fund Association (IRFA) in 1911 with specific purpose to promote scientific medical research in India. IRFA took upon itself the role of a promoter of scientific medical research and gave necessary impetus to research activities in the country, specially relating to malnutrition, malaria, rabies, plague, cholera, leprosy and kala-azar etc. Some of the Centres where such work had started developed into full fledged institutes in due course. The Malaria Institute of India at Kasauli was developed in 1926 from the Central Malaria Bureau and was entrusted with the main function of treatment of malaria and of advising the Government on antimalarial measures.[27] The Association had put up two schemes, one for establishing a Central Medical Research Institute at Dehradun and a Public Health Institute at Calcutta. The Calcutta scheme, supported by the initiative of the Rockefeller Foundation, had a better reception and the All India Institute of Hygiene and Public Health was set up in 1928. The activities of the Association were restricted due to the economic depression during the early thirties and thus the position did not improve until the end of the Second World War. During this period there was a change in the status of the Association, which became an autonomous body on March 22, 1938.[28]

Health Survey and Development Committee was appointed under the chairmanship of Sir Joseph Bhore in 1942 to meet both health care delivery services and medical education facilities, specially postgraduate education. The Bhore Committee reviewed the position of medical research in India and submitted its report in 1946. The Committee highlighted the lack of organised research in medical colleges and emphasised the need for a strong central organisation for medical research, which was suggested to be the National Research Council of India. In the field of medical research the Bhore Committee's recommendations are the landmark, as they, in fact, formed the basis for the development of medical research.

In 1949 the IRFA was renamed as the Indian Council of Medical Research (ICMR). ICMR is an apex body in India for the formation, co-ordination and promotion of biomedical research. It discharges its primary function of promoting biomedical research, mainly through its permanent research institutes, centres of advanced research, regional medical research centres, national multicentric co-ordinated projects and through a large number of adhoc research schemes generated by working scientists, in biomedical institutions and universities in India. A major objective of ICMR is to strengthen indigenous capability and develop a broad-based and balanced cadre of able research personnel and facilities to cope with the present and future health problems of India.[29] ICMR is a very well organised network of 21 permanent Research Institutes and Centres, 6 Regional Medical Research Centres, and 8 Centres for Advanced Research. The 21 permanent institutes and centres which are engaged to address issues of specific diseases, are: Central JALMA Institute for Leprosy, Agra; National Institute of Occupational Health, Ahmedabad; National Institute of Epidemiology, Chennai; Tuberculosis Research Centre, Chennai; Malaria Research Centre, Delhi; Food and Drug Toxicology Research Centre, Hyderabad; National Centre for Laboratory Animal Science, Hyderabad; National Institute of Nutrition, Hyderabad; National Institute of Cholera and Enteric Diseases, Kolkata; Centre for Research in Medical Entomology, Madurai; Enterovirus Research Centre, Mumbai; ICMR Genetic Research Centre, Mumbai; National Institute for Research in Reproductive Health, Mumbai; Institute of Immunohaematology, Mumbai; Institute for Research in Medical Statistics, New Delhi; Institute of Cytology and Preventive Oncology, New Delhi; Institute of Pathology, New Delhi; Rajendra Memorial Research Institute of Medical Sciences, Patna; and Vector Control Research Centre, Pondicherry; National AIDS Research Institute, Pune; and National Institute of Virology, Pune.

ICMR's six Regional Medical Research Centres are: Regional Medical Research Centre, Bhubaneshwar; Regional Medical Research Centre, Dibrugarh; Regional Medical Research Centre for Tribals, Jabalpur; Desert Medicine Research Centre, Jodhpur; Regional Medical Research Centre, Port Blair; Regional Medical Research Centre, Belgaum. ICMR has eight Centres for Advanced Research such as ICMR-NIC Centre for Biomedical Information, New Delhi; Centre for Advanced Research for Clinical Pharmacology in Traditional Medicine, Mumbai; Centre for Advanced Research for Drug Development from Natural/ Plant Products, Lucknow; Advanced Centre for Cellular and Molecular Reproduction, Bangalore; Centre for Advanced Research on Clinical Pharmacology, Mumbai; Centre for Advanced Research on Aging and Brain, Hyderabad; Centre for Advanced Research in Molecular Medical Microbiology, Bangalore; and Advanced Centre for Liver Diseases, New Delhi.

Some of the significant areas in which ICMR is focused are tuberculosis, cholera, leprosy, malaria, filariasis, leishmaniasis and diarrhoeal diseases, nutritional disorders and nutritional surveys, food and drug toxicology, immunohaematology, reproduction, medical statistics and viral diseases like HIV/ AIDS, malaria, dengue and kala-azar.

4.3.1 Post-graduate Medical Education and Research

After Independence, the ICMR took stock of the situation and, instead of confining activities merely to infectious diseases, it began to pay attention to a broad spectrum of medical topics both in fundamental and applied research. Important areas in which it expanded its activities included communicable diseases, cancer, nutrition, cardiovascular diseases, maternal and child health, mental health, reproductive physiology, medical education, occupational health, environmental medicine and health practices.

The recommendations of the Bhore Committee also stressed upon the need for organised research in medical colleges and the setting up of an institute for training of highly qualified teachers and research workers. In 1947, India had only 16 medical colleges and today there are more than 160 recognised medical colleges and institutions with an annual enrolment of 16,000 students. In addition, there are a number of national institutes and specialty centres spread around the country in different disciplines. After independence, there was a rapid growth of medical colleges all over the country. To meet the growing needs of teachers for these colleges and institutions and to create an environment for high quality research, All India Institute of Medical Sciences (AIIMS) as an autonomous institution of national importance was established at New Delhi in 1956 by an Act of the Parliament. This was followed by the establishment of several other such institutes like Post-Graduate Institute of Medical Education and Research (PGIMER), Chandigarh, Pondicherry, Calcutta and later in Lucknow also. The National Institute of Neurosciences and Mental Health (NIMHANS), Bangalore, and Sri Chitra Tirunal Institute for Medical Sciences and Technology, Thiruvananthapuram were started to meet the growing needs of medical research in the country. The Government of India also created centres of excellence in different medical colleges by upgrading certain departments for post-graduate education. Post-graduate centres in medical sciences were established in Ahmedabad, Calcutta, Chandigarh and Pondicherry by taking over and strengthening the existing institutions. The Post-Graduate Institute of Indian Medicine was set up at the Banaras Hindu University in 1963. Separate faculties for Ayurvedic studies have been established in the Universities of Indore, Jammu and Kashmir, Jiwaji, Kerala, Lucknow, Marathwada, Poona, Rajasthan and Ravishankar. The Gujarat Ayurvedic University was set up at Jamnagar in 1967.[30]

Besides this, a number of institutes have been created by the Indian Council of Medical Research, Council of Scientific and Industrial Research, Department of Biotechnology (DBT) and several other agencies which are actively engaged in biomedical research. These organisations have introduced centres to address issues of specific diseases. In addition to the ICMR, several scientific agencies have created research centres in specialised fields related to medical sciences like the National Institute of Immunology, New Delhi, National Centre for Cell Sciences, Pune; Centre for DNA Fingerprinting and Diagnostics, Hyderabad; National Brain Research Centre, Manesar; Functional Genomic Research Unit at Centre for Biochemical Technology, Delhi by DBT. Likewise the Central Drug Research Institute, Lucknow; Indian Institute of Chemical Biology, Kolkata; Indian Institute of Chemical Technology and Centre for Cellular and Molecular Biology, Hyderabad; Industrial Toxicology Research Centre (ITRC), Lucknow; and Central Institute of Medicinal and Aromatic Plants, Lucknow were established by the CSIR and Radio-pharmaceutical Centre and Cancer Research Centre by the Atomic Energy Commission. Thus a network of centres provides the infrastructure for medical research in the country. Research and Development in the medical field is also being carried out at medical colleges, major hospitals and research centres in the country. In recent years a few research centres have been established by the major pharmaceutical industries and private organisations. No doubt these developments have resulted in a significant improvement in our health indices. Life expectancy at birth which was around 30 years in 1947, is already 60+. The infant mortality has come down from 140 to 72 per 1000 live births and maternal mortality to 4.6 per thousand. Important contributions of national and international significance have been made in recent years in every sphere of biomedical research such as BCG trial, the oral polio vaccine studies, the iodine deficiency syndromes, the indigenously developed leprosy vaccine trials or the bio-environmental approaches to control malaria, epidemiological studies on cholera, malaria, filaria, leprosy, tuberculosis, cataract, coronary heart disease, stroke and cancer.[31]

4.4 DEFENCE RESEARCH

Until the nineteen thirties, the application of science and technology to defence was very limited and mostly restricted to testing defence stores and equipment. The Second World War brought with it a number of technical problems connected with procurement, maintenance, storage, preservation and modification of equipment and stores to suit local conditions and the utilisation of indigenous materials. The emerging need of the time led to the expansion and improvement of laboratories and technical development establishments. During the forties, these units were further expanded and restructured. As a result of this the Defence Science Organisation was set up in 1948 to advise and assist the Defence Services on scientific problems and to execute research in the domain of defence issues. To study all aspects of the application of science in defence, the Defence Production Board was created to provide an integrated control over research, design, development, production and inspection.[32]

In 1958, the Defence Research and Development Organisation (DRDO) was constituted by amalgamating the units of Defence Science Organisation and the Technical Development Establishments of three services. It was set up to observe the organisations for defence production and inspection. With this as the nucleus, many organisations have now been built up to meet the growing scientific needs relevant to national security. Later a separate Department of

Defence R&D was constituted in 1980 to improve organisational administrative efficiency. DRDO is the largest scientific establishment of the country. DRDO handles a network of 51 research laboratories/establishments in close partnership with about 40 academic institutions, 15 national S&T agencies, 50 PSUs and 250 private sector enterprises.

In pre-independence phase, the technical requirements of the Defence Forces were provided to only a limited extent through a number of technical development establishments (TDEs). Since independence, India has come a long way to achieve a larger measure of self-reliance in terms of defence items. In 1948, the Defence Science Organisation was set up to avoid dependance on long-term basis on imports of required defence materials in the country. DRDO consists of a chain of laboratories spread all over the country, carrying out research and development in the physical, chemical, biological and engineering sciences.

The Department of Defence R&D executes various R&D programmes and projects through a network of 51 laboratories and establishments of the DRDO spread over different parts of the country and a Centre for Military Airworthiness and Certification (CEMILAC). It also governs the Aeronautical Development Agency (ADA) which is involved in design and development of the Light Combat Aircraft (LCA). DRDO has made much progress in the necessary infrastructure and competence in different disciplines of science and technology. These laboratories and establishments execute R&D programmes and projects in various fields of armaments, rockets, missiles, aeronautics, combat vehicles, naval science and technology, electronics and instrumentation, advanced computing and networking, engineering, food and agriculture, life sciences, and advanced materials technology. At present, the network of DRDO laboratories is backed by more than 5000 scientists and about 25,000 other scientific, technical and supporting personnel. DRDO has formed four research boards which are playing key role to nurture and exploit expertise in academic institutions, universities, R&D centres and industry. The organisation extends necessary facilities to promote basic research, nurture and exchange of ideas with R&D agencies to expand and enrich the knowledge pool in their respective domains.

DRDO also organises specialised training programmes in these areas of expertise to the scientists, engineers and technologists who are engaged in the R&D programmes in universities and other research organisations. It has constituted two training institutions namely, Institute of Armament Technology (IAT) at Pune and the Institute of Technology Management (ITM) at Mussoorie. These institutes extend specialised training programmes to the scientists in different areas of specialisation. In addition, a number of laboratories and establishments, such as Defence Food Research Laboratory, Mysore and Defence Research and Development Establishment, Gwalior also offer specialised training programmes in their respective domains.

4.5 ATOMIC RESEARCH

The Atomic Energy Commission was set up in August 1948 under the Atomic Energy Act of 1948. The Commission's decisions were executed through the Department of Scientific Research and later through the Ministry of Natural Resources and Scientific Research. In the light of the Commission's activities, the need for a full-fledged atomic energy programme was felt, and the Government of India set up the Department of Atomic Energy (DAE) on August 3, 1954[33] with the objectives like building research reactors, the generation of safe, economically competitive electricity, utilisation of isotopes produced therein for use in agriculture, medicine, industry and research, to facilitate development in areas such as accelerators, lasers, biotechnology, information technology and strategic materials like thorium, encouraging technology transfers and interaction with industry, support to basic research in nuclear energy, encouraging international cooperation in advanced areas of research and contributing to national safety. The atomic energy programmes develop and utilise nuclear energy for peaceful purposes. The Tata Institute of Fundamental Research (TIFR) established in 1945 was the only institution carrying out research in the field of atomic energy before independence. TIFR is a leading Centre for research in basic nuclear sciences and theoretical physics and covers a wide spectrum of basic and applied research activities.

The Atomic Energy Establishment, Trombay (AEET), was created in January 1954 by the Atomic Energy Commission for furtherance of research and development of atomic energy. Initially, the establishment has been concentrating on chemistry and metallurgy, to which the theoretical physics, nuclear physics and electronics groups, that were functioning at the Tata Institute of Fundamental Research on behalf of the Commission, were added. Later, groups working in biology and medicine at the Indian Cancer Research Centre, Bombay, on behalf of the Commission, were also merged with the establishment. The contribution of the TIFR to the early activities of the Commission was very significant for the development of atomic energy programmes of the country.

The AEET was renamed after its founder and the first Director, Dr. H. J. Bhabha on 12 January 1967 as Bhabha Atomic Research Centre (BARC). It is an unique research centre of its type in the whole country which blends research reactors, and basic facilities for nuclear research, and strengthens infrastructure and trained manpower in all disciplines that come under the umbrella of nuclear energy. The R&D work of Bhabha Atomic Research Centre is a valuable contribution in various fields which include a broad spectrum of activities such as basic nuclear physics, reactor physics, fusion-related research, condensed matter, lasers and applications, plasma physics, basic and analytical chemistry, health physics, and radiological protection.

The Department of Atomic Energy (DAE) is a multidisciplinary organisation combining basic and applied research, technology development and their transformation in industrial application. There are Research Centres under the Department of Atomic Energy, such as Bhabha Atomic Research Centre (BARC), Mumbai; Indira Gandhi Centre for Atomic Research (IGCAR), Kalpakkam; the Atomic Minerals Directorate for Exploration and Research (AMD), Hyderabad; Centre for Advanced Technology (CAT), Indore; and Variable

Energy Cyclotron Centre, Kolkata which are harnessing the nuclear energy for various applications. There are industrial organisations under DAE namely, the Heavy Water Board (HWB), Mumbai; the Board of Radiation and Isotope Technology (BRIT), Mumbai; and the Nuclear Fuel Complex (NFC), Hyderabad. The public sector units are the Nuclear Power Corporation of India Limited (NPCIL), Mumbai; the Electronics Corporation of India Limited (ECIL), Hyderabad; Indian Rare Earths Limited (IRE), Mumbai; and the Uranium Corporation of India Limited (UCIL), Jaduguda. DAE also financially supports autonomous research institutes, such as the Tata Institute of Fundamental Research, Mumbai; Harish Chandra Research Institute, Allahabad (Formerly known as Mehta Research Institute of Mathematics and Mathematical Physics, Allahabad); Tata Memorial Centre, Mumbai; Saha Institute of Nuclear Physics, Kolkata; Institute of Physics, Bhubaneshwar; Institute of Mathematical Sciences, Chennai; the Institute of Plasma Research, Ahmedabad; and Atomic Energy Education Society, Mumbai which are involved in basic research activities applied in broad range of disciplines.

The DAE also provides several opportunities to scientists working in other organisations and abroad to interact and collaborate on research activities. It is a network of trained scientists and engineers who have given invaluable contribution for the societal benefit such as application of radiation technology in health care, radio-isotopes and tracer techniques in industry and in improving crop varieties to increase food and agricultural production in the country.

4.6 ELECTRONICS AND INFORMATION TECHNOLOGY

The Government of India recognised the pivotal role which electronics and information technology (IT) could play in modern S&T. As such the need for the growth of this vital sector in a balanced manner was also felt. In 1963, the Government of India appointed the Electronics Committee under the Chairmanship of Dr. H. J. Bhabha. The Committee had the mandate to assess the total requirements of the country in respect of various items of electronics components and equipment and to recommend measures for the planned development of electronics, so that the country as a whole might become self-sufficient in the field in the quickest and most economical manner. There has been a steady growth in the electronics industry in India since the Bhabha Committee submitted its recommendations in 1966. As a result, the Department of Electronics (DOE) was set up on June 26, 1970 and the Electronic Commission in February 1991. The DOE is entrusted with the responsibility of development of electronics and co-ordination among the various users. The Electronics Commission is an apex body to formulate policies and programmes for the development of electronics. Electronics and its applications have tremendous impact on extensive range of national activities. India produces a wide range of electronics requirements such as radios, television sets, broadcasting equipment, telecommunication, switching and transmission equipment, radars, earth stations, nuclear reactor control power electronics, under-water systems and so on. A large part of the material and components required for all this is produced within the country, except for specialised items needed in relatively small quantities.[34]

4.6.1 Research and Development

In order to have appropriate environment, a strong base of research and development in electronics has been built up in the form of research laboratories coming under the purview of various scientific agencies, such as the *Atomic Energy*: Bhabha Atomic Research Centre, Bombay; Tata Institute of Fundamental Research, Bombay; Saha Institute of Nuclear Physics, Kolkata; *Space and Electronics Commissions*: Vikram Sarabhai Space Centre, Ahmedabad; ISRO Satellite Centre, Bangalore; *Council of Scientific and Industrial Research*: National Physical Laboratory, New Delhi; Central Electronics Engineering Research Institute, Pilani; Central Scientific Instruments Organisation, Chandigarh; *Defence Research and Development Organisation*: Naval Physical & Oceanographic Laboratory, Cochin; Defence Electronics Applications Laboratory, Dehradun; Electronics and Radar Development Establishment, Bangalore, etc. as also in various educational institutions such as the IITs and the universities.

In addition to this, a number of production agencies like Bharat Electronics Limited, Electronics Corporation of India Limited, Central Electronics Limited, KELTRON, Bharat Heavy Electricals Limited, Indian Telephone Industries, etc. now have strong in-house R&D groups. Major Government Departments have also set up R&D facilities for work in areas of their direct interest, such as Doordarshan (Television), All India Radio, P&T Department/Ministry of Communications, Department of Civil Aviation and Tourism.

4.6.2 Systems Engineering Groups

A number of systems engineering groups have been created in the country, which have successfully been executed, or are in the process of executing, major integrated systems. Some of these are the electronic capabilities of the radio engineering network for the Indian Army, the air defence ground environment system for the Indian Air Force, communication systems for off-shore oil, entire telecommunication network, etc. By the effort of the Technology Development Council and the National Radar Council of the Department of Electronics, many R&D groups have been nucleated in contemporary areas.

Various projects of very specific nature with national relevance have also been undertaken. It includes a series of computer systems and peripherals; strategic microwave components; ultra high frequency (UHF) and microwave communication equipment; software development and management information systems; liquid crystal displays; industrial control and instrumentation for industries, such as paper, pulp, sugar, etc; safety equipment for railway systems; automatic test equipment; wind finding and weather analysis radars; route surveillance radars, etc. An integrated approach has been formulated in the area of microprocessors relating to technology development, education, application engineering, information and research. Major facilities which have been accomplished include the Semi Conductor Complex Ltd. at Chandigarh for the manufacture of advanced semiconductor devices involving large scale integration, National Computer Centre viz the National Centre for Software Development and

Computing Technologies (Bombay), and the National Informatics Centre (NIC, New Delhi), and a number of Regional Computer Centres.

4.6.3 Electronics and Information Technology

Department of Electronics was established to achieve the set goals, to review the field of electronics with regards to research, development and industrial operations, to formulate policy in the fields of electronics and information technology, and to attain self-reliance. In 1975, the Government of India decided to take effective steps for the development of information systems, utilisation of information resources, to introduce and promote computer-based decision support system in ministries and departments to facilitate planning and programme implementation for the economic and social development of the country. To achieve IT based economy, the Central Government created a new Ministry of Information Technology (MIT) in 1999 by merging the Department of Electronics (DOE), National Informatics Centre (NIC) and Electronics and Software Export Promotion Council. During the 1970s and 1980s, many state and central electronics corporations, such as KELTRON, MELTRON, UPTRON, WEBEL, HARTRON, ESPL, KEONICS, ELCOT, BEL, ECIL, were constituted to develop electronics industry in the states. Along this, various policy announcements like the Import Policy (1983), Computer Policy (1984), Electronic Policy (1985) and Software Policy (1986) laid the foundations for the liberalised growth of electronics and information technology industry in India. Significant growth in the electronics and information technology sector has been recorded in the decades of 1980s and 1990s. This growth has not only increased our software exports but also offered great potential of employment opportunities in the country. Information Technology Act (2000) and Communication Convergence Bill (2001) of the Government has also given new direction to catering all types of technologies, such as Internet, Datacom, Telecom, Wireless, Wireline, Fixed, Mobile, Cellular, Satellite Communication, etc. including e-commerce in a single communication network. National Task Force on Information Technology and Software

Development (1998) of the Central Government had prepared a plan of action to make India an IT superpower in the world. Introduction of computer education in schools, establishment of Indian Institutes of Information Technology (IIITs), IT Parks, Hardware Parks and Software Technology Parks in the country has promoted and encouraged the growth of IT education, services, industry and economic, social and rural development of India.[35]

The MIT has taken initiatives to implement a comprehensive action plan to make India an IT Superpower to promote software exports and accelerate the Internet revolution and web-based online services. The thrust areas of the Ministry are to spread IT education, e-commerce, electronics and computer hardware manufacturing and exports, development of IT enabled services in every discipline and Internet based enterprises. To meet these challenges, the Ministry of Information Technology has set up several autonomous organisations to address the needs of different sectors of IT, such as Centre for Development of Telematics (C-DOT) (1984); National Informatics Centre (NIC) (1977); Centre for Development of Advanced Computing (C-DAC); Computer Maintenance Corporation (CMC) Ltd. (1976); Standardisation, Testing & Quality Certification (STQC) Directorate; Controller of Certification Authority (CCA); National Centre for Software Technology (NCST); Society for Applied Microwave Electronics Engineering and Research (SAMEER); Education and Research Network (ERNET) Society; Department of Electronics Accreditation of Computer Courses (DOEACC) Society (1990); Centre for e-Governance; Centre for Electronics Design and Technology of India (CEDTI); Semiconductor Complex of India (SCI); Electronics Research & Development Centre of India (ER&DCI); ET&T; Electronics and Software Promotion Council; National Radar Council; National Photonics Council; Electronics Materials Development Council. These organisations are playing an active role the training and development of manpower for electronics and computer industry. Moreover, they offer help and guidance to the electronics industry by providing infrastructure, consultancy, policy support, training, testing, accreditation, market support and are engaged in R&D programmes in their specific areas. Following are the major areas of electronics and information technology where significant success has been achieved through sponsored R&D projects: *Appropriate Automation Programme* – Retrofit Automation, Energy Management, Process Controls, Robotics Welding System; Automatic Data Handling Systems for Plan ADGES; Axle Counter and Chopper Control Equipment and Interlocking System for Indian Railways; *Communication, Broadcast and Telemetry* – Digital Mobile Radio, Subtitling in regional languages, Spread Spectrum Radio Modem; 'PARAM series of Super computers; Meteorological instruments, i.e. Cyclone Warning Radar, Radiosonde, MST Radar; Pollution-free vehicles; Telemedicine Networks; *Electronics Industry Development Project (Manpower Component)* – Project IMPACT' Fibre Optics Application Programme (FOSAPP); Future Air Navigation Systems (FANS) programme in Airport navigation; Instrumentation for Paper and Pulp, Textiles, Tea, Sugar and Jute Industry; Microprocessor Application Programme; Software for Indian Languages; Technologies for Internet, e-Governance and e-Commerce; and Vehicle Tracking System based on GPS technology. These R&D projects are run at research institutes, industries, academic institutes and research laboratories.[36]

4.7 OCEANOGRAPHIC RESEARCH

India is a peninsula with an extensive coastline, which also includes island groups in the Indian ocean. Hence, Oceanography has an important role to play in the country's development where the coastline is about 8000 km. India has had a long sea-faring tradition. It is only since independence that major thrusts in the construction of ports and harbours, enlargement of the shipping fleet, ship design and construction facilities, and tapping of fishery resources have occurred. Oceanographic research and development has particularly grown since the last three decades with the setting up of the National Institute of Oceanography (NIO). The work of the Oil and Natural Gas Commission (ONGC) relating to off-shore hydrocarbons, studies by naval research groups and participation in major instrumental programmes like IIOE and

GRAPMONEX have also played a big role.[37] India has varied interests in the fields of oceanography, off-shore hydrocarbons, fishery resources to support food supplies, particularly proteins, mineral resources, pollution, understanding of weather, specially the monsoon and easterly weather structures across the Bay of Bengal, etc. Consequently, a major thrust is put on R&D in the area of oceanography.

The Government of India established an Ocean Science and Technology Agency (OSTA) in the Department of Science and Technology in 1976 with the basic objective to plan, co-ordinate and develop indigenous capability in oceanographic research in the country. The Governing Board is headed by the Prime Minister. The activities of this agency are controlled by the Governing Board and Standing Committee which have been instituted for this purpose. A separate Marine Research and Development Fund was instituted under OSTA to support R&D in this area of interest of the country.

The Department of Ocean Development (DOD) was established in July 1981 under the Ministry of Science and Technology to organise, co-ordinate and promote ocean R&D programmes in the country. The Government of India issued the Ocean Policy Statement in 1982 where more emphasis was given to control, management and utilisation of the internal resources available in the sea, and development of appropriate technologies to harness the marine wealth. From March 1982, the DOD has been functioning as a separate nodal department in line with the Ocean Policy Statement of 1982. The Department's programmes are mainly directed towards technology development for future applications, marine living and non-living resources programme, fishery resources to support food supplies, marine environment, ocean atmosphere and climatology, understanding of weather, capacity building for self-sufficiency and creation of public awareness of the ocean, its potential and uses. The Department also concerns itself with the multi-institutional and multi-disciplinary Polar Science programme and Antarctic Expeditions.

In order to harness the sea resources, various institutions of ocean research were established, such as National Institute of Ocean Technology (NIOT) at Chennai, National Centre for Antarctic and Ocean Research (NCAOR) at Goa, and Indian National Centre for Ocean Information Services at Hyderabad. Besides the existing institutes, academic research institutes and other science departments have significantly contributed to DOD R&D programmes. National Institute of Oceanography (NIO), Goa, is one of the CSIR institutes which has extended information services on several disciplines relating to marine research and development programmes. NIOT has been carrying out multi-disciplinary marine surveys in various parts of the country by using sophisticated equipment. The scientific research and technology development programmes are formulated, co-ordinated and executed through autonomous institutes of the Department.

The Department deals with new areas and emerging programmes of ocean development at national and international levels. The Department is the nodal agency for international programmes in the ocean sector and represents the country in International Governmental Oceanographic Commission (IOC) of UNESCO, Regional Committee of IOC in Coastal Indian Ocean (IOCINDIO), International Sea-Bed Authority (ISBA), and the State Parties of the United Nations Convention on the Law of the Seas (UNCLOC), the Antarctic Treaty System (ATS) and its scientific and managerial organs – Commission on Conservation of Antarctic Marine Living Resources (CCAMLR), Council of Managers of National Antarctic Programme (COMNAP), and Scientific Committee on Antarctic Research (SCAR). The Department is making efforts to strengthen the marine research and capacity building and promote basic research in marine science and introduce centres of excellence in academic institutions. During the last two decades, the department has made significant achievements in the area of Ocean Science and Technology, such as Antarctic Programme, National Data Buoy Programme (1997), Ocean Thermal Energy Conservation, Development of Potential Drugs from Ocean, Polymetallic Nodules Programme.[38]

The Department of Ocean Development (DOD) has achieved significant progress in various fields of ocean research during the past few years. Systematic surveys and exploration of marine living and non-living resources in the Exclusive Economic Zone and the continental shelf of the country is being carried out by two vessels FORV Sagar Sampada and ORV Sagar Kanya. The polymetallic nodules programme is an important programme of DOD which consists of survey and exploration, extractive metallurgy (processing) and mining, and environmental studies. R&D work on extractive metallurgy continued to be carried out in the RRL Bhubaneswar, NML at Jamshedpur, Hindustan Zinc Ltd at Udaipur and Hindustan Copper Ltd at Khetri.

4.7.1 Antarctic Programme

The Antarctic programme of India is a national effort towards establishing a place for Indian science in the polar regions. Antarctic research activities began in 1981 with the launching of the first scientific expedition and India has successfully launched twenty multi-disciplinary and multi-institutional expeditions so far. The first expedition set up a base camp named Dakshin Gangotri. The second expedition selected another site for building a permanent station besides continuing scientific studies. These expeditions collected rock samples from nearly 100 locations in the Humboldt Massif of the Wohlthat Mountains for Geological Survey of India. The airborne magnetic surveys conducted by the National Geophysical Research Institute over an area of 12,000 sq. km. was the first such kind of Indian effort in Antarctica, followed by 20 line km of ground magnetic surveys in the Humboldt Massif area.

The first Indian permanent station was established in 1983 at Dakshin Gangorti and later an indigenously built modern new station Maitree was set up in 1988-89. Biological and geophysical studies were carried out in the Wohlthat region. Metallic mineralisation was recorded at five places in the Schirmacher ranges and meteorological studies were also undertaken.[39] Protection of the marine environment and monitoring of marine pollutants in the seas around India is an important interdisciplinary programme. In this programme, during 1988-89, DOD had established two marine pollution monitoring centres, one at Mumbai on the west coast and another at Kolkata on the east coast. A Marine Research and Development Fund (MRDF) has been created in DOD as a part of its effort to encourage meaningful ocean-related activities in different institutions of the country. The Department initiates activities towards manpower development in the frontier area of oceanography. It also offers Fellowships and Associateships to Universities/Institutions, national laboratories in this field. Universities are given financial support towards development of marine science programmes.

4.8 SPACE RESEARCH

In 1963, the Government of India established Indian National Committee for Space Research (INCOSPAR) under the Department of Atomic Energy. But the Committee was reconstituted in 1969 under the Indian National Science Academy and made responsible for liaison with other national and international organisations and United Nations agencies interested in space research. On August 15, 1969 activities in the field of space research were entrusted to the newly constituted organisation called the Indian Space Research Organisation (ISRO) set up under the DAE.

With the formation of the Space Commission and a separate Department of Space on June 1, 1972, DAE was absolved of the responsibility of space research. The responsibilities of the Space Commission include the formulation of the policy of the Department of Space, preparation of the budget of the Department and implementation of government policy in all matters concerning outer space. The Department of Space (DOS) is responsible for the execution of activities in the country in space applications, space technology and space sciences through the ISRO.[40] The DOS and Space Commission were set up to promote development and application of space technology in the areas of telecommunications, television broadcasting, tele-education, disaster management, meteorology, resources survey and management. The DOS also looks after the development of satellites, launch vehicles and related ground equipment systems. First Indian Satellite Aryabhata was launched on April

19, 1975. India launched the Satellite Instructional Television Experiment (SITE) in 1975-76 to telecast a series of educational TV programmes on health, family planning, agriculture and adult education to the rural community.

The Indian National Satellite (INSAT) system is a joint venture of Department of Space (DOS), Department of Telecommunications (DOT), Indian Meteorological Department and Ministry of Information and Broadcasting. It is a multi-purpose satellite system that provides indigenous services in telecommunications, TV broadcasting and radio and TV programme distribution, meteorology and disaster warning. The INSAT system was commissioned in 1983 with the launch of INSAT-1B satellite on August 30, 1983 and now it has become one of the largest domestic satellite systems in the world. First generation INSAT-1D was launched on June 12, 1990, second generation satellites INSAT-2B on July 23, 1993, INSAT-2C on December 7, 1995, and INSAT-2E on April 3, 1999. In INSAT-3 series of satellites, five satellites have been planned and the first satellite INSAT-3B was launched on March 22, 2000, INSAT-3C was launched on January 24, 2002. INSAT-3A a multipurpose communication and meteorological satellite was successfully launched on April 10, 2003 and INSAT-3E was launched in September 28, 2003.

The Indian Remote Sensing Satellite (IRS) system was operational with the establishment of IRS-1A on March 17, 1988. IRS-1B was second operational Remote Sensing Satellite launched on August 29, 1991. The other satellites launched are IRS-1C on December 28, 1995, IRS-P3 on March 21, 1996 and IRS-1D on September 29, 1997, IRS-P4 on May 26, 1999. Data from IRS is used for estimation of acreage and yield of important crops like wheat, rice, oil seeds and sugarcane and other applications, such as forest survey, forecasting drought conditions, flood mapping and demarcation of flood-risk zones, land use and land cover mapping for agroclimatic planning, waste land mapping, snow-cover and snow-melt run-off estimation of Himalayan rivers for optimal use of water and several other purposes like urban planning, alignment of roads and pipelines, marine resources survey, mineral resources prospecting and so on.

To strengthen indigenous technological capabilities, India started satellite launch vehicle development in the early 1970s. The first experimental launch vehicle SLV-3 was launched on May 31, 1980. An augmented version of this vehicle, ASLV was launched successfully on May 20, 1992 and on May 4, 1994 carrying the Stretched Rohini Satellite Series (SROSS) satellites into low earth orbit. With the successful development of Polar Satellite Launch Vehicle (PSLV), India has now acquired a significant achievement in the satellite launch vehicle area. PSLV-D2 was launched on 15 October 1994 and PSLV-D3 test was done on 21 March 1996. PSLV is being used to launch the satellites of other countries and in this direction it has launched two small satellites, one for Korea (KITSAT-3) and another for Germany (TUBSAT) along with India's IRS-P4 into orbit on May 26, 1999. PSLV-C3 was successfully launched on October 22, 2001 placing three satellites, i.e., India's TES, Belgian PROBA and German BIRD, into Polar sun-synchronous orbit. The Geo-synchronous Satellite Launch Vehicle (GSLV-D1) made its successful flight on April 18, 2001 and second developmental test flight of GSLV (GSLV-D2) was made on May 8, 2003. Beside this, other satellite KALPANA-1, an exclusive meteorological satellite was launched by PSLV on September 12, 2002. RESOURCESAT-1, the most advanced remote sensing satellite built by ISRO, was launched by ISRO's PSLV-C5 on October 17, 2003.

Overall direction to the technical, scientific and administrative functions are provided by both DOS and ISRO headquarters located at Bangalore. The R&D activities under the space programme are conducted at Vikram Sarabhai Space Centre (VSSC) at Thiruvananthapuram, the ISRO Satellite Centre (ISAC) at Bangalore, the SHAR Centre at Sriharikota, the Space Applications Centre (SAC) at Ahmedabad, the Liquid Propulsion Systems Centre (LPSC) at Bangalore, Trivandrum and Mahendragiri, the Development and Educational Communication Unit (DECU) at Ahmedabad, the ISRO Telemetry, Tracking and Command Network (ISTRAC) with its headquarters at Bangalore, the Master Control Facility (MCF) at Hassan, the ISRO Inertial Systems Unit (IISU) at Thiruvananthapuram, the Physical Research Laboratory (PRL) at Ahmedabad, the National Remote Sensing Agency (NRSA) at Hyderabad and the National Mesosphere, Stratosphere, Troposphere Radar Facility (NMRF) at Gadanki. Five Regional Remote Sensing Service Centres (RRSSCs) have been established by the DOS at Bangalore, Jodhpur, Kharagpur, Dehradun and Nagpur, North Eastern-Space Applications Centre (NE-SAC) at Shillong and Antrix Corporation Limited at Bangalore.

India is taking international cooperation from the inception of the Indian space programme. Several developed countries such as USA, former Soviet Union, France, Germany and international space agencies are engaged in the establishment of the Equatorial Rocket Launching Station at Thumba, in the conduct of space application demonstrations, like Satellite Instructional Television Experiment (SITE) 1975-76 and Satellite Telecommunication Experiment Project (STEP) 1977-79 and launches of experimental satellites, like Aryabhata on April 19, 1975, Bhaskara-I on June 7, 1979, Bhaskara-II on November 20, 1981 and APPLE (Ariane Passenger Payload Experiment) June 19, 1981. India has developed satellites, three types of launch vehicles, conducted several successful flights, established an elaborate infrastructure to design, build and test communication and remote sensing satellites, their launch, and their in-orbit management as well as their data processing and application.

The Department of Space operates as the nodal agency for the evolution and establishment of the National Natural Resources Management System, in which all the central ministries/agencies and state/union territory governments concerned participate. The Department of Space is mainly responsible for the development of integrated data based on remote sensing and thereafter analysis and dissemination of information derived from data, while subsequent activities relating to utilisation of the information are carried out by the respective Central and State Government agencies.

4.9. DEPARTMENT OF SCIENCE AND TECHNOLOGY

Government of India had established several scientific

departments to achieve the specific objectives in different disciplines. The Department of Science and Technology (DST) was one of them to achieve the S&T progress in the country. The DST was established in May 1971 under the Ministry of Science and Technology with the objective to promote new areas of science and technology and act as a nodal centre for the promotional activities in the area of science and technology in the country. Since then it has been playing a significant role in the promotion of basic research and technology development in the country. The Department also assists in the formulation of policy statements, guidelines and mechanism for the coordination between various institutions. After independence, Government of India gave prime importance to the establishment of modern S&T infrastructure in the country. The Government set up the Technology Development Board (TDB) in September 1996 to provide funds to industrial undertakings and agencies towards promotion of indigenous technology and adoption of foreign technology for wider domestic applications.

R&D programmes of the DST are undertaken through the Science and Engineering Research Council (SERC), an apex body of eminent scientists and technologists from universities, national laboratories, institutes and industry. It extends support for the establishment of centres of excellence and setting up of national research facilities for the scientists and training programmes for young scientists. The Council promotes and strengthens research in different areas like structural and reproduction biology, plant physiology, genetic engineering and biotechnology, neurobiology, laser spectroscopy, condensed matter physics, organic chemistry, solid state chemistry and climate research, drugs and pharmaceuticals, etc. Regional Sophisticated Instrument Centres (RSICs) and Sophisticated Instrument Facilities (SIFs) offer the facilities of sophisticated analytical instruments to scientists working in universities, research organisations and industry. A programme called 'Fund for Improvement of S&T Infrastructure in Universities and Other Higher Educational Institutions (FIST) has been initiated to strengthen R&D infrastructure and nurture congenial environment of promoting R&D in universities and other institutions. A National Science & Technology Management Information System (NSTMIS) has been established to collect, collate, analyse and disseminate S&T information to strengthen decision support system at national level. Various surveys and documents have been brought out which are being well received by the science community in the country and abroad.

DST has launched new schemes in the Human Resources Development in Science and Technology called *Swarnajayanti* Fellowships and *Kishore Vaigyanik Protsahan Yojana (KVPY)* to encourage the young scientists and young students to take up research as a career. These programmes identify new talents and offer them financial assistance in the form of fellowships, scholarship schemes and training programmes for researchers. In addition, scientists are also offered partial financial assistance to attend and participate in international conferences and workshops.

There are several autonomous research institutes of DST which have contributed significantly to research at national and international levels. These high quality autonomous scientific research institutions are engaged in R&D in the emerging areas of astronomy and astrophysics, microbiology, modern biology, medical sciences and technology, palaeobotany, Himalayan geology, geomagnetism and several other areas. These autonomous bodies have set up national facilities of research to the scientific community of researchers. Autonomous institutes of DST are: Agharkar Research Institute, Pune; Birbal Sahni Institute of Palaeobotany, Lucknow; Bose Institute, Kolkata; Indian Institute of Astrophysics, Bangalore; Indian Institute of Geomagnetism, Mumbai; Indian Institute of Tropical Meteorology, Pune; International Advanced Research Centre for Powder Metallurgy and New Materials (ARCI), Hyderabad; Jawaharlal Nehru Centre for Advanced Scientific Research, Bangalore; Raman Research Institute, Bangalore; S N Bose National Centre for Basic Sciences, Kolkata; Sree Chitra Tirunal Institute for Medical Sciences and Technology, Thiruvananthapuram; Wadia Institute of Himalayan Geology, Dehradun; Indian Association for the Cultivation of Science, Kolkata; Vigyan Prasar, New Delhi; National Accreditation Board for Testing and Calibration Laboratories, New Delhi;

Technology Information, Forecasting and Assessment Council (TIFAC), New Delhi; Indian National Science Academy, New Delhi; Indian Academy of Sciences, Bangalore; Indian Science Congress Association, Kolkata; National Academy of Sciences, Allahabad; Indian National Academy of Engineering, New Delhi.

DST pursues its agenda of technology development through the Technology Development Board (TDB). Technology Information, Forecasting and Assessment Council (TIFAC), an autonomous body, was established to enable a Technology Information System and generate documents on technology forecasting, technology assessment and techno-market survey in different areas of science and technology. TIFAC has worked on a long-term Technology Forecasting exercise and brought out Technology Vision 2020 documents in 17 different areas. Technopreneur Promotion Programme (TePP) was initiated jointly by DST, DSIR and TIFAC for providing financial assistance, project advice, R&D facilities and expertise and to tap the vast innovative potential of Indian innovators. A Patent Facilitating Centre (PFC) has been set up in TIFAC to provide information related to patenting and intellectual property to the scientific community.

Various Science and Technology programmes have been initiated to change the rural economy and address the problems of rural people and keeping in view the needs for weaker sections of the society. Variety of technologies has been developed in both farm and non-farm sectors, and for the upgradation of traditional ones and for evolving women-friendly technologies for rural development. Rural Technology Parks have been introduced in the North-Eastern India. Three Women Technology Parks have been established at Dehradun, Manipal and Barmer. A National Award has also been instituted to honour individual or organisational work for the benefit of women. National Science and Technology Entrepreneurship Development Board (NSTEDB), Science and Technology Entrepreneurship Parks and Entrepreneurship Programmes (TEDPs) at academic and research organisations have been set up to encourage promotion of new and existing entrepreneurs. A National Resources Data Management System (NRDMS) that involves several R&D institutes, universities and NGOs has been set up to enable decision-making process for local area management and development of data management at the district level.[42]

The National Council of Science and Technology Communication (NCSTC) was established to popularise and stimulate scientific and technological temper among people. The Council conducts the National Children's Science Congresses (NCSCs) and number of other initiatives like *Bharat Jan Vigyan Jathas* (BJVJ), television serials, video programmes and radio programmes. Vigyan Prasar was constituted in 1989 to promote and popularise scientific temper through *Vigyan Prasar Information System* and network of science clubs.

4.10 DEPARTMENT OF SCIENTIFIC AND INDUSTRIAL RESEARCH

The Department of Scientific and Industrial Research (DSIR) was created by the Ministry of Science and Technology in 1985. The Department has a wide spectrum of activities which include all matters relating to the Council of Scientific and Industrial Research, the National Research Development Corporation, Central Electronics Limited, the National Information System for Science and Technology (NISSAT), UNCTAD and WIPO (World Intellectual Property Organisation), Registration and Recognition of In-house R&D Unit in Industry, and the national register of foreign collaborations.

4.10.1 Scientific and Industrial Research

After the two world wars science gained great prominence in most parts of the world and the government of the concerned countries which started taking active interest, assured direct responsibility for it. India was no exception. Several universities and other research institutions have been in the forefront in carrying out notable work in basic sciences, but the need for applied science research in the country was felt strongly. Hence, every one felt the acute need for an organisation which could respond to the needs of industry. Way back in 1918, the Indian Industrial Commission had urged the

Government of India to promote applied research. Seventeen years after that the Government established a Bureau for Industrial Intelligence and Research. Later on, the Bureau was superseded by a Board of Scientific and Industrial Research to advise the Government on industrial research and development of Indian industry. Dr. Shanti Swarup Bhatnagar was appointed as Director, Scientific and Industrial Research. Later the Government converted this Board into an Advisory Board to a new organisation designated as the Council of Scientific and Industrial Research, constituted in 1942.[43]

In fact a systematic attempt to carry out applied research in India commenced with the establishment of the Council of Scientific and Industrial Research (CSIR) in India in 1942. Scientific and industrial research has received a major boost with the establishment of the CSIR. The major objectives of CSIR were defined to be "research and development projects of national priority and research and development directed towards continuous improvement of indigenous technology and adoption and development of imported technology". It has built up interface with industries in the public and private sectors under which sponsored research programmes are taken up by the CSIR. CSIR is multidisciplinary network of 38 laboratories/institutes and 39 regional centres which are engaged in fundamental and applied research and development in all areas of science and technology. This network is served by around 8000 scientists and engineers of repute and 10,000 technical support personnel. Science and technology have become the important factors of economic and social development of society, and are playing significant role in the industry, and in such fields as health, agriculture, transport, etc. They are imperative for harnessing and utilisation of all natural resources for the development and welfare of the human beings.

CSIR has divided the network of its R&D laboratories and institutes in five categories. There are five laboratories in Physical Sciences, such as Central Electronics Engineering Research Institute, Pilani; Central Scientific Instruments Organisation, Chandigarh; National Geophysical Research Institute, Hyderabad; National Institute of Oceanography, Goa;

National Physical Laboratory, New Delhi. Seven laboratories in Chemical Sciences are Central Electrochemical Research Institute, Karaikudi; Central Leather Research Institute, Chennai; Central Salt & Marine Chemical Research Institute, Bhavnagar; Indian Institute of Chemical Technology; Hyderabad; Indian Institute of Petroleum, Dehradun; Regional Research Laboratory, Jorhat; and National Chemical Laboratory, Pune. There are eleven laboratories in Biological Sciences which are : Central Drug Research Institute, Lucknow; Central Food Technological Research Institute, Mysore; Central Institute for Medicinal and Aromatic Plants, Lucknow; Institute of Genomics and Integrative Biology, Delhi; Centre for Cellular & Molecular Biology, Hyderabad; National Botanical Research Institute, Lucknow; Indian Institute of Chemical Biology, Kolkata; Industrial Toxicology Research Centre, Lucknow; Institute of Microbial Technology, Chandigarh; Regional Research Laboratory, Jammu; and Institute of Himalayan Bioresource Technology, Palampur. Thirteen laboratories in Engineering Sciences are: Central Building Research Institute, Roorkee; Central Fuel Research Institute, Dhanbad; Central Glass & Ceramic Research Institute, Kolkata; Central Mining Research Institute, Dhanbad; Central Road Research Institute, New Delhi; National Aerospace Laboratories, Bangalore; National Metallurgical Laboratory, Jamshedpur; National Environmental Engineering Research Institute, Nagpur; Regional Research Laboratory, Thiruvananthapuram; Regional Research Laboratory, Bhopal; Regional Research Laboratory, Bhubaneshwar; Structural Engineering Research Centre, Chennai; Central Mechanical Engineering Research Institute, Durgapur. There are only two laboratories in information sciences, i.e., National Institute of Science Communication and Information Resources, New Delhi; and National Institute of Science, Technology and Development Studies, New Delhi, which are disseminating information to the scientific community of researchers in India and abroad.

CSIR has made several scientific achievements such as the induction of precocious flowering of bamboo through tissue culture, discovery of multifunctional, small protein, seminal plasmin, the first combined genetic and physical map of the whole Vibrio cholerae genome; the development of a salt sensitive expression vector used successfully to clone and express six divergent genes, the elucidation of the mechanisms for delaying the formation of cataract in the human eye. CSIR declared an Intellectual Property Policy in 1995 and filed around 406 patents in India and around 491 patents abroad in 2003-2004. In addition, CSIR was the first to launch buffalo milk for infant food, introduced the wholly indigenous tractor Swaraj, developed a cost-effective process for drugs for mass use, built an all-composite two-seater small aircraft Hansa. CSIR offers R&D services in different areas of science such as aerospace and aeronautics, bio-sciences and bio-technology, chemicals and chemical technology, coal, gas and petroleum, construction technology, drugs and pharmaceuticals, earth and ocean resources, ecology and environment, electronics and instrumentation, food processing, leather and leather products, machinery and equipment, new materials, mining and metallurgy.

CSIR maintains S&T co-operation with appropriate research organisations in several countries through bilateral and multilateral agreements, co-operation and exchange programmes. It has been playing a key role in the activities of the Commonwealth Science Council, the Association for Science Cooperation in Asia, the South Asia Association for Regional Cooperation (SAARC), the World Association of Industrial and Technological Research Organisations, the Canadian International Development Research Centre, and the Third World Academy of Sciences (TWAS). CSIR offers fellowships both for Post-Doctoral Research and for Post-Graduate studies in CSIR laboratories with Third World Academy of Sciences.[44]

CSIR publishes primarily scholarly science journals to disseminate the scientific knowledge among scholars and scientists engaged in R&D programmes in the area of Science and Technology. It brings out bulletins on distinct areas of science, such as fuel science and technology, mining research, mechanical engineering, electro-chemistry, medicinal and aromatic plant sciences and so on.

4.11 DEPARTMENT OF BIOTECHNOLOGY

National Biotechnology Board (NBB) was instituted by the Government to nurture, promote and strengthen the R&D programmes and infrastructure in the field of biotechnology. Likewise Department of Biotechnology (DBT) was established in 1986 under the Ministry of Science and Technology. Since then, both the organisations are engaged in the R&D programmes of newly emerging discipline. The scenario of biotechnology is changing speedily in the whole world. Innovations are being done in the area of agriculture, health care, environment, bio-industrial development and other allied areas to harness the biological wealth of the nation. The thrust areas are research support towards scientific excellence, involvement of user agencies and industries, development of products and processes for welfare of the society, innovations for patenting purpose, demonstrations at large scale, technology development and transfer. In addition, emphasis is also being laid on other activities such as R&D programmes and support in priority areas, expansion of bioinformatics network, establishing new centres of excellence and human resource development. All biotechnology innovations and tools are used to exploit the biological wealth of the nation for the welfare of society, economic development and prosperity of the nation.

Department of Biotechnology has taken several initiatives to encourage the biotechnology R&D programmes in the country. The Department has established several autonomous institutes and centres of excellence in various relevant areas of biotechnology. These are: National Centre for Plant Genome Research (NCPGR), New Delhi; National Brain Research Centre (NBRC), Manesar; National Centre for Cell Science (NCCS), Pune; National Institute of Immunology (NII), New Delhi, that was set up by DST and was later transferred to DBT; Centre for DNA Fingerprinting and Diagnostics (CDFD), Hyderabad; Institute of Bioresources and Sustainable Development (IBSD), Imphal; and Institute of Life Sciences, Bhubaneswar. These centres offer infrastructure support to the scientists and researchers engaged in the serious research work in the area of biotechnology and allied disciplines.

The DBT has initiated four Jai Vigyan National S&T Missions in the areas of the development of new generation vaccines for infectious diseases, herbal products development, biotechnological approaches for coffee improvement and set up of mirror sites for genomic research and biotechnological databases. Several biotechnology programmes have been initiated for the benefit of society in rural areas, particularly women, SC/ST and weaker sections and human resource development. A Women's Biotechnology Park and a Biovillage have been set up for the women of rural areas and weaker sections. Various R&D and demonstration programmes have been strengthened and introduced in different areas of biotechnology for the benefit of society. These includes food technology, biofertilisers, basic research in new areas, plant biotechnolgy, biological pesticides, animal biotechnology, aquaculture and marine biotechnology, plant tissue culture, Micropropagation Technology Parks at NCL, Pune and TERI, New Delhi, bioprospecting and molecular taxonomy, seri-biotechnology, medicinal and aromatic plants, medical biotechnology, agriculture, crop biotechnology, human genetics and genome analysis, bioethics and biodiversity conservation and environment,. Several technologies like vaccines for leprosy, drug formulation for septic shock, diagnostic kits for HIV, hepatitis, dengue, assessment of reproductive hormones, plant tissue culture protocols, formulation of biofertilisers, have been transferred to different industries to develop products for the societal use.

In addition, National Bioresource Development Board (NBDB) has been instituted for the development of a broad policy framework and application of effective scientific approaches for the utilisation of bioresources. Universities, national laboratories, state government institutes, krishi vigyan kendras and NGOs have been engaged for implementing special biotechnological programmes for the benefit of SC/ST population, women and rural people in the areas of biopesticides, biofertilisers, sericulture, floriculture, mushroom cultivation, medicinal plant production, poultry, fish farming and improvement of human health care. Department is providing scientific and technical advice and awareness to the states for establishing Biotechnology Parks/Cities and other endeavours in this direction. A Women's Biotechnology Park has been introduced in Chennai. The Department has established a large number of facilities, repositories and centres of excellence to achieve the objective of facilitating research and offering services across the country. In this regard, an International Depository Authority has been established at Institute of Microbial Technology (IMTECH), Chandigarh for conservation of microbial biodiversity in accordance with the Budapest Treaty. Other new facilities introduced are the National Containment Facility for Transgenic Plant Material and the National Facility for Virus Diagnosis and Quality Control of tissue culture raised plants at Indian Agricultural Research Institute (IARI), New Delhi. Moreover, it has enlarged the bioinformatics network in the country for easy access, retrieval and dissemination of data information resources through its distributed information centre, establishing international databases, establishing new centres and training. Department has introduced human resource development programme for scientists and students at the post-graduate, post-doctoral, post-MD/MS levels across the country. Post-doctoral Fellowship programme and Biotechnology Associateships are extended to train scientists and upgrade the knowledge in advanced areas of biotechnological research, short-term, long-term and industrial training programmes to enhance career opportunities. Numerous awards such as Biology Scholarships for top students, National Bioscience Award for Career Development for mid-career scientists and National Woman Bioscientist Award have been instituted to recognise the works, encourage and promote excellence. Conferences, seminars, symposia and lectures are also being conducted to promote the biotechnological experiments in the country. Several programmes of S&T priority of national interest such as human reproduction, environment, genetic disorders, agriculture, health and industrial applications have been identified and implemented for further international collaboration with developed and developing nations. These programmes have been demonstrated with Belarus, China, Cuba, France, Germany, Israel, Italy, Japan, Myanmar, Poland,

Russia, Sri Lanka, Sweden, Switzerland, UK, USA and Vietnam. Programmes with S&T agencies in Australia, Hungary and the Philippines and multilateral collaborations with SAARC, G-15 and the ASEAN countries have also been initiated to develop international linkages for the welfare of the society.[45]

In a nutshell, it can be said that there is a long history of the development of pure and applied research in India. In the contemporary stage a large network of education and research organisations of India is in severe crisis of financial constraints. Their laboratories, libraries and research facilities are out of fashion or not available to scientists and research scholars due to the limited allocation of funds, falling of the standard of quality of higher education. Quality in the higher education can be assured if the researchers and teachers in the system are dedicated, accountable and responsible towards their profession, work and duties to enlighten and prosper the future of the nation.

The growth of technology does offer us strength and hope to meet the challenge of educating the nation. In this direction, satellite, television, computers and Internet, etc. can be effective tools to meet the challenges. Indian Space Research Organisation has followed the space technology for education and development. These efforts began with the Satellite Instructional Television Experiment and have continued over the years. Satellite based information and communication technology enabled education would offer a wide range of delivery modes like TV broadcast, Interactive TV, video conferencing, computer conferencing, web-based instruction, etc. with the right kind of satellite support. No doubt, information and communication technologies have contributed tremendously to the research and development at global level. To support the school, higher and professional education and education in science and technology, a fully-dedicated satellite is required to achieve the desired target. Knowledge is power and it is growing and changing at a rapid pace. To keep pace with the developments, only satellite supported education is the best response to keep the nation updated. For this purpose EDUSAT, an exclusive satellite, will be used to provide a sustainable distance education service in India.[46]

REFERENCES

1. Saha, J. Special libraries and information services in India and in the USA Metuchen, NJ: The Scarecrow Press, 1969. P.5-6.
2. Aggarwal, D. S. Lectures on universe of knowledge. Delhi: Academic Publications, 1985.
3. Rao, C. N. R. and Mohan Ram, H. Y., eds. Science in India: 50 Years of the Academy. New Delhi: Indian National Science Academy, 1985. P.109.
4. *Ibid.*, p.110.
5. UNESCO. National science policy and organisation of scientific research in India. Paris: UNESCO, 1972. P.9.
6. *Ibid.*, p.9.
7. IIT Review Committee, 1986, Ministry of Human Resource Development, Government of India.
8. Nehru, Jawaharlal. The Discovery of India. New Delhi: Jawaharlal Nehru Memorial Fund, 1981. 582p.
9. Annual Report 2003-2004. New Delhi: University Grants Commission. 212p.
10. Dongaonkar, Dayanand. Higher education in India: The varied dimensions – convocation address. *University News*, 42(21), 2004, 22-25, 28.
11. Nehru, Jawaharlal. Convocation address. University of Allahabad, 1947.
12. Bhatnagar, S. S. Seventh convocation address. University of Rajputana, Jaipur, 1954. P.3.
13. INSA. Pursuit and promotion of science: The Indian experience. New Delhi: Indian National Science Academy, 2001, 399p.
14. UNESCO, *op.cit.*, p.10.
15. India. Education Commission (1964-66) (Chairman: D. S. Kothari) Report. 275p.
16. UNESCO, *op.cit.*, p.11.
17. Deshmukh, C. D. Reflections on finance education and society. Delhi: Motilal Banarsidass, 1972. 238p.

18. Government of India, Ministry of Education. Report of the Education Commission (1964-66), 1966. 278p.
19. National Policy on Education (1986). P.14.
20. Dongaonkar, *op.cit.*, 22-25, 28.
21. Mulimani, V. H. Science education in universities. *University News,* 42(2), January 12-18, 2004, 13-15.
22. Rao and Mohan Ram, *op.cit.*, p.19-20.
23. UNESCO, *op.cit.*, p.14.
24. Prabhakar, A. S. and others. Higher agricultural education in India: Thoughts for future planning. *University News,* 39(24), June 11-17, 2001, 7-9.
25. Annual Report DARE/ICAR 2003-2004. 261p. 26 April 2005. Available: http://www.icar.org.in/anrep/200304/index.htm
26. UNESCO, *op.cit.*, p.15-16.
27. Rao and Mohan Ram, *op.cit.*, p.40.
28. UNESCO, *op.cit.*, p.15-16.
29. Rahman, Abdur, ed. Science and technology in India, Pakistan, Bangladesh and Sri Lanka. Essex: Longman, 1990. P.38.
30. UNESCO, *op.cit.*, p.15-16.
31. INSA, *op.cit.*, p.170-189.
32. UNESCO, *op.cit.*, p.16.
33. *Ibid.*, p.17.
34. Rahman, *op.cit.*, p.28-29.
35. INSA, *op.cit.*, p.358-368.
36. *Ibid.*, p.358-368.
37. Status report on science and technology in India: 1994. New Delhi: Council of Scientific and Industrial Research, 1994. P.25.
38. INSA, *op.cit.*, p.350-357.
39. Rahman, *op.cit.*, p.97.
40. *Ibid.*, p.24.

41. Department of Space Annual Report 2003-2004. ISRO: Bangalore, 77p.

42. INSA, *op.cit.*, p.279-293.

43. 25 Years of CSIR. New Delhi: Council of Scientific and Industrial Research, 1968. P.1.

44. INSA, *op.cit.*, p.250-257.

45. *Ibid.*, p.323-336.

46. Mukhopadhyay, Marmar. Educating the nation: Need for a dedicated satellite. Ahmedabad: ISRO, 2003. 35p.

5

Information and Communication Technology in Scientific and Technical Libraries

5.0 GENERAL

Information has been accepted as a vital input in the socio-economic development of a nation. This has led to tremendous growth in the field of Information Technology (IT). Advances in the field of information technology have in turn replaced traditional manual operations in the library with modern machine added operations. These changes have taken place more in the scientific and technical libraries. And in fact, these scientific and technical libraries in India have taken lead in the implementation of several new information technologies basically for bibliographic utilities, full text databases, online reference services and storage of information. The application of information technology became world-wide phenomena as early as in 1960s. The application of computer based information systems, particularly in scientific and technical libraries and information units is now common every where in the information world. All the leading institutions have taken initiatives to introduce new technologies into the libraries to manage the information resources and offer quality services. Information technologies have become ubiquitous in the libraries of developed as well as developing nations.

There have been many technological developments during the past few years which have affected the operations of libraries and information centres. One of the major developments has been the emergence of microcomputer systems, with increasingly advanced features which can be used for a variety of library operations. The other major technological development has been the introduction of telecommunications networks and their availability in the information world with the decrease in the cost and the increase in availability. The libraries such as academic, special and research use these networks to gain access to external services, such as online shared cataloguing systems, online resources and online search services. A further technological development has been the advent of videotext. The combination of computing and telecommunications for the acquisition, processing, storage and transmission of vocal, pictorial, textual and numeric information is referred as 'information technology'. The fast technological developments in the area of telecommunication, multimedia and digital technologies have significantly changed the activities of the libraries, such as collection development and their organisation, sharing, use and transmission of information. These technologies have produced the alternatives of fast and effective access to the information. These changes have made a significant impact on the contemporary roles of the libraries of all kinds.

Libraries have developed integrated automated systems which support core processing functions of libraries, such as acquisitions, serials control, cataloguing and circulation. Star and Ruhleder's[1] (1996) state that "Integrated library systems are embedded in the work practices of libraries and depend upon certain jobs and relationships in addition to specific technologies. They support the processing of materials and resources at multiple sites and enable remote access to cataloguing and other databases twenty-four hours a day. Upon joining the community, both staff and patrons learn to use the systems and to develop certain expectations of services. Integrated library systems embody national and international standards, both library-specific (e.g., MARC, Z39.50) and general technical standards (e.g., Unicode, TCP/IP). These systems build upon an installed base — usually consisting of cataloguing records, holdings records, and other records, in standard formats – an established practice".

5.1 IMPACT OF INFORMATION TECHNOLOGY ON LIBRARY SERVICE

The computer is one of the most powerful forces in the information world of the modern society. It is being used every where - in homes, offices and in research organisations of all sizes and libraries and information centres. Family, colleagues, friends all rely on e-mail to communicate to each other. Impact of information technology on the society and its influence, no doubt, is continuously increasing. All facets of life have been affected. There are so many people who are working on different aspects of information technology, such as creating web pages, writing software, marketing of products and services, advertising, designing and graphics, information technology related jobs, marketing research and business on the web. Even it has made the communication system very fast and cheap. Moreover, other information as stock prices, travel information, banking services and publishing, etc. all spheres of life have changed. It is difficult to think that accelerated growth and application of information technology has not affected any areas of the society. Most of the activities of research, writing, editing and publishing, etc. whether it is in print or electronic publishing, involve computer and communication network. Like other institutions, libraries could no longer function in the absence of computer and information networks. They depend on the computer networks to provide access to information resources.

In the present age, electronic devices and media have increasingly invaded our society. These devices and computers have an effect on traditional library methods, practices and routine housekeeping functions of the libraries. The new information technology has affected all aspects of library operations from acquisition, cataloguing, circulation, serials control to management and staff activities of the libraries. This paradigm shift has taken place from print to electronic resources such as full text journals databases, indexing and abstracting databases, encyclopedias, directories and other full text reference sources. These technologies have made the libraries as "one-stop shopping" and shrink the job and activities of the librarian and information professionals. Digital technologies have developed the concept of paperless library or paperless office and it is one of the major benefit to the entire organisation to reduce paper expenses, increase productivity, save the time of the staff, avoid duplication efforts of the staff and bring people close to each other. It has opened several avenues of communication, of sharing of knowledge among colleagues and break communication barrier across the organisation.

For shift from traditional library and information services to electronic machines and computers, the effective use of the computers is inevitable. Computers are being used in research and scientific and technical libraries for ordering and acquisition, cataloguing, circulation, serials control, CAS (Current Awareness Service) and SDI (Selective Dissemination of Information), communication, access of information, transmission and sharing of online resources. Now a days libraries rely on computers, networks and electronic resources to render information to their users. They use the computers and other information technologies in selecting, acquiring, organizing, preserving, conserving books, journals and other reading material and provide access to information and collection. They offer a wide range of information services to the users working in the organisation.

A number of online databases of abstracting and indexing journals, full text journals, encyclopedias, patents, standards, online cataloguing data, etc. is being made available for the vast majority of documents acquired by libraries throughout the world through co-operative and consortia bases networks such as OCLC. With the advancement of technology in providing digitised document delivery services of transmission at the national, regional or any geographic level, focus in the coming decade is on network of information and networking of the people. The recent introduction of databases in compact discs, such as CD-ROM, DVD (Digital video disc) which is cheap and portable medium for archiving text and other online publications and access of online databases through Internet and the rapid evolution and convergence of many disparate technologies such as computers and telecommunications, augmented by micro computers, micro-electronics, video and optical discs and advanced communication systems video-web conferencing, etc. - have brought about profound changes in every aspect of the library. As yet, the computerised library network has had little effect on patrons of S&T libraries, but the new information technologies have enhanced the ability of patrons to access, store and obtain relevant information from these libraries for their future use. Broadly speaking, new technology has maximised the use of libraries and caused an development of the libraries as well as librarianship.

The advent of information technology has tremendous impact on libraries and information centres. Traditional library operations has been replaced by the computers, networks and other digital technologies. It has also brought about economy, speed in transmitting of information, organizing, expanding the scope of library services, preserving and conserving resources and efficiency in access and overall operations. At the same time it has also posed challenge to the librarians. It is rightly pointed out that yesterday's backward nations were those which missed out on industrial revolution and tomorrow's backward nations would be those which would miss out on information and communication technology and application of intranet and internet technology to access electronic information. With this changing environment, if the libraries of contemporary world do not change themselves, it will ultimately become increasingly uncompetitive and will go out of the race of information world.[2]

The impact of computer and information technology can be seen in the retrieval of information from the unlimited number of records without loss of time. As Sanders pointed out, "A New York surgeon contacted a medical library when a near-term pregnant woman lapsed into a hepatic coma. He needed immediate information on exchange blood transfusions for the woman. Using a computer terminal and retrieval programme, the librarian searched more than a half-million medical documents in a few minutes to get the information the surgeon needed to perform an emergency blood transfusion. The patient recovered fully from the hepatitis. Most information retrieval tasks obviously don't involve life-or-death decisions, but quick computer assisted retrieval saves time and aggravation for many people."[3] The present Information Technology revolution is inescapable and it affects the availability of and access to information in which the library has very important role to play.

5.2 ADVANTAGES OF APPLICATION OF INFORMATION AND COMMUNICATION TECHNOLOGY

There are a number of advantages of the application of computer and information technology in the libraries. These advantages have been discussed in the following sections.

5.2.1 Time Saving of Professional Staff

The libraries so far resorted manual operations to perform even advanced functions and services, such as depth classification, advanced cataloguing, bibliographic services, literature search, indexing, abstracting, etc. These are the important but time consuming functions. Not only these are time consuming but they also require enough professional staff to manage them. The advent of computers and information technology has minimised the need for depth classification and advanced cataloguing to organise reading material. By applying the information technology, all sorts of works and processes can be performed in providing bibliographic services, literature search, indexing, etc. even transmission of full text resources and thus a lot of time of professional staff could be saved and the task would easily be handled by employing less number of professionals. It avoids duplication of efforts of staff to maintaining and managing information.

5.2.2 Quick, Accurate and Easy Access to Information

The information technology has enhanced the recall and precision value of information available in the library. Entire gamut of information available in various forms in the library could be accessed without wasting much time. Indigenous databases developed by the library are such an effective medium that enables one to ascertain very quickly as to what is available in the library pertaining to his/her interest. Since the use of technology has increased the possibility of access to the vast store of information from different angles, the probability of any thing relevant being left out is not there.

5.2.3 Availability of Relevant and Condensed Information

The exponential growth of published information in every discipline has posed a challenge to the information officer in storing, retrieving and disseminating right information to the right people at the right time. The pace with which information is exploding, it is difficult to obtain and select relevant bibliographic records from millions of bibliographic sources so easily. The effort in this regard proves to be time consuming process and delay in providing services. But the emergence and use of electronic media, such as CDs and other online databases have made the job not only easy but have also brought about accuracy, speed and relevancy in the dissemination of information.

5.2.4 Quick Retrieval and Better Quality of Information Services

In the fast growing multi-disciplinary approaches it is probably difficult to avoid the false drops in manually retrieved information. Sometimes, it so happens that information provided by the use of traditional methods fails to achieve the required objective. The computer aided technologies have reduced these false drops and improved quality of information resources and services.

5.2.5 Fast Communication and Receiving of Information

The use of computer technology, telecommunication, satellite, etc. has brought about revolution in the transmission of information to the users at global level. These tools have created an environment in which any one having requisite infrastructure could access and share the information available in any part of the world easily and timely.

5.2.6 Avoiding Duplication of Resources and Works

This is possible simply because in-house databases help to check out available literature in the library without loss of time and thus the acquisition of literature is streamlined in the manner that duplication is avoided. Secondly, organisation can also get into an understanding with similar organisation to rationalise their resources and documentation works. The application of information technology has reduced the duplication work and efforts of the staff to create and develop the manual records. Electronic records and information can be harnessed unlimited times.

5.2.7 Use of Bibliographic and Full-Text Databases through Networks

The development of the nation depends to a large extent on availability of and access to information. Through networks, the libraries and information centres of the scientific and technical institutes can search the bibliographic and full-text databases at regional, national and international levels. In the present context of information world, no library and information centre can be fully equipped on its own to meet the demands of their clients. They have to depend on the co-operative exchange of information and resources to achieve the desired goals of their parent bodies. There is a thrust of exchange of information, programmes, databases, advanced communication technologies and setting up of regional networks to establishment of International Information Systems among the nations for better communication and exchange of information. Many developed countries have established and produced a large number of online bibliographic and full-text databases and networks.

5.2.8 Saving of Space

The library being a dynamic organisation keeps collecting literature which go on accumulating. At the same time other activities also expand. These cause space problems. Efforts have been made to solve this problem by using various information technologies. The present information technologies such as, microfilms, microfiches, slides, audio/visual media, CD-ROMs, DVDs, optical discs, Internet, etc. are the media and their use in scientific and technical libraries would help the information specialists and librarians to overcome the space problems arising due to the storage of multi-volume reference sources for their accommodation and management in the available space. The Encyclopaedia Americana and the New Encyclopaedia Britannica are the best examples which occupy only a small space in CD-ROM in comparison to the hard and print copy.

5.2.9 Knowledge Sharing Workspace

Sharing of knowledge across the organisation and its units is significant approach of the application of information technology in libraries. Platform of sharing of ideas, insights and knowledge that resides among the intellectuals can be developed to nurture, strengthen and regenerate the knowledge. Web space collaboration applications are new tools which enhance the communication and knowledge sharing capabilities for intellectual works. Dynamic sharing environment through intranet makes an organisation more productive and responsive by providing access to critical resources. Other collaboration tools such as e-mail, web conferencing, discussion groups, alerts, workflow and document sharing are essential components of knowledge sharing. These tools offer resource sharing among scientists, researchers and technical personnel of various units across the organisation. This approach assists to preserve, leverage and share the tacit knowledge easily and effectively – both inside and beyond the firewall. Though e-mail works well for sharing of information but Web Space in the organisation offers rich sharing environment to workout the critical issues. It eliminates the geographic boundaries by providing online workplace to the team of scientists, faculty, research scholars, planners and intellectuals working in the organisation to accomplish the mission together online and to collaborate on policies, procedures, documents, issues, discussions, complicated tasks, evaluations and assessments.

In competitive environment, it is important that people access information, databases and share the same when they need. This can be done only if organisation has well established IT infrastructure and shared space. It integrates employees and knowledge workers with each other on a single and open platform and thinks over the issues in collective efforts. The users can work together and respond more quickly, accurately and efficiently in well-equipped networked environment. Having access to timely and accurate information is key to helping scientists with their technical and complicated decisions.[4] The advent of information technologies has offered solution to many problems being faced by the modern scientific and technical libraries. These technologies would help to retrieve the exact, timely and accurate information by handling of large data and to improve the quality of library and information services in respect of labour saving, cost-effectiveness, avoiding duplication of resources, enhancing the efficiency of library staff.

5.3 USE OF SPECIFIC TECHNOLOGIES IN SCIENTIFIC AND TECHNICAL LIBRARIES

There is a wide array of computer equipment already in use in research libraries and that many of the libraries regularly make use of time-sharing services for searching databases. The use of computers in these scientific and technical libraries is for a variety of information automation, library automation and information dissemination tasks. The libraries are at present applying one or more of the following technological applications: computers, online database services networks such as OCLC (Online Computer Library Centre) and RLIN (Research Libraries Information Network), automated information systems, electronic bulletin boards, optical disk technologies, such as videodisk and CD-ROM, facsimile, and microfiche and related equipment. These are the primary technologies and technological applications in use today and among the most likely to be found in libraries within the next years.

5.3.1 Online Database Services

Online databases can be accessed by the users directly from producers of databases or vendors of these databases. DIALOG is one of the most widely used online information service in different areas, such as business, science, engineering, finance and law. There are a number of other online information services which are BRS, ORBIT, OCLC, BLAISE (British Library Automated Information Service, London), ESA-IRS (European Space Agency Information Retrieval Service) and so on. At the end of 1997, DIALOG had around fifty times more content than all of the world wide web (WWW).[5]

There are a number of publications which regularly update the growth of online databases and other information. Gale Directory is the most prominent among these. These publications update information in terms of the number of vendors, database producers, databases, database records and online searches, etc. According to Walker and Janes (1993)[6], the first major online dial-up service was MEDLINE, which was the online version of MEDLARS, followed in 1972 by the offer of commercial online services from DIALOG and ORBIT. During the 1970s and 1980s, other online services vendors Data Star, BRS and other major organisations have initiated their efforts to create and develop online bibliographic reference databases. During the past few years, most of the producers of databases and vendors have started providing full text online services (including graphics and pictures). DIALOG started its services in 1972 with six databases and remained a major player of online databases with more than 900' databases. There are other vendors which are providing online services, such as BRS, ORBIT and STN.

In the sixties and seventies, most databases were produced by the government organisations, such as NASA (National Aeronautics and Space Administration), AEC (Atomic Energy Commission). In the eighties commercial databases arose expeditiously. Their growth rose from 22% of all online databases in 1977 to 57% in 1985 and 65% in 1988. From 1985 to 1988 the number of bibliographic databases increased from

1094 to 1162. Other kinds of databases that grew over this period were full text-535 to 1285, directory-287 to 613, and dictionary-10 to 32. In 1985, the total number of online databases was 3010, which rose to 4042 in 1988. In 1998 the number of databases on major subjects were: business 1815, consumer interests 186, general 301, health and life sciences 433, humanities 84, law 441, academic 29, news 428, social sciences 460, and science, technology and engineering 1184.[7] Williams (1998)[8] states that online databases in business are 27% of the total, whereas science and technology databases represent 17%, law databases 11%, health and life science databases 10%, humanities and social science databases 6% and so on.

Electronic journals are growing very rapidly and publishers have captured the internet and transferred their journals on internet. The major giants of electronic journals like Information Access Company (IAC), Universal Microfilms International (UMI) and EBSCO, etc. get permission from a variety of publishers to distribute their reading materials electronically. They pay royalty to the publishers, i.e. based on the use and sale of units. They package all magazines in a single database and offer their product online or CD-ROM, e.g. IAC includes popular computing magazines and publishes multititle CD-ROM publication *Computer Select.* EBSCO Subscription Services is the world's largest subscription agent with 150 databases which are being used in over 80 countries world wide. EBSCO has brought its online bibliographic and full text databases in the field of business, management and education, i.e. Academic Search Premier, Business Source Premier, etc. All databases are available through internet and can be accessed 24 hours a day, 7 days a week for 365 days a year. Other giants in this field are ABI/INFORM, IAC, JSTOR, SWETS and ACM, Blackwell, Cambridge University Press, Elsevier Science (ScienceDirect), Emerald, IEEE, M. E. Sharpe, Oxford University Press, Kluwer Academic Publishers and Springer-Verlag merged in 2004, Sage Publications, Taylor and Francis Group, Wiley InterScience, etc. that are engaged as vendors of their products and producers of the databases. The vendors and institutions of these databases have introduced user-friendly software that lessens both the need for trained searchers and the costs of online searching. Online databases and other computerised retrieval systems cover a wide variety of continually expanding subject areas. They provide libraries greater flexibility in the choice of format and access to previously unavailable information. The use of these services also allows the library to be less dependent on paper and print media.

5.3.2 Library Communication Networks

Communication networks can be formed by two or more libraries utilizing information technologies to enhance the exchange of materials, information and other services. In India the Indian Commercial Computer Communication Network (INDONET), the Education and Research Network (ERNET), National Informatics Network (NICNET)), the Gateway Packet Switching System (GPSS), Remote Area Business Message Network (RABMN) and the National Packet Switched Data Network (INET) are the communication networks which are working to support education, commerce, health and application of IT in the country. The formation of Local, State, Regional, and National Networks has significantly altered the operation of libraries. There are several types of networks which have been developed for bibliographic utility, regional service organisations and subject-oriented networks. Although bibliographic utilities began as a means for libraries to reduce costs of cataloging, their primary function today is for resource sharing, such as DELNET (Developing Library Network), CALIBNET (Calcutta Library Network) and OCLC. OCLC is a major computer-based co-operative network founded in 1967. At present more than 50,000 libraries in 96 countries use OCLC services.[9] (OCLC Newsletter, No.267, January-March 2005). The OCLC network assists librarians in acquiring and cataloguing materials, initiating interlibrary loan, locating materials in member libraries, and gaining access to other databases. More and more depository libraries are using OCLC databases for reference purposes to assist in searching books, articles, the government documents and grey literature. There were 39,517 libraries participating in the OCLC network in March 2001 and this number has now increased to 50,000. Moreover, OCLC provides electronic access to such information as abstracts, full-texts, indexes, bibliographies, etc. The centre helps libraries deliver this information by the best means – whether online or through interlibrary loan, document supplier or library archive to their customers. In March 2001, there were 3,189 journals available online in Electronic Collections online and now it offers access to more than 5,000 titles in a wide range of subject areas from over 70 publishers of academic and professional journals. OCLC has introduced one specific information about BioOne in mid-2001. BioOne is an aggregated collection of electronic journals in the field of biological, ecological and environmental sciences. It is being developed by SPARC (the Scholarly Publishing and Academic Resources Coalition), the American Institute of Biological Sciences (AIBS), the University of Kansas, the Big 12 Plus Libraries Consortium, and Allen Press.

These networks are undergoing changes in their structure and functions. Areas affected include autonomy for members, changes in the telecommunication infrastructure, decentralised versus centralised control, the development of more integrated systems for libraries that permit greater emphasis on local resource sharing and interlibrary co-operation. As a result of the network changes, the libraries are also changing. They are automating their information systems that assist the librarians and information specialists in performing specific library tasks, such as inventory, acquisitions, cataloguing, circulation, administration, personnel, budgeting, and providing connectivity with the regional, national and international networks.

5.3.3 Electronic Bulletin Boards

Bulletin board is an excellent forum for sharing thoughts, ideas and information. Electronic bulletin boards are being used in support of library operations, such as interlibrary loan (ILL), resource sharing functions, for access to current information located elsewhere, storing presentation material, site photographs, interesting writeups, project updates, newspaper cuttings/clippings, etc. It has the advantages of being reasonable in terms of price and, in fact, being less costly than the previous system; increase the speed of communication and transition of information, network and internet facility; capability to store and track the requests in a database; minimises the amount of paper used to support the ILL system and enhances utility of the computer in the information centres.

There is no need to send attachment or document to all users from the mail box, since it makes many number of copies on the server which slows down the mail transferring process. An attachment is uploaded on the bulletin board to create a document link and then send to all users in the mail memo. Its advantage is that only the link goes to all the users and the document or attachment remains at one place on the server. The users can access the document from bulletin board.

5.3.4 Optical Disks

CD-ROM has become an important media that can store huge amounts of data and disseminate information very speedily. CD-ROM databases contain text, numeric data, pictures (graphics and images) and sound. In initial stage, CD-ROMs were used to capture mainly bibliographical, textual and numeric data. But now CD-ROM databases have covered wide spectrum of information sector, such as bibliographic databases, full text materials, encyclopaedias, dictionaries, directories, patent specifications, newspapers and so on. Now a days CD-ROM has emerged with the multimedia applications. Optical disk is being put into the use in scientific and technical libraries for both technical services purposes and for reference services. Today the library and information communities are at the forefront of testing and using the various optical media in digital data publishing and storage applications. These technologies can provide improved access to a variety of information sources and are a means of preserving important documents and information. They are convenient to the users.

The use of CD-ROMs in Indian libraries, particularly in scientific and technical libraries, has increased during the beginning of last decade. Today they are available with variety of diverse information. The product of CD-ROM has been brought about due to the co-operation of major libraries, publishers and manufacturers. It is becoming obvious that information supplied on CD-ROM can be more directly comparable to the printed publication than online retrieval services. Scientific and technical libraries of CSIR have shown their keen interest to acquire enough optical disk technologies in their respective research domain for reference services. The CD-ROM (Compact Disk-Read Only Memory) is an optical storage medium capable of holding up to 700 MB of data, about 80 minutes of high-fidelity audio, or a combination of the two. Today CD-ROMs are in common use for text, graphics, data, audio and video and large volume data storage applications - especially multimedia and software distribution. These can store huge data, text, graphics, audio and video.

The following factors make CD-ROMs increasingly important and popular in academic, research and S&T libraries and information centres for database creators:

1. Tremendous storage capacity of CD-ROM, one disc can store up to 700 megabytes of data or more.
2. Unlimited access to the CD-ROM databases. Its cost is fixed and users can make number of searches and can take amount of time as necessary for conducting searches.
3. CD-ROM searches are less expensive as compared to online information search.
4. Easy to carry, handle and light in weight as compared to magnetic tape/disks and microfiche.
5. It is not dependent on telecommunication as compared to online information retrieval through Internet that needs telephone links, modem, telecommunication software, etc. CD-ROM technology needs only computer and CD-ROM drive.
6. It provides ability to perform searches themselves without a trained librarian.
7. CD-ROM discs are not affected by common environmental problems, such as humidity, heat,

frequent power fluctuations/failure, etc. Moreover, users can only read, copy and save data and information from the CD-ROM and cannot change, tamper with, overwrite and erase data.

5.3.4.1 Disadvantages of the CD-ROM

On the other hand, there are some disadvantages in the use of CD-ROM in library and information centres. These are:

1. Infrastructure required to access the CD-ROM databases such as CD-ROM drive involves additional expenditure.
2. For speedy access, new CD-ROM databases require more powerful and latest hardware, such as the latest versions of the operating system, fast CD-ROM drive and more expensive networking requirements. These technological changes compel the organisation to keep pace with technological advances.
3. Searches through CD-ROM are slower than online searching and its fast access largely depend on the speed of the computer processor. If the systems are old and slow, the searching processes are always very frustrating and painful for users.
4. Searching process in large databases is poor, irritating, time-consuming and frustrating as compared to small databases.
5. CD-ROM databases obtained in the library from time to time cannot be updated frequently as compared to more frequent updating of online databases. Thus, it is difficult to obtain current information from a CD-ROM database.

Despite the lack of common information access and retrieval standards, an ever increasing number of vendors are introducing publications and database services on CD-ROM. Use of a CD-ROM usually requires a Pentium CD-ROM drive and CD-ROM. Reference materials and large textual or statistical databases are now available in the CD-ROM format in S&T libraries and information centers. Reference materials are especially well suited to CD-ROM because they save shelf space and do not require frequent updating. Online databases are also available on CD-ROMs. The primary advantage of having these databases on disk is that the user may sit at a terminal for any time and do not incur high connect charges. This allows the untrained users to perform his/her own search. The user-oriented characteristic of CD-ROM explains some of the technology's popularity. There are a number of other factors to be taken into account by libraries when this technology is introduced and applied. Therefore, CD-ROMs are not practical for time-sensitive data. Different databases require different access software and indexing structures. The use of different search and retrieval software packages by vendors results in difficulty for librarians when "putting up" a new disk. This requires additional expertise and training on the part of the libraries. Finally, a PC and a CD-ROM reader are necessary, and this entails additional expense in the library. Digital video disc (DVD) is a new technology that has enormous capacity to store, video as well as audio and text data to retrieve and speedily access information. Its single-layer, single-sided disc has a capacity of 4.7 GB as compared to 700 MB of data of CD-ROM and double-layer disc achieves a capacity of 8.5 GB and the double-sided and double-layer disc will have a capacity of 17GB.[10] Its enormous capacity will help to store the large amount of data and integrate reference sources and backup of data on a single disc. Higher price and extra hardware requirement on PC are hurdles in the growth and use of this technology in libraries and information centres.

5.3.5 Multimedia Systems

Multimedia has been developed to offer variety of multimedia applications. This technology has been introduced for education, entertainment of the young children and enhance computer-based training of participants. In the multimedia application systems, textual, audio and video information is used to train the participants of training programmes. Moreover, this technology is widely used in the World Wide Web (WWW) and other areas such as marketing of products, maintenance, banking and finance, entertainment, production and manufacturing. Jeffcoate[11] defines the multimedia as 'A computer platform, communications network or software tool is a *multimedia system* if it supports the interactive use of at least one of the following types of information – audio, still image or motion video – in addition to text and graphics'.

5.3.6 Facsimile

An important technological method used in the libraries and information centres is facsimile or fax transmission which is being employed for document delivery through terrestrial or satellite links. Fax is the transmission of information such as letter, order form, interlibrary loan request from one location to another by encoding the printed materials into digitised form. The information is converted back to its original form once it is received. Through this technology message can be sent via cable, telephone lines and other means. Usually telephone lines are used to send messages since it is much more economical than other means. It can deliver and receive information within a few minutes. This service is widely used in governmental, non-governmental, business and industrial organisations to eliminate the geographical gap.

5.3.7 Electronic Mail

Electronic mail is popularly known as E-mail. All organisations whether it is academic, business and research require ways to efficiently distribute information such as news releases, seminar announcements, memos, training programmes, resource sharing, electronic document delivery and other academic work across teams, customers, suppliers and functional departments. It is very popular means of faster communication that takes only a few seconds for a message to reach to any place of the world. The objective of electronic mail is to improve the efficiency and effectiveness of written communication by utilizing the power of the computer and the speed of data transmission. Its purpose is to make it faster, cheaper and easier to transmit information from office to office by applying the latest developments in data processing technology.

Electronic mail helps in the following ways:

1. It increases the speed of communication of information;

2. It is very useful and convenient method to send notices, short note and memo in the offices. It has made publishing, discussing and communicating the academic conferences, seminars very easily and inexpensively in academic, research and business world;
3. It is not limited to transfer the text but also allows the transfer of images, graphics, sound and programmes;
4. It is very reliable source to deliver the message. In postal and other services some times messages are lost;
5. It increases the cost of communication by utilizing the existing data network to process messages and eliminates the postage, stationary and interoffice mail costs;
6. It improves the effectiveness of communication by providing a simple, easy-to-use system for the creation, transmission, retrieval and follow up of messages;
7. It also lessens the print service in business, offices. Many information technology related organisations keep their important messages and records in electronic form than in print;
8. It lessens the use of photocopying machines;
9. It is helpful in solving the space problem; and
10. It helps the management to speed up the better decisions on important matters quickly and makes easy and more convenient for readers to share the knowledge and information resources of other libraries promptly. In the present era of information technology, i.e., in networks, electronic mail can help in resources sharing in libraries in more effective and efficient manner.

Despite all of the advantages, it needs infrastructure such as computer, modem, telephone facility and ISP facility which is beyond the access of a common man. Another negative development which emerged recently is "junk e-mail and flood of unsolicited and unwanted commercial e-mail. The processing of sending junk e-mail to many sites simultaneously is known as *spamming*. This is a serious problem and is a type of abuse of the e-mail system. Since it is time consuming process and tedious job to check the flood of spams, it is also difficult to check, read and respond e-mail on regular basis. However, despite its disadvantages, its advantages are great and useful for the society.

5.3.8 Digital Technology

Digital information is the need of the 21st century libraries and it should be motive of each library to digitise its physical collection and huge amount of paper-based information into electronic format. The libraries of developed countries have already taken initiative in this direction and now developing world is also pursuing the same path to digitise its in-house resources. Digitisation of research studies and other publications and easy access to those resources on web is an invaluable contribution to the academic and research community. Before digitisation, it must be ensured that quality of digitised product should meet the national and international standards of printing and publishing. Borgman et al. (1996)[12] stated that digital libraries are a set of electronic resources and associated technical capabilities for creating, searching and using information. In this sense they are an extension and enhancement of information storage and retrieval systems that manipulate digital data in any medium (text, images, sounds; static or dynamic images) and exist in distributed networks. The content of digital libraries includes data, metadata that describe various aspects of the data (e.g., representation, creator, owner, reproduction rights) and metadata that consist of links or relationships to other data or metadata, whether internal or external to the digital library. Digital libraries serve the users through electronic collection such as books, journals, reports, theses, dissertations, reports, audio-visual material, online databases, etc. with the help of electronic devices. Current research studies, projects, occasional paper series, training programme reports and proceedings, etc. can be uploaded on the website to disseminate the results of the research. The main goal of the non-profit making organisations is to disseminate published and unpublished resources to the wide spectrum of scholars in the area of their respected research.

5.3.9 Intranet and Extranet

The term 'intranet' refers to a computer network built upon Internet technologies in which access is restricted to a particular group of users, typically employees of the organisation. When that network is expanded to include other authorised users, the term 'extranet' is sometimes used.[13] Intranet is apparently a powerful tool to constitute highly skilled experts and competent investment managers, by its "capacity to generate, transmit, store and integrate knowledge".[14] Lang (2001)[15] stated, "That all human knowledge could be put into one book". Intranet is a network technology that connects people of the organisation to access the organisational restricted information. It is a pool of the organisational knowledge that stores, generates, shares and disseminates the knowledge across the organisation and brings people close to each other. Organisation must lay down emphasis on to develop and strengthen the intranet activities of the organisation to handle various types of internal information among employees. Easy access to the information system is important for timely and effective decision-making during meetings and research and development programme. Major goal of any information system is to structure the unstructured information scattered in the organisational units in such fashion that can be easily leveraged and shared in the organisation. Further, it will assist the decision-making body to make decisions, evaluation of scientists, faculty members, employees and observe to what extent the organisation has achieved its goals. Scientists, faculty members and publication department can furnish the books, research works, articles, technical reports and proceedings without any hesitation to strengthen the knowledge pool of the organisation. Through this the management and decision-making body can take decision regarding recruitment of scientists, faculty and staff for research, training, group meetings, research technology, planning and policy and web development. Beside this, decision-making body takes instant decisions in the area of faculty assessment, students evaluation, financial stability, infrastructure and growth and development of the organisation.

All organisational publications and unpublished works can be made available on the intranet and Internet, such as books, journals and newsletters, research studies, occasional papers, training programmes' reports, dissertations, theses, etc. All kinds of forms used in the organisation are made available in portable document format (PDF) and HTML (Hypertext markup language) on intranet. Every organisation must emphasise to build a system which could capture all the organisation's internal knowledge and integrate the same with useful outside knowledge such as educational news from the web and e-mail communications with intellectual groups, discussions, talks, etc. The main purpose of the intranet is to create one-stop-pool for knowledge rather than having to go to several places for the information one needs. Other organisational information such as budget information, financial benefits, work-in-progress documents, sale of documents, archived e-mail discussions of internal and external intellectuals, data and manpower directory, etc. can be accessed through out the organisation through intranet and extranet.[16]

Moreover, other information which cannot be uploaded on the website is accessible and shared on intranet, e.g. online databases and information about official circulars. Sharing of ideas on intranet radically improves an organisation's development and breaks communication barrier across the organisation. Indeed, an intranet is one step closer to the paperless office and probably it is a one of the major benefits to the entire organisation in reducing paper expenses, increasing the productivity and morale, saving the time of the staff and bringing people closer to each other. Norris et al (2003) states, "Transactable e-knowledge and knowledge networking will become the lifeblood of knowledge sharing. They will support a 'Knowledge Economy' based on creating, distributing and adding value to knowledge, the very activities in which colleges and universities are engaged. Yet few colleges and universities have taken sufficient account of the need to use their knowledge assets to achieve strategic differentiation".[17]

To disseminate or access the information beyond the

firewall, a password-protected extranet enables the faculty, research scholars and decision makers to share the internal and external pool of information and knowledge with the colleagues all over the world. They can contribute information to the knowiedge pool from any part of the world. In an organisational environment, intranet can act as a facilitator in the knowledge managing process by harnessing tacit knowledge on an intra-organisational web.

5.3.10 Knowledge Management System

Knowledge Management System (KMS) brings a platform of sharing of ideas, insights and knowledge reside among the intellectuals working in the organisation. It is a process to integrate various databases and processes of the organisation in order to bring efficiency, effectiveness, productivity, quality and qualitative change in the working of entire organisation. It will assist the decision makers, policy makers and administrators in making decisions and strengthen decision support system, document management, communication, dissemination of information and develop knowledge products. The best way to share and deliver knowledge to the research community of the organisation is through dynamic portal contents.

Besides this, KMS will embrace activities of all sections/ departments/units of the organisation. Financial information, publications, document management, knowledgeable products and all kinds of forms used in the organisation would also assist the administrators to take quick decisions. Directory of training participants, resource persons, and directory of the Institute's manpower are important resources that help the administrators and decision makers to use the skilled personnel in the thrust areas to fulfill the needs of the different units of the organisation.[18] This system familiarises the individuals as well as new comers about the policies and work culture of the organisations.

5.4 NETWORKING AND NETWORKS: INTERNATIONAL AND NATIONAL SCENARIO

Due to information explosion, the libraries not only in

developing countries but also in developed countries are facing problems in storing, handling, retrieving and disseminating information effectively. At the same time they are also faced with problems of financial constraints. The solution to these problems lies in networking and consortia arrangement among libraries for the purposes of strengthening and maximising use of their resources for rationalisation of acquisition in the library and sharing of resources. This is done through an agreement which formalises the involvement of the libraries or organisations to exchange information, resources and services for the benefit of users of their parent bodies. It is a co-operative arrangement which allows an effective linkage among group of individuals, computers, equipment, or institutions that are interconnected to form a system to achieve some significant objectives. The telephone system is the best example of an effective network. Networks can be implemented on various levels for variety of purposes. The document delivery largely depends on the postal and courier facilities but digitisation has revolutionised the storage of electronic information and electronic document delivery services. Networking has forced the libraries to acquire more and more electronic resources to strengthen the knowledge pool and delivery of information to a large extent.

The decade of 1990s has witnessed the most exciting phase in terms of electronic communications and networking developments in India and abroad. This phase has also seen the expansion of existing electronic networks and their uses in leading S&T libraries and many other research libraries. The success and survival of resource sharing is, however, contingent largely upon adequate reprographic facilities, efficient communication, postal and courier services, adequate bibliographical control over the resources of participating libraries in the network. As Kent has suggested, "The success and survival of big libraries will depend on how much and to what extent libraries co-operate with each other in future".[19] The information specialists and scientists should strive to develop a national network to increase the bibliographical and physical access to library resources to all the special users of research and S&T libraries and other special libraries. The goal of the network is to extend the facilities of exchange of information, data, and messages among scientists, technologists, academicians, research scholars and policy-makers and provide the facilities to communicate the results of R&D programmes.

Recognising the importance of networks and networking, various types of networks have been established all the world over. Some of the important networks have been discussed in succeeding pages.

5.4.1 Information Networks

Initially, there were information retrieval networks on agro-economic, socio-economic and administrative data. Preference was given to food and agriculture, industry, health, education, electricity, water, oil and transport. The National Information System for Science and Technology (NISSAT), Department of Scientific and Industrial Research took up initiatives for the design and development of library networks in India in 1985 in order to share the resources available in the libraries located in various parts of the country. During the past two decades some important data networks, namely, Internet, NICNET, ERNET, SIRNET, ADINET, BONET, CALIBNET, DELNET, INFLIBNET, MALIBNET, MYLIBNET and PUNENET, etc. have been established. The networking system is the most effective infrastructure for most forms of information handling. The main objectives of these library networks were to prepare union catalogue of books, periodicals, non-book material, theses, dissertations, and to promote and encourage the interlibrary loan among the member libraries, document delivery services and create centralised database of resources, etc. so that resource sharing among these libraries could be expedited and duplication of resources is avoided and the limited funds are utilised for the useful purposes.

5.4.2 The Internet

Internet is one of the most important and useful means in existing networks. It is a co-operative computer network of networks that links governments, schools, libraries, corporations, individuals, and others to each other and to a vast information resources. Borgman (2003) explains, "The Internet is a network of networks, linking many layers of networks within organisations, within local geographic areas, within countries, and within larger geographical regions".[20] It is used in all spheres of life to access and exchange of information. Internet came into being in 1969. The Internet protocol links up many disparate and independent networks together so that they appear as a single network to the user. This US system allows access to most existing types of electronic communications, such as electronic mail, bulletin boards, OPACs, and electronic publishing all over the world. It has continued to demonstrate its usefulness, and has been utilised as a primary network by the information specialists and librarians of the scientific and technical institutions and other research organisations. The Internet is receiving more and more international acceptability as more users such as leading scientific and technical libraries and information units, research organisations and other information centres have recognised its importance and uses. Tremendous growth of information shows that number of publicly accessible web pages and hosts are growing exponentially. Public access databases and online public access catalogues (OPACs) are becoming accessible in several forms. Thousands of leading libraries, publishers and organisations, particularly in the academic and research sectors, spread all over the world have made their catalogues, databases and products accessible via the Internet.

5.4.3 Networks in India

(a) NICNET

The National Informatics Centre (NIC) was established in 1975 by the Government of India for promotion of informatics culture in the government at various levels. It has the following objectives:

1. To design, develop and implement advanced computer-based methodologies;
2. To promote adoption of computer-based data management techniques;

3. To generate specialised manpower in the field of informatics; and
4. To build intra-city and inter-city computer networks for interconnecting various ministries/departments of the Central Government and autonomous organisations for a distributed governmental information system.

The NIC is providing network backbone and e-governance support to Central Government, State Governments, UT Administrations, Districts and other Government bodies. It is the only Government organisation in India that offers network services over Ku-band (TDMA, FTDMA, IPA and DVB, and SCPC VSATs, video conferencing facility, Wireless Metropolitan Area Networks (MANs) and Local Area Networks (LANs) for intranet application, and with NICNET Gateway for Internet resources, e-commerce, multimedia information system and Geographical Information System. It has set up a countrywide satellite based VSAT network (NICNET) and has linked 600 districts, 28 State Governments, 7 NCT/UT Administrations and Central Government departments. NIC has set up its VSAT based network in all the blocks of North-Eastern States. At present there are more than 1800 VSATs in different parts of the country.[21]

NICNET offers services such as e-mail, Internet access, Electronic Data Interchange, databases of medical literature MEDLARS, the district information system (DISNIC), Intellectual Property and Know-How Services, Courts Information Systems (COURTIS) that provide information on pending cases in the High Court and Supreme Court of India, traditional sciences and technologies of India, GISTNIC (General Information Services Terminal of NIC), Community Information Centres (CICs) in the North-East, Land Records Computerisation and the Research and Education Network of the NIC (RENNIC) that share information at global level, and meets the information needs of academic and research community of the nation.

(b) ERNET

During the Seventh Plan (1986-91), the Department of Electronics, New Delhi took one of the major initiatives to establish Education and Research Network (ERNET) with support from the Government of India and United Nations Development Programme (UNDP) with the specific aim to provide academic and research institutions with electronic mail, networking and Internet facilities. During the last few years, ERNET has established itself as a major operational facility. It is being used by academic, research and scientific and technical establishments in the country. The centre provides variety of applications and services, such as e-mail, network bulletin board service, file transfer, remote login, database access, WWW and networks in other countries. It has achieved international connectivity through gateways at New Delhi, Mumbai, Bangalore and Kolkata. It connects 92 universities, 215 research and development institutions and 334 other institutions in the country.[22] ERNET works on the projects of high-speed networking, network management, electronic publishing, multimedia, ATM and digital libraries.

ERNET has been initiated to fulfill the objectives of:

i) setting up a nationwide computer network for the academic and research community;

ii) undertaking R&D in the design and development of and advanced research in networking and related technologies; and

iii) carrying out training and consultancy for manpower development.

In addition, it provides state-of-the-art communication infrastructure and services to academic and research institutions, Government organisations, private sector R&D organisations and other non-governmental organisations (NGOs).

ERNET is engaged to provide Internet and intranet to various academic and research institutions of the country for their research and development. Main activities of the ERNET are:

1. UGC - Infonet – In partnership with the ERNET India and University Grants Commission to connect 150 universities and higher learning institutions on intranet and Internet.
2. AICTE - Net – Provide connectivity to All India Council for Technical Education (AICTE) recognised colleges and regional centres spread over the entire country. 48 institutions connected.
3. ICAR - NET – Provide intranet and Internet for 104 Agricultural Universities and Research Institutions affiliated to Indian Council of Agricultural Research (ICAR).
4. Navodaya Vidyalaya Samiti - Net - Provide NVS – Net connectivity to 100 Navodaya Vidyalayas situated in different parts of the country.
5. Vidya Vahini – Provide intranet and Internet for 140 schools in 7 districts of 6 states, information and communication technology infrastructure, training to teachers to use ICT to impart education and different learning resources which include curriculum and other learning material.
6. Gyan Vahini

In addition, the centre imparts training to the persons who are engaged in education and research organisations of the country to build, configure and manage the Local and Wide Area Networks.

(c) SIRNET

Scientific and Industrial Research Network (SIRNET) of INSDOC is a computer communication network initially started for exchange of information among CSIR laboratories. It is a fast expanding network and it targets to link S&T organisations and establishments throughout the country. All CSIR laboratories are connected to SIRNET. About 130 S&T establishments and organisations of the country are connected with this network. SIRNET has its network management centres at Delhi, Bangalore, Calcutta and Madras. In Bombay,

INSDOC has arrangements with Western Regional Instrumentation Centre (WRIC) for providing information service in the western region. The Unix-based SIRNET node at INSDOC-WRIC Information Service acts as the network management centre for SIRNET at Bombay at the University Campus, Vidyanagari, Kalina, Santacruz (E), Bombay. The SIRNET's main node at INSDOC, New Delhi is connected to Education and Research Network (ERNET) set up by the Department of Electronics (DOE) through leased line. Through ERNET, SIRNET has access to Unix User Network (UUNET), an international network and hence to JANET, CSNET and BITNET. The software used for SIRNET is Basic Networking Software (UUCP) with standard UNIX package to communicate with other UNIX Systems. Besides e-mail, it also offers access to indigenous databases of INSDOC, document copy supply and CAPS (Contents, Abstracts and Photocopies Service).

The objectives of the SIRNET are to help organise indigenous online database services on food technology, natural products, chemistry, radio physics and medicinal plants. It provides access to the databases, such as the National Union Catalogue of Scientific Serials in India (NUCSSI), the Current Contents of Indian Journals, Polymer Science, the Material Science bibliographic database, the Catalogue of Scientific and Technical Conference Proceedings. It plans to set up a bulletin board service and teleconferencing facilities through the network, and to facilitate the flow of routine administrative and financial information and the exchange of library resources.

(d) DELNET

It was in 1988 when a group of library professionals in Delhi took a major initiative to launch a network of libraries in Delhi known as DELNET (Delhi Library Network). It was initially sponsored by the National Information System for Science and Technology (NISSAT), Department of Scientific and Industrial Research, Government of India. It is currently being promoted by the National Informatics Centre, Ministry of Communications and Information Technology, Government of India and India International Centre, New Delhi. It was conceived as a channel for promoting the creation of databases of libraries situated in Delhi. Subsequently, it was registered as a Society on June 30, 1992 and now it has developed into an important resource centre for the libraries such as academic, public and research in Delhi. Delnet was established with the objective to promote resources sharing among the libraries by developing a network of libraries, by collecting, storing and disseminating information and by offering computerised services to the users to co-ordinate efforts for suitable collection, development and reducing unnecessary duplication wherever possible. DELNET has opened a Co-ordination Unit in Bangalore to co-ordinate the interlibrary loan (ILL) and document delivery operations among the member libraries. On September 13, 2000, it was renamed from Delhi Library Network to Developing Library Network (DELNET).

DELNET attempts to bring the uniformity in the creation of bibliographic records. For this purpose the participating libraries set up a committee on the standardisation of DELNET programme. In a short period, DELNET has succeeded in converting records into machine readable form by the participating libraries. It was for the first time that creation of the union catalogue of books in machine readable form has been taken up in India. It has been engaged in creating the databases, such as Union Catalogue of Books, Union List of Periodicals, Union Catalogue of Periodicals, CD-ROM Database, Specialists' Database, Database of Journal Articles, Union List of Video Recordings, Union List of Sound Recordings, Urdu Manuscripts' Database, Database of Theses and Dissertations and several other databases.

As on 31 March 2005, DELNET had 878 libraries of India and abroad related to all disciplines as its members. Its membership has grown from 743 on April 1, 2004 to 878 on March 31, 2005. In 1992-93, 26 libraries were members of DELNET, 30 libraries in 1993-94, 43 libraries in 1994-95, 57 libraries in 1995-96, 69 libraries in 1996-97, 76 libraries in 1997-98, 106 libraries in 1998-99, 153 libraries in 1999-2000, 233 libraries in 2000-2001, 393 libraries in 2001-2002, 565 libraries in 2002-2003, 743 libraries in 2003-2004 and 878 libraries in 2004-2005. Out of 878 libraries, 629 libraries belong to Science and Technology, 101 Social Sciences, 123 general and 25 Humanities of the 878 member libraries, 866 are Indian and 12 are foreign libraries.[23] More than 70 percent (71.6%) libraries of DELNET belong to the area of Science and Technology.

(e) TIFACLINE (Technology Information System)

Technology Information System was initiated as a national network for online technology information. It was introduced in 1990 by the Technology Information, Forecasting and Assessment Council (TIFAC), the Department of Science and Technology, New Delhi. It became operational in 1991. TIFAC extends a number of value added technology and industry oriented databases in co-operation with the reputed organisations in the country which are accessible online in India through TIFACLINE Information System on Indonet and I-net. TIFACLINE offers access to various databases, such as Composites, Environmental Technologies, Food Technology, Non-Ferrous Materials, Expertsbase, Standards Directory, Technology Sourcing World-Wide to its members. Its operations are managed by the Technology Applications Group (TAG) of CMC Ltd., which is a premier IT company of the Government of India. TAG offers technology support and consultancy services to Technology Sourcing, Project Feasibility Studies, Project Reports, etc. TIFAC brings out a bulletin on Intellectual Property Rights (IPR) for dissemination.[24]

(f) CALIBNET

The Calcutta Library Network as a metropolitan network was inaugurated on 21 December 1993 by Prof. S. K. Sen, Minister-in-Charge for Power, Science and Technology and NES, Government of West Bengal, at Jadavpur University Campus. This project was financially supported by NISSAT (National Information Systems for Science and Technology). This computer-based library network was introduced to provide a cost-effective solutions to the information problems of academic, research and management libraries. CALIBNET was established with a view to meet the increasing demand of information, to counter the problem of financial constraints, space, and to avoid the import of expensive books and journals by saving the foreign exchange. Its prime objective is create the databases of holdings of libraries in Calcutta and facilitate remote online access to the databases of books, serials, inter-library co-operation and document delivery among the member libraries of the network for effective resource sharing.

In future the CALIBNET plans to have linkages with the other regional and national networks that have emerged in the country. Its Services Centre offers electronic access to global information services to participating member libraries of Kolkata. Other services, such as access to union catalogue, databases and national and international networks, are also offered to the libraries. CALIBNET has developed its own software, earlier 'MAITRAYEE' now 'SANJUKTA', to support the centralised databases and complete automation of house-keeping operations of participating libraries.

It has followed UNIMARC format after obtaining views and opinions of international specialists and experts on exchange formats to enhance the scope for eventual exchange of information with library and information centres in other nations. It has also developed PARAPAR conversion software package to facilitate and support the conversion of bibliographic data from USMARC, CCF or any non-standard format to UNIMARC standard which has been accepted as International Standard for networking of libraries.

(g) INFLIBNET

INFLIBNET (Information and Library Network) is an autonomous Inter-University Centre (IUC) of the University Grants Commission (UGC). It is a major UGC programme initiated in 1991 and located at Gujarat University Campus, Ahmedabad. Initially, it was stated as a project under the IUCAA, later it became an independent Inter-University Centre in 1996. INFLIBNET was initiated to modernise the university libraries in India and connect the same with a nation-wide high speed network to promote sharing of resources across the country. INFLIBNET is a co-operative library network which will contribute to pooling, sharing and optimisation of the library resources, services and facilities in universities and R&D

institutions. This network will cover all universities and is expected to support 400 libraries and information centres of the university system and other R&D institutions of the country in information storage and retrieval. It was established to develop a computer communication network at national level for modernisation and linking of universities, R&D institutions and information units during the period of 8th Five Year Plan so that research activities could be encouraged. The major objectives of INFLIBNET are to evolve a national network to access, share and disseminate the information and increase awareness among the academic and research community of the country. It interconnects various libraries and information centres in universities, deemed to be universities, colleges, UGC information centres, institutions of national importance and research and development (R&D) institutions for efficient sharing of resources and avoid duplication of efforts.

INFLIBNET has developed several databases, such as of books, serials, theses, university experts, experts database in science and technology. The centre is engaged in various activities like networking, software development, database development, library automation and human resource development. It offers services to the academic and research community of the country through document delivery service, bibliographic information services, online registration of experts, register projects and database CD-ROMs.

To achieve the mission to provide relevant and quality education to the academic and research community of the Indian universities and colleges, UGC launched a major programme namely, UGC-INFONET: E-journals Consortium to facilitate free access to scholarly journals and databases in all areas of learning to the academic and research community of the nation. It offers access to more than 4000 full text e-journals from 20+ publishers from all areas of learning through this programme.[25] INFLIBNET is the nodal agency that co-ordinates and facilitates linkage between ERNET and universities. Moreover, INFLIBNET Centre has been organizing several training programmes to create awareness among the academic and research community for accessing and browsing the e-journals of the UGC-Infonet E-journals consortium.

(h) MALIBNET

In 1991, academicians, scientists and heads of major institutions felt the need of interconnecting libraries and information centres in Madras, now Chennai. In this direction, INSDOC now NISCAIR (National Institute of Science Communication and Information Resources) convened a meeting of librarians of important institutions in September 1991 to discuss the possibility of establishing a Madras Library Network (MALIBNET). Thereafter, feasibility study was taken up by INSDOC. That study categorised the libraries in Madras into the following major disciplines: 1. Applied Science and Technology; (2) Medical Sciences; (3) Arts and Basic Sciences; and (4) Industries.

Due to the non-availability of funds, heads of major institutions, universities and industries and other academicians of Madras through a co-operative effort realised the need of the establishment of MALIBNET. As a result, MALIBNET was registered as a Society in Madras in February 1993 to share the resources among the libraries of the city. MALIBNET was established with the objectives to foster growth of knowledge in the fields of library, documentation, and information science and technologies; to undertake scientific research in the area of library documentation and information science and technologies; to evolve network of libraries and information centres in and around Madras, initially, and in other parts of the state latter; to facilitate sharing of resources among the libraries and information centres and promote information dissemination through computerised network; and to establish appropriate linkages with other regional, national and international libraries, information and documentation centres at networks and organise lectures, conferences, workshops and seminars. MALIBNET offers services to its member libraries such as access to the list of current serials subscribed by the member libraries, online databases, e-mail and interlibrary loan, etc.

(i) BONET

Sponsored by NISSAT, BONET (Bombay Library Network) is the latest network in the chain of projects like DELNET, CALIBNET and PUNENET. BONET was inaugurated by Shri N. Vittal, Secretary, Department of Electronics, Government of India at the National Centre for Software Technology, (NCST), Mumbai on November 6, 1992. Its objective is to build up a library information system of metropolitan libraries in academic, research, scientific and technical and business fields, etc. which can be linked to the other libraries and networks in and outside Mumbai. It aims to enhance networking, increase facilities and promote inter-library co-operation among the participating libraries in and around Mumbai.

BONET renders services, such as access to online catalogue of books and periodicals, promote co-operation among libraries of Mumbai and interlibrary loan service and online access to foreign catalogues and commercial databases. Moreover, participating libraries will computerise their own operations and strengthen resource sharing with each other. BONET will offer training related to library automation and networking and speed up computerisation of the libraries of the city.

(j) PUNENET

Like other library network projects, Pune Library Network (PUNENET) was funded and supported by NISSAT. It is a joint programme of the University of Pune, Centre for Development of Advanced Computing and the National Chemical Laboratory (NCL). Its objective is to create and maintain the databases of books, periodicals and other resources available in the participating libraries situated around Pune and enhance the co-operation among participating libraries to strengthen the resource sharing efficiently and effectively.[26]

(k) MYLIBNET

The Mysore Library Network (MYLIBNET) was established during May 1995 in the city of Mysore under the financial assistance from NISSAT. MYLIBNET is housed at the Central Food Technological Research Institute (CFTRI) campus. Its objectives are to share resources among the S&T libraries, to provide e-mail, to develop software for the better management of library resources, to set up information bases in collaboration with industry, to conduct seminars, conferences and training programmes for library professionals about the development of modern IT infrastructure, etc. Moreover, it extends services to automate the library operations, access to various databases, e-mail to libraries under ERNET. For the better and faster communication among the libraries, MYLIBNET has been subscribing the e-mail facility from ERNET, Department of Electronics, Government of India.[27]

(l) ADINET

ADINET (Ahmedabad Library Network) was established to strengthen the resource sharing among the libraries situated in and around Ahmedabad. It was registered as a Society in October 1994. It is supported by NISSAT, Department of Scientific and Industrial Research, Government of India. Rapid growth in the published literature and their escalating costs has urged the libraries of all disciplines to share their resources with each other. The prime objective of ADINET is to promote sharing of resources, dissemination of information among participating libraries through networking, creation of centralised Union catalogue of books, serials, non-book material, etc. of all the participating libraries. Moreover, other objectives are to co-ordinate with other regional, national and international networks, libraries and information centres for exchange of information and technical guidance to member libraries. ADINET extends services to the users of member libraries such as access to database of current periodicals, inter-library loan, training programme for information professionals on the application of latest technologies.

5.5 FUTURE OF ELECTRONIC RESOURCES AND WEB ENABLED SERVICES

Web enabled services will continue to exist and grow

with the passage of time and developments. According to Jasperse[28] and Clausen,[29] CD-ROM technology is a low cost and portable medium for text archives and a medium for back-up of electronic and online publications, It will continue to play an important role in the storing of information. Jeffery Galt, President of the DIALOG Corporation states that the future of industry is tied up with the development of customised services which can save customers from the information overload in future. These customised services should be able to exploit and harness the Internet, intranet, extranet and other new technologies to survive the web-enabled services.[30] The development of DVD is another technology which has an enormous capacity of storage, speedy access and for the preservation of data in future.

The financial constraints of the organisations and libraries are a universal problem. Not only developing countries but developed ones are also not immune to this problem. The gradual fall in the annual budgets of the organisation and libraries is universal that hinders the development of the research work of the organisation. E-resources, which are cheap in comparison to the printed resources, are a solution to all problems. Online resources have replaced the printed resources, such as books, journals, reference sources and reports, etc. The significant factors are the possibilities of rapid publication, rapid updating and economics of electronic distribution. It is a fact that electronic resources can be published frequently and updated whenever needed. The various kinds of important reference sources like statistical data, business information, encyclopedias, dictionaries, directories, compilations of data and books of facts, are produced in electronic because electronic technology can search and sort large data quickly in a different manners. Encyclopedia Britannica has gained more popularity and earned more income from web-based electronic version than from print publication. In addition, indexing and abstracting journals are also important reference sources which are being publishing electronically. A major advantage of online resources is that electronic information in journals, books and proceedings, etc. can be accessed any time and at every place throughout the world. Such types of information are more suited in electronic format than others. Internet is not only the source of providing information but it offers so many opportunities of publishing, establishing networks, web conferencing, interactive services and broadcasting.[31]

A survey report covering technology predictions at colleges and universities, published in the issue of Campus Trends (American Council on Education), indicates that 68 percent of the colleges and universities feel more courses using electronic materials in the coming year, 47 percent foresee more courses offered through distance learning, and 34 percent see more assignments submitted electronically.[32] Such electronic trends have revolutionised the world of scholars to conduct programmes and amalgamate the electronic publications and use other information technologies in teaching and distance learning. In the support of electronic documents, Ward (1998)[33] stated that the value of electronic documents and information is proliferating by leaps and bounds. According to the Electronic Document Systems Foundation (EDSF), the worldwide value of electronic document revenue in 1991 stood at $46.9bn; by 1996 this had grown to $85.7bn. The value of electronic documents is doubling every five years and it will reach $600bn by 2010.

Mashelkar[34] indicates that tomorrow's society will be a knowledge based society and every one should have access to knowledge so that a knowledgeable worker could generate the national wealth and prosperity for the nation. In today's electronic environment, the wealth of a nation is measured in terms of knowledge-based society and not by the physical assets like land, buildings, etc. He has further stated that economics of knowledge would dominate the 21st century. It is the need of the hour that preservation of knowledge should not be documented but also digitised so that this digitised information could be exploited by the chain of research organisations. Digitised information or electronic information can be preserved for a longer period of time. Developed countries like USA and the UK have already launched operations to preserve information for future in electronic format. He further stated that the market for knowledge society will be knowledge markets and its wars will be fought not by conventional weapons, guns and missiles but in the knowledge markets with the new thermonuclear weapon which is called 'information and knowledge'. These weapon can be used if we take the initiative to change with the new technology.

The libraries are gradually moving in this direction and some of the libraries have already taken initiatives to digitise its resources and have been subscribing to e-journals' databases through consortia based subscription of e-journals to provide round the clock access to their users. E-publications have brought a solution to the libraries and organisations which have the space problem in today's metropolitan cities and industrialised society. It is impossible to predict the future of online resources but it is a fact that it largely depends upon the speed of transition of information. An advanced technology and systems are required to adopt the change in our traditional systems but it is only possible if we accept and prefer electronic publications besides printed publications. King et al. (2003)[35] examined that the electronic collection and services offer benefits of lower prices per title, less time of staff and savings in space. These resources can be reallocated into additional or better services to users. Users benefit in flexibility of several times access, saving of time in searching, locating and obtaining the articles round-the-clock. Moreover, electronic collection offers new and useful features for better access and increase in the number of journals in databases.

It is a fact that financial constraints and lack of infrastructure in electronic environment have affected the Research and Development (R&D) in academic as well as research organisations of Third World countries. Our library systems need change in their traditional setups, because old collections of printed resources, whether it is journal or a monograph, need to be preserved and converted into digital format. Through web-enabled services, libraries are expanding their wider array of services, such as all online services through intranet, extranet and Internet and digital resources and distance learning. Libraries with their limited resources are meeting the greater demands of services through electronic resources, consortia of libraries and web enabled services.

CONCLUSION

In order to promote effective flow of information for profitable use by the scientists, research scholars, engineers and technologists, strengthening of the existing information centres through co-ordination, co-operation and proper communication linkages is essential. It is, therefore, necessary for the managers of information centres and libraries to adapt the use of new information technologies for better and speedy access to information which in turn would result into the social and economic prosperity of the country. The S&T libraries have taken lead in adopting the new information technologies like Internet, intranet, CD-ROMs, DVDs, online bibliographic and full text databases of journals, etc. to improve their functioning for effective communication and dissemination of R&D results among information specialists and scientists, technologists, entrepreneurs, academicians and decision-makers. Budd and Harloe[36] stated that in future, in the first decades of the 21st century, it is more likely that evolution of a mixed system - part print, and increasingly electronic would continue in libraries.

Emergence of Internet and intranet technology has posed some exciting challenges and opportunities to explore the ways of exploiting resources and benefit the users through quick transfer of information. Many governmental and non-governmental organisations have initiated their efforts towards the digitisation and have launched their digital products free of cost on the Internet so that right information at the right time to the needy users can be accessed and disseminated. Ladendorf[37] remarks that "in today's information-rich environment, those who exploit these information resources most effectively are the ones who will succeed." So, it is imperative for CSIR laboratories to develop a national database system for CSIR libraries for free flow of S&T information and make it available to other research organisations in the country through online searching system and other effective systems also.

REFERENCES

1. Star, S. L. and Ruhleder, K. Steps toward an ecology of infrastructure: Design and access for large information spaces. *Information Systems Research,* 7(1), 1996, 111-134.
2. Thakur, D. S. Value of information and online information resources. In: *Emerging Digital Library Initiatives and Future of Business and Management Information in India: Proceeding 5th National MANLIBNET Convention.* XLRI, Jamshedpur, March 6-8, 2003, 303-310.
3. Sanders, Donald H. Computers today. 3rd edition. New York: McGraw-Hill Book Company, 1988.
4. Thakur, D. S. and Thakur, K.S. Approaches to knowledge management in higher education. *Annals of Library and Information Studies,* 52(4), 2005, 115-118.
5. Skyrme, David J. Knowledge networking: Creating the collaborative enterprise. Oxford: Butterworth-Heinemann, 1999. 311p.
6. Walker, G. and Janes, J. Online retrieval: A dialogue of theory and practice. Englewood, CO: Libraries Unlimited, 1993.
7. Chowdhury, G. G. Introduction to modern information retrieval. London: Library Association Publishing, 1999. 452p.
8. Williams, M. E. The state of databases today: 1998. In: Braun, Erin E. (ed) Vol. 1: Online databases; Vol.2 : CD-ROM, diskette, magnetic tape, handheld and batch access database products. Detroit, MI, Gale, 1998, xvii-xxix.
9. OCLC Annual Report 2003/2004. Ohio: OCLC, 2004. 41p. 5 May 2005. Available: http://www.oclc.org/news/publications/annualreports/2004.pdf
10. Cunningham, S. and Rosebush, J. Electronic publishing on CD-ROM. Bonn: O'Reilly, 1996.
11 Jeffcoate, J. Multimedia in practice: Technology and applications. New York: Prentice-Hall, 1995.

12. Borgman, Christine L. et al. Social aspects of digital libraries: Final report to the National Science Foundation, 1996, 35p. Available: http://www.ifla.org/documents/libraries/net/ucladl01.pdf

13. Watson, Ian. Internet, intranet and extranet: Managing the information bazaar. *Aslib Proceedings*, 51(4), 1999, 109-114.

14. Edenius, Mats and Borgerson, Janet. To manage knowledge by intranet. *Journal of Knowledge Management*, 7(5), 2003, 124-136.

15. Lang, J. Managerial concerns in knowledge management. *Journal of Knowledge Management*, 5(1), 2001, 43-57.

16. Thakur, D. S. and Thakur, K. S. Online information resources and intranet: A case study of NIEPA library. In: Shokeen, Ashu, Madhusudhan, Margam and Singh, D. V. (eds). *Knowledge Organisation in Digital Environment in Libraries (KODEL): Introspect and Prospects*. Seminar papers of 50th All India Conference, M. S. University of Baroda, Vadodara, 1-4 December 2004. Delhi: Indian Library Association, 2004, 438-455.

17. Norris, Donald M. and others. A revolution in knowledge sharing. *EDUCAUSE Review*, September/October 2003, 14-26.

18. Thakur, D. S. and Thakur, K. S. Knowledge acquisition, management and sharing in higher education. In: Kamalavijayan, D. et al. (eds). *International Conference on Information Management in a Knowledge Society*. Vol.2. IASLIC, Mumbai, February 21-25, 2005. New Delhi: Allied, 2005, 703-709.

19. Kent, A. and Galvin, Thomas. Library resource sharing proceedings of the 1976 conference on resource sharing in libraries, Pitsburg, Pennsylvania. New York: Marcel Dekker, 1977.

20. Borgman, Christine L. The invisible library: Paradox of the global information infrastructure. *Library Trends*, 51(4), Spring 2003, 652-674.

21. Information Technology Annual Report 2003-04. New

Delhi: Ministry of Communications and Information Technology, 2004. 106p.

22. *Ibid.*, p.70-72.
23. Director's report 2004-2005. New Delhi: Developing Library Network (DELNET), 2005. 24p.
24. TIFAC technology information services - TIFACLINE Available: http://corporatepark.com/tifac/tifaclin.html
25. UGC INFONET: E-journals consortium: A key to E-resources. Ahmedabd: INFLIBNET Centre, 2005. 312p.
26. Rao, Siriginidi Subba. Networking of libraries and information centres: Challenges in India. *Library Hi Tech,* 19(2), 2001, 167-178.
27. Rao, S. N. Krishna. Mysore Library Network: MYLIBNET (Network with a difference). *Information Today & Tomorrow,* 21(1), 2002, 13-14, 30. Available: http://www.mylibnet.org/nissat/vol21/mylibnet.html
28. Jasperse, J. Are we losing a generation of manuscripts? *Online and CD-ROM Review,* 21(2), 1997, 30-32.
29. Clausen, H. Online, CD-ROM and Web: is the same difference. *Aslib Proceedings,* 19(7), 1997, 177-183.
30. Galt, J. S. Does the future of online industry lie in individually customised services? How online hosts are adapting to the future. In: Raitt, D. I., Blake, P. and Jeaps, B. (eds). *Online Information 97: Proceedings of the 21st International Online Information meeting,* London, 9-11 December 1997. Oxford: Learned Information Europe, 1997, 13-18.
31. Thakur, D. S. and Thakur, K. S. Electronic publishing and its future. In: Mujoo-Munshi, Usha (ed.). *Information Management in New Millennium.* 19th Annual Convention and Conference of Society for Information Science, Indian National Science Academy (INSA), New Delhi, 27-29 January 2000. New Delhi: Allied Publishers, 2002, 354-366.
32. Hitchingham, Eileen. Collection management in light of electronic publishing. *Information Technology and Libraries,* March 1996, 38-41.

33. Ward, Gareth. Publishing in the digital age. London: Bowerdean Publishing Company Limited, 1998. P17-18.

34. Mashelkar, R. A. Wealth creation through knowledge. *New India Digest,* 4(6), November 1999 - February 2000, 28-33, 144-146.

35. King, Donald W. et al. Library economic metrics: Examples of the comparison of electronic and print journal collections and collection services. *Library Trends,* 51(3), 2003, 376-400.

36. Budd, John M. and Harloe, Bart M. Collection development and scholarly communication in the 21st century: From collection management to content management. In: Gorman, G. E. and Miller, Ruth H. (eds). *Collection Management for the 21st Century: A Handbook for Librarians.* Westport: Greenwood Press, 1997, 3-25.

37. Ladendorf, Janice. The special librarian in the modern world. *Special Libraries,* 61, December 1970, 535.

6

Specialised Information Centres in India

The tremendous growth in the scientific and technical literature in the form of research results has created an acute problem of information assessment, their selection and acquisition and organisation for the information specialists working in scientific and technical institutions and organisations. They have realised the need for an effective and efficient system for handling information by applying Information Technology. Scientists and technologists need to keep themselves abreast of information relating to research works and activities in a specialised field for avoiding duplication in researches already done by others in the same specialised field. Information about the researches done in the same subject field helps in avoiding duplication and saves a lot of money, time and effort of the scientists and researchers in that field. In order to fulfil the need for precise and accurate information in the field of science and technology, the Government took major initiatives to establish National Information System for Science and Technology (NISSAT) for an over all development and prosperity of the country and developing a strong information system for the support of R&D.

The Government of India realised the importance of having a National Information System for the first time in 1971. On the request of Government of India, UNESCO provided the services of Peter Lazar in March-April, 1972 to advice the National Institute of Science Communication and Information Resources (formerly known as INSDOC), to set up a Network of National Information System in science and technology. During this period, the Government of India had established a high powered apex body, the National Committee of Science and Technology (NCST), in October 1971 and entrusted it with the task of preparation and continuous updating of national scientific and technological plans, both Five Year Plans and Perspective Plans. The NCST then prepared a comprehensive Science and Technology Plan for a five year period, with a view to integrating the S&T Plan with the Nation's Fifth Five Year Plan (1974-79). A panel of experts was appointed to deal with the "Information Sector" in this Plan on S&T. The panel examined the recommendations of Peter Lazar and prepared a report in 1973 and favoured the recommendations for the establishment of a National Information System for Science and Technology. Thus NISSAT formed an integral part of our Science and Technology Plan for the years 1974-79. It was implemented in June 1977.[1]

NISSAT came into existence as a project under the Department of Science and Technology (DST), Government of India, in June 1977. It aims to promote and support the development of a compatible and effective set of information systems for science and technology and interlinking these into an effective information network. It operates as a co-ordinating agency to bring the existing and future information centres, systems and services to a higher level of an effective network to better meet the information needs of the national community of information users. It also identifies the existing research gaps and avoid the duplication of research efforts.

NISSAT functions for fulfilling the following objectives:

1. Provision of national information services to meet the present and future needs of users, generators, processors and disseminators of information.
2. Optimum utilisation of existing information services and systems and the development of new ones.
3. Promotion of national and international co-operation and liaison for exchange of information.
4. Support and provide active encouragement for the development of facilities for education and training in information science and technology.

5. Support and promotion of research, development and innovation in information technology.

Promotion and support to the development of a compatible set of information systems on science and technology and interlinking these into a network, NISSAT has established fourteen sectoral information centres (See Table 6.1). These centres in turn bring about information awareness and meet the information requirements of scientists, academicians, technologists, entrepreneurs and decision makers.

Table 6.1 National Information Centres (NICs)

Sl.No.	*Subject Area*	*Host Institution*
1.	Leather Technology (NICLAI)	Central Leather Research Institute, Chennai.
2.	Drugs and Pharmaceuticals (NICDAP)	Central Drug Research Institute, Lucknow.
3.	Food Technology (NICFOS)	Central Food Technological Research Institute, Mysore.
4.	Machine Tools and Production Engineering (NICMAP)	Central Manufacturing Technology Institute, Bangalore (formerly known as Central Machine Tool Institute).
5.	Textiles and Allied Subjects (NICTAS)	Ahmedabad Textile Industry's Research Association, Ahmedabad.
6.	Chemicals & Allied Industries (NICHEM)	National Chemical Laboratory, Pune.
7.	Advanced Ceramics (NICAC)	Central Glass and Ceramics Research Institute, Kolkata.
8.	Crystallography (NICRYS)	Department of Crystallography & Biophysics, University of Madras, Chennai.
9.	Bibliometrics Communication (NCB)	National Institute of Science Communication and Information Resources (NISCAIR), New Delhi (formerly known as INSDOC).

Sl.No.	Subject Area	Host Institution
10.	CD-ROM (NICDROM)	National Aerospace Laboratories, Bangalore.
11.	Management Sciences (NICMAN)	Indian Institute of Management, Ahmedabad
12.	Marine and Aquatic Sciences (NICMAS)	National Institute of Oceanography, Goa
13.	Publications on CD-ROMs	Foundation for Innovation and Technology Transfer (FIIT), New Delhi
14.	Tea Manufacturing and Marketing (NICMAT)	Tea Board, Kolkata.

These sectoral information centres were built around the existing information resources and facilities. In order to ensure proper information service to science community, these centres were well equipped with wide range of documents and advanced information technology infrastructure. They house an extensive collection of published and unpublished documents in the form of books, periodicals, research reports, development and trade reports, conference proceedings, standards, patents, etc. pertaining to the relevant subject areas. Monthly technical publications which are brought out on regular intervals by these sectoral centres include Current Awareness, Current Highlights, Industry Highlights, Patents Awareness in respective sectors and also semi-technical and popular ones in the form of digests.

The following Sectoral Information Centres of the NISSAT are functioning and providing information services to their clients at national level.

6.1 NATIONAL INFORMATION CENTRE FOR LEATHER AND ALLIED INDUSTRIES (NICLAI)

National Information Centre for Leather and Allied Industries (NICLAI) is one of the sectoral centres functioning under NISSAT, Department of Scientific and Industrial Research, Government of India. It was established in 1977 in Chennai.

6.1.1 Objectives

The main objectives of the NICLAI are identification of users at various levels, determine versatile range of information required by the different sectors, develop the existing infrastructure into a specialised library for leather and allied subjects, identify design and develop an appropriate information system, build up a Technological Information Bank, provide reprographic services to R&D and industrial services, and develop technical and popular write-ups, special publications and printing services.

6.1.2 Publications and Services of the Centre

NICLAI has the following 5 databases which could be accessed by scientists, industrialists and students:

i) LESA (Leather Science Abstracts)

ii) PERHOL (Periodical Holdings)

iii) LETHAS (Leather Thesarus)

iv) LEACAT (Library Catalogue)

v) LEAINST (International Leather Institutes)

The Centre is also providing online international database services like DIALOG.

The library of CLRI at the NICLAI has 33,719 volumes in their collection, including 13,728 books and reference books, 16,116 back volumes of periodicals, 126 theses/dissertations, 466 research reports, 355 conference proceedings, 1622 standards, specifications and patents and 1240 reprints. In addition, they possess 64 microfiches in collection. Annually 203 current and core journals are being received in the library, both Indian as well as foreign, to foster the R&D activities of the Institute. The library offers reference and referral services and document delivery services.NICLAI brings out a monthly journal entitled "Leather Science Abstracts (LESA)" and several bibliographies.[2]

6.2 NATIONAL INFORMATION CENTRE FOR DRUG AND PHARMACEUTICALS (NICDAP)

National Information Centre for Drug and

Pharmaceuticals (NICDAP) is a Sectoral Information Centre set up under the National Information System for Science and Technology (NISSAT), Department of Scientific and Industrial Research (DSIR), Government of India. It was established at the Central Drug Research Institute (CDRI), Lucknow, in October 1977 to cater to the information needs of scientists, researchers and academicians in the area of drugs and pharmaceuticals.

6.2.1 Objectives

The NICDAP collects, organises, stores, retrieves and disseminates information in the field of drugs and pharmaceuticals. The main objective of the Centre is to create information awareness and to meet the information requirements of scientists, technologists, academicians, executives, entrepreneurs and decision makers in the sphere of drugs and pharmaceuticals. The expert group of information scientists, librarians and technical personnel provide the NICDAP information services.

6.2.2 Publications and Services of NICDAP

The NICDAP utilises the library and information resources of the CDRI Library to keep scientists, research scholars and users abreast of the R&D programmes related to the drugs and pharmaceuticals. It maintains a rich collection of 21248 books, reference books and 60746 bound volumes of periodicals. Beside this, it holds a good collection of theses, research reports, conference proceedings, standards, patents, etc. The Centre subscribes to 281 core journals, both Indian and foreign, in the area of drugs and pharmaceuticals and biomedical research. (CDRI Annual Report 2003-04). It has a specialised collection of non-book materials - such as microfiches, audio cassettes, video cassettes, CD-ROMs and online databases.

NICDAP has strengthened the collection of CD-ROMs to provide the latest information to its users working on different areas of R&D in drugs and pharmaceuticals. It houses the following databases: Chemical Abstracts, Biotechnology Abstracts, International Pharmaceutical Abstracts, Drug

Information Sources – Full Text, Excerpta Medica (Drugs and Microindex, Pharmacology), Current Contents, MEDLINE, POPLINE and R&D Insight.

NICDAP offers online access to international databases available through DIALOG and STN. Moreover, it extends full text research articles, monographs and complete patent specification services to its scientists and research scholars. The centre extends information on biotechnology related queries relating to drugs and pharmaceuticals.[3] The Centre has access to electronic journals subscribed through consortia based subscription of e-journals.

NICDAP brings out two current awareness bulletins like Industry Highlights (Monthly), Current R&D Highlights and Ocean Drugs Alert (Quarterly) on regular basis to keep users abreast about the latest developments in the area of drugs and pharmaceuticals. Beside this, a number of adhoc publications are also brought out. The services like bibliographic services, document supply services for research articles, patent literature searches, reprographic services, micrographic and translation services, are offered to the scientists and other users in response to and in anticipation of their needs in the area of drugs and pharmaceuticals.

An Industrial Information Cell operating within the Centre is equipped with experts and specialists to fulfill the needs and queries of industry and R&D institutions. In addition, the Sectoral Information Centre is the focal point for Lucknow Special Libraries Consortium (LUSIC). In LUSIC, member institutions participate in resource sharing activities such as interlibrary loan, referral service, document supply service to achieve its objective. NICDAP is also a Collaborating Centre of WHO on drug/vaccines acquired HEALTHNET linkages for retrieval and dissemination of health based drug information. The Centre has collected and disseminated information pertaining to drugs and pharmaceuticals to the South-East Region which includes besides India, Bangladesh, Bhutan, Indonesia, Democratic Republic of Korea, Maldives, Mangolia, Myanmar, Nepal, Sri Lanka and Thailand.

The following databases have been developed at NICDAP

and these are also being updated periodically for enhancing their utility and currency:

1. ***Natural Products Database***: It covers Taxonomical, Chemical and Biological Information on medicinal plants.
2. ***Folklore Database***: This database is developed on traditional use of medicinal plants.
3. *Letters of Intent and Industrial Licenses*
4. ***Research Project Database***: NICDAP has developed this database on various on-going research projects in India in the area of drugs and pharmaceuticals.
5. ***Union Catalogue of Periodicals***: It has maintained the Union Catalogue of Periodicals of special libraries in Lucknow to meet the consequences of financial shrinking of the libraries. This database contains information on periodicals subscribed to by these special libraries of Lucknow.

NICDAP has planned to develop and strengthen more databases on different areas like medicinal plants, marine flora and fauna, various chemical compounds synthesised, integrating drug information system, authority file of scientists and researchers, and biotechnology applied to drugs and pharmaceuticals.

6.3 NATIONAL INFORMATION CENTRE FOR FOOD SCIENCE AND TECHNOLOGY (NICFOS)

National Information Centre for Food Science and Technology (NICFOS) is one of the sectoral information centres established with the support of NISSAT in October 1977. This Sectoral Information Centre utilises the library and documentation infrastructural facility of the Central Food Technological Research Institute (CFTRI), Mysore to provide the information services. The information centre of CFTRI has been recognised as a reference centre for Food Science and Technology Information on national and international level. The information services of NICFOS are generated by the professional information specialists. The Centre offers a wide range of information services, such as current awareness service, document delivery, backup service, database search service, and membership service to its users. NICFOS also provides inputs of Indian food literature to international database of the International Food Information Services (IFIS) of UK.

6.3.1 Objectives

This Sectoral Information Centre was set up with the following objectives:

- To cater to information requirements of R&D institutions and academic institutions, industries and individuals involved in R&D and training programmes in Food Science and Technology areas, through CAS, SDI, bibliographies, document delivery service, reprographic service, translation service and computerised information service.
- To provide backup service for publications by supplying copies of original documents on payment basis.

6.3.2 NICFOS Databases

NICFOS has created the databases with the help of the modern computer facility which offers online search facility related to current as well as retrospective literature for R&D institutions, industries and trade organisations, universities, government departments and other agencies. NICFOS databases include Indian Food Science and Technology Database, bibliographies in specified areas, directory of on-going projects in food technology in India, directory of processed food industries in India, directory of equipment and machinery for food processing, CFTRI Publications (Reprints) (1950-1990), directory of food technology experts in India, CFTRI theses and dissertations, CFTRI library holdings, Mysore City S&T libraries' holdings, food technology database, etc. These directories and databases are very useful tools for referral services for the scientists and technologists.

6.3.3 Library and Information Resources

CFTRI has a well-equipped library with modern computer facilities, called the Food Science and Technology Information Service (FOSTIS) which serves as the base for providing information related activities. It has 25428 books, 3770 directories, yearbooks and handbooks, 40341 back volumes of periodicals, 12187 Indian standards/specifications, 83633 patent specifications, 1837 dissertations and theses, 1906 annual reports, 156 project reports and 4502 microfiches in the area of food, science and technology. In addition, FOSTIS has 5 in-house databases and 298 CD-ROM databases and reference sources in the area of food technology. Annually 418 current Indian and foreign journals are received by the library to assist the R&D programmes of the laboratory, specially in food and allied areas.[4]

NICFOS provides search service for world literature in Food Science and Technology areas through international database available with abstracts. It has access to a wide range of full text online journals subscribed on consortia basis.

6.3.4 CFTRI Publications

The Centre is compiling and publishing regularly service oriented publications to meet the information requirements of scientists, academicians, technologists, managers, traders and entrepreneurs. Its each publication caters to the needs of the definite target group in time. It has a database of research papers published by the CFTRI scientists since the inception of the institute.

6.3.5 Databases

Food Technology Abstracts (Monthly)

In the age of information explosion, the R&D information pertaining to food is published in hundreds of journals. It is not possible for researchers, scientists and other users to spend their valuable time in scanning relevant literature from these journals. Food Technology Abstracts provides information on world food literature to satisfy the information requirements of R&D personnel in the food science and technology areas which includes about 39444 records condensed or abstracted by the specialists and experts.

Food Digest (Quarterly)

This publication caters to the specific needs of industry, planners, management personnel, etc. It has 11551 records which covers wide areas such as recent food raw materials ready for exploitation, new products and processes, waste management, latest equipment and machinery, trade and commercial information, raw material availability and industrial production, regulatory information, food hygiene in an industrial environment and the new industries.

Food Patents (Quarterly)

Patents are important sources of information, particularly for the trade, business and industries. The experts scan the world patent literature and collect relevant and useful items for the benefit of entrepreneurs and abstracts of those patents which are registered in India are provided. The Centre has 23127 records of food patents till March 2004.

Microform Information Services (Quarterly)

A large amount of latest information is also being obtained in the area of food technology and allied areas in machine readable form especially microfiche. Such materials received in non-paper form are pooled, classified and provided to all concerned users through this quarterly publication.

Library Bulletin

The Centre brings out the library bulletin to keep users abreast, aware and up-to-date with the latest publications received in the library. The Centre has 526 library bulletins which include publications such as books, monographs, proceedings, state-of-the-arts reports, annual reports, directories and bibliographies and other publications in food and allied fields.

Bibliographies

The Centre compiles and provides bibliographies on request in food science and technology areas. It compiles bibliographies of all the researches done in the past on a specific subject on the request of users through in-house database search facility.

Reprographic Services

The Centre provides photocopies of articles from its rich collection of books, back volumes of journals as well as from the latest journals received in the library on requests. Besides this, the Centre also provides the following services:

1. Guidance in establishing new libraries and information centres in food science and technology and its allied areas by providing the list of books, journals and other important and relevant materials useful in the area.
2. The Centre also organises training programmes for information personnel to orient them with method of using latest information technology in information handling efficiently and effectively.
3. The Centre provides current contents service based on journals received in the CFTRI library.
4. The Centre also helps in resolving immediate and top priority queries of the users. It uses electronic facilities such as telex, fax and electronic mail facilities to transmit information quickly to the users.

NICFOS has strengthened the information base through computerised and electronic information services with the use of new information and communication technologies. It has linkages with national and international databases in the area of food science and technology.

6.4 NATIONAL INFORMATION CENTRE FOR MACHINE TOOLS AND PRODUCTION ENGINEERING (NICMAP)

National Information Centre for Machine Tools and Production Engineering (NICMAP) is one of the Sectoral Information Centre functioning at the Central Manufacturing

Technology Institute (CMTI), Bangalore, formerly known as Central Machine Tool Institute, under NISSAT, programme of the Department of Scientific & Industrial Research (DSIR), Government of India, to cater to the information needs of the engineering industries. It was established in 1977 and since its inception, the Centre has been providing information services to its users. NICMAP has well equipped library which has rich collection of books, reference books, back volumes of periodicals and non-book material. It focuses on to develop its own specialised databases, initiating computer-aided technical information services and the Industrial Membership Scheme. During the last few years, NICMAP has developed bibliographical enquiry services for its users. It offers facilities to its users, such as bibliographical databases, non-bibliographical databases, patent search facility and Internet access facility.

NICMAP renders library reference services, technical enquiry services such as bibliographies, product information, techno-economic data, patent information, standards information, document supply services, consultancy and training, and internet search services. Moreover, the Centre extends bibliographic services, SDI services, full text information, customised search service and comprehensive search service.[5]

6.4.1 Publications of NICMAP

NICMAP brings out the following publications to its users:

1. Manufacturing Technology Today – Monthly Periodical
2. Buyers Guide – Adhoc publication

6.4.2 Bibliographical Databases

Besides this, NICMAP provides the following services:

Metalworking Database: Started in 1983, it contains bibliographical records from leading journals, books, reports and reprints and has been maintained for providing relevant and detailed information on the concerned topics.

Patent Database: It was started in 1989 and contains records of Indian patents on metalworking appearing in Gazette of India.

6.4.3 Non-bibliographical Databases

Production database covers production statistics of machine tools in the country in terms of specific machine, type and size. Cutting tools are also covered.

Export-Import database provides import and export data on specific machine tools and allied equipment in number and value.

The Centre provides information on the production, import and export statistics of metal-cutting and metal-forming machine tools for the leading machine tool manufacturing countries.

Census database: Under the sponsored project of the Ministry of Industry, NICMAP organised and completed the census of machine tools in the country. It contains the data on size-wise and year-wise listing of the machine tools installed in the country in different segments of industries and also the data on imported machine tools. The data thus generated were published in a hardcopy form and distributed to various machine tool industries in the country.

Buyers' guide database: It covers the records of all types of machine tools and allied equipment manufactured in India, including the names and addresses of manufacturers and suppliers.

Agents' database: It includes data on machine tools and allied equipment of foreign manufacturers along with the names and addresses of manufacturers and their Indian representatives.

Spec database: It comprises of records with detailed specifications of machine tools manufactured in India with names and addresses of manufacturers and their collaborators.

The Centre commenced technical enquiry service in 1984, which provides bibliographies on specific subject areas, addresses of manufacturers, suppliers and agents and statistical information. It offers technical information services to the metalworking industries, academic and R&D institutions, libraries, individuals and other public and private organisations on payment basis or against membership. NICMAP has made efforts for rationalisation of periodical acquisitions in the city of Bangalore to avoid duplication of acquisition and save the foreign exchange.

It brings out a number of publications, including two monthly publications, i.e. Metalworking Abstracts and Metalworking Bulletin.

The Centre plans to strengthen the existing bibliographical databases and also to update the non-bibliographical databases on a continuing basis.

Subcontract Register: NICMAP intends to compile, on spare capacity, a subcontract register for manufacturing for the city of Bangalore and extend to other industrial pockets gradually.

Directory of foreign collaborations: In its future plans, NICMAP proposes to compile a directory of foreign collaborations specifically for machine tools and allied products like cutting tools and metrology equipment.

6.4.3 Initiation of SDI and Retrospective search

The Centre has taken initiative to render SDI and retrospective search to their users in their particular area of research.

Due to non-availability of specialised database on metalworking, NICMAP has created a database on Metal Working which may allow access to users both in India and abroad.

6.5 NATIONAL INFORMATION CENTRE FOR TEXTILE AND ALLIED SUBJECTS (NICTAS)

National Information Centre for Textile and Allied Subjects (NICTAS) is one of the national chain of information centres set up on different subjects under NISSAT programme of Department of Scientific & Industrial Research, Government of India, at the Ahmedabad Textile Industry's Research

Association (ATIRA), Ahmedabad in 1987. Indian textile industry witnessed unprecedented structural changes since 1960's. Today's effective operation of managers, technologists, entrepreneurs, traders as well as policy makers requires latest input of information. NICTAS was born out of this need of the textile and allied industries in India. It is a co-operative venture of all textile research associations in India. NICTAS became functional in 1987 and its activities gained momentum with the release of the first issue of TEXINCON from January 1989.

6.5.1 Objectives

NICTAS functions to fulfil the following objectives:

- to integrate the economic, scientific and technical information systems and services related to textile and allied subjects into an effective network
- with the co-operation of textile research institutions, industry, trade and their associations, Government and other agencies, and
- through links and communication with similar information centres outside India.
- to build up a comprehensive collection of textile information from all available sources in the world with special emphasis on India.
- to develop resources and disseminate information in ways appropriate to the needs of Indian users.
- to create familiarity amongst all groups of users and to educate them in the optimum utilisation of available resources and information.

6.5.2 Library Collection and Services

The library collection of books, bound volumes of journals, translation and photocopy is a valuable source for NICTAS to offer a wide range of services to the users. Its collection is in textiles and allied subjects as well as in several other subjects, such as engineering, electronics, energy, environment, pollution control, fashion design, chemistry and chemical technology, total quality management, information technology, management science and statistics, etc. ATIRA library is one of the richest libraries of textile information in India having more than 41000 books, reference books, and bound volumes of journals. It subscribes to about 185 journals and receives 100 journals on gratis both Indian and foreign. Its rich collection is used by research scientists, teaching staff, students of various academic institutions and industry members.

NICTAS has strengthened the web-enabled services to fulfil the diverse needs of its users. It offers comprehensive patent search on any subject filed in any part of the world, free US and European patent search facilities, full text patent from any country, in any language and subject and translation of non-English patents into English at nominal charges. It has procured all Indian standards to enrich the collection of standards on textile. Its users are from the fields of chemicals, dyestuffs, engineering, pharmaceuticals, export and import trade and textile and environment pollution control. NICTAS provides services to its users from NACID (NISSAT Access Centre for International Data Centre) and from other various online databases.[6]

6.5.3 Information Services and Publications of NICTAS

Literature Search: It provides a list of documents published on a specified subject during a specified period for the benefit of users.

Document Procurement: The Centre procures published papers, conference proceedings, directories, reports, patents, standards, etc. from national and international sources for in-house and outside users.

Translation Service: The Centre provides translation of technical literature into English and Indian languages.

Referral Service: The Centre gives reference to other organisations which possess the required information.

Reference Service: Responds to a variety of queries raised by the organisations about the names and addresses of manufacturers and suppliers in India and abroad, patents on a particular topic or item and standards on test methods and products, etc.

Reprographic Service: The Centre extends the facilities of reprographic service such as supplying photocopies.

Contents of Periodicals: To keep scientists and researchers abreast of new arrivals and current literature, the Centre supplies photocopies of contents pages of journals received by ATIRA and NICTAS so that they could go through the original articles of their interests.

CULT (Current Universal Literature on Textiles): The Centre offers pinpointed and current information to each user according to the users profile for which regular and permanent profits are maintained.

6.5.4 Publications

TEXINCON

It is a quarterly periodical publication which provides summarised information to identified users' groups in the textile and allied industries in developing countries.

State-of-the-Art Reports

NICTAS brings out several reports in textile and its well defined allied areas so as to keep the users up-to-date and posted with the developments in their areas.

6.5.5 Online Databases

NICTAS is equipped with the latest IT infrastructure supported by computerised facilities. It has an access centre for online international information sources which offers global information on variety of subjects.

The following computerised databases and files have been maintained for the consultation of the users:

1) *ISTAS (Information System of Textile and Allied Subjects)*: It contains about 4,00,000 records of published textile literature of the world.

2) *ALIRS (ATIRA Library Information Retrieval System)*: This covers more than 40,000 records of ATIRA Library books, bound volumes of periodicals and other items.

3) *PMS (Periodicals Management Systems)*: Provides information about periodicals received in the ATIRA Library.

4) *TEXINCON (Textile Information Condensed)*: It is a unique database containing lead articles in condensed summary form for easy access by users.

NICTAS has computerised textile information in an abstract form starting from 1978 to till date 2004. Such kind of fast, pinpointed and low cost facility is not available in any library of India.[6]

Recent Additions to Library Users' Group Interaction: A Textile Information Users' Group (TIUG) has been formed to provide a venue for exchange of ideas, needs and experience. Through this publication, the following details are disseminated for awareness, such as advance information about conferences/ trade fairs, state-of-the-art review publications, information on R&D progress in India, information consultancy and training, preparation and maintenance of Union Catalogue of Textile, periodicals available in Indian libraries, regulatory information on licensing, imports, exports, etc. information on annual reports of Indian textile companies, textile machinery information, statistical information on textiles, and directory of source of information.

It has planned to publish summaries of standards produced by the International Organisation for Standardisation (ISO), British Standards Institute (BSI), Deutsches Institut fur Normung (DIN), etc. in the field of textiles and related fields. The following types of services are being arranged extensively:

- Summaries for TEXINCON prepared by subject specialists.
- Strengthening and ensuring full utilisation of NICTAS services by various identified user groups.
- To bring out state-of-the-art report.

- To collect and disseminate information useful to exporters of textiles.
- To explore the possibilities of selling NICTAS information abroad.

6.6 NATIONAL INFORMATION CENTRE FOR CHEMISTRY AND CHEMICAL TECHNOLOGY (NICHEM)

NICHEM is a Sectoral Information Centre (SIC) established in 1986 under the NISSAT programmes. This information centre functions around the resources of library and documentation services of National Chemical Laboratory (NCL), Pune. Its objectives are to identify users and their information needs, to provide library facilities, to provide bibliographical services, online services, specialised current awareness services (CAS), maintain union catalogue of periodicals in chemistry and chemical technology, provide information on patents, develop computerised databases in chemistry and chemical technology, provide translation services and reprographic services, conduct user education programmes, organise in-house training programmes for information workers of the Centre, tools for information storage and handling, promote and develop Associate Information Centres (AIC) by offering advisory and technical assistance and to maintain communication link with other information centres in the country and abroad to exchange ideas, expertise and techniques in the storage and handling of information.

6.6.1 NICHEM: Its Collection

NICHEM has a rich collection of books, reference books, back volumes of journals, online journals and technical reports on chemicals and chemicals industry. The library holds a comprehensive collection of 424,000 volumes, including 55,000 books and reference books, 65,000 back volumes of periodicals, 1000 theses/dissertations, 2000 research/project reports and 300,000 conference proceedings, standards, specifications, patents, pamphlets and reprints in chemistry and chemical technology. The information centre possesses a rich collection of Indian patents and it functions as an Inspection Centre for Indian Patents. Beside this, it contains a good collection of 1000 reports on chemistry and chemical technology, like reports of British Intelligence Objective Sub-Committee (BIOS), Combined Intelligence Objective Sub-Committee (CIOS) and Field Information Agency Technical (FIAT), etc. which describe the industrial plants and processes of Germany upto Second World War.

The Centre holds a large collection of scientific and technical periodicals. It receives 250 (200 foreign and 50 Indian) important current core journals, both Indian as well as foreign in chemistry and chemical technology. It also acquires important and significant indexing and abstracting periodicals like Chemical Abstract (CAS), USA; Analytical Abstract: Royal Society of Chemistry, UK; Science Citation Index, ISI; Indian Science Abstracts, INSDOC; Theoretical Chemical Engineering Abstracts, UK.

The Centre offers access to a wide range of digital resources, such as Chemical Abstracts (1977 onwards), Current Contents, Chemical Business News base on the intranet and online access to a large number of electronic journals from leading publishers, like Elsevier Science, American Chemical Society, Royal Society of Chemistry and Wiley Interscience. NCL also subscribes to patent databases like DELPHION and SCIFINDER. The library has launched its all informative products and services on intranet that furnish the details about the library. All the users can access information about the library and services from their desktops. It has taken initiative to digitise the old documents from 1868 onwards and converted into CD, and printed material has been preserved as archive.[7]

6.6.2 Reference and Information Services

The Centre assists the users in the use of library and its resources, locating specific documents, bibliographic search and provides information on specific topics. It arranges referral services to the readers like location of other sources of information. Its all registered members are allowed to borrow documents from the Library and Information Centre. Most of its services are used by chemical and pharmaceutical industry. The Centre extends services, such as document supply, translations, reprographic, patents search and online search of articles and databases. The Centre holds a large number of electronic resources which can be accessed through Internet.

6.6.3 Reprographic Services

The Centre provides reprographic facilities like photocopies of documents from microfiches of the collection of chemistry and chemical technology. The information centre possesses a rich collection on chemistry and chemical technology and provides photocopies of required materials on the request of users.

6.6.4 Translation Services

Presently, the Centre provides translation of scientific and technical literature of foreign languages – French, German, Russian, Japanese, Czech, Polish and Chinese – into English on specific demands.

6.6.5 Consultancy Services and Training Programmes

NICHEM offers consultancy services and technical assistance in the development of associate information centres in the field of chemistry and chemical technology. It also organises training programmes for the information professionals in the area of information storage, handling and management.

6.6.6 Online Access

NCL - a Regional Centre of NISSAT, operates as NISSAT Access Centre for International Database service (NACID). It was established in May 1989 to conduct online searches of several databases, such as bibliographic, factual and full text databases. The Centre is equipped with the modern ICT infrastructure which provides access to various online databases such as DIALOG and STN international. All the important online databases on science and technology as well as techno-economic, ScienceDirect and several other databases can be accessed through NICHEM. In addition, it organises seminars, workshops, symposia and other various activities in the country for imposing information services.

6.7 NATIONAL INFORMATION CENTRE ON ADVANCED CERAMICS (NICAC)

The National Information Centre for Advanced Ceramics (NICAC) is a Sectoral Information Centre set up under the NISSAT in 1989. This Centre is established at the Central Glass and Ceramic Research Institute (CGCRI), Kolkata.

6.7.1 Objectives

The Centre collects, collates, consolidates, stores, retrieves and disseminates information and data on Advanced Ceramics in conformity with the needs of the national community of users. It performs the following functions under the guidance of an Advisory Committee to achieve the objectives, such as create and maintain computerised databases on advanced ceramics, including optical materials, ceramic composites, ceramic coating and high temperature ceramic superconductors, establishing linkages with data and information centres on advanced ceramics and allied areas in different countries, generate and provide information services on the advanced ceramics and its related areas for the national community of scientists and technologists.

6.7.2 Publications and Services of the NICAC

The Sectoral Information Centre has the databases on advanced ceramics and its related fields, such as advanced ceramics, optical materials, ceramic composites and coatings, and high temperature superconductors.

The information centre publishes documentation lists of (i) Glass and Ceramics: a documentation list. (ii) Superconductors Abstracts. (iii) Ceramic Update (Quarterly alerting service) (iv) Directory on Glass and Ceramics Industries. It also prepares and arranges bibliographies for scientists, research scholars and industries and provides these services on the request of users. The Centre provides industrial and techno-economic information services on different areas such as (i) information on manufacturers/suppliers of the related raw materials, (ii) machinery and equipment, (iii) products, and (iv) status of the industry in the country.

The Centre has access to online databases and updating these databases from time to time. NICAC is an important resource and information centre for meeting the information requirements of the scientists and other users in the field of advanced ceramics.[8]

6.8 NATIONAL INFORMATION CENTRE FOR CRYSTALLOGRAPHY (NICRYS)

The National Information Centre for Crystallography (NICRYS) was set up under NISSAT programme. The Centre is functioning since August 1982 at the Department of Crystallography & Biophysics, University of Madras. This Centre operated during 1978-81 as National Crystal Data Centre (NCDC) under a project funded by Science and Engineering Research Council (SERC) of the Department of Science and Technology.

6.8.1 Objectives

The Centre provides Crystallographic Data relating to organic and organometallic compounds to the scientists and research scholars in India. It is the only one of its kind dealing with hard data services besides bibliographic and textual information.

6.8.2 Publications and Services of NICRYS

The Centre provides relevant information on compounds. It supplies data in India on charge basis to other organisations. Special programmes like PLUTO and GEOM available in the Cambridge Data Centre have been put into operation. It conducts and participates in various training programmes, seminars, workshops, both at national and international levels. Online access of NICRYS from 1990 has been made available to potentially a wider community of users.

NICRYS aims at the expansion as well as extension of utilisation of the Cambridge Data Bank to its fullest extent possible, by extending the database to other crystallographic and closely related regional level activities (Asia/Pacific). NICRYS plans to procure crystallographic databases like Power Data, Inorganic and Metal Data, Crystal Data from National Bureau of Standards, USA, to form a more comprehensive crystallographic database. The two databases on Nucleic Acid Sequence Data (Genbank) and Structural and Sequence Data on Proteins have also been obtained by the NICRYS.

NICRYS also runs a Newsletter service.

6.8.3 Research and Development Activity

NICRYS also procures the protein structural data, sequence data, and nucleic acid sequence data (GENBANK). These databases are also made available for online access. With the NICRYS going online on INDONET, the direct demand from all over India on graphic and visual output for crystallographic information/data is bound to multiply.[9]

6.9 NATIONAL CENTRE ON BIBLIOMETRICS (NCB)

National Centre on Bibliometrics started functioning from April 1988 with the support of NISSAT. Its activities include the research output analysis, citation studies and organisation of short-term training courses.

6.9.1 Objectives

The Centre aims to fulfil the following objectives:

1. To create a Science Citation Index Database of Indian contributions appearing in Indian scientific journals;
2. To develop tools, techniques and methodologies for the analysis of research output;
3. To analyse the research output of scientific institutions and organisations, individual scientists, universities and other bodies in India and generate indicators useful for planning, management and decision making;
4. To provide bibliometric services to any scientist and

technologist as well as institutions and organisations on demand;

5. To conduct training courses and such other activities to disseminate knowledge of bibliometrics and to make people aware of the utilities of this field;
6. To forge linkages with national and international bodies to further the cause of bibliometrics.

6.9.2 Publications and Services of NCB

1. Bibliometric Analysis of Papers.
2. CSIR Research Output - a Bibliometric Analysis.
3. Commemorative volume of CSIR contributions in the advancement of scientific knowledge.
4. Citation analysis of contribution of hundreds of scientists in the country, including several Bhatnagar awardees and the prospective Bhatanagar awardees.
5. Indian Science Citation Index (ISCI).
6. Consultancy: Evaluation of the UGC supported projects (under COSIST programme).
7. CD-ROM and SCI SEARCH: SCI search on CD-ROM is extensively used for citation analysis of productivity of various scientists.[10]

The Centre takes up consultancy projects for bibliometric evaluation of departments of various universities and some renowned institutions and organise short-term training programme on bibliometrics. It offers access of various national and international databases of NISCAIR.

6.10 NATIONAL INFORMATION CENTRE ON CD-ROM (NICDROM)

National Information Centre on CD-ROM (NICDROM) is a Centre for Information on Compact Disks founded in 1989 at the Information Centre for Aerospace Science and Technology (ICAST) in National Aerospace Laboratory in Bangalore. The Centre caters to the information needs of the Indian aerospace community, engineers and technical personnel justifying its recognition as a National Information Centre for Aerospace by UNESCO, DSIR and AR&DB. ICAST is well-known for its aerospace collection of books, journals, non-book material and specifically technical reports on aerospace from NASA, DLR, ONERA, NLR, ARL and UTIAS. The Centre offers access to about 2000 e-journals, CD-ROM and Internet based literature search services to the users. ICAST is an ISO 9001: 2000 certified centre along with its parent organisation. The Centre offers information services to professionals and institutions by providing information on CD-ROM products, their suppliers, reference collection of books, journals and databases on CD-ROM and technology trends, and thus help Indian users adopt the technology.

ICAST has developed its collection systematically in the areas of aeronautics, aerospace engineering, computer science, composites, metallurgy, mechanical engineering, materials science, mathematics, etc. to provide exhaustive, effective and timely information to the aerospace community. ICAST has about 350000 bibliographic records of documents which include 80232 books, conference proceedings and theses, 224247 technical reports (87744 reports in hardcopy and 136503 reports in microfiche), 39597 back volumes of periodicals, 3512 standards and patents and 235 CD-ROMs. The Centre subscribes to 359 journals in the core area of aerospace and allied subjects.[11]

This sectoral information centre of NISSAT was set up for fulfilling the objectives to create and develop information base on CD technology, disseminate information about the developments in CD-ROM technology, collect and provide information on: hardware/software developments, manufacturers and suppliers of CD-drives, availability of databases, producers and suppliers of databases, CD-ROM systems available in the country. Moreover, it provides necessary information for establishing in-house CD-ROM systems in an organisation, organise workshops, training programmes and lectures on CD-ROM searching for the benefit of library and information professionals and users.

NICDROM is equipped with the modern ICT

infrastructures and qualified and experienced staff.

6.10.1 Resources

It has the databases on NTIS (U.S. Government Reports) and LISA (Library and Information Science Abstracts) on CD-ROM. NICDROM has the core journals on CD-ROM such as CD-ROM Librarian (1989+), CD-ROM Professional (1990+), Online 3 (1989+) and Database (1989+).

These journals are important source of latest information on CD-ROM technology and applications related to hardware, software and other peripherals in the CD-ROM area.

The core reference documents of the Centre include 5th Annual Conference on Optical Information Systems (London June 1988), CD-ROM - the new papyrus 1986, The Brady Guide to CD-ROM, CD-ROM fundamentals to applications, CD-ROMs in print: 1988-89 and CD-ROM standards - the book.

These documents are extremely useful sources for providing information on CD-ROM.

6.10.2 Professional Services

The Centre provides professional services like technical guidance for setting up CD-ROM system, bibliographic search service on LISA and NTIS databases for various organisations in Bangalore and other parts of the country. The major use of LISA will be for providing hands-on training to users for better comprehension of retrieval operations, preparation of search strategy, etc. and workshop and practical training on CD-ROM. It shares the databases with other organisations to avoid duplication of CD-ROM databases in Bangalore.

6.10.3 Resource Sharing

Since the databases are very expensive and the centre avoids the duplication of the CD-ROMs and other databases at least in Bangalore by sharing these databases with other research organisations.

The Centre provides the bibliographic search and SDI services at national level to the R&D organisations at a very nominal cost. All the research organisations, such as CSIR,

DRDO, IITs, Universities, Public Sector Undertakings and other R&D organisations utilise the facility for both retrospective search and SDI service. NICDROM brings out CD-FOCUS, a bi-monthly publication highlighting the developments in CD-technology and other news items reported in the journals.

6.11 NATIONAL INFORMATION CENTRE ON MANAGEMENT (NICMAN)

The National Information Centre on Management (NICMAN) is a joint project of the Indian Institute of Management, Ahmedabad (IIMA) and NISSAT, Department of Scientific and Industrial Research, Government of India. It has been set up at the Vikram Sarabhai Library of the Indian Institute of Management, Ahmedabad and is sponsored by the NISSAT. It was formally inaugurated in 1996 as a national information centre to serve and disseminate timely business and management information to the managers, faculty and researchers to improve the management practices in the country.

6.11.1 Objectives of the NICMAN

The objectives of the Centre are to serve the information needs of management students, faculty, researchers and managers; prepare value added information products and services; strengthen the resource base and provide access of management information and international databases to organisations; collect, process and disseminate information on various sectors of the economy and conduct studies on the industry and sectors; establish a network of management and other allied libraries to strengthen the resource base; and use appropriate information technology for internal management, networking and marketing of products and services. Moreover, it conducts training programmes for information professionals and librarians in organising, designing, developing and marketing of information products and services.

6.11.2 Functions of NICMAN

1. Conduct research for assessing user needs, developing

appropriate products and services and marketing strategies.

2. Conduct information technology assessment and develop innovative applications for storage, retrieval and dissemination.
3. Develop and organise training programmes for internal librarians and information professionals working in other libraries to improve marketing and decision making skills.
4. Analyse information and prepare reports and studies on industry and sectors.
5. Strengthen resource base and offer library facilities.
6. Provide documentation and online information services.
7. Develop co-operation among libraries and information centres for the exchange of information and strengthen resource sharing.

6.11.3 Resources of NICMAN

NICMAN consists of 1,50,000 books, 45000 bound volumes of periodicals, 2000 working papers, 180 dissertations, 50 educational videocassettes and 650 CDs. The Centre subscribes to 610 Indian and foreign journals in the core area of management, finance and allied disciplines.

Vikram Sarabhai Library of IIMA is recognised as a national Information Centre on Management under NISSAT programme of Department of Scientific and Industrial Research, Government of India. The Centre is equipped with rich resources of management and electronic databases, such as Proquest, EBSCOHost, Informs, ACM Digital Library, Blackwell Synergy, Wiley InterScience, Taylor and Francis, IEL Collection (IEEE journals), Indlaw, ScienceDirect, Springer, GMID, Jstor, Emerald Full Text, JCC; and company and industry Databases, such as ISI-Emerging Market, CMIE, CAPITALINE, Insight, Mag India, CrisInfac, India Stat.com, etc. The library is a member of INDEST which offers online access to thousands of journals in the area of finance, management, IT and allied areas on the consortia basis.

6.11.4 Services of NICMAN

The Centre offers services, such as indexing of journal articles, Current Contents of Periodicals (CCP), Executive Briefings/Digest, database search, electronic document delivery and document delivery service, photocopying of journal articles, etc. to the students, researchers, faculty and managers.

6.11.5 Publications

NICMAN has been bringing out the information alert services like Information Bulletin on Management: Executive Briefings (Quarterly), Current Index of Management: Marketing (Quarterly), and Current Contents in Management: Marketing (Quarterly), to meet the information needs of students, researchers and faculty.

Moreover, NICMAN brings out other bulletins such as Information Bulletin on Mergers and Acquisitions; Marketing Management: A Literature Update; Information Bulletin on Supply Chain Management; and Information Bulletin on Capital Markets and Portfolio Management, etc.[12]

6.12 NATIONAL INFORMATION CENTRE ON MARINE SCIENCES (NICMAS)

The library of National Institute of Oceanography (NIO), Goa has been recognised as the National Information Centre on Marine Sciences (NICMAS) under the NISSAT programme of Department of Scientific and Industrial Research, Government of India. It has been set up at the library of National Institute of Oceanography. The Centre serves and disseminates information on marine science to the scientists, researchers and technologists engaged in research in the field of marine sciences, both in India and outside India.

The Centre maintains databases on Marine Science Studies in Indian Ocean, Directory of Indian Marine Scientists, and contributions of NIO scientists, Union catalogue of periodical holdings of sciences libraries in Goa, bibliographic database of literature on Indian Ocean. Its electronic resources can be accessed by the scientists of NIO on the intranet library server. NICMAS also extends services using ASFA (Aquatic

Sciences and Fisheries Abstracts), Current Contents on Diskettes (CCOD) on:

(i) Physical, Chemical and Earth Science.

(ii) Agriculture, Biology and Environmental Sciences, and

(iii) Engineering, Computing and Technology.

NICMAS maximises its resource utilisation by offering services to the marine scientists and researchers through databases. It extends electronic delivery of documents for speed transmission of information and photocopying services according to the requirements of the users. It offers contents of periodicals, literature search and document delivery services to its members. Its membership is open to Indian individuals and academic and research organisations.

6.12.1 IndOcean

The Centre has compiled a Database of Abstracts on Indian Ocean and Adjacent Waters, named IndOcean which is updated every year. This database has more than 34000 records and is available on CD for academic and research organisations on annual membership fee.

6.12.2 ASFA

NICMAS is a centre of ASFA (Aquatic Sciences and Fisheries Abstracts). The Centre monitors the literature on aquatic sciences and allied areas published in the Indian journals and other sources. Central Institute of Fishery Technology (CIFT) in India is also involved for input activities in ASFA. The quality input of about 1000 items is sent to ASFA every year to make available the Indian research to rest of the world.

Besides the bibliographic database and IndOcean — a database of abstracts — NICMAS has also developed a website (www.indian-ocean.org) to offer a gateway to the information on Indian Ocean to researchers. The Centre also looks after the development and maintenance of a website (www.mangroveindia.org) of Indian mangroves database that contains literature and appropriate information on flora and fauna of mangrove ecosystem in India. Moreover, the Centre has offered expertise in the capacity building in African continent which has recognised NICMAS at international level.

An Indian National Oceanographic Internet Server (INOIS) has been established under NICMAS. The bibliographic databases of NICMAS have been transferred into web server (INOIS). The NICDAP has developed a unique oceanographic search engine MANTHAN on the web which would facilitate locating the oceanographic information and data available on the web.[13]

6.13 NATIONAL COLLECTION CENTRE FOR CD-ROMS PUBLISHED IN INDIA AND ON INDIA (NCCC)

National Collection Centre for CD-ROMs published in India and on India (NCCC) [The National Centre on Publications on CD-ROM (NCPC)] was set up by NISSAT in 1996 at Foundation for Innovation and Technology Transfer (FITT), IIT Delhi, to promote usage of CD-ROMs for basic and applied research and also to build up a national repository of CD-ROMs by collecting systematically CDs produced in India and on India.

6.13.1 Objectives

1. To systematically procure all CD-ROMs published in India and on India and build up a national repository.
2. To act as a single window information service Centre for Indian CD-ROMs.
3. To create awareness about usage of CD-ROMs.
4. To keep regular updates of CD-ROM technology trends in India.
5. To provide information services to the clients from Indian and other CD-ROMs.

6.13.2 Services

The Centre offers various services, such as search service from the CD-ROMs available at the NCCC, compilation of Union catalogue of CD-ROMs available in the libraries and information centres in India, conduct workshops and practical training programmes on CD-ROM and Internet and review of

CD-ROM products published in India and on India, and also other CD-ROMs.

6.13.3 Activities

NCCC extends the facility to create awareness among users to get information regarding the Indian CD-ROM products. The Centre has developed a mechanism for the vendors and publishers of CD-ROM where they can inform about the launch of their new products. It has developed a common catalogue of Indian CD-ROM products and disseminated/distributed to the government organisations as well as industrial organisations. Moreover, the Centre has also compiled Union Catalogue of CD-ROMs available in Indian libraries and information centres and distributed the soft copy to all the respondents. To disseminate the services of the CD-ROM products at global level, the Centre has listed all CD-ROM products of NCCC on the Web.[14]

6.14 NATIONAL INFORMATION CENTRE ON TEA MANUFACTURING AND MARKETING (NICMAT)

National Information Centre on Tea Manufacturing and Marketing (NICMAT) was established in Tea Board, Kolkata in 1999 to facilitate timely information on latest techniques and practices in tea production and manufacturing and to provide latest market information to the scientists, decision makers and tea producers.

Tea is one of the major export items of India. Tea plantation and manufacturing is the traditional industry of the country and an important livelihood for the people of North East and South. To promote tea research in the country and maintain linkages with various information centres, including Tea Research Information Centre in the country and abroad, a network with Tea Board as nodal agency has been established to promote research and development in the regional centres:

(i) Tea Research Association (TRA), TOCKLAI, Jorhat

(ii) UPASI Tea Research Foundation, Valparai, Coimbatore

(iii) Institute of Himalayan Bio-Resource Technology (IHBRT), Palampur, Himachal Pradesh, and

(iv) Darjeeling Tea Research Centre (DTRC), Kurseong.[15]

6.15 ONLINE AND SDI SERVICES

On the pattern of developed countries, NISSAT has established eleven National Access Centres to International Database Services (NACIDS) in India to provide online access to international database services such as Dialog and STN databases to the community of scientists, researchers, technologists and entrepreneurs. These centres are heavily used by the users and centres charge the full cost of the access to information.

NACIDS was floated during the Seventh Five Year Plan after several rounds of demonstration and experimentation. In 1987, 5 centres were established at CLRI, Chennai; IACS,

Table 6.2 : National Access Centres to International Database Services (NACIDS)

S.No.	*Place*	*Host Institution*
1.	Ahmedabad	Ahmedabad Textiles Industry's Research Association (ATIRA)
2.	Bangalore	National Aerospace Laboratory (NAL)
3.	Kolkata	Indian Association for Cultivation of Science (IACS)
4.	Chennai	Central Leather Research Institute (CLRI)
5.	Hyderabad	Centre for Cellular and Molecular Biology (CCMB)
6.	Mumbai	Victoria Jubilee Technical Institute (VJTI)
7.	New Delhi	National Institute of Science Communication and Information Resources (NISCAIR)
8.	Pune	National Chemical Laboratory (NCL)
9.	Thiruvananthapuram	Kerala State Industrial Development Corporation (KSIDC)

Kolkata; NISCAIR, New Delhi; NAL, Bangalore; and NCL, Pune. Encouraged by success of these centres, NISSAT established four more centres during the 8th Five Year Plan — KSIDC, Thiruvananthapuram; CCMB, Hyderabad; VJTI, Mumbai; apart from the centre at ATIRA, Ahmedabad.[16] All these centres are now established and absorbed by the parent organisations.

Selective Dissemination of Information (SDI) is provided regularly to the science community on the basis of their information profile by using modern information technologies such as CD-ROM databases and online databases.

CONCLUSION

In the present age of information explosion and deluge, these Sectoral Information Centres of NISSAT are making efforts in providing information to the scientists and research scholars of CSIR laboratories at national and international levels by sharing the wide resources of the nation. Out of the fourteen, eight Sectoral Information Centres have been established at the heart of information centres of the CSIR laboratories. In order to meet the information needs of the scientists and research scholars of other research fields, NISSAT intends to set up more information centres to boost up the research programmes of the nation in different fields, such as geology, electronics, environmental studies, etc. These Sectoral Information Centres also strive to improve the existing information resources and services with the modern information infrastructure facilities and from time to time to gauge the research activities of the CSIR laboratories and other research organisations, businesses and industrial sectors, etc. However, it is imperative to provide adequate finance to equip these information centres with the latest information technologies and qualified, trained and experienced staff to handle and manage the information for the overall development and prosperity of the nation. In fact, there is a dire need for making changes in information services scenario necessitated by the developments in information and communication technologies and effectiveness of their use.[17]

REFERENCES

1. Khanna, J. K. Handbook of library information systems and services. New Delhi: Beacon Books, 1996. P.288-314.
2. Thakur, D. S. Effectiveness and use of library and information services of the laboratories of Council of Scientific and Industrial Research in India. Ph. D. Thesis. Gwalior: Jiwaji University, 1997. P.169-206.
3. Zaidi, J. A. et al. Emergence of new technologies in biomedical information: A CDRI perspective. In: Kaul, H. K. and Das, B. B. (eds). *Library and Information Networking: NACLIN 2003.* New Delhi: DELNET, 2004, 421-431.
4. Central Food Technological Research Institute Performance Report 2003-2004. Mysore: CFTRI, 2004. 138p.
5. NICMAP, Bangalore. 26 April 2005. Available: http://dsir.nic.in/division/nissat/nisnat/nics/nicmap.html
6. Ahmedabad Textile Industry's Research Association: Report of the Council of Administration 2003-2004. Ahmedabad: ATIRA, 2004. 79p.
7. National Chemical Laboratory Annual Report 2003-2004. Pune: NCL, 2004. 163p.
8. Thakur, *op.cit.*, p.169-206.
9. *Ibid.*, p.169-206.
10. Thakur, *op.cit.*, p.169-206.
11. National Aerospace Laboratories Annual Report 2003-2004. Bangalore: NAL, 2004. 217p.
12. NICMAN, Ahmedabad. 26 April 2005. Available: http://www.nicmaniima.org
13. NICMAS, Goa. 26 April 2005. Available: http://www.nio.org/nicmas/Nicmas.jsp Available: http://dsir.nic.in/division/nissat/nisnat/nics/go.html
14. NCCC, New Delhi. 26 April 2005. Available: http://dsir.nic.in/division/nissat/nisnat/nccc/nccc.html
15. DSIR Annual Report 2002-2003. P.74-81.

16. National Access Centres to International Data Services (NACIDS). 26 April 2005. Available: http://dsir.nic.in/division/nissat/nisnat/nacid/nnacid.html
17. Thakur, *op.cit.*, p.169-206.

7
An Assessment of Scientific and Technical Libraries

The exponential growth of scientific and technical literature has compelled to set up scientific and technical libraries. These libraries were established to acquire, collect, organise and disseminate information regarding the research and development programmes of the institutions to scientists and research scholars of the parent organisations. With the passage of time these libraries have grown from small units to a full fledged institutions. Some of them have adopted modern approaches and technologies too. In this chapter an attempt has been made to present a profile of Library-In-Charges and libraries as well. The profile of libraries covers the growth of CSIR libraries, staff, budget, resources, services and reading facilities which reflect the status of scientific and technical libraries of CSIR. The library activities includes acquisition of reading material, processing of material and making the material available to the library clientele for use. Human resources in the form of library staff are required to perform effective service. The effective and efficient service cannot be performed without having adequate financial resources, for the acquisition and processing of reading material and appointment of skilled and trained staff. The effectiveness and evaluation of library's performance depend on the resources, the staff, users satisfaction and cost. These four factors — resources, users satisfaction, staff and financial support – are the important criteria for evaluating the library performance. There are important yardsticks, such as quantity and quality of library resources, users satisfaction, staffing structure, financial support, library services and application of computer and information technology to assess the effectiveness and performance of the library.

7.1 DISTRIBUTION OF RESPONDENTS, LABORATORY-WISE

Out of 40 libraries belonging to five groups, the responses from only 34 libraries were received. Five libraries belonging to ESG and one library of BSG have not responded.

Table 7.1 : Distribution of Respondents, Laboratory-Wise

Group of Libraries	*Distribution of Total Number of Libraries*	*Number of Responding Libraries*	*Percentage*
PESG	5	5	14.7
CSG	7	7	20.6
BSG	11	10	29.4
ESG	14	9	26.5
ISG	3	3	8.8
Total	40 (100.0)	34 (85.0)	100.0

7.1.1 Sex-Wise Distribution of Respondents

It is surprising to note that out of 34 library heads, only 4 are females. It is evident from Table 7.2 that the position of head in CSIR libraries are predominated by males. There are three groups namely PESG, CSG and ISG which don't have even single female head.

Table 7.2 : Sex-Wise Distribution of Respondents

	Library Head		
Group of Libraries	*Male*	*Female*	*Row Total*
PESG	5 (100.0)	-	5 (14.7)
CSG	7 (100.0)	-	7 (20.6)
BSG	9 (90.0)	1 (10.0)	10 (29.4)
ESG	6 (66.7)	3 (33.3)	9 (26.5)
ISG	3 (100.0)	-	3 (8.8)
Total Column	30 (88.2)	4 (11.8)	34 (100.0)

7.1.2 Age of Respondents

Since the data pertains to librarians which happens to be the top slot in administrative hierarchy in a library set up, it is not surprising to note that a very few librarians are in the younger age group i.e. 26-35 years. As expected, higher proportion of librarians are in the older age group, i.e., 46-55 and above. Because it is prerequisite for any professional to accumulate enough skill and competence through years of works experience before reaching the top, therefore, by the time one moves up to the position of librarian, he enters the middle age-group or in some cases higher. At the same time data also contain some respondents who are in the age group of 36-45. However, the proportion is only 29.4 percent.

Table 7.3 : Age of the Librarians of CSIR Libraries

Group of Libraries	*Age Group of Librarians*				
	26-35	*36-45*	*46-55*	*56+*	*Row Total*
PESG	-	2	1	2	5
		(40.0)	(20.0)	(40.0)	(14.7)
CSG	-	-	3	4	7
			(42.9)	(57.1)	(20.6)
BSG	2	3	2	3	10
	(20.0)	(30.0)	(20.0)	(30.0)	(29.4)
ESG	-	3	2	4	9
		(33.3)	(22.2)	(44.4)	(26.5)
ISG	-	2	1	-	3
		(66.7)	(33.3)		(8.8)
Column Total	2	10	9	13	34
	(5.9)	(29.4)	(26.5)	(38.2)	(100.0)

7.1.3 Academic Qualifications of the Librarians

Any productive activity and efficient library service requires trained and experienced professional staff in the library. Professionally trained staff can manage and organised the library material and services for the maximum benefit of the organisation. If the resources of the library are fully meeting the requirement of users, the overall effectiveness and performance of the library cannot be effective without trained, experienced and competent library staff to render effective services. Ifidon (1986) indicates three most important factors, i.e., size, qualifications and skills, which influence staffing and staffing performance.[1]

Data in Table 7.4 indicate that only a few librarians possess Ph.D. degree, and majority is of those who hold only graduate degree. A good number of librarians are also postgraduate degree holders. Those who have done M.Phil. constitutes only 11.8 percent of the respondents.

Table 7.4 : Academic Qualifications of the Librarians

Group of Libraries	*Academic Qualifications*				
	Graduation	*Post-graduation*	*M.Phil.*	*Ph.D.*	*Row Total*
PESG	1 (20.0)	8 (80.0)	-	-	5 (14.7)
CSG	4 (57.1)	1 (14.3)	-	2 (28.6)	7 (20.6)
BSG	5 (50.0)	2 (20.0)	3 (30.0)	-	10 (29.4)
ESG	3 (33.3)	4 (44.4)	1 (11.1)	1 (11.1)	9 (26.5)
ISG	1 (33.3)	2 (66.7)	-	-	3 (8.8)
Column Total	14 (41.2)	13 (38.2)	4 (11.8)	3 (8.8)	34 (100.0)

7.1.3.1 Professional Qualifications of the Librarians

Persuasion of higher qualification in library science does not seem to be an issue as only one librarian had this degree. However, none have gone for M.Phil. There are comparatively larger number of respondents with MLISc. It is surprising that there are two respondents who have had only Diploma/CLISc to their credit. It may be summed up that educational profile of librarians is not very impressive.

Table 7.5 : Professional Qualifications of the Librarians

Professional Qualifications	*Group of Libraries*					
	PESG	*CSG*	*BSG*	*ESG*	*ISG*	*Row Total*
Diploma/CLISc	-	1 (14.3)	-	1 (11.1)	-	2 (5.9)
AIS/ADRTC	1 (20.0)	2 (28.6)	3 (30.0)	1 (11.1)	2 (66.7)	9 (26.5)
BLISc	1 (20.0)	1 (14.3)	1 (10.0)	2 (22.2)	-	5 (14.7)
MLISc	2 (40.0)	2 (28.6)	3 (30.0)	5 (55.6)	1 (33.3)	13 (38.2)
M.Phil.	-	-	-	-	-	-
Ph.D.	1 (20.0)	-	-	-	-	1 (2.9)
Not stated	-	1 (14.3)	3 (30.0)	-	-	4 (11.8)
Column Total	5 (14.7)	7 (20.6)	10 (29.4)	9 (26.5)	3 (8.8)	34 (100.0)

7.1.4 Growth of the CSIR Laboratories and Their Libraries

The analysis of the growth of CSIR laboratories and their libraries in Table 7.6 shows that from 1950-1960, libraries were established along with the laboratories. However, this trend did not continue onwards, e.g. during 1961-70 six laboratories were established but only four libraries came up during that period. Similarly, two laboratories were established during 1971-80 but only one laboratory established its library during this period.

Table 7.6 : Growth of the CSIR Laboratories and Their Libraries

Decades	*Laboratories*	*Libraries*
Before 1950	7	7
	(20.6)	(20.6)
1951-60	16	16
	(47.1)	(47.1)
1961-70	6	4
	(17.6)	(11.8)
1971-80	2	1
	(5.9)	(2.9)
1981-90	3	5
	(8.3)	(14.7)
1991+	-	1
		(2.9)
Total Column	34	34
	(100.0)	(100.0)

7.1.5 Staffing Structure of the CSIR Libraries

Analysis of library staff structure in Table 7.7 indicates that the majority of staff working in the CSIR libraries consisted of professionals, followed by non-professional staff. The semi-professional staff who assist the professionals in carrying out various library operations accounted for only 10.0 percent of the total staff. It may be inferred that the CSIR libraries are being manned by professionals.

Table 7.7 : Staffing Structure of the CSIR Libraries

Group of Libraries	*Response*			*Row Total*
	Professional	*Semi-professional*	*Non-professional*	
PESG	30 (53.6)	11 (19.6)	15 (26.8)	56 (13.0)
CSG	65 (59.1)	5 (4.5)	40 (36.4)	110 (25.5)
BSG	54 (46.5)	17 (14.7)	45 (38.8)	116 (26.9)
ESG	46 (46.0)	3 (3.0)	51 (51.0)	100 (23.1)
ISG	22 (44.0)	7 (14.0)	21 (42.0)	50 (11.6)
Column Total	217 (50.2)	43 (10.0)	172 (39.8)	432 (100.0)

7.2 LIBRARY BUDGET

Adequate availability of funds to procure the resources of the library for rendering effective information services to the users is necessary. The budget of the scientific and technical libraries may be allocated to fulfil the needs of the different types of resources such as books, journals and other non-printed material.

The survey of CSIR libraries showed that budget allocations in most of the CSIR libraries were inadequate to meet the present requirements. It has been seen that largest part of the budget is being spent on the subscription of journals than on books, grey literature and non-book materials. The scientific and technical libraries of CSIR are not in a position to acquire non-book materials, such as microfilms/ microfiches, audio-visual materials, slides, CD-ROMs, online databases, transparencies, etc.

7.2.1 Distribution of the Library Budget for the Year 1992-93

The analysis of the distribution of the 1992-93 library budget of the CSIR laboratories in Table 7.8 shows that maximum number of libraries (23.5%) had budget of Rs.10-15 lakh, 20.6 percent of libraries had budget of Rs.15-20 lakh, 17.6 percent libraries had budget provisions between Rs.20-30 lakh and Rs.30-50 lakh.

Group-wise analysis indicates that the 44.4 percent libraries of ESG had a budget of Rs.10-15 lakh, followed by 42.9 percent of libraries of CSG having budget of Rs.20-30 lakh. Only two libraries of CSG and BSG had library budget of Rs.50-65 lakh for the year 1992-93.

Table 7.8 : Distribution of the Library Budget for the Year 1992-93

Range of the Budget (in Rs)	*1992-93*					
	PESG	*CSG*	*BSG*	*ESG*	*ISG*	*Row Total*
6,00000–10,00000	-	-	2	2	1	5
			(20.0)	(22.2)	(33.3)	(14.7)
10,00001-15,00000	2	-	1	4	1	8
	(40.0)		(10.0)	(44.4)	(33.3)	(23.5)
15,00001-20,00000	2	2	2	1	-	7
	(40.0)	(28.6)	(20.0)	(11.1)		(20.6)
20,00001-30,00000	-	3	2	1	-	6
		(42.9)	(20.0)	(11.1)		(17.6)
30,00001-50,00000	1	1	2	1	1	6
	(20.0)	(14.3)	(20.0)	(11.1)	(33.3)	(17.6)
50,00001-65,00000	-	1	1	-	-	2
		(14.3)	(10.0)			(5.9)
Column Total	5	7	10	9	3	34
	(14.7)	(20.6)	(29.4)	(26.5)	(8.8)	(100.0)

7.2.1.1 Distribution of the Library Budget (Books) for the Year 1992-93

Table 7.9 indicates the budget allocation for books for the year 1992-93. The majority of the libraries, i.e., 44.1 percent had budgetary allocation for books between Rs.2-5 lakh, and 20.6 percent had the budgetary allocation of up to Rs.1,00000 and between Rs.1-2 lakh for books. Group-wise analysis shows that most of the libraries in all groups had budget of Rs.2-5 lakh. There was one library which spent Rs.10-15 lakh for purchasing books during 1992-93.

Table 7.9 : Distribution of the Library Budget (Books) for the Year 1992-93

Range of the Budget (in Rs.)	*Group*					*Row Total*
	PESG	*CSG*	*BSG*	*ESG*	*ISG*	
Up to 1,00000	1	1	3	2	-	7
	(20.0)	(14.3)	(30.0)	(22.2)		(20.6)
1,00001-2,00000	-	2	2	2	1	7
		(28.6)	(20.0)	(22.2)	(33.3)	(20.6)
2,00001-5,00000	3	3	4	4	1	15
	(60.0)	(42.9)	(40.0)	(44.4)	(33.3)	(44.1)
5,00001-10,00000	-	-	-	1	1	2
				(11.1)	(33.3)	(5.9)
10,00001-15,00000	-	1	-	-	-	1
		(14.3)				(2.9)
Not stated	1	-	1	-	-	2
	(20.0)		(10.0)			(5.9)
Column Total	5	7	10	9	3	34
	(14.7)	(20.6)	(29.4)	(26.5)	(8.8)	(100.0)

7.2.1.2 Distribution of the Library Budget (Journals) for the Year 1992-93

Distribution of the library budget for journals indicates that all libraries of the CSIR were spending most of their budget on the subscription of journals rather than on books and non-printed materials (See Table 7.10). The majority of libraries (26.5%) spent Rs.5-10 lakh for the subscription of journals.

Similarly, 20.6 percent of libraries had budget allocation of Rs.10-15 lakh, Rs.15-20 lakh and Rs.20-30 lakh. Group-wise analysis reveals that 66.7 percent libraries of ISG had a budget of Rs.5-10 lakh for journals. About 43 percent libraries of CSG had budget for journals between Rs.15-20 lakh and Rs.20-30 lakh, for 1992-93.

Table 7.10 : Distribution of the Library Budget (Journals) for the Year 1992-93

Range of the Budget (in Rs.)	*Group*					
	PESG	*CSG*	*BSG*	*ESG*	*ISG*	*Row Total*
5,00000 – 10,00000	-	-	2 (20.0)	5 (55.5)	2 (66.7)	9 (26.5)
10,00001-15,00000	4 (80.0)	-	1 (10.0)	2 (22.2)	-	7 (20.6)
15,00001-20,00000	-	3 (42.9)	3 (30.0)	1 (11.1)	-	7 (20.6)
20,00001-30,00000	-	3 (42.9)	2 (20.0)	1 (11.1)	1 (33.3)	7 (20.6)
30,00001-63,50000	1 (20.0)	1 (14.3)	1 (10.0)	-	-	3 (8.8)
Not stated	-	-	1 (10.0)	-	-	1 (2.9)
Column Total	5 (14.7)	7 (20.6)	10 (29.4)	9 (26.5)	3 (8.8)	34 (100.0)

7.2.1.3 Distribution of the Library Budget (Other Items) for the Year 1992-93

It is seen from the analysis (Table 7.11) that all the libraries of CSIR were utilizing most of their budget for the books and journals. Only two or three libraries were spending a small amount of budget for other items, such as non-book material and binding, etc. Only one library of CSG was spending Rs.60 thousand for items other than books and journals. In PESG, there was also one library which was having a budget of Rs.27 thousand for other items.

Table 7.11 : Distribution of the Library Budget (Other Items) for the Year 1992-93

Range of the Budget (in Rs.)	*Group*					
	PESG	*CSG*	*BSG*	*ESG*	*ISG*	*Row Total*
27000	1	-	-	-	-	1
	(20.0)					(2.9)
30000	-	-	1	-	-	1
			(10.0)			(2.9)
60000	-	1	-	-	-	1
		(14.3)				(2.9)
Not stated	4	6	9	9	3	31
	(80.0)	(85.7)	(90.0)	(100.0)	(100.0)	(91.2)
Column Total	5	7	10	9	3	34
	(14.7)	(20.6)	(29.4)	(26.5)	(8.8)	(100.0)

7.2.2 Distribution of the Library Budget for the Year 1993-94

Distribution of the library budget of CSIR laboratories in Table 7.12 indicates that majority of the libraries (32.3%) had budget provision of Rs.10-20 lakh, and 26.5 percent of libraries had budgetary provision of Rs.30-50 lakh. Some of the libraries also had Rs.50-94 lakh as library budget. Group-wise analysis shows that the majority of libraries of PESG and ESG had the library budget between Rs.10-20 lakh.

Table 7.12 : Distribution of the Library Budget for the Year 1993-94

Range of the Budget (in Rs.)	*1993-94*					
	PESG	*CSG*	*BSG*	*ESG*	*ISG*	*Row Total*
6,00000 – 10,00000	-	-	1	2	1	4
			(10.0)	(22.2)	(33.3)	(11.8)
10,00001-20,00000	4	-	2	4	1	11
	(80.0)		(20.0)	(44.4)	(33.3)	(32.3)
20,00001-30,00000	-	3	3	2	-	8
		(42.8)	(30.0)	(22.2)		(23.5)
30,00001-50,00000	1	3	3	1	1	9
	(20.0)	(42.8)	(30.0)	(11.1)	(33.3)	(26.5)
50,00001-94,00000	-	1	1	-	-	2
		(14.3)	(10.0)			(5.9)
Column Total	5	7	10	9	3	34
	(14.7)	(20.6)	(29.4)	(26.5)	(8.8)	(100.0)

7.2.2.1 Distribution of the Library Budget (Books) for the Year 1993-94

Budget allocation for books, as given in Table 7.13, shows that 41.2 percent of libraries had budgetary allocation of Rs.2-5 lakh for books, and 23.5 percent of libraries had allocated Rs.1-2 lakh towards books.

Table 7.13 : Distribution of the Library Budget (Books) for the Year 1993-94

Range of the Budget (in Rs.)	*Group*					
	PESG	*CSG*	*BSG*	*ESG*	*ISG*	*Row Total*
Up to 1,00000	-	1 (14.3)	1 (10.0)	2 (22.2)	-	4 (11.8)
1,00001-2,00000	1 (20.0)	-	4 (40.0)	2 (22.2)	1 (33.3)	8 (23.5)
2,00001-5,00000	3 (60.0)	5 (71.4)	4 (40.0)	1 (11.1)	1 (33.3)	14 (41.2)
5,00001-10,00000	-	-	-	3 (33.3)	-	3 (8.8)
10,00001-23,50000	-	1 (14.3)	-	1 (11.1)	1 (33.3)	3 (8.8)
Not stated	1 (20.0)	-	1 (10.0)	-	-	2 (5.9)
Column Total	5 (14.7)	7 (20.6)	10 (29.4)	9 (26.5)	3 (8.8)	34 (100.0)

7.2.2.2 Distribution of the Library Budget (Journals) for the Year 1993-94

Allocation of library budget for journals during 1993-94 shows that 26.5 percent of libraries were spending Rs.20-30 lakh on journals, 17.6 percent were spending Rs.5-10 lakh and an equal percent between Rs.10-15 lakh. There were libraries which were reported to have spent Rs.50-75 lakh.

Table 7.14 : Distribution of the Library Budget (Journals) for the Year 1993-94

Range of the Budget (in Rs.)	*Group*					
	PESG	*CSG*	*BSG*	*ESG*	*ISG*	*Row Total*
5,00000-10,00000	-	-	1 (10.0)	4 (44.4)	1 (33.3)	6 (17.6)
10,00001-15,00000	2 (40.0)	-	2 (20.0)	1 (11.1)	1 (33.3)	6 (17.6)
15,00001-20,00000	2 (40.0)	2 (28.6)	-	1 (11.1)	-	5 (14.7)
20,00001-30,00000	-	3 (42.9)	3 (30.0)	2 (22.2)	1 (33.3)	9 (26.5)
30,00001-50,00000	1 (20.0)	1 (14.3)	2 (20.0)	1 (11.1)	-	5 (14.7)
50,00001-75,00000	-	1 (14.3)	1 (10.0)	-	-	2 (5.9)
Not stated	-	-	1 (10.0)	-	-	1 (2.9)
Column Total	5 (14.7)	7 (20.6)	10 (29.4)	9 (26.5)	3 (8.8)	34 (100.0)

7.2.2.3 Distribution of the Library Budget (Other Items) for the Year 1993-94

There don't seem to be budgetary allocation for items other than books and journals in CSIR libraries as only two libraries belonging to CSG had respectively spent Rs.40 thousand and Rs.50 thousand for the purchase of other items.

Table 7.15 : Distribution of the Library Budget (Other Items) for the Year 1993-94

Range of the Budget (in Rs.)	*Group*					*Row Total*
	PESG	*CSG*	*BSG*	*ESG*	*ISG*	
40000	-	1 (14.3)	-	-	-	1 (2.9)
50000	-	1 (14.3)	-	-	-	1 (2.9)
Not stated	5 (100.0)	5 (71.4)	10 (100.0)	9 (100.0)	3 (100.0)	32 (94.1)
Column Total	5 (14.7)	7 (20.6)	10 (29.4)	9 (26.5)	3 (8.8)	34 (100.0)

7.2.3 Adequacy of the Library Budget

The data collected regarding adequacy of the library budget (Table 7.16) indicates that the majority of libraries in all the groups, 66.7 percent, felt that the present budget of their libraries was inadequate. Only 23.5 percent libraries in all the groups indicated the library budget as adequate to meet the users' needs. Group-wise analysis reveals that almost 80 percent of libraries of PESG stated that the present budget of their libraries was inadequate. Similarly 71.4 percent of CSG libraries and 70.0 percent of BSG libraries indicated the budget to be insufficient.

Table 7.16 : Adequacy of the Library Budget

Group of Libraries	*Response*			
	Adequate	*Fairly Adequate*	*Inadequate*	*Row Total*
PESG	1 (20.0)	-	4 (80.0)	5 (14.7)
CSG	1 (14.3)	1 (14.3)	5 (71.4)	7 (20.6)
BSG	2 (20.0)	1 (10.0)	7 (70.0)	10 (29.4)
ESG	3 (33.3)	1 (11.1)	5 (55.6)	9 (26.5)
ISG	1 (33.3)	-	2 (66.7)	3 (8.8)
Column Total	8 (23.5)	3 (8.8)	23 (67.7)	34 (100.0)

7.2.4 Percentage of Increase in the Total Library Budget

The analysis in Table 7.17 indicates that the majority of libraries of all the groups have required 36-50 percent enhancement in the total budget of their libraries. Another 17.6 percent of libraries have stated that the budget of their libraries may be increased from 16-25 percent and yet another 17.6 percent require an increase of 26-35 percent in the total budget of the library. Group-wise analysis reveals that the majority of libraries (42.9%) of CSG require enhancement in their library budget from 26-35 percent.

Table 7.17 : Percentage of Increase in the Total Budget of the Library

Percentage	*Group of Libraries*					
	PESG	*CSG*	*BSG*	*ESG*	*ISG*	*Row Total*
10 – 15%	2	-	2	-	-	4
	(40.0)		(20.0)			(11.8)
16 – 25%	-	2	2	2	-	6
		(28.6)	(20.0)	(22.2)		(17.6)
26 – 35%	1	3	1	1	-	6
	(20.0)	(42.9)	(10.0)	(11.1)		(17.6)
36 – 50%	1	1	2	2	2	8
	(20.0)	(14.3)	(20.0)	(22.2)	(66.7)	(23.5)
Not stated	1	1	3	4	1	10
	(20.0)	(14.3)	(30.0)	(44.4)	(33.3)	(29.4)
Column Total	5	7	10	9	3	34
	(14.7)	(20.6)	(29.4)	(26.5)	(8.8)	(100.0)

7.3 LIBRARY COLLECTION

The collection of scientific and technical libraries is developed to fulfil the objectives of the organisation. The collection of these libraries comprises books, reference books, back volumes of periodicals, theses/dissertations, research reports, seminar/conference proceedings, pamphlets and reprints, standards, specifications and patents. In addition, contemporary scientific and technical libraries hold the rich collection of non-book material, such as microfilm/microfiches, audio-visual material, CD-ROMs and online databases, maps/atlases, etc. which are very useful to make library impressive in modern times.

In order to evaluate effectiveness of library and its services, it is necessary to find out whether the present collection of the library of different kinds is adequate to meet the information requests of scientists and research scholars in the organisation.

The performance of a library as a service organisation depends to a very large extent on the quantity and quality of the various resources of the library. Clapp and Jordan[2] have since challenged the accepted doctrine and assert that the adequacy of a library cannot be measured by the number of volumes it possesses. Ifidon[3] proved beyond all reasonable doubt that there is a positive relationship between qualitative and quantitative assessments of the library collection. The assessment of the library collection which will significantly influence the library performance is based on the gross size of the resources. The writer has used gross size to refer not only to the resources of a single library but also to other resources which are available to supplement the library's own collection. This is because there are co-operative links among libraries by way of co-operative acquisition schemes, interlibrary loan and photocopying requests. This concept is known as the rating of the total (internal and external) resources' adequacy. He further stated that adequacy of the collection is enhanced by the qualifications and skills of the library staff members.[4]

7.3.1 Adequacy of the Library Collection

The data in Table 7.18 reveals that majority of the libraries' collection of books was moderately adequate to meet the information requirements of scientists and research scholars. On the other hand half of the respondents indicated that the collection of back volumes of periodicals was fully adequate to meet the requests of users. Further, the non-book material, also needs a serious attention of the librarians which is really absent in most of the libraries. The grey literature is not fully adequate to meet the information requests of users. It requires a serious attention of librarians and research scholars.

Table 7.18 : Adequacy of the Library Collection

Types of Collection	*Response* Partially Adequate	Moderately Adequate	Fully Adequate	No Response	Row Total
Books	3 (8.8)	18 (52.9)	13 (38.2)	-	34 (100.0)
Bound volumes of journals	2 (5.9)	15 (44.1)	17 (50.0)	-	34 (100.0)
Non-book material	17 (50.0)	11 (32.4)	3 (8.8)	3 (8.8)	34 (100.0)
Theses/research, conference proceedings, pamphlets and reprints	19 (55.9)	14 (41.2)	1 (2.9)	-	34 (100.0)
Standards, specifications and patents	13 (38.2)	19 (55.9)	2 (5.9)	-	34 (100.0)

It is inferred from the analysis of data that almost all libraries of CSIR are required to pay more attention towards the grey literature and theses/dissertations, research and project reports, seminar/conference proceedings, pamphlets and reprints, standards, specifications and patents, etc.

It is noteworthy that the present collection of libraries, except books and back volumes of periodicals, needs to be strengthened. The collection of grey literature and non-book material of all types are not satisfactory to meet the information requirements of users.

7.3.2 Distribution of Libraries by Number of Books

Analysis of data on book collection, as given in Table 7.19, shows that a large number of libraries (35.3%) have collection between 15,001-30,000. A good number of libraries (14.7%) are reported to have collection of 30,001-50,000 and 50,001-75,000 books respectively, and 11.8 percent libraries are such as have the collection numbering below 5,000. Group-wise analysis of data indicates that a larger number of libraries belonging to PESG (80.0%), BSG (40.0%) and ESG (33.3%) are having collection between 15,001-30,000. Whereas majority of libraries belonging to CSG and ISG have the collection of 5,001-15,000 and 50,001-75,000 respectively. However, there are four libraries belonging to BSG and ESG which have collection of books below 5000.

Table 7.19 : Distribution of the Libraries by Number of Books

Number of Books	*Group of Libraries*					
	PESG	*CSG*	*BSG*	*ESG*	*ISG*	*Row Total*
Below 5,000	-	-	3 (30.0)	1 (11.1)	-	4 (11.8)
5,001-15,000	-	4 (57.1)	2 (20.0)	1 (11.1)	1 (33.3)	8 (23.5)
15,001-30,000	4 (80.0)	1 (14.3)	4 (40.0)	3 (33.3)	-	12 (35.3)
30,001-50,000	-	1 (14.3)	1 (10.0)	3 (33.3)	-	5 (14.7)
50,001-75,000	1 (20.0)	1 (14.3)	-	1 (11.3)	2 (66.7)	5 (14.7)
Column Total	5 (14.7)	7 (20.6)	10 (29.4)	9 (26.5)	3 (8.8)	34 (100.0)

7.3.2.1 Adequacy of the Libraries by Books

Group-wise analysis of data in Table 7.20 suggests that the book collection of the libraries is perceived to be moderately adequate by the majority of the librarians. A good number of librarians also feel that the book collection in their respective libraries is fully adequate to meet the users requirements. Partial adequacy of collection is indicated only by a few librarians. Leaving minor variation, pattern seems to be the same in group-wise analysis as well. The majority of librarians working in CSG feel that the collection is moderately adequate.

However, an equal proportion of them consider the collection partially and fully adequate. Situation in PESG, ESG and ISG seems to be also similar. As majority of their librarians consider their book collection moderately adequate. Contrary to this, an equal proportion of respondents of BSG rate their book collection as moderately and fully adequate. It is true that in today's context, it is not possible for any library to be self reliant in terms of collection. Still, as far as book collection is concerned, it needs to be adequate that too fully. It is only expected that the libraries which are able to meet users' requirements only moderately through their collection must be streamlined.

Table 7.20 : Adequacy of Libraries by Books

Group of Libraries	*Response*			*Row Total*
	Partially Adequate	*Moderately Adequate*	*Fully Adequate*	
PESG	-	3	2	5
		(60.0)	(40.0)	(14.7)
CSG	2	3	2	7
	(28.6)	(42.9)	(28.6)	(20.6)
BSG	-	5	5	10
		(50.0)	(50.0)	(29.4)
ESG	1	5	3	9
	(11.1)	(55.6)	(33.3)	(26.5)
ISG	-	2	1	3
		(66.7)	(33.3)	(8.8)
Column Total	3	18	13	34
	(8.8)	(52.9)	(38.2)	(100.0)

7.3.3 Distribution of Libraries by Number of Bound Volumes of Journals

Collection of bound volumes of journals, as given in Table 7.21, shows that a sizable proportion of libraries are having library collection between 5.001-15,000 and 15,001-30,000 volumes. Only a small proportion of libraries, i.e. 5.9

percent is in possession of 60,001-1,00000 bound volumes of journals. Out of five groups, libraries belonging to the three groups, namely PESG, ESG and ISG, have not responded to this question. Group-wise analysis shows that there is no uniform pattern of collection of bound volumes of journals. The majority of libraries in PESG have a collection of 5,001-15,000, whereas libraries in CSG have a collection of 15,001-30,000. An equal proportion of libraries belonging to BSG are, however, having collection of 15,001-30,000 and 30,001-60,000. Similarly, the group of PESG is also composed of a good number of libraries which are having collection up to 5,001-15,000. The response is equally divided in case of ISG.

Table 7.21 : Distribution of Libraries by Number of Bound Volumes of Journals

Number of Bound Volumes of Journals	*Group of Libraries*					
	PESG	*CSG*	*BSG*	*ESG*	*ISG*	*Row Total*
Up to 5,000	-	-	2	2	1	5
			(20.0)	(22.2)	(33.3)	(14.7)
5,001-15,000	3	2	2	1	-	8
	(60.0)	(28.6)	(20.0)	(11.1)		(23.5)
15,001-30,000	-	3	3	2	-	8
		(42.9)	(30.0)	(22.2)		(23.5)
30,001-60,000	1	1	3	1	-	6
	(20.0)	(14.3)	(30.0)	(11.1)		(17.6)
60,001-1,00000	-	1	-	-	1	2
		(14.3)			(33.3)	(5.9)
Not stated	1	-	-	3	1	5
	(20.0)			(33.3)	(33.3)	(14.7)
Column Total	5	7	10	9	3	34
	(14.7)	(20.6)	(29.4)	(26.5)	(8.8)	(100.0)

7.3.3.1 Adequacy of Libraries by Bound Volumes of Journals

In many cases, science articles, published in journals, don't loose their relevance even after years of their publication.

That is why libraries take utmost care to preserve back volumes of journals. It is interesting to note that the majority of librarians find the collection of back volumes of journals to be fully adequate. However, there emerges a little variation when data is analysed group-wise. It is apparent that the majority of librarians of CSG, BSG and ISG considered the collection of bound volumes of journals as fully adequate, and majority of PESG and ESG librarian rated their collection as moderately adequate.

Table 7.22 : Adequacy of Libraries by Bound Volumes of Journals

Group of Libraries	*Response*			*Row Total*
	Partially Adequate	*Moderately Adequate*	*Fully Adequate*	
PESG	1 (20.0)	3 (60.0)	1 (20.0)	5 (14.7)
CSG	-	3 (42.9)	4 (57.1)	7 (20.6)
BSG	-	2 (20.0)	8 (80.0)	10 (29.4)
ESG	1 (11.1)	6 (66.7)	2 (22.2)	9 (26.5)
ISG	-	1 (33.3)	2 (66.7)	3 (8.8)
Column Total	2 (5.9)	15 (44.1)	17 (50.0)	34 (100.0)

7.3.4 Distribution of Libraries by Number of Non-book Material

Analysis of non-book material (Table 7.23) shows that a good number of respondents have not given any response. And also 8.8 percent of respondents have indicated non-availability of non-book material in their libraries. Most of the libraries are in possession of 501-2,000 items of non-book material, followed by 14.7 percent of libraries having 101-500 items of non-book material. There is only one library which has collection of between 5,001-1,25000 items of non-book material. Group-wise analysis reveals that only 40 percent of libraries of BSG are such as are having 101-500 items of non-book material.

Table 7.23 : Distribution of Libraries by Number of Non-book Material

Number of Non-Book Material	*Group of Libraries*					
	PESG	*CSG*	*BSG*	*ESG*	*ISG*	*Row Total*
Up to 100	-	1 (14.3)	-	2 (22.2)	1 (33.3)	4 (11.8)
101-500	1 (20.0)	-	4 (40.0)	-	-	5 (14.7)
501-2,000	1 (20.0)	1 (14.3)	2 (20.0)	1 (11.1)	1 (33.3)	6 (17.6)
2,001-5,000	1 (20.0)	1 (14.3)	1 (10.0)	1 (11.1)	-	4 (11.8)
5,001-1,25000	-	-	-	1 (11.1)	-	1 (2.9)
Not stated	2 (40.0)	4 (57.1)	2 (20.0)	3 (33.3)	-	11 (32.4)
Not available	-	-	1 (10.0)	1 (11.1)	1 (33.3)	3 (8.8)
Column Total	5 (14.7)	7 (20.6)	10 (29.4)	9 (26.5)	3 (8.8)	34 (100.0)

7.3.4.1 Adequacy of Libraries by Non-book Material

Non-book material includes a wide range of sources, such as microfiche, microfilms, audio-visual aids, CD-ROMs, maps, etc. They are considered valuable additions in the library. It is clear from the Table 7.24 that majority of the librarians feel that the collection of non-book material in their libraries is only partially adequate. Similar response prevails across all the libraries, except ESG, where the majority is of the view is that the collection is moderately adequate. There are only a few librarians who have termed the collection fully adequate. It signifies that since whatever is available with them meets only partial requirement. As such the libraries need to upgrade the collection.

Table 7.24 : Adequacy of Libraries by Non-book Material

Group of Libraries	*Response*				
	Partially Adequate	*Moderately Adequate*	*Fully Adequate*	*Not Stated*	*Row Total*
PESG	3	1	1	-	5
	(60.0)	(20.0)	(20.0)		(14.7)
CSG	6	1	-	-	7
	(85.7)	(14.3)			(20.6)
BSG	4	4	1	1	10
	(40.0)	(40.0)	(10.0)	(10.0)	(29.4)
ESG	2	5	1	1	9
	(22.2)	(55.6)	(11.1)	(11.1)	(26.5)
ISG	2	-	-	1	3
	(66.7)			(33.3)	(8.8)
Column Total	17	11	3	3	34
	(50.0)	(32.4)	(8.8)	(8.8)	(100.0)

7.3.5 Distribution of Libraries by Number of Theses/ Dissertations, Research/Project Reports, Conference Proceedings, Pamphlets and Reprints

Analysis of collections (Table 7.25) shows that over 20.6 percent of libraries are having collection of theses/dissertations, research reports, conference proceedings, pamphlets and reprints up to 1000, and 14.7 percent of libraries have such a collection of between 1,001-3,000 documents. There are two libraries which have collection between 15,001-90,000. In group-wise analysis, only 30.0 percent of libraries of BSG have collection of theses/dissertations, reports, conference proceedings, etc. up to 1000.

Table 7.25 : Distribution of Libraries by Number of (Theses/ Dissertations, Research/Project Reports, Conference Proceedings, Pamphlets and Reprints

Number of Documents	*Group of Libraries*					
	PESG	*CSG*	*BSG*	*ESG*	*ISG*	*Row Total*
Up to 1000	-	1	3	2	1	7
		(14.3)	(30.0)	(22.2)	(33.3)	(20.6)
1,001-3,000	1	1	2	-	1	5
	(20.0)	(14.3)	(20.0)		(33.3)	(14.7)
3,001-5,000	1	1	1	-	-	3
	(20.0)	(14.3)	(10.0)			(8.8)
5,001-7,500	1	1	2	-	-	4
	(20.0)	(14.3)	(20.0)			(11.8)
7,501-15,000	1	2	-	1	-	4
	(20.0)	(28.6)		(11.1)		(11.8)
15,001-90,000	1	-	-	1	-	2
	(20.0)			(11.1)		(5.9)
Not stated	-	1	2	5	1	9
		(14.3)	(20.0)	(55.6)	(33.3)	(26.5)
Column Total	5	7	10	9	3	34
	(14.7)	(20.6)	(29.4)	(26.5)	(8.8)	(100.0)

7.3.5.1 Adequacy of the Libraries by (Theses/Dissertations, Research/Project Reports, Conference Proceedings, Pamphlets and Reprints

It is clear from Table 7.26 that the majority is of the view that their collection of theses, etc. in CSIR libraries meets only partial requirement, meaning that the collection in the area is inadequate. Barring only minor variation, situation is almost the same across the groups. Unlike in USA, there is no agency in India which acquires theses, etc. for various disciplines and makes them available to the interested users. Thus, there remain only very restricted sources for laboratories under study to acquire such documents. In all probability, theses, etc. are made available to those laboratories' libraries by internal scientists who obtain Ph.D./M.Phil or those who seek some support from these laboratories while carrying out Ph.D./ M.Phil.

Table 7.26 : Adequacy of the Libraries by Theses/ Dissertations, Research/Project Reports, Conference Proceedings, Pamphlets and Reprints

Group of Libraries	*Response*				
	Partially Adequate	*Moderately Adequate*	*Fully Adequate*	*Not Stated*	*Row Total*
PESG	2	2	1	-	5
	(40.0)	(40.0)	(20.0)		(14.7)
CSG	5	1	-	-	7
	(71.4)	(28.6)			(20.6)
BSG	5	5	-	-	10
	(50.0)	(50.0)			(29.4)
ESG	4	5	-	-	9
	(44.4)	(55.6)			(26.5)
ISG	3	-	-	-	3
	(100.0)				(8.8)
Column Total	19	14	1	-	34
	(55.9)	(41.2)	(2.9)		(100.0)

7.3.6 Distribution of Libraries by Number of Standards, Specifications and Patents

Data in Table 7.27 indicates that 47.1 percent of libraries have not responded about standards, specifications and patents. It is, therefore, difficult to say whether they are in possession of such a collection or not. However, out of 34 libraries, 14.7 percent possess the collection up to 2,000 documents. An equal proportion of libraries, i.e. 11.8 percent have collection between 2,001-5,000 and 5,001-20,000 documents.

Table 7.27 : Distribution of Libraries by Number of Standards, Specifications and Patents

Number of Standards, Specifications and Patents	*Group of Libraries*					
	PESG	*CSG*	*BSG*	*ESG*	*ISG*	*Row Total*
Up to 2,000	-	2	2	1	-	5
		(28.6)	(20.0)	(11.1)		(14.7)
2,001-5,000	-	-	2	2	-	4
			(20.0)	(22.2)		(11.8)
5,001-20,000	1	1	-	1	1	4
	(20.0)	(14.3)		(11.1)	(33.3)	(11.8)
20,001-1,50000	1	1	1	-	-	3
	(20.0)	(14.3)	(10.0)			(8.8)
1,50001-3,00000	-	1	1	-	-	2
		(14.3)	(10.0)			(5.9)
Not stated	3	2	4	5	2	16
	(60.0)	(28.6)	(40.0)	(55.6)	(66.7)	(47.1)
Column Total	5	7	10	9	3	34
	(14.7)	(20.6)	(29.4)	(26.5)	(8.8)	(100.0)

7.3.6.1Adequacy of Libraries by Standards, Specifications and Patents

The collection of standards, specifications and patents, as indicated by the librarians, is moderately adequate to meet users' requirements. Group-wise analysis, however, depicts some variation. Librarian belonging to PESG, CSG and ESG reported that their collection in this area meets the requirements moderately. On the other hand librarians working in BSG and ISG felt that the collection met only partial requirement (See Table 7.28).

Table 7.28 : Adequacy of Libraries by Standards, Specifications and Patents

Group of Libraries	*Response*				*Row Total*
	Partially Adequate	*Moderately Adequate*	*Fully Adequate*	*Not Stated*	
PESG	2 (40.0)	3 (60.0)	-	-	5 (14.7)
CSG	2 (28.6)	5 (71.4)	-	-	7 (20.6)
BSG	6 (60.0)	4 (40.0)	-	-	10 (29.4)
ESG	1 (11.1)	6 (66.7)	2 (22.2)	-	9 (26.5)
ISG	2 (66.7)	1 (33.3)	-	-	3 (8.8)
Column Total	13 (38.2)	19 (55.9)	2 (5.9)	-	34 (100.0)

7.3.7 Distribution of Libraries by Number of Journals Subscribed

Journals are considered the most important and popular collection in scientific and technical libraries. Table 7.29 indicates that maximum number of libraries (35.3%) are subscribing to between 101-200 journals, and 32.4 percent are subscribing to between 201-300 journals. There is one library belonging to ISG which subscribes to between 801-3200 journals. Group-wise analysis reveals that majority of the libraries of BSG and ESG are subscribing to 101-200 journals, whereas in PESG and CSG, the majority of libraries are subscribing to 201-300 journals.

Table 7.29 : Distribution of Libraries by Number of Journals Subscribed

Number of Journals Subscribed	*Group of Libraries*					
	PESG	*CSG*	*BSG*	*ESG*	*ISG*	*Row Total*
Up to 100	-	-	1	1	-	2
			(10.0)	(11.1)		(5.9)
101-200	2	1	5	4	-	12
	(40.0)	(14.3)	(50.0)	(44.4)		(35.3)
201-300	3	4	1	2	1	11
	(60.0)	(57.1)	(10.0)	(22.2)	(33.3)	(32.4)
301-500	-	1	3	2	-	6
		(14.3)	(30.0)	(22.2)		(17.6)
501-800	-	1	-	-	1	2
		(14.3)			(33.3)	(5.9)
801-3200	-	-	-	-	1	1
					(33.3)	(2.9)
Column Total	5	7	10	9	3	34
	(14.7)	(20.6)	(29.4)	(26.5)	(8.8)	(100.0)

7.3.7.1 Distribution of Libraries by Number of Indian Journals Subscribed

Distribution of libraries by Indian journals subscription in CSIR libraries shows that 58.8 percent of the libraries are subscribing up to 50 Indian journals, and 26.5 percent are subscribing to 51-100 Indian journals. There is only one library which is subscribing to 201-850 Indian journals (See Table 7.30).

Table 7.30 : Distribution of Libraries by Number of Indian Journals Subscribed

Number of Indian Journals Subscribed	*Group of Libraries*					
	PESG	*CSG*	*BSG*	*ESG*	*ISG*	*Row Total*
Up to 50	5 (100.0)	3 (42.9)	5 (50.0)	6 (66.7)	1 (33.3)	20 (58.8)
51-100	-	3 (42.9)	3 (30.0)	2 (22.2)	1 (33.3)	9 (26.5)
101-150	-	-	2 (20.0)	-	-	2 (5.9)
151-200	-	1 (14.3)	-	-	-	1 (2.9)
201-850	-	-	-	-	1 (33.3)	1 (2.9)
Not stated	-	-	-	1 (11.1)	-	1 (2.9)
Column Total	5 (14.7)	7 (20.6)	10 (29.4)	9 (26.5)	3 (8.8)	34 (100.0)

7.3.7.2 Distribution of Libraries by Number of Indian Journals Received on Gift and Exchange Basis

The analysis of data in Table 7.31 shows that 70.6 percent of libraries are receiving up to 50 Indian journals on gift and exchange basis, and 14.7 percent of libraries are also receiving between 51-100 journals on gift and exchange basis. Only one library of ISG is such which is receiving 301-850 Indian journals on gift and exchange basis.

Table 7.31 : Distribution of Libraries by Number of Indian Journals Received on Gift and Exchange Basis

Number of Journals Received	*Group of Libraries*					
	PESG	*CSG*	*BSG*	*ESG*	*ISG*	*Row Total*
Up to 50	4 (80.0)	6 (85.7)	8 (80.0)	5 (55.6)	1 (33.3)	24 (70.6)
51-100	1 (20.0)	1 (14.3)	-	3 (33.3)	-	5 (14.7)
101-300	-	-	-	-	1 (33.3)	1 (2.9)
301-850	-	-	-	-	1 (33.3)	1 (2.9)
Not stated	-	-	2 (20.0)	1 (11.1)	-	3 (8.8)
Column Total	5 (14.7)	7 (20.6)	10 (29.4)	9 (26.5)	3 (8.8)	34 (100.0)

7.3.7.3 Adequacy of Libraries by Number of Indian Journals Subscribed

It is interesting to note that subscription to journals of Indian origin is reported to be adequate to the extent of being able to meet users' requirements moderately as well as fully. A good number of librarian (38.2%) felt that Indian journals as subscribed by them meets users requirements fully.

This is followed by 47.1 percent of respondents who have expressed moderate satisfaction with Indian journals. Group-wise analysis indicates that all the libraries belonging to ISG are fully satisfied with the subscription to Indian journals. However, satisfaction is moderate in case of CSG and ESG. The respondents are divided in case of PESG. But if we take moderate and full satisfaction into account, the response is satisfactory (See Table 7.32).

Table 7.32 : Adequacy of Libraries by the Indian Journals Subscribed

Group of Libraries	*Response*			*Row Total*
	Partially Adequate	*Moderately Adequate*	*Fully Adequate*	
PESG	1	2	2	5
	(20.0)	(40.0)	(20.0)	(14.7)
CSG	2	4	1	7
	(28.6)	(57.1)	(14.3)	(20.6)
BSG	1	4	5	10
	(10.0)	(40.0)	(50.0)	(29.4)
ESG	1	6	2	9
	(11.1)	(66.7)	(22.2)	(26.5)
ISG	-	-	3	3
			(100.0)	(8.8)
Column Total	5	16	13	34
	(14.7)	(47.1)	(38.2)	(100.0)

7.3.7.4 Distribution of Libraries by Number of Foreign Journals Subscribed

The analysis of Table 7.33 reveals that majority of the libraries (38.2%) are subscribing to 51-100 foreign journals and 23.5 percent of the libraries are subscribing upto 101-150 journals. Group-wise analysis indicates that 57.1 percent libraries of CSG are subscribing to 51-100 foreign journals. It is significant to note that 51-100 foreign journals are also being subscribed to by the libraries of ESG (44.4%) and PESG (40.0%). Only one library of BSG is subscribing to 301-350 foreign journals. The rise in periodical subscription rates and financial problems may be the reason behind less number of journals being subscribed to in these scientific and technical libraries.

Table 7.33 : Distribution of Libraries by Number of Foreign Journals Subscribed

Number of Foreign Journals Subscribed	*Group of Libraries*					
	PESG	*CSG*	*BSG*	*ESG*	*ISG*	*Row Total*
Up to 50	-	-	1	1	-	2
			(10.0)	(11.1)		(5.9)
51-100	2	4	2	4	1	13
	(40.0)	(57.1)	(20.0)	(44.4)	(33.3)	(38.2)
101-150	1	1	2	3	1	8
	(20.0)	(14.3)	(20.0)	(33.3)	(33.3)	(23.5)
151-200	1	1	3	-	-	5
	(20.0)	(14.3)	(30.0)			(14.7)
201-300	1	1	1	-	1	4
	(20.0)	(14.3)	(10.0)		(33.3)	(11.8)
301-350	-	-	1	-	-	1
			(10.0)			(2.9)
Not stated	-	-	-	1	-	1
				(11.1)		(2.9)
Column Total	5	7	10	9	3	34
	(14.7)	(20.6)	(29.4)	(26.5)	(8.8)	(100.0)

7.3.7.5 Distribution of Libraries by Number of Foreign Journals Received on Gift and Exchange Basis

Table 7.34 indicates that the majority of libraries (44.1%) are receiving foreign journals on gift and exchange basis up to 25, and 20.6 percent libraries from 26-50 journals. Group-wise analysis shows that almost all libraries of PESG (100.0%) are receiving journals on gift and exchange basis up to 25. Similarly, 40.0 percent libraries of BSG and ESG are also receiving foreign journals up to 25 on gift and exchange basis. Only one library of ISG is receiving 401-1350 foreign journals on gift and exchange basis.

Table 7.34 : Distribution of Libraries by Number of Foreign Journals Received on Gift and Exchange Basis

Number of Journals Received	*Group of Libraries*					
	PESG	*CSG*	*BSG*	*ESG*	*ISG*	*Row Total*
Up to 25	5	2	4	4	-	15
	(100.0)	(28.6)	(40.0)	(44.4)		(44.1)
26-50	-	2	2	2	1	7
		(28.6)	(20.0)	(22.2)	(33.3)	(20.6)
51-100	-	1	1	2	-	4
		(14.3)	(10.0)	(22.2)		(11.8)
101-400	-	-	1	-	1	2
			(10.0)		(33.3)	(5.9)
401-1350	-	-	-	-	1	1
					(33.3)	(2.9)
Not stated	-	2	2	1	-	5
		(28.6)	(20.0)	(11.1)		(14.7)
Column Total	5	7	10	9	3	34
	(14.7)	(20.6)	(29.4)	(26.5)	(8.8)	(100.0)

7.3.7.6 Adequacy of Libraries by Foreign Journals Subscribed

Analysis of data in Table 7.35 shows that majority of libraries are moderately satisfied as to the number of foreign journals are subscribed and also a good number of libraries have full satisfaction in this regard. Group-wise analysis shows that the majority of respondents of BSG and ISG libraries are fully satisfied, whereas majority of respondents of PESG, CSG and ESG have moderate satisfaction. Number of libraries across the group have just shown partial satisfaction.

Table 7.35 : Adequacy of Libraries by Foreign Journals Subscribed

Group of Libraries	*Response*			*Row Total*
	Partially Adequate	*Moderately Adequate*	*Fully Adequate*	
PESG	2	3	-	5
	(40.0)	(60.0)		(14.7)
CSG	1	5	1	7
	(14.3)	(71.4)	(14.3)	(20.6)
BSG	1	3	6	10
	(10.0)	(30.0)	(60.0)	(29.4)
ESG	1	7	1	9
	(11.1)	(77.8)	(11.1)	(26.5)
ISG	-	1	2	3
		(33.3)	(66.7)	(8.8)
Column Total	5	19	10	34
	(14.7)	(55.9)	(29.4)	(100.0)

7.3.8 Availability of Non-book Material in CSIR Libraries

Analysis of availability of non-book material in CSIR libraries in Table 7.36 indicates that in most cases, only two types of non-book material, i.e., microfilms/microfiche and maps/atlases are reported to be available. Other non-book material, such as audio-cassettes, videocassettes, slides, CD-ROMs, picture transparencies, etc. are generally not available. Group-wise analysis indicates that PESG is the only group in which majority of the libraries are in possession of microfilms/microfiche, CD-ROMs and atlases, whereas in other groups the possession is confined to microfilms/microfiche and maps/atlases only. It may be pointed out that the use of CD-ROM databases have not yet become common in the CSIR laboratories.

Table 7.36 : Availability of Non-book Material in CSIR Libraries

Availability of Non-book Material	*Group of Libraries*									
	PESG		*CSG*		*BSG*		*ESG*		*ISG*	
	Yes	*No*	*Yes*	*No*	*Yes*	*No*	*Yes*	*No*	*Yes*	*No*
Microfilms/ microfiches	4 (80.0)	1 (20.0)	6 (85.7)	1 (14.3)	7 (70.0)	3 (30.0)	7 (77.8)	2 (22.2)	1 (33.3)	2 (66.7)
Audiocassettes	1 (20.0)	4 (80.0)	1 (14.3)	6 (85.7)	2 (20.0)	8 (80.0)	4 (44.4)	5 (55.6)	-	3 (100.0)
Videocassettes	1 (20.0)	4 (80.0)	-	7 (100.0)	3 (30.0)	7 (70.0)	3 (33.3)	6 (66.7)	-	3 (100.0)
Slides	1 (20.0)	4 (80.0)	-	7 (100.0)	2 (20.0)	8 (80.0)	3 (33.3)	6 (66.7)	-	3 (100.0)
CD-ROM databases	3 (60.0)	2 (40.0)	2 (28.6)	5 (71.4)	4 (40.0)	6 (60.0)	2 (22.2)	7 (77.8)	1 (33.3)	2 (66.7)
Online databases	1 (20.0)	4 (80.0)	1 (14.3)	6 (85.7)	3 (30.0)	7 (70.0)	2 (22.2)	7 (77.8)	2 (66.7)	1 (33.3)
Maps/atlases	4 (80.0)	1 (20.0)	5 (71.4)	2 (28.6)	8 (80.0)	2 (20.0)	7 (77.8)	2 (22.2)	2 (66.7)	1 (33.3)
Pictures/transpa-rencies/photos	-	5 (100.0)	-	7 (100.0)	2 (20.0)	8 (80.0)	2 (22.2)	7 (77.8)	-	3 (100.0)

7.4 TECHNICAL PROCESSING AND CIRCULATION ACTIVITIES

7.4.1 Classification Schemes Used in CSIR Libraries

Analysis of use of various classification schemes in CSIR libraries shows that majority of the libraries across the group are following UDC. The use of CC and DDC is equally divided. Group-wise analysis shows that CC system is being used in the libraries belonging to four groups, whereas DDC system is being used in the libraries of two groups.

Table 7.37 : Use of Classification Schemes

Group of Libraries	*Response*				
	CC	*DDC*	*UDC*	*Not stated*	*Row Total*
PESG	2 (40.0)	-	3 (60.0)	-	5 (14.7)
CSG	1 (14.3)	-	5 (71.4)	1 (14.3)	7 (20.6)
BSG	1 (10.0)	4 (40.0)	5 (50.0)	-	10 (29.4)
ESG	1 (11.1)	-	8 (88.9)	-	9 (26.5)
ISG	-	1 (33.3)	2 (66.7)	-	3 (8.8)
Column Total	5 (14.7)	5 (14.7)	23 (67.6)	1 (2.9)	34 (100.0)

7.4.2 Coverage of Catalogue

All CSIR libraries are maintaining catalogue but coverage of the catalogue is just partial in many cases. The majority of the libraries appear to be maintaining catalogue of their entire collections. Group-wise analysis shows that an overwhelming majority of the libraries across the group maintain catalogue of their entire collection. But a good number of ISG and BSG libraries have the catalogue which is just partial (Table 7.38).

Table 7.38 : Coverage of Catalogue

Group of Libraries	*Catalogue Coverage*		
	Entire	*Partial*	*Row Total*
PESG	4	1	5
	(80.0)	(20.0)	(14.7)
CSG	6	1	7
	(85.7)	(14.3)	(20.6)
BSG	7	3	10
	(70.0)	(30.0)	(29.4)
ESG	7	2	9
	(77.8)	(22.2)	(26.5)
ISG	2	1	3
	(66.7)	(33.3)	(8.8)
Total Column	26	8	34
	(76.5)	(23.5)	(100.0)

7.4.3 Type of Catalogue Maintained in CSIR Libraries

Table 7.39 indicates the use of different types of catalogue in CSIR libraries. The majority (38.2%) of the libraries are following dictionary catalogue, and 35.3 percent of the libraries have classified catalogue. Use of dictionary/classified catalogue in CSIR libraries is in fact evenly distributed. About 24 percent of the libraries are those which are following dictionary/classified catalogue.

Table 7.39 : Type of Catalogue Maintained in CSIR Libraries

Group of Libraries	*Response*				
	Dicti-onary	*Classi-fied*	*Dictionary/ Classified*	*Compute-rised*	*Row Total*
PESG	1 (20.0)	2 (40.0)	2 (40.0)	-	5 (14.7)
CSG	2 (28.6)	3 (42.9)	2 (28.6)	-	7 (20.6)
BSG	9 (90.0)	-	1 (10.0)	-	10 (29.4)
ESG	1 (11.1)	4 (44.4)	3 (33.3)	1 (11.1)	9 (26.5)
ISG	-	3 (100.0)	-	-	3 (8.8)
Column Total	13 (38.2)	12 (35.3)	8 (23.5)	1 (2.9)	34 (100.0)

7.4.4 Catalogue Code Used in CSIR Libraries

Library catalogue is an effective tool which offers access to the library collection without spending much time. Proper use of catalogue code provides easy and quick access to documents in the library. Table 7.40 indicates the data regarding catalogue codes used in the CSIR libraries. The majority of the libraries are using AACR-2 whereas an equal proportion of libraries are using AACR-1, CCC-5 and ALA catalogue code. On the other hand 2.9 percent libraries are such which are using CCC and AACR-2 and have computerised catalogue.

Group-wise analysis of libraries indicates that the majority of the libraries (44.1%) are following AACR-2, particularly CSG (42.9%), BSG (60.0%) and ISG (100%) libraries. But AACR-1 is being followed in the majority of the libraries belonging to PESG (40.0%) and ESG (33.3%). In each group, except ISG, there are some libraries which follow CCC-5 and ALA codes also.

Table 7.40 : Catalogue Code Used in CSIR Libraries

Types of Catalogue Code Used	*Group of Libraries*					
	PESG	*CSG*	*BSG*	*ESG*	*ISG*	*Row Total*
AACR-1	2	-	-	3	-	5
	(40.0)			(33.3)		(14.7)
AACR-2	1	3	6	2	3	15
	(20.0)	(42.9)	(60.0)	(22.2)	(100.0)	(44.1)
CCC-5	1	2	1	1	-	5
	(20.0)	(28.6)	(10.0)	(11.1)		(14.7)
ALA	1	1	2	1	-	5
	(20.0)	(14.3)	(20.0)	(11.1)		(14.7)
AACR-1 & ALA	-	1	1	-	-	2
		(14.3)	(10.0)			(5.9)
CCC & AACR-2	-	-	-	1	-	1
				(11.1)		(2.9)
Computerised	-	-	-	1	-	1
				(11.1)		(2.9)
Column Total	5	7	10	9	3	34
	(14.7)	(20.6)	(29.4)	(26.5)	(8.8)	(100.0)

7.4.5 Circulation System of CSIR Libraries

The data collected regarding circulation system of the libraries reveals that the majority of the libraries are following Newark and Browne system for issuing and returning documents whereas seven libraries are those which are using their own system for circulation of documents. Only two libraries have computerised circulation system (Table 7.41).

Group-wise analysis indicates that almost an equal number of the libraries of all groups, except ISG, are following Newark and Browne system for issuing and returning of documents. Only two libraries belonging of BSG are using both Newark and Browne systems for circulation. It is clear that the computerised system of circulation has not yet picked up in CSIR libraries leave aside use of bar code technology.

Table 7.41 : Circulation System of CSIR Libraries

Circulation System	*Group of Libraries*					
	PESG	*CSG*	*BSG*	*ESG*	*ISG*	*Row Total*
Newark	2 (40.0)	2 (28.6)	3 (30.0)	2 (22.2)	2 (66.7)	11 (32.4)
Browne	2 (40.0)	2 (28.6)	4 (40.0)	3 (33.3)	-	11 (32.4)
Newark & Browne	-	-	2 (20.0)	-	-	2 (5.9)
Own System	1 (20.0)	2 (28.6)	1 (10.0)	2 (22.2)	1 (33.3)	7 (20.6)
Computerised	-	1 (14.3)	-	1 (11.1)	-	2 (5.9)
Not responded	-	-	-	1 (11.1)	-	1 (2.9)
Column Total	5 (14.7)	7 (20.6)	10 (29.4)	9 (26.5)	3 (8.8)	34 (100.0)

7.4.6 Availability of Book Reservation Facility

An analysis of data regarding the availability of reservation facility given in Table 7.42 reveals that the majority of the libraries are providing book reservation facilities for their users.

Table 7.42 : Availability of Book Reservation Facility

Book Reservation	*Group of Libraries*					
	PESG	*CSG*	*BSG*	*ESG*	*ISG*	*Row Total*
Yes	4 (80.0)	5 (71.4)	6 (60.0)	7 (77.8)	2 (66.7)	24 (70.6)
No	1 (20.0)	2 (28.6)	4 (40.0)	2 (22.2)	1 (33.3)	10 (29.4)
Column Total	5 (14.7)	7 (20.6)	10 (29.4)	10 (26.5)	3 (8.8)	34 (100.0)

7.4.6.1 Utilisation of Book Reservation Facility

Data given on the use of book reservation facility in Table 7.43 reveals that the majority of the libraries are utilizing book reservation facility on regular basis whereas 32.4 percent of the libraries indicated the use of book reservation facility only occasionally. Significant percentage of the libraries are of the view that they are not providing such facility.

Group-wise analysis of the libraries reveals that users of majority of libraries of PESG (60.0%) utilise the book reservation facility occasionally, followed by 40.0 percent of users of the libraries of BSG. Whereas the users of CSG and ESG are utilizing this facility on regular basis. There are few libraries which are not providing the book reservation facility to their users.

Table 7.43 : Utilisation of Book Reservation Facility

Group of Libraries	*Response*			
	Regularly	*Occasionally*	*Not at All*	*Row Total*
PESG	1	3	1	5
	(20.0)	(60.0)	(20.0)	(14.7)
CSG	4	1	2	7
	(57.1)	(14.3)	(28.6)	(20.6)
BSG	2	4	4	10
	(20.0)	(40.0)	(40.0)	(29.4)
ESG	5	2	2	9
	(55.6)	(22.2)	(22.2)	(26.5)
ISG	1	1	1	3
	(33.3)	(33.3)	(33.3)	(8.8)
Column Total	13	11	10	34
	(38.2)	(32.4)	(29.4)	(100.0)

7.4.7 Availability of Interlibrary Loan Facility

Growth of published literature has created so many problems to the users and libraries to acquire everything in the library. No single library is self-sufficient to meet every information requirement of the scientists and research scholars. The co-operation between the libraries to acquire the reading material from each other is the interlibrary loan system. Before the advent of technologies like computer and networks, it was an established system of sharing the reading material between the libraries. This established system is still continuing to meet the information needs of the users. It is imperative for the librarian to provide the patrons the required documents on request as well as ensure that required information is obtained as quickly as possible.

On account of information explosion, no library is self sufficient in acquiring and affording all kinds of material required by its clientele/patrons. To avoid such problems, sharing of resources between the libraries through interlibrary loan or other means have become imperative to meet the needs of their clientele. CSIR laboratories' libraries have interlibrary loan arrangements among them and with university libraries and other libraries of the scientific and technical organisations.

The data collected from the libraries in Table 7.44 indicates that almost all libraries of PESG, CSG and ISG are providing interlibrary loan facilities to their users. A slight variation is reported in BSG and ESG libraries which are also providing interlibrary loan facility to their users.

Table 7.44 : Availability of Interlibrary Loan Facility

Interlibrary	*Group of Libraries*					
Loan	*PESG*	*CSG*	*BSG*	*ESG*	*ISG*	*Row Total*
Yes	5	7	9	7	3	31
	(100.0)	(100.0)	(90.0)	(77.8)	(100.0)	(91.2)
No	-	-	1	2	-	3
			(10.0)	(22.2)		(8.8)
Column Total	5	7	10	9	3	34
	(14.7)	(20.6)	(29.4)	(26.5)	(8.8)	(100.0)

7.4.7.1 Utilisation of Interlibrary Loan Facility

The data on use of interlibrary loan facilities in Table 7.45 reveals that almost all libraries (100%) of ISG are utilizing the interlibrary loan facility on regular basis whereas the libraries of PESG (60.0%) and BSG (50.0%) are also utilizing this facility to the extent indicated in parenthesis. There are a few libraries in all the groups which are providing this facility occasionally.

Table 7.45 : Utilisation of Interlibrary Loan Facility

Group of	*Response*			
Libraries	*Regularly*	*Occasionally*	*Not at All*	*Row Total*
PESG	3	2	-	5
	(60.0)	(40.0)		(14.7)
CSG	3	4	-	7
	(42.9)	(57.1)		(20.6)
BSG	5	4	1	10
	(50.0)	(40.0)	(10.0)	(29.4)
ESG	4	3	2	9
	(44.4)	(33.3)	(22.2)	(26.5)
ISG	3	-	-	3
	(100.0)			(8.8)
Column Total	18	13	3	34
	(52.9)	(38.2)	(8.8)	(100.0)

7.5 LIBRARY SERVICES AND FACILITIES

7.5.1 Availability of Resource Sharing Facility

The analysis of data in Table 7.46 indicates that 70.6 percent libraries of CSIR have the provision of resource sharing facilities. Group-wise analysis indicates that almost all the libraries of ISG are providing the resource sharing facilities to their users. Even 80.0 percent of the libraries of BSG are offering the resource sharing facilities. A slight variation is recorded in the availability of resource sharing facilities in three groups namely, ESG, CSG and PESG.

Table 7.46 : Availability of Resource Sharing Facility

Resource Sharing	*Group of Libraries*					
	PESG	*CSG*	*BSG*	*ESG*	*ISG*	*Row Total*
Yes	3	4	8	6	3	24
	(60.0)	(57.1)	(80.0)	(66.7)	(100.0)	(70.6)
No	2	3	2	3	-	10
	(40.0)	(42.9)	(20.0)	(33.3)		(29.4)
Column Total	5	7	10	9	3	34
	(14.7)	(20.6)	(29.4)	(26.5)	(8.8)	(100.0)

7.5.2 Procurement of Material from Other Countries on Request

It is interesting to note from Table 7.47 that the most of the libraries have arrangement to procure documents from other countries for the users of the library. This is done on the request of users. Group-wise analysis shows that this facility is available in majority of the libraries of CSG, ESG and ISG. But situation is altogether different in PESG and BSG where majority of the libraries do not have this facility.

Table 7.47 : Procurement of Material from Other Countries on Request

Procurement of Material from Other Countries	*Group of Libraries*					
	PESG	*CSG*	*BSG*	*ESG*	*ISG*	*Row Total*
Yes	2	6	4	7	2	21
	(40.0)	(85.7)	(40.0)	(77.8)	(66.7)	(61.8)
No	3	1	6	2	1	13
	(60.0)	(14.3)	(60.0)	(22.2)	(33.3)	(38.2)
Column Total	5	7	10	9	3	34
	(14.7)	(20.6)	(29.4)	(26.5)	(8.8)	(100.0)

7.5.2.1 Necessity for Procurement of Material from Other Countries

Table 7.48 indicates that 60 percent each of the libraries of PESG and BSG (60.0%) have the need to procure the reading material from other countries. Even significant number of the libraries of three groups also desired to procure such material from other countries.

Table 7.48 : Necessity for Procurement of Material from Other Countries

Necessity for Procurement of Material	*Group of Libraries*					
	PESG	*CSG*	*BSG*	*ESG*	*ISG*	*Row Total*
Yes	3	1	6	2	1	13
	(60.0)	(14.3)	(60.0)	(22.2)	(33.3)	(38.2)
No	2	6	4	7	2	21
	(40.0)	(85.7)	(40.0)	(77.8)	(66.7)	(61.8)
Column Total	5	7	10	9	3	34
	(14.7)	(20.6)	(29.4)	(26.5)	(8.8)	(100.0)

7.5.3 Need for Users' Education

User education involves providing orientation to the library users on how to use more beneficially the library and its resources so that they can be exposed to the resources available in the library for their effective use. User education is very essential activity for maximisation of the library utilisation. In order to assess the need for such programme, librarians were asked to indicate their response.

Data presented in the Table 7.49 shows that an overwhelming majority of the libraries in each group have expressed need for users' education. However, some variation is noticeable in response rate. The need for users' education is 100 percent in CSG, BSG and ESG whereas it is only by 60 percent and 66.7 percent of the libraries in the group of PESG and ISG respectively.

Table 7.49 : Need for Users' Education

Need for Users' Education	*Group of Libraries*					
	PESG	*CSG*	*BSG*	*ESG*	*ISG*	*Row Total*
Yes	3	7	10	8	2	30
	(60.0)	(100.0)	(100.0)	(88.9)	(66.7)	(88.2)
No	2	-	-	1	1	4
	(40.0)			(11.1)	(33.3)	(11.8)
Column Total	5	7	10	9	3	34
	(14.7)	(20.6)	(29.4)	(26.5)	(8.8)	(100.0)

7.5.4 Provision of Library Services

In the present world, it is very difficult for research scholars, scientists and technologists to keep pace with the growing knowledge and keep themselves aware of the development in their area of specialisation. Dr. S. R. Ranganathan has defined reference service as "the process of establishing contact between a reader and his document in a personal way".[5] It is a direct personal service or aid which is given by library staff to the users either on demand or in anticipation. Reference service may be provided to the users by selecting and organising the reading material according to the requirements of users. In research libraries this service has its own significance by locating the specific information or document to the engaged scientific community of users in their research works. This service is very valuable in saving the time of the users.

The main objective of the scientific and technical libraries is to store information related to their research in different disciplines and to provide the pinpointed and condensed information to their scientists and research scholars in an effective way to achieve better results out of researches. The services of the modern libraries and mode of delivery have gone under tremendous change.

The analysis indicates that an overwhelming majority of libraries provide the list of journals subscribed or discontinued in the CSIR libraries. Whereas almost an equal proportion of respondents indicated that the libraries also bring out the list of new additions, bibliographic services on demand and literature search. Only bibliographic service in anticipation is not seriously taken by the libraries. Also response on indexing and abstracting services, contents of periodicals, SDI services are also not very encouraging.

The practice of providing digest of scientific, technical and industrial information and service is rare. As 82.4 percent libraries are such which don't render the digest of scientific, technical and industrial information to the users. The response in Table 7.50 indicates that libraries attached with CSIR are providing almost all advanced library services to their clienteles.

Table 7.50 : Provision of Library Services

Library Services	*Response*		
	Yes	*No*	*Row Total*
1. Bringing out new additions	28 (82.4)	6 (17.6)	34 (100.0)
2. List of journals subscribed/ discontinued	32 (94.1)	2 (5.9)	34 (100.0)
3. Indexing/abstracting services	20 (58.8)	14 (41.2)	34 (100.0)
4. Bibliographical services	30 (88.2)	4 (11.8)	34 (100.0)
a) On demand	29 (85.3)	5 (14.7)	34 (100.0)
b) In anticipation	11 (32.4)	23 (67.6)	34 (100.0)
5. Literature search	29 (85.3)	5 (14.7)	34 (100.0)
6. Contents pages of periodicals	18 (52.9)	16 (47.1)	34 (100.0)
7. SDI services	21 (61.8)	13 (38.2)	34 (100.0)
8. Digest of scientific, technical and industrial information	6 (17.6)	28 (82.4)	34 (100.0)

7.5.4.1 Library Services Offered by CSIR Libraries

Analysis of different library services offered by CSIR laboratories in Table 7.51 indicate that some of the services such as list of new additions, list of journals subscribed/ discontinued, bibliographic services, literature search, are being offered by the majority of the libraries belonging to their groups. However, proportion of such libraries varies from group to group. It is seen that PESG is one such group in which an overwhelming majority of the libraries are offering a number of services but some library services such as contents of periodicals and digest of scientific, technical and industrial information, are offered only by a few libraries. Similar, is the situation in CSG in which a number of library services, such as list of new additions, journals subscribed/discontinued, bibliographical services and literature search are offered by a sizable proportion of libraries but other important services which include bibliography in anticipation, SDI services, contents of periodicals and digest of scientific, technical and industrial literature are provided by a limited number of libraries. It is, however, interesting to note that the majority of the libraries belonging to BSG, ESG and ISG are offering the most of the services. The number of such services which are not offered by these groups does not go beyond two.

Table 7.51 : Library Services Offered by CSIR Libraries

Provision of Services	*Group of Libraries*									
	PESG		*CSG*		*BSG*		*ESG*		*ISG*	
	Yes	*No*	*Yes*	*No*	*Yes*	*No*	*Yes*	*No*	*Yes*	*No*
Bringing out new	5	-	6	1	7	3	8	1	2	1
additions	(100.0)		(85.7)	(14.3)	(70.0)	(30.0)	(88.9)	(11.1)	(66.7)	(33.3)
List of journals subs-	5	-	6	1	10	-	8	1	3	-
cribed/ discontinued	(100.0)		(85.7)	(14.3)	(100.0)		(88.9)	(11.1)	(100.0)	
Indexing/abstracting	2	3	4	3	6	4	7	2	1	2
services	(40.0)	(60.0)	(57.1)	(42.9)	(60.0)	(40.0)	(77.8)	(22.2)	(33.3)	(66.7)
Bibliographical services	5	-	6	1	8	2	8	1	3	-
	(100.0)		(85.7)	(14.3)	(80.0)	(20.0)	(88.9)	(11.1)	(100.0)	
On demand	5	-	6	1	7	3	8	1	3	-
	(100.0)		(85.7)	(14.3)	(70.0)	(30.0)	(88.9)	(11.1)	(100.0)	
In anticipation	1	4	1	6	5	5	4	5	-	3
	(20.0)	(40.0)	(14.3)	(85.7)	(50.0)	(50.0)	(44.4)	(55.6)		(100.0)
Literature search	5	-	6	1	7	3	8	1	3	-
	(100.0)		(85.7)	(14.3)	(70.0)	(30.0)	(88.9)	(11.1)	(100.0)	
Contents pages of	2	3	3	4	3	7	8	1	2	1
periodicals	(40.0)	(60.0)	(42.9)	(57.1)	(30.0)	(70.0)	(88.9)	(11.1)	(66.7)	(33.3)
SDI services	4	1	3	4	6	4	7	2	1	2
	(80.0)	(20.0)	(42.9)	(57.1)	(60.0)	(40.0)	(77.8)	(22.2)	(33.3)	(66.7)
Digest of scientific,	1	4	1	6	2	8	2	7	-	3
technical and industrial information	(20.0)	(80.0)	(14.3)	(85.7)	(20.0)	(80.0)	(22.2)	(77.8)		(100.0)

7.5.4.2 Bringing out New Additions

The special library provides indepth and condensed information to the users who are different in terms of their specialisation and need from the other types of libraries. The staff of these libraries makes effort to disseminate new information as quickly and efficiently as possible to the researchers and scientists of the organisation. The staff of the libraries must be acquainted with the latest happenings and R&D programmes. The value and effectiveness of the library and its services can be measured in terms of the queries responded to.

In order to familiarise all clientele of the library about

new publications, lists and bulletins of new additions are prepared. Such type of lists may be alphabetical or subject-wise. To give a better information about books, pamphlets, proceedings, journals, etc. these items may be included in such lists. These lists may be circulated among the scientists and researchers or displayed on the display boards. Table 7.52 indicates that 82.4 percent libraries are bringing out lists of new additions. Group-wise analysis indicated that all libraries belonging to PESG bring out lists of new additions. A little over 85 percent of libraries of CSG and ESG should also attempt to bring out new additions in their libraries. Even a good number of respondents of BSG and ISG also indicated such provision. It is clear from the analysis that almost an overwhelming majority of libraries, irrespective of group, have provision for this service.

Table 7.52 : Bringing out Lists of New Additions

Bringing out New Additions	*Group of Libraries*					
	PESG	*CSG*	*BSG*	*ESG*	*ISG*	*Row Total*
Yes	5	6	7	8	2	28
	(100.0)	(85.7)	(70.0)	(88.9)	(66.7)	(82.4)
No	-	1	3	1	1	6
		(14.3)	(30.0)	(11.1)	(33.3)	(17.6)
Column Total	5	7	10	9	3	34
	(14.7)	(20.6)	(29.4)	(26.5)	(8.8)	(100.0)

7.5.4.3 List of Journals Subscribed/Discontinued

The majority of libraries indicated that they are providing the list of journals being subscribed or discontinued in the library. This type of service is very useful to keep clientele aware of the recent arrivals and discontinued journals in their area of specialisation. Group-wise analysis (Table 7.53) indicates that an overwhelming majority of libraries of PESG, BSG and ISG are providing such services to the users. As compared to other groups, the proportion of such libraries in CSG and ESG is less.

Table 7.53 : List of Journals Subscribed/Discontinued

List of Journals Subscribed/ Discontinued	*Group of Libraries*					
	PESG	*CSG*	*BSG*	*ESG*	*ISG*	*Row Total*
Yes	5	6	10	8	3	32
	(100.0)	(85.7)	(100.0)	(88.9)	(100.0)	(94.1)
No	-	1	-	1	-	2
		(14.3)		(11.1)		(5.9)
Column Total	5	7	10	9	3	34
	(14.7)	(20.6)	(29.4)	(26.5)	(8.8)	(100.0)

7.5.4.4 Provision of Indexing and Abstracting Services

Analysis of provision of indexing and abstracting services given in Table 7.54 indicates that 58.8 percent libraries are offering these services. Further analysis of data of groups shows that majority of libraries belonging to PESG and ISG do not have facility for this service. Whereas majority of libraries in the group of CSG, BSG and ESG have provision for this service.

Table 7.54 : Provision of Indexing and Abstracting Services

Provision of Indexing and Abstracting Services	*Group of Libraries*					
	PESG	*CSG*	*BSG*	*ESG*	*ISG*	*Row Total*
Yes	2	4	6	7	1	20
	(40.0)	(57.1)	(60.0)	(77.8)	(33.3)	(58.8)
No	3	3	4	2	2	14
	(60.0)	(42.9)	(40.0)	(22.2)	(66.7)	(41.2)
Column Total	5	7	10	9	3	34
	(14.7)	(20.6)	(29.4)	(26.5)	(8.8)	(100.0)

7.5.4.5 Provision of Bibliographical Services

Analysis of data on libraries providing bibliographical services, as given in Table 7.55, shows that 88.2 percent of libraries are having provision of bibliographical services. Group-wise analysis of data is also similar. An overwhelming majority of libraries, irrespective of group affiliation, are offering this service. The status, however, is different in PESG and ISG where all libraries have this facility.

Table 7.55 : Provision of Bibliographical Services

Provision of Bibliographical Services	*Group of Libraries*					
	PESG	*CSG*	*BSG*	*ESG*	*ISG*	*Row Total*
Yes	5 (100.0)	6 (85.7)	8 (80.0)	8 (88.9)	3 (100.0)	30 (88.2)
No	-	1 (14.3)	2 (20.0)	1 (11.1)	-	4 (11.8)
Column Total	5 (14.7)	7 (20.6)	10 (29.4)	9 (26.5)	3 (8.8)	34 (100.0)

7.5.4.6 Provision of Bibliographical Services on Demand and in Anticipation

The analysis of data in Table 7.56 is based on the response of libraries regarding provision of bibliographical facilities. It is interesting to note that almost all the groups respond to the demand of users for bibliographical services but they are not that forthcoming in preparation of bibliographies in anticipation. Except BSG, where 50 percent of libraries are also providing bibliographical services in anticipation, the majority of libraries in each group though offer this service on demand, they do not attempt in the similar manner to prepare it in anticipation.

Table 7.56 : Provision of Bibliographical Services on Demand and in Anticipation

Group of Libraries	*Bibliographical Services*				
	On demand		*In anticipation*		
	Yes	*No*	*Yes*	*No*	*Row Total*
PESG	5	-	1	4	5
	(100.0)		(20.0)	(80.0)	(14.7)
CSG	6	1	1	6	7
	(85.7)	(14.3)	(14.3)	(85.7)	(20.6)
BSG	7	3	5	5	10
	(70.0)	(30.0)	(50.0)	(50.0)	(29.4)
ESG	8	1	4	5	9
	(88.9)	(11.1)	(44.4)	(55.6)	(26.5)
ISG	3	-	-	3	3
	(100.0)			(100.0)	(8.8)
Column Total	29	5	11	23	34
	(85.3)	(14.7)	(32.4)	(67.6)	(100.0)

7.5.4.7 Provision of Literature Search

Literature search is very important activity often done by researchers themselves at different levels of their work. However, due to lack of time, library staff's help is also sought. In the Table 7.57, an attempt has been made to find out provision of such service in CSIR libraries. Data indicate that an overwhelming majority of libraries, 85.3 percent, provide literature search facility to users. Group-wise analysis also indicates that majority of libraries in each group are offering this facility. However, the proportion of such libraries is higher in PESG and ISG.

Table 7.57 : Provision of Literature Search

Provision of Literature Search	*Group of Libraries*					
	PESG	*CSG*	*BSG*	*ESG*	*ISG*	*Row Total*
Yes	5	6	7	8	3	29
	(100.0)	(85.7)	(70.0)	(88.9)	(100.0)	(85.3)
No	-	1	3	1	-	5
		(14.3)	(30.0)	(11.1)		(14.7)
Column Total	5	7	10	9	3	34
	(14.7)	(20.6)	(29.4)	(26.5)	(8.8)	(100.0)

7.5.4.8 Provision of Contents Pages of Periodicals

Contents pages of periodicals help an user to identify article/write-up of his interest. It is done in the library using a simple method of getting photocopies made of contents pages of periodical received in the library and then circulating among members. It is surprising to find that except two groups, namely ESG and ISG, majority of other groups are not providing this service.

Table 7.58 : Provision of Contents Pages of Periodicals

Provision of Contents Pages of Periodicals	*Group of Libraries*					
	PESG	*CSG*	*BSG*	*ESG*	*ISG*	*Row Total*
Yes	2	3	3	8	2	18
	(40.0)	(42.9)	(30.0)	(88.9)	(66.7)	(52.9)
No	3	4	7	1	1	16
	(60.0)	(57.1)	(70.0)	(11.1)	(33.3)	(47.1)
Column Total	5	7	10	9	3	34
	(14.7)	(20.6)	(29.4)	(26.5)	(8.8)	(100.0)

7.5.4.9 Provision of SDI Services

Out of 34 libraries, only 21 libraries of different groups of CSIR laboratories are providing SDI services. Across the group of libraries, 80.0 percent of PESG and 77.8 percent of ESG libraries are reported to have provision for the SDI services. Some libraries in other groups are also engaged in providing SDI services. On the other hand, 66.7 percent of the libraries of ISG and 57.1 percent of libraries of CSG are reported to have no provision of SDI services. It is clear from the analysis of data that even scientific and technical libraries are lagging behind in providing pinpointed and condensed information to the scientists and research scholars.

Table 7.59 : Provision of SDI Services

Provision of SDI Services	*Group of Libraries*					
	PESG	*CSG*	*BSG*	*ESG*	*ISG*	*Row Total*
Yes	4	3	6	7	1	21
	(80.0)	(42.9)	(60.0)	(77.8)	(33.3)	(61.8)
No	1	4	4	2	2	13
	(20.0)	(57.1)	(40.0)	(22.2)	(66.7)	(38.2)
Column Total	5	7	10	9	3	34
	(14.7)	(20.6)	(29.4)	(26.5)	(8.8)	(100.0)

7.5.4.10 Provision of Digest of Scientific, Technical and Industrial Information

Table 7.60 reveals that data collected from 34 libraries of CSIR indicates that only 6 libraries maintained the digest of scientific, technical and industrial information. The majority of libraries indicated to have no such service. Almost all libraries of ISG indicated non-availability of digest of scientific, technical and industrial information, as also 85.7 percent libraries of CSG. Other groups, like PESG, BSG and ESG also indicated the absence of this service.

Table 7.60 : Provision of Digest of Scientific, Technical and Industrial Information

Provision of Digest of Scientific, Technical & Industrial Information	*Group of Libraries*					
	PESG	*CSG*	*BSG*	*ESG*	*ISG*	*Row Total*
Yes	1	1	2	2	-	6
	(20.0)	(14.3)	(20.0)	(22.2)		(17.6)
No	4	6	8	7	3	28
	(80.0)	(85.7)	(80.0)	(77.8)	(100.0)	(82.4)
Column Total	5	7	10	9	3	34
	(14.7)	(20.6)	(29.4)	(26.5)	(8.8)	(100.0)

7.5.5 Provision of Translation Service

In scientific and technical libraries, efforts should be made to create some provisions to provide translation of foreign language journal articles and other reading material. The provision of in-house current awareness service, which includes translation service, should be made or there should be some provision to provide the service through other agency. The librarian or information officer should be familiar with the location of expertise and rates of translators who can undertake such assignments. This is required in cases where library staff is not able to discharge this work. There is limited number of such translation centres which can provide the translation service to the needy users. The INSDOC, now NISCAIR, being the National Science Library has such provisions to provide translation service of foreign language reading material. But the efforts should be made to set up more translation centres in each specific discipline at the state level as well as the national level to meet the requirements of users without delay.

A look at the Table 7.61 indicates that except ISG and PESG, a good number of libraries in each group have the provision of translation service.

Table 7.61 : Provision of Translation Service

Provision of Translation Service	*Group of Libraries*					
	PESG	*CSG*	*BSG*	*ESG*	*ISG*	*Row Total*
Yes	1	5	6	9	1	22
	(20.0)	(71.4)	(60.0)	(100.0)	(33.3)	(64.7)
No	4	2	4	-	2	12
	(80.0)	(28.6)	(40.0)		(66.7)	(35.3)
Column Total	5	7	10	9	3	34
	(14.7)	(20.6)	(29.4)	(26.5)	(8.8)	(100.0)

7.5.5.1 Provision of Translation Service in Different Languages in CSIR Libraries

The data collected from the 34 libraries of CSIR laboratories reveals that only 16 libraries are providing translation service in different languages through various agencies. The foreign languages covered by these laboratories include English, Russian, French, Japanese, German, Spanish and Chinese. The majority of the libraries, 15 (44.1%), offer translation service of French language, whereas 41.2 percent libraries reported to be offering translation in German language. Translation service in Russian and Japanese languages was available at 35.3 percent libraries, followed by translation in Spanish language in 32.4 percent of libraries. In addition, there are some libraries in other groups which also offer translation of foreign languages, such as Chinese and English which constitute 29.4 percent and 26.5 percent respectively.

Table 7.62 : Provision of Translation Service in Different Languages

Languages	*Response*				
	Yes	*No*	*Not Stated*	*Not Available*	*Row Total*
English	9	7	6	12	34
	(26.5)	(20.6)	(17.6)	(35.3)	(100.0)
Russian	12	4	6	12	34
	(35.3)	(11.8)	(17.6)	(35.3)	(100.0)
French	15	1	6	12	34
	(44.1)	(2.9)	(17.6)	(35.3)	(100.0)
Japanese	12	4	6	12	34
	(35.3)	(11.8)	(17.6)	(35.3)	(100.0)
German	14	2	6	12	34
	(41.2)	(5.9)	(17.6)	(35.3)	(100.0)
Spanish	11	5	6	12	34
	(32.4)	(14.7)	(17.6)	(35.3)	(100.0)
Chinese	10	6	6	12	34
	(29.4)	(17.6)	(17.6)	(35.3)	(100.0)

7.5.5.2 Panel of Translators

Out of 16 libraries, only 4 libraries have a panel of translators (Table 7.63). There are some libraries which are utilising the services of outside agencies in place of internal translators.

Table 7.63 : Panel of Translators

Group of Libraries	*Panel of Translators*			
	Yes	*No*	*Not Available*	*Row Total*
PESG	-	1 (20.0)	4 (80.0)	5 (14.7)
CSG	1 (14.3)	1 (14.3)	5 (71.4)	7 (20.6)
BSG	1 (10.0)	1 (10.0)	8 (80.0)	10 (29.4)
ESG	1 (11.1)	-	8 (88.9)	9 (26.5)
ISG	1 (33.3)	-	2 (66.7)	3 (8.8)
Column Total	4 (11.8)	3 (8.8)	27 (79.4)	34 (100.0)

7.5.6 Availability of Reprographic Services

Analysis of reprographic services, as given in Table 7.64, indicate that of the various devices available, only photocopying is commonly used across the groups. But in a number of libraries belonging to CSG and ESG, even photocopying service is not available. Some of the services, such as ammonia printing, slide making, are available in one or two laboratories only. It is difficult to point out the reason for non-availability of such things. But it is certain that CSIR laboratories are lagging behind in picking up advancement.

Table 7.64 : Availability of Reprographic Services

Availability of Reprographic Services	*Group of Libraries*									
	PESG		*CSG*		*BSG*		*ESG*		*ISG*	
	Yes	*No*	*Yes*	*No*	*Yes*	*No*	*Yes*	*No*	*Yes*	*No*
Micro-filming	1	4	-	7	-	10	-	9	1	2
	(20.0)	(80.0)		(100.0)		(100.0)		(100.0)	(33.3)	(66.7)
Microfiche	1	4	-	7	2	8	1	8	1	2
	(20.0)	(80.0)		(100.0)	(20.0)	(80.0)	(11.1)	(88.9)	(33.3)	(66.7)
Photocopying	5	-	6	1	10	-	8	1	3	-
	(100.0)		(85.7)	(14.3)	(100.0)		(88.9)	(11.1)	(100.0)	
Ammonia printing	-	5	-	7	-	10	1	8	-	3
		(100.0)		(100.0)		(100.0)	(11.1)	(88.9)		(100.0)
Reader printer	2	3	2	5	3	7	3	6	1	2
	(40.0)	(60.0)	(28.6)	(71.4)	(30.0)	(70.0)	(33.3)	(66.7)	(33.3)	(66.7)
Slide making	1	4	-	7	-	10	2	7	1	2
	(20.0)	(80.0)		(100.0)		(100.0)	(22.2)	(77.8)	(33.3)	(66.7)

7.5.7 Availability of the Air-conditioned Facilities

Maximum utilisation of the resources does not depend only on good number of books and other resources. Rather it is very important to create conducive environment for the same. Air-conditioned facilities help in creating conducive environment within the libraries. It is found from the Table 7.65 that the majority of the libraries (64.7%) are having this facility.

Group-wise analysis shows that almost all libraries belonging to ISG are equipped with this facility. Also the majority of libraries belonging to PESG, CSG and ESG are having air-conditioned facilities.

Table 7.65 : Availability of Air-conditioned Facilities

Availability of the Air-conditioned Facilities	*Group of Libraries*					
	PESG	*CSG*	*BSG*	*ESG*	*ISG*	*Row Total*
Yes	3	4	5	7	3	22
	(60.0)	(57.1)	(50.0)	(77.8)	(100.0)	(64.7)
No	2	3	5	2	-	12
	(40.0)	(42.9)	(50.0)	(22.2)		(35.3)
Column Total	5	7	10	9	3	34
	(14.7)	(20.6)	(29.4)	(26.5)	(8.8)	(100.0)

7.6 APPLICATION OF COMPUTER AND INFORMATION TECHNOLOGY

In the present world of information, all libraries are unable to manage the information requirements of users. These information requirements can be met through resource sharing among libraries by following the networking of libraries and information centres. In the recent years, several special libraries of reputed R&D organisations in India have adopted the computer and other information technologies. These libraries are Council of Scientific and Industrial Research, Indian Council of Medical Research, Indian Council of Agricultural Research and the Defence Research and Development Organisation. Some of the other important libraries of public and private sector research organisations, such as BHEL and Steel Authority of India Limited (SAIL), and international organisations such as International Crops Research Institute for the Semi-Arid Tropics (ICRISAT) have also made useful contributions in the field of information technology.[6]

These scientific and technical libraries are among the very first to adopt the new information technologies, such as computers, CD-ROMs, online searching to national and international databases to assist in performance and operations of the library. It enhances the client access to the resources and saves the time of users.

7.6.1 Availability of Computer Facility

It is interesting to note that an overwhelming majority (85.3%) of the libraries are having computer facilities. All the libraries belonging to the two groups, i.e. PESG and ISG are having computer facilities. CSG is the only group where a relatively a higher proportion of libraries are not having computer facilities.

Table 7.66 : Availability of Computer Facility

Availability of the Computer Facility	*Group of Libraries*					
	PESG	*CSG*	*BSG*	*ESG*	*ISG*	*Row Total*
Yes	5	5	8	8	3	29
	(100.0)	(71.4)	(80.0)	(88.9)	(100.0)	(85.3)
No	-	2	2	1	-	5
		(28.6)	(20.0)	(11.1)		(14.7)
Column Total	5	7	10	9	3	34
	(14.7)	(20.6)	(29.4)	(26.5)	(8.8)	(100.0)

7.6.2 Year of Computerisation of the CSIR Libraries

Year-wise computerisation of CSIR libraries shows that the maximum number of libraries opted for computerisation during 1991-92. Some of the libraries have also started computerisation during 1985-86 and 1987-88. The majority of libraries (20.6%) have not indicated the year in which computerisation of the libraries was taken up. Group-wise analysis reveals that the majority of the libraries of BSG (40.0%) are such which started the computerisation of their libraries in 1993-94, whereas 66.7 percent libraries of ISG started computerisation of libraries during 1989-90. There are some libraries which do not have the computer facilities; these constitute 14.7 percent (Table 7.67).

Table 7.67 : Year of Computerisation of CSIR Libraries

Year of Computerisation of the Library	*Group of Libraries*					
	PESG	*CSG*	*BSG*	*ESG*	*ISG*	*Row Total*
1985-86	2 (40.0)	1 (14.3)	1 (10.0)	-	-	4 (11.8)
1987-88	1 (20.0)	1 (14.3)	1 (10.0)	1 (11.1)	-	4 (11.8)
1989-90	-	-	1 (10.0)	-	2 (66.7)	3 (8.8)
1991-92	1 (20.0)	1 (14.3)	1 (10.0)	2 (22.2)	1 (33.3)	6 (17.6)
1993-94	-	1 (14.3)	4 (40.0)	-	-	5 (14.7)
Not stated	1 (20.0)	1 (14.3)	-	5 (55.6)	-	7 (20.6)
Not applicable	-	2 (28.6)	2 (20.0)	1 (11.1)	-	5 (14.7)
Column Total	5 (14.7)	7 (20.6)	10 (29.4)	9 (26.5)	3 (8.8)	34 (100.0)

7.6.3 Computerised Activities of the CSIR Libraries

Analysis of data in Table 7.68 shows that various library activities which could be rendered using computer technology have not received due momentum in CSIR libraries. Normally, cataloguing and serial control are the two activities which are given priority when computerisation is taken up. However, in CSIR laboratories only 38.2 percent libraries have computerised this service.

It seems acquisition of documents is computerised. As a result 47.1 percent of respondents have indicated to be in the process of bringing out computerised accession list. Retrospective literature search and CAS are the other two important services which have been computerised in a good number of libraries. It shows that there is lack of integrated approach in computerisation of libraries.

Table 7.68 : Computerised Activities of CSIR Libraries

Computerised Activities	*Group of Libraries*			
	Yes	*No*	*Not Available*	*Row Total*
Accession list	16 (47.1)	13 (38.2)	5 (14.7)	34 (100.0)
Book order list	11 (32.4)	18 (52.9)	5 (14.7)	34 (100.0)
CAS	14 (41.2)	15 (44.1)	5 (14.7)	34 (100.0)
Circulation	7 (20.6)	22 (64.7)	5 (14.7)	34 (100.0)
Cataloguing	13 (38.2)	16 (47.1)	5 (14.7)	34 (100.0)
Document delivery	2 (5.9)	27 (79.4)	5 (14.7)	34 (100.0)
Retrospective literature search	16 (47.1)	13 (38.2)	5 (14.7)	34 (100.0)
Serial control	13 (38.2)	16 (47.1)	5 (14.7)	34 (100.0)
SDI service	10 (29.4)	19 (55.9)	5 (14.7)	34 (100.0)

7.6.4 Availability of the Computerised Library Services

The analysis of data (Table 7.69) regarding various computerised services reveal that some of the services are being offered in the libraries belonging to each group. But their number is limited. Computerised library services offered by majority of libraries in PESG include accession list, book order list and CAS. Whereas libraries belonging to BSG have confined their services to CAS and cataloguing. ISG is another group which offers computerised library services, such as accession list, book order list, cataloguing and serial control. However, the case of CSG is different as there is not a single service which is offered by the majority of its libraries.

Table 7.69 : Availability of Computerised Library Services

Availability of Computerised Library Services	*Group of Libraries*											
	PESG		*CSG*		*BSG*		*ESG*		*ISG*		*Not Stated*	*Row Total*
	Yes	*No*	*Yes*	*No*	*Yes*	*No*	*Yes*	*No*	*Yes*	*No*		
Accession list	3 (60.0)	2 (40.0)	1 (14.3)	4 (57.1)	4 (40.0)	4 (40.0)	5 (55.6)	3 (33.3)	3 (100.0)	-	5 (14.7)	34 (100.0)
Book order list	3 (60.0)	2 (40.0)	2 (28.6)	3 (42.9)	1 (10.0)	7 (70.0)	3 (33.3)	5 (55.6)	2 (66.7)	1 (33.3)	5 (14.7)	34 (100.0)
CAS	3 (60.0)	2 (40.0)	1 (14.3)	4 (57.1)	5 (50.0)	3 (30.0)	4 (44.4)	4 (44.4)	1 (33.3)	2 (66.7)	5 (14.7)	34 (100.0)
Circulation	2 (40.0)	3 (60.0)	1 (14.3)	4 (57.1)	1 (10.0)	7 (70.0)	3 (33.3)	5 (55.6)	-	3 (100.0)	5 (14.7)	34 (100.0)
Cataloguing	2 (40.0)	3 (60.0)	1 (14.3)	4 (57.1)	5 (50.0)	3 (30.0)	2 (22.2)	6 (66.7)	3 (100.0)	-	5 (14.7)	34 (100.0)
Document delivery	-	5 (100.0)	1 (14.3)	4 (57.1)	-	8 (80.0)	1 (11.1)	7 (77.8)	-	3 (100.0)	5 (14.7)	34 (100.0)
Retrospective literature search	4 (80.0)	1 (20.0)	3 (42.9)	2 (28.6)	2 (20.0)	6 (60.0)	6 (66.7)	2 (22.2)	1 (33.3)	2 (66.7)	5 (14.7)	34 (100.0)
Serial control	1 (20.0)	4 (80.0)	2 (28.6)	3 (42.9)	3 (30.0)	5 (50.0)	4 (44.4)	4 (44.4)	3 (100.0)	-	5 (14.7)	34 (100.0)
SDI services	3 (60.0)	2 (40.0)	2 (28.6)	3 (42.9)	1 (10.0)	7 (70.0)	3 (33.3)	5 (55.6)	1 (33.3)	2 (66.7)	5 (14.7)	34 (100.0)

7.6.5 Library Software Used in the CSIR Libraries

Since the last few years, several institutions have been engaged in the development of library software for the automation activities. Some notable institutions, such as SAIL, INSDOC, NIC, BHEL R&D, ICRISAT, Defence, Scientific Information and Documentation Centre (DESIDOC), IIT Kanpur, etc. have developed library software to achieve the objectives of system in metropolitan and other cities. CMC Ltd., a public sector computer company, has developed a software 'MAITRAYEE' which has successfully been applied in CALIBNET.[7]

Table 7.70 indicates that majority of libraries of CSIR laboratories are using the CDS/ISIS and dBase software to automate their library activities. But there are some other packages which have been put into use for the automation of library activities.

Table 7.70 : Library Software Used in CSIR Libraries

Library Software	*Group of Libraries*				
	Yes	*No*	*Not Stated*	*Not Available*	*Row Total*
CDS/ISIS	16 (47.1)	10 (29.4)	3 (8.8)	5 (14.7)	34 (100.0)
dBase	14 (41.2)	12 (35.3)	3 (8.8)	5 (14.7)	34 (100.0)
Fox base	2 (5.9)	24 (70.6)	3 (8.8)	5 (14.7)	34 (100.0)
FoxPro	4 (11.8)	22 (64.7)	3 (8.8)	5 (14.7)	34 (100.0)
LibSys	3 (8.8)	23 (67.6)	3 (8.8)	5 (14.7)	34 (100.0)
RDBMS	1 (2.9)	25 (73.5)	3 (8.8)	5 (14.7)	34 (100.0)
WILISYS	1 (2.9)	25 (73.5)	3 (8.8)	5 (14.7)	34 (100.0)
UNIFY	1 (2.9)	25 (73.5)	3 (8.8)	5 (14.7)	34 (100.0)
COBOL in-house software	1 (2.9)	25 (73.5)	3 (8.8)	5 (14.7)	34 (100.0)

7.6.6 Provision of Online Searching to National and International Databases

Table 7.71 shows that only 32.4 percent of libraries of five groups of CSIR laboratories are having facilities for online searching to national and international databases. Group-wise analysis shows that it is more of ISG than the other groups which have facilities for online searching to national and international databases.

Table 7.71 : Provision of Online Searching to National and International Databases

Online Searching to National and International Databases	*Group of Libraries*					
	PESG	*CSG*	*BSG*	*ESG*	*ISG*	*Row Total*
Yes		3	3	3	2	11
		(42.9)	(30.0)	(33.3)	(66.7)	(32.4)
No	5	4	7	6	1	23
	(100.0)	(57.1)	(70.0)	(66.7)	(33.3)	(67.6)
Column Total	5	7	10	9	3	34
	(14.7)	(20.6)	(29.4)	(26.5)	(8.8)	(100.0)

7.6.7 Availability of Telex Facility

Modern communication facilities have become inseparable part of modern libraries. Being fastest mode of communication, facilities like telex, fax and E-mail help the library staff to obtain necessary information from various sources and also to transmit the same whenever need arises. An attempt has been made to examine availability of these facilities in CSIR laboratories.

Analysis in Table 7.72 reveals that the majority of libraries, 67.6 percent, have telex facilities. Group analysis indicates that ISG is having this facility in all the libraries, whereas this is not true in the case of other groups. PESG is another group where 80.0 percent of libraries are connected with these facilities, followed by 70.0 percent of BSG libraries.

It is noted that the groups like CSG and ESG are not equipped in this respect in a similar manner.

Table 7.72 : Availability of the Telex Facility

Availability of the Telex Facility	*Group of Libraries*					
	PESG	*CSG*	*BSG*	*ESG*	*ISG*	*Row Total*
Yes	4	4	7	5	3	23
	(80.0)	(57.1)	(70.0)	(55.6)	(100.0)	(67.6)
No	1	3	3	4	-	11
	(20.0)	(42.9)	(30.0)	(44.4)		(32.4)
Column Total	5	7	10	9	3	34
	(14.7)	(20.6)	(29.4)	(26.5)	(8.8)	(100.0)

7.6.8 Availability of Fax Facility

Now-a-days when fax has become an instrument of common availability in the organisations irrespective of their size and activities, it is surprising to note that a good number of libraries belonging to CSIR are not in possession of this facility. ISG and PESG, however, are exceptions in having this facility. Situation remains almost the same in respect of other groups, barring minor variation in BSG, where compared to telex facility, only 60.0 percent of libraries have fax.

Table 7.73 : Availability of the Fax Facility

Availability of Fax Facility	*Group of Libraries*					
	PESG	*CSG*	*BSG*	*ESG*	*ISG*	*Row Total*
Yes	4	4	6	5	3	22
	(80.0)	(57.1)	(60.0)	(55.6)	(100.0)	(64.7)
No	1	3	4	4	-	12
	(20.0)	(42.9)	(40.0)	(44.4)		(35.3)
Column Total	5	7	10	9	3	34
	(14.7)	(20.6)	(29.4)	(26.5)	(8.8)	(100.0)

7.6.9 Availability of E-mail Facility

Similar pattern is evident in respect of availability of E-mail facility in CSIR libraries. This facility is available in almost all libraries of ISG, followed by 80.0 percent of PESG. A good number of ESG libraries are also having E-mail facility. There appears to be no change in respect of CSG.

Table 7.74 : Availability of E-mail Facility

Availability of the E-mail Facility	*Group of Libraries*					
	PESG	*CSG*	*BSG*	*ESG*	*ISG*	*Row Total*
Yes	4	4	6	6	3	23
	(80.0)	(57.1)	(60.0)	(66.7)	(100.0)	(67.6)
No	1	3	4	3	1	11
	(20.0)	(42.9)	(40.0)	(33.3)		(32.4)
Column Total	5	7	10	9	3	34
	(14.7)	(20.6)	(29.4)	(26.5)	(8.8)	(100.0)

7.7 PARTICIPATION OF THE CSIR LIBRARIES IN THE INFORMATION AND COMMUNICATION NETWORKS

With the increasing cost of reading material and shrinking of the library budgets, more and more emphasis is being laid on resource sharing. Emergence of various information networks could be attributed to this phenomena partially. The need for resource sharing and rationalisation of acquisition is more in scientific and technical libraries as compared to other libraries. It is, therefore, presumed that CSIR libraries have surged ahead in establishing their participation in any information network. It is surprising to note that only 55.9 percent libraries are participating in information and communication networks (Table 7.75).

Table 7.75 : Participation of CSIR Libraries in the Information and Communication Networks

Participation in the Networks	*Group of Libraries*					
	PESG	*CSG*	*BSG*	*ESG*	*ISG*	*Row Total*
Yes	2 (40.0)	3 (42.9)	6 (60.0)	5 (55.6)	3 (100.0)	19 (55.9)
No	3 (60.0)	4 (57.1)	4 (40.0)	4 (44.4)	-	15 (44.1)
Column Total	5 (14.7)	7 (20.6)	10 (29.4)	9 (26.5)	3 (8.8)	34 (100.0)

7.7.1 Information Networks

Table 7.76 shows that there are over 85 percent of libraries which are not participating in any information network which have developed at different cities. It may be pointed out that these networks have their area of operation confine to particular cities. As such it may not be possible for other libraries located at different places to participate in those information networks. That may be one of the reasons for their non-participation in information network. Only a few libraries are participating in the networks, such as DELNET, MALIBNET and HYLIBNET.

Table 7.76 : Participation of CSIR Libraries in the Information Networks

Information Networks	*Group of Libraries*					
	PESG	*CSG*	*BSG*	*ESG*	*ISG*	*Row Total*
BONET	-	-	-	-	-	-
CALIBNET	-	-	-	-	-	-
DELNET	-	-	-	1 (11.1)	2 (66.7)	3 (8.8)
MALIBNET	-	1 (14.3)	-	-	-	1 (2.9)
PUNENET	-	-	-	-	-	-
HYLIBNET	-	-	1 (10.0)	-	-	1 (2.9)

Not stated	2 (40.0)	2 (28.6)	5 (50.0)	3 (33.3)	1 (33.3)	13 (38.2)
Not applicable	3 (60.0)	4 (57.1)	4 (40.0)	5 (55.6)	-	16 (47.1)
Column Total	5 (14.7)	7 (20.6)	10 (29.4)	9 (26.5)	3 (8.8)	34 (100.0)

7.7.2 Communication Networks

Analysis of data in Table 7.77 suggests that the participation of CSIR libraries is more in communication networks as compared to information networks. A good number of libraries are participating in various communication networks. It is also observed that their participation concentrates largely on SIRNET. Participation in other communication networks is, however, marginal.

Table 7.77 : Participation of CSIR Libraries in the Communication Networks

Communication	*Group of Libraries*					
Networks	*PESG*	*CSG*	*BSG*	*ESG*	*ISG*	*Row Total*
ERNET	-	-	1 (10.0)	-	-	1 (2.9)
NICNET	-	-	-	-	-	-
SIRNET	2 (40.0)	3 (42.9)	2 (20.0)	3 (33.3)	3 (100.0)	13 (38.2)
NICNET and SIRNET	-	-	1 (10.0)	-	-	1 (2.9)
ERNET and SIRNET	-	-	1 (10.0)	1 (11.1)	-	2 (5.9)
NICNET, SIRNET and ENVIS	-	-	1 (10.0)	-	-	1 (2.9)
Not stated	-	-	-	1 (11.1)	-	1 (2.9)
Not applicable	3 (60.0)	4 (57.1)	4 (40.0)	4 (44.4)	-	15 (44.1)
Column Total	5 (14.7)	7 (20.6)	10 (29.4)	9 (26.5)	3 (8.8)	34 (100.0)

7.7.3 Participation of CSIR Libraries in the International Information Network Agencies

Table 7.78 indicates that 73.5 percent libraries are not participating in any international information network agency. Out of 34 libraries, only 9 libraries (26.5%) are participating in international information networks. Group-wise analysis indicates that only 40.0 percent libraries of BSG are participating in international information network agencies, followed by 22.2 percent libraries of ESG. Three libraries of PESG, CSG and ISG are participating in different international information network agencies.

Table 7.78 : Participation of CSIR Libraries in International Information Network Agencies

Participation in International Information Network Agencies	*Group of Libraries*					
	PESG	*CSG*	*BSG*	*ESG*	*ISG*	*Row Total*
Yes	1	1	4	2	1	9
	(20.0)	(14.3)	(40.0)	(22.2)	(33.3)	(26.5)
No	4	6	6	7	2	25
	(80.0)	(85.7)	(60.0)	(77.8)	(66.7)	(73.5)
Column Total	5	7	10	9	3	34
	(14.7)	(20.6)	(29.4)	(26.5)	(8.8)	(100.0)

7.7.3.1 Participation of CSIR Libraries in Different International Information Network Agencies

Participation of libraries in international information network agencies, Table 7.79, indicates that out of 34 libraries only 9 libraries are participating in different international information network agencies. Group-wise analysis shows that libraries belonging to ISG are participating in a number of such agencies, followed by BSG. However, the participation of ESG, CSG and PESG is confined to 3, 2 and 1 only.

Table 7.79 : Participation of CSIR Libraries in Different International Information Network Agencies

International Information Network Agencies	*Group of Libraries*					
	PESG	*CSG*	*BSG*	*ESG*	*ISG*	*Row Total*
ASFIS	1	-	-	-	-	1
BTNET	-	-	1	-	-	1
DATASTAR	-	-	-	-	1	1
DIALOG	-	1	1	2	1	5
ECHO	-	-	-	-	1	1
ESAIRS	-	-	-	-	1	1
IRPTC	-	-	1	-	-	1
NASA	-	-	-	1	-	1
STN	-	1	-	-	1	2
UUNET	-	-	1	-	-	1
Column Total	1	2	4	3	5	15

DISCUSSIONS AND CONCLUSIONS

Staff Profile

It is found that almost all libraries belonging to PESG, CSG and ISG (i.e. 34 libraries covered under the study) are headed by males. However, ESG and BSG libraries have relatively more female librarians as compared to other groups, their percentage being 33.3 and 10.0 respectively. About 38 percent of librarians of CSIR libraries are in the age group of 56 years and above, 29.4 percent in the age group of 36-45 years and 26.5 percent in the age group of 46-55 years. In ISG libraries, 66.7 percent librarians are in the age group of 36-45 years, whereas in BSG libraries, 20.0 percent librarians are in the age group of 26-35 years. The age distribution of librarians is more or less balanced in CSIR libraries with the exception of ISG, which has younger librarians in large numbers.

About 41 percent and 38.2 percent of librarians of the

CSIR libraries are graduates and postgraduates, respectively. The majority of librarians of PESG (80.0%) have postgraduate degree, whereas 57.1 percent of librarians of CSG are graduates against 50.0 percent librarians of BSG. Only 30.0 percent librarians of BSG are M.Phil., followed by 11.1 percent librarians of ESG libraries being M.Phil. While 28.6 percent librarians of CSG and 11.1 percent of ESG have Ph.D. degrees in the subject other than Library and Information Science.

The study identifies that 38.2 percent librarians of CSIR libraries have MLISc degree, whereas 26.5 percent are AIS/ADRTC. Only 20.0 percent librarians of PESG have Ph.D. degree and another 14.7 percent hold BLISc degree. There are 14.3 percent librarians in CSG and 11.1 percent in ESG who hold Diploma and CLISc respectively. Thus, the librarians in CSIR libraries are mostly professionally qualified with adequate knowledge and skills.

Staffing Pattern

Five groups of CSIR libraries are managed by majority of professionals (50.2%). On the other hand, only 10.0 percent staff is semi-professional and about 40 percent library staff is non-professional. CSG libraries have 30.0 percent professionals, followed by 24.9 percent in BSG libraries. Only ESG has 51.0 percent of non-professionals against 46.0 percent professionals. It is interesting to note that ISG libraries have only 44.0 percent professional staff.

Growth and Development

Around 47 percent of libraries were established along with their laboratories between 1951-60, whereas 20.6 percent libraries were established with their laboratories before 1950. Another 2.9 percent libraries with laboratories were established in 1991. It is interesting to note that during 1961-70, 11.8 percent libraries were established against 17.6 percent laboratories which was followed all through the years.

Budget and Expenditure Pattern

About 24 percent libraries had the budget of Rs.10-15

lakh for the year 1992-93. Another 20.6 percent libraries had an annual budget of Rs.15-20 lakh, whereas 17.6 percent libraries had a budget of Rs.20-30 lakh, and Rs.30-50 lakh respectively. The budget of 5.9 percent libraries ranged between Rs.50 and Rs.65 lakh for the year 1992-93. The major portion of the budget of these libraries was spent on subscription to periodicals. About 27 percent libraries had paid Rs.5-10 lakh towards subscription to journals in 1992-93, whereas an equal proportion of libraries (20.6%) had each spent an amount of Rs.10-15 lakh, Rs.15-20 lakh and Rs.20-30 lakh on the subscription to journals during 1992-93. In 1993-94, 32.3 percent libraries were spending Rs.10-20 lakh and 26.5 percent of the libraries were spending Rs.30-50 lakh on subscription to journals.

About 44 percent libraries have indicated expenditure of Rs.2-5 lakh on the acquisition of books in 1992-93, whereas 41.2 percent of the libraries spent the same amount on the acquisition of books in 1993-94. On the other hand, 20.6 percent libraries spent Rs.1 lakh and Rs.1-2 lakh for the acquisition of books in 1992-93.

About 68 percent libraries of the CSIR laboratories indicated that the budget allocation to be inadequate for the acquisition of reading material. Only 23.5 percent of the respondents of CSIR libraries were satisfied with their present budget. As such, it is desirable that the annual budget wherever necessary should be increased in the light of the fact that prices of the documents are increasing day by day. About 24 percent of respondents have desired that the present budget of their libraries need to be enhanced by 36-50 percent.

In regards to acquisition of non-print material, libraries of PESG (20.0%), CSG (14.3%) and BSG (10.0%) spent up to Rs.27-60 thousand out of their budget on non-print material and book binding in 1992-93. In 1993-94, only 14.3 percent libraries of CSG spent Rs.40-50 thousand on the non-print material. During interview, it was revealed that most of these libraries do not acquire electronic material because of the absence of trained staff to handle them for the use of users. It is, therefore, desirable that qualified and trained staff should be appointed so that electronic material could be acquired and used. Alternatively, the staff members may be given adequate training to handle the same. There is also inadequacy of budget provision for such material.

Library Collection

The collection of CSIR libraries as indicated in five groups of laboratories is follows:

1. The collection of majority of libraries meets the users' requirements moderately. Only 38.2 percent libraries expressed their collection of books to be meeting their requirements fully. It has been seen that 28.6 percent of the libraries were partially fulfilling users' needs.
2. The library collection of bound volumes of periodicals has been found to be adequate to fully meet users' needs.
3. All CSIR libraries are partially satisfied with the non-book material available in their libraries. ESG is an exception where 55.6 percent libraries are meeting the requirements of users moderately.
4. In about 56 percent of the libraries of CSIR laboratories, the collection of theses/dissertations, research/project reports, grey literature, conference proceedings and pamphlets and reprints, partially meet the requirements of their users. Only 41.2 percent of libraries stated that such a collection moderately satisfied the need of their users. It is surprising to note that all libraries of ISG are partially satisfied with the collection of such material. About 56 percent of libraries of ESG and 50.0 percent of libraries of BSG are moderately satisfied with such collection.
5. About 56 percent of the libraries are moderately satisfied with the collection of standards, specifications and patents. Whereas 38.3 percent of the libraries stated that such collection is partially satisfying the requirements of their users. The majority of the libraries of CSG (71.4%) marked the collection of standards,

specifications and patents as moderately satisfying the needs of their users.

Non-Book Material

Availability of non-book material in CSIR libraries is reported to be inadequate. Only microfilms/microfiches are available in these libraries. About 67 percent of libraries of ISG have online databases whereas CD-ROM databases are available in 60.0 percent of libraries of PESG. The majority of libraries of all groups indicate possession of maps/atlases. The picture, transparencies, photos, are not available. Almost all libraries of PESG, CSG and ISG indicated non-availability of pictures/transparencies, photos. Other collection of audio-visual cassettes, slides, etc. is indicated as totally negligible by CSG and ISG libraries.

Subscription to Indian and Foreign Journals

About 35 percent libraries are subscribing to 101-200 journals, while 32.4 percent libraries are subscribing to 201-300 Indian and foreign journals. Another 5.9 percent libraries are subscribing to 100 journals. Sixty percent libraries of PESG are subscribing to 201-300 journals. Subscription to periodicals varies in CSIR libraries. There are 33.3 percent libraries in ISG which are subscribing to 801-3200 Indian and foreign journals.

About 59 percent libraries are subscribing up to 50 Indian journals in different areas of specialisation. There are 26.5 percent of the libraries which are subscribing to 51-100 Indian journals and 33.3 percent libraries of ISG are subscribing to 201-850 Indian journals. The majority of libraries (70.6%) are receiving up to 50 journals on gift and exchange basis. ISG is an exception, receiving as many as 301-850 Indian journals on gift and exchange basis. About 38 percent of libraries are subscribing to 51-100 foreign journals whereas 23.5 percent of libraries are subscribing to 101-150 foreign journals. Only BSG libraries (10.0%) are receiving 301-350 foreign journals. About 44 percent libraries receive up to 25 foreign journals on gift and exchange basis while 20.6

percent libraries are such which are receiving 26-50 foreign journals on gift and exchange basis.

About 47 percent of libraries are moderately satisfied with the subscription to Indian journals. There are 38.2 percent libraries which are fully satisfied with the subscription of Indian journals. The majority of libraries of ESG (66.7%) and CSG (57.1%) indicated moderate satisfaction with these journals.

About 56 percent of the libraries are moderately satisfied with the subscription to foreign journals. The majority of libraries of ESG (77.8%), CSG (71.4%) and PESG (60.0%) are moderately satisfied with the quantity of foreign journals which fulfill the requirements of their libraries. On the other hand, 66.7 percent libraries of !SG and 60.0 percent of BSG have shown their full satisfaction with the subscription to these journals.

Cataloguing and Classification Techniques

UDC is being used by 67.6 percent of scientific and technical libraries of CSIR, whereas 14.7 percent of libraries are using CC and another 14.7 percent DDC schemes to classify documents for shelve arrangements. About 89 percent libraries in ESG are following the UDC scheme in their libraries. The majority of libraries (76.5%) have the entire catalogue of documents whereas 23.5 percent libraries have maintained partial catalogue. About 38.2 percent libraries are following dictionary catalogue whereas 35.3 percent libraries maintain classified catalogue. All libraries of ISG have maintained classified catalogue whereas 90.0 percent libraries of BSG have dictionary catalogue.

The AACR-2 is used for cataloguing in 44.1 percent of libraries. An equal number of libraries (14.7%) are following AACR-1, CCC-5 and ALA catalogue code. For the circulation of documents, an equal proportion of libraries (32.4%) are following Newark and Browne circulation systems. About 21 percent of libraries are using their own system for circulation whereas 5.9 percent of libraries have the computerised circulation system.

Facilities and Services

More than 70.6 percent libraries are providing book reservation and resource sharing facility to users whereas inter library loan service is offered by 91.2 percent libraries. Majority of CSIR libraries (88.2%) of all groups feel the need for users' education. Similar percentage of libraries (85.3%) are rendering bibliographic services on demand and literature search whereas 94.1 percent libraries are providing list of journals subscribed/ discontinued, and 82.4 percent are bringing out list of new additions. SDI services are offered by only 61.8 percent libraries whereas contents of periodicals are rendered by 52.9 percent of the libraries. Digest of scientific, technical and industrial information service is offered by 17.6 percent of the libraries. Only 64.7 percent libraries are providing translation services in English, Russian, French, Japanese, German, Spanish and Chinese. All libraries of CSIR laboratories are having photocopying services. There are 64.7 percent of libraries which are air-conditioned whereas 35.7 percent libraries do not have such facility.

Information and Communication Technology Services

About 85 percent libraries are having computer facility but computerized services are not offered by most of these libraries. Another 47.1 percent libraries are using CDS/ISIS package whereas only 8.8 percent libraries are using LibSys package for library operations and other services.

About 32.4 percent libraries are having the facility for online searching to national and international databases. Majority of CSIR libraries (65%) have indicated the availability of telex, fax and e-mail facilities. To strengthen the resource sharing activities among libraries, 55.9 percent libraries are participating in information and communication networks. Another 73.5 percent libraries are not participating in any international information network. Only 26.5 percent libraries are participating in international information networks to offer services to scientists. It is surprising to note that such a large network of national laboratories is not harnessing the optimum use of information and communication technology.

In this chapter, data collected from 34 libraries in terms of budget, collection, services, use of ICT and participation in national and international networks have been analyzed. The CSIR libraries and information centres are playing a significant role in research and development work of its laboratories. In any organization, the performance of the library depends to a large extent on quality and quantity of available resources, services and quality of professional and other staff. The collection of grey literature, theses/dissertations, research and project reports, government documents, conference proceedings, and standards, specifications and patents and non-book material (audio-video cassettes, CD-ROM databases and online databases) is poor in these libraries. Authorities must pay attention towards improvement of the collection of these libraries, which is the necessary condition for making a library effective. Necessary interventions are required to augment use of ICT for storing, processing, filtering, generating, sharing and disseminating online information and services to scientists and engineers across the CSIR laboratories. All libraries of multidisciplinary network of CSIR laboratories should subscribe online databases and/or join the consortia based subscription of e-journals to provide round-the-clock access to scientists, engineers and technologists.

REFERENCES

1. Ifidon, Sam E. The evaluation of performance. *Libri*, 36(3), 1986, 231.
2. Clapp, V. W. and Jordan, R. T. Quantitative criteria for adequacy of academic library collection. *College and Research Libraries*, 26(5), 1965, 371-380.
3. Ifidon, S. E. A quantitative assessment of adequacy of Nigerian University library collections in the humanities and the social sciences in relation to postgraduate research. Ph. D. Thesis. University of Ibadan, 1977. 286p.
4. Ifidon, *op.cit*, p.227.
5. Ranganathan, S. R. Reference service. 2nd ed. Bombay: Asia Publishing House, 1961. P.53.

6. Haravu, L. J. Library automation and networking in India - An overview of recent developments. *Annals of Library Science and Documentation*, 40(1), 1993, 32-40.

7. *Ibid.*, p.33.

8

Perceptions of Users About Scientific and Technical Libraries

There are many yardsticks that could be applied to evaluate the efficiency of the library operation in terms of services and also in terms of infrastructure facility provided by the library to the user satisfaction. In our context, users' opinion has been taken up as the basis to analyse strengths and weaknesses of library services and facilities, etc. The present study has been conducted using questionnaire. It was distributed to four types of users namely: Scientist A&B, Scientist C, Senior Scientist and research scholars working in CSIR laboratories. Responses thus received have been analysed in the proceeding pages.

8.1 BACKGROUND INFORMATION

This section deals with information about users of the CSIR libraries which include sex, position, scientist category, highest level of qualifications, area of specialisation, membership of associations, number of conferences attended at national and International level, and number of contributions of research papers and articles made during the last five years.

8.1.1 Distribution of Respondents - Laboratory-Wise

About 500 questionnaires were distributed among scientists and research scholars of the five groups of CSIR laboratories. About 380 filled-in questionnaires were received back. Since an overwhelming majority of respondents of BSG (34.5%) responded to our questionnaires, they emerged as the largest group followed by ESG. Out of the total responses, the percentage of respondents belonging to CSG, PESG and ISG appears to be comparatively low. But in view of the total number of users in these groups, the response rate is significant enough to form the basis for analysis.

Table 8.1 : Distribution of Respondents, Laboratory-Wise

Sr. No.	*Group of CSIR Laboratories*	*Number of Respondents*	*Percentage*
1.	PESG	53	13.9
2.	CSG	57	15.0
3.	BSG	131	34.5
4.	ESG	94	24.7
5.	ISG	45	11.8
Total		380	100.0

8.1.2 Sex-Wise Distribution

Sex-wise distribution of respondents among the CSIR libraries shows predominance of males in all the groups. Similar is the trend in academic libraries too. Singh in his study reported predominance of male professionals (83.1%) over female professionals (16.9%) in university libraries in UP, MP, Punjab and Haryana.[1] Male users constitute over ninety percent of respondents in PESG, CSG and ESG. In other groups also, male users constitute majority but the presence of female users is also significant. The female users constitute 21.4 percent and 33.3 percent in BSG and ISG respectively.

Table 8.2 : Sex-Wise Distribution

Group of Laboratories	*Sex*		
	Male	*Female*	*Row Total*
PESG	51 (96.2)	2 (3.8)	53 (13.9)
CSG	55 (96.5)	2 (3.5)	57 (15.0)
BSG	103 (78.6)	28 (21.4)	131 (34.5)

ESG	93 (98.9)	1 (1.1)	94 (24.7)
ISG	30 (66.7)	15 (33.3)	45 (11.8)
Total Column	332 (87.4)	48 (12.6)	380 (100.0)

8.1.3 Distribution of Respondents

In order to find out the composition of respondents, data regarding their designation have been given in Table 8.3. Data reveals that the group of respondents is largely composed of scientists only. Research scholars figure marginally. Even group-wise representation also does not reveal any variation. Each group is represented largely by scientists.

Table 8.3 : Distribution of Respondents, Designation-Wise

Group of Laboratories	*Research Scholars*	*Scientists*	*Row Total*
PESG	1 (1.9)	52 (98.1)	53 (13.9)
CSG	2 (3.5)	55 (96.5)	57 (15.0)
.BSG	17 (13.0)	114 (87.0)	131 (34.5)
ESG	-	94 (100.0)	94 (24.7)
ISG	1 (2.2)	44 (97.8)	45 (11.8)
Total Column	21 (5.5)	359 (94.5)	380 (100.0)

8.1.4 Position-Wise Distribution of Scientists

Table 8.4 depicts the position-wise distribution of respondents. The group of respondents constitutes 48.4 percent of senior scientists, and scientists C 32.4 percent. A look at the table reveals similar distribution of respondents, particularly senior scientists and scientists C in each group except ISG where the majority is of scientists A&B. But in other groups, majority of respondents are the senior scientists. The presence of scientists A&B and research scholars is visible in each group barring exception but not very significant.

Table 8.4 : Position-Wise Distribution of Scientists

Group of Laboratories	*Scientist A&B*	*Scientist C*	*Senior Scientists*	*Research Scholars*	*Row Total*
PESG	6	14	32	1	53
	(11.3)	(26.4)	(60.4)	(1.9)	(13.9)
CSG	-	19	36	2	57
		(33.3)	(63.2)	(3.5)	(15.0)
BSG	7	40	67	17	131
	(5.3)	(30.5)	(51.1)	(13.0)	(34.5)
ESG	15	35	44	-	94
	(16.0)	(37.2)	(46.8)		(24.7)
ISG	24	15	5	1	45
	(53.3)	(33.3)	(11.1)	(2.2)	(11.8)
Total Column	52	123	184	21	380
	(13.7)	(32.4)	(48.4)	(5.5)	(100.0)

8.1.5 Educational Background of the Respondents

Table 8.5 analyses the data regarding levels of qualification possessed by the respondents of CSIR libraries. It reveals that over 75 percent of the respondents hold Ph.D. degree and the rest are M.Sc. Those engaged in pursuance of Post Doctoral Fellowship are only a few. Group-wise analysis also indicates that except ISG majority of users in all the groups hold Ph.D. degree. Though those holding Ph.D. degree are in majority in ISG as well, their percentage is much less as compared to other groups. 46.7 percent respondents of ISG are just M.Sc. BSG is the only exception where a few respondents are engaged in Post-Doctoral Fellowship.

Table 8.5 : Educational Level of the Respondents

Group of Laboratories	*M.Sc.*	*Ph.D.*	*Post-doctoral Fellow*	*Row Total*
PESG	9	44	-	53
	(17.0)	(83.0)		(13.9)
CSG	6	51	-	57
	(10.5)	(89.5)		(15.0)
BSG	23	105	3	131
	(17.6)	(80.2)	(2.3)	(34.5)
ESG	27	67	-	94
	(28.7)	(71.3)		(24.7)
ISG	21	24	-	45
	(46.7)	(53.3)		(11.8)
Column Total	86	291	3	380
	(22.6)	(76.6)	(.8)	(100.0)

8.1.6 Area of Specialisation of the Respondents

Table 8.6 reveals that majority of respondents of CSG (89.5%) are working in the area of chemistry and chemical technology, whereas 25.2 percent respondents of BSG are also engaged in the field of chemistry and chemical technology. This indicates that a large number of respondents are working in the area of chemistry and chemical technology. But it does not mean that there is absence of other areas of specialisation. 44.7 percent respondents of ESG and 37.7 percent respondents of PESG have their specialisation in engineering science.

On the other hand, 35.9 percent respondents of BSG are those who are working in the biological sciences whereas 27.5 percent respondents of BSG have their specialisation in medical sciences. 25.2 percent respondents of BSG and 19.1 percent respondents of ESG are in the areas of chemistry and chemical technology while 22.6 percent respondents of PESG have shown their specialisation in the field of physical sciences. A little over 18 percent respondents of PESG and ESG have their specialisation in the fields of earth sciences and physical sciences.

It is apparent from the analysis that 28.9 percent respondents of CSIR libraries belong to chemistry and chemical technology whereas 17.1 percent respondents are from the engineering sciences. Biological sciences and information science and technology areas comprise 13.4 percent and 12.4 percent of respondents respectively.

Table 8.6 : Area of Specialisation of the Respondents

Area of Specialisation	*Group of Laboratories*					
	PESG	*CSG*	*BSG*	*ESG*	*ISG*	*Row Total*
Agricultural Sciences	-	-	10 (7.6)	-	-	10 (2.6)
Biological Sciences	2 (3.8)	2 (3.5)	47 (35.9)	-	-	51 (13.4)
Chemistry and Chemical Technology	8 (15.1)	51 (89.5)	33 (25.2)	18 (19.1)	-	110 (28.9)
Earth Sciences	10 (18.9)	-	-	8 (8.5)	-	18 (4.7)
Engineering Sciences	20 (37.7)	3 (5.3)	-	42 (44.7)	-	65 (17.1)
Environmental Sciences	1 (1.9)	1 (1.8)	4 (3.1)	8 (8.5)	-	14 (3.7)
Information Science and Technology	-	-	1 (.8)	1 (1.1)	45 (100.0)	47 (12.4)
Medical Sciences	-	-	36 (27.5)	-	-	36 (9.5)
Physical Sciences	12 (22.6)	-	-	17 (18.1)	-	29 (7.6)
Column Total	53 (13.9)	57 (15.0)	131 (34.5)	94 (24.7)	45 (11.8)	380 (100.0)

8.1.7 Membership of Associations

In order to find out the involvement of scientists in professional activities beyond their organisations, the respondents of CSIR laboratories were asked to indicate the membership of associations, i.e., state, national and international professional bodies, societies and associations. Table 8.7 indicates that majority of respondents, 82.9 percent, have the membership of one or the other professional associations whereas 17.1 percent are not member of any of these associations, etc.

Group-wise analysis of respondents regarding membership of professional associations indicates that an overwhelming majority of respondents across the groups have membership of profssional association. However, there is marginal variation in response rate.

Table 8.7 : Membership of Associations

Group of Laboratories	*Response*		
	Yes	*No*	*Row Total*
PESG	47 (88.7)	6 (11.3)	53 (13.9)
CSG	49 (86.0)	8 (14.0)	57 (15.0)
BSG	103 (78.6)	28 (21.4)	131 (34.5)
ESG	85 (90.4)	9 (9.6)	94 (24.7)
ISG	31 (68.9)	14 (31.1)	45 (11.8)
Total Column	315 (82.9)	65 (17.1)	380 (100.0)

8.1.7.1 Membership of State Associations

Data collected from the users of CSIR libraries regarding membership of state level professional associations as given in

Table 8.8 reveals that majority of respondents (78.4%) are not member of any state level professional association. Only 17.4 percent respondents are those who are member of a state level professional association. There are only a few respondents with membership of 2 to 3 professional associations.

On the other hand, group-wise analysis of membership of state professional associations indicates that over 80 percent respondents of BSG and PESG are not member of any professional body. Similarly, 77.8 percent respondents of ISG also do not have the membership. The case of CSG and ESG is also the same.

The membership of one professional association is shown by 24.6 percent respondents of CSG followed by ESG 22.3 percent. 17.8 percent respondents of ISG and 17.0 percent respondents of PESG have membership of one professional association of state level. Also a little over 4 percent respondents of BSG, ISG and ESG have membership of 2 associations.

It is clear from the above analysis that scientists working in CSIR laboratories are not interested in state level associations. May be that the state associations are not as functional as they should be to attract scientists, etc.

Table 8.8 : Membership of State Associations

Group of Laboratories	*Membership of State Associations*				
	0	*1*	*2*	*3*	*Row Total*
PESG	43 (81.1)	9 (17.0)	1 (1.9)	-	53 (13.9)
CSG	42 (73.7)	14 (24.6)	-	1 (1.8)	57 (15.0)
BSG	109 (83.2)	14 (10.7)	7 (5.3)	1 (.8)	131 (34.5)
ESG	69 (73.4)	21 (22.3)	4 (4.3)	-	94 (24.7)
ISG	35 (77.8)	8 (17.8)	2 (4.4)	-	45 (11.8)
Column Total	298 (78.4)	66 (17.4)	14 (3.7)	2 (.5)	380 (100.0)

8.1.7.2 Membership of National Associations

Respondents of CSIR libraries were (Table 8.9) asked to indicate their membership of professional bodies/associations. The majority of respondents, 29.2 percent, were members of two associations of national level, whereas 24.7 percent respondents indicated that they were members of one association only. There are also 20.3 percent respondents who are not member of any national association. At the same time, there are 16.3 percent of respondents who are associated with three associations.

Group-wise analysis suggests that the majority of respondents of PESG (41.5%), CSG (33.3%) and ESG (29.8%) are members of two national associations, whereas the majority of respondents belonging to BSG (25.2%) and ISG (31.1%) are associated with one association only. At the same time there are a few respondents in each group who have membership of 3-5 associations. It shows that the respondents are actively involved in sharing their views and ideas. In fact, information on membership of associations is a kind of index of maturity of the profession. These are the right platforms for the members concerned to deliberate upon various contemporary issues.

Table 8.9 : Membership of National Associations

Group of	*Membership of National Associations*						
Laboratories	*0*	*1*	*2*	*3*	*4*	*5*	*Row Total*
PESG	9 (17.0)	10 (18.9)	22 (41.5)	7 (13.2)	3 (5.7)	2 (3.8)	53 (13.9)
CSG	11 (19.3)	16 (28.1)	19 (33.3)	9 (15.8)	2 (3.5)	-	57 (15.0)
BSG	31 (23.7)	33 (25.2)	30 (22.9)	19 (14.5)	13 (9.9)	5 (3.8)	131 (34.5)
ESG	10 (10.6)	21 (22.3)	28 (29.8)	25 (26.6)	5 (5.3)	5 (5.3)	94 (24.7)
ISG	16 (35.6)	14 (31.1)	12 (26.7)	2 (4.4)	1 (2.2)	-	45 (11.8)
Column Total	77 (20.3)	94 (24.7)	111 (29.2)	62 (16.3)	24 (6.3)	12 (3.2)	380 (100.0)

8.1.7.3 Membership of International Associations

Respondents response on membership of international associations is presented in Table 8.10. It reveals that majority of them (73.2%) do not have membership of any international association. Only 20.5 percent respondents are member of one international association followed by 5.5 percent who are member of two international associations. Group-wise analysis of data shows that 91.1 percent respondents of ISG are those who are not member of any international association followed by BSG (72.5%) and ESG (72.3%). A good number of respondents in each group, except ISG, are member of international association. It may be mentioned that membership fee of international associations is often very high and beyond the means of individuals. In respect of subscribers who have obtained membership of international associations, it is difficult to explain the source of fund to pay the subscriptions. However, in many such cases institutional support has helped in obtaining such membership.

Table 8.10 : Membership of International Associations

Group of	*Membership of International Associations*				
Laboratories	*0*	*1*	*2*	*3*	*Row Total*
PESG	35	15	2	1	53
	(66.0)	(28.3)	(3.8)	(1.9)	(13.9)
CSG	39	16	2	-	57
	(68.4)	(28.1)	(3.5)		(15.0)
BSG	95	21	13	2	131
	(72.5)	(16.0)	(9.9)	(1.5)	(34.5)
ESG	68	23	3	-	94
	(72.3)	(24.5)	(3.2)		(24.7)
ISG	41	3	1	-	45
	(91.1)	(6.7)	(2.2)		(11.8)
Column Total	278	78	21	3	380
	(73.2)	(20.5)	(5.5)	(.8)	(100.0)

8.1.8 Number of National Conferences Attended During the Last Five Years

Data regarding number of national conferences attended during the last five years (Table 8.11) reveals that 42.1 percent respondents have attended 1-3 national conferences during the last five years (1990-94), and 32.1 percent respondents have attended 4-6 conferences of national level during these years. There are also 10.0 percent of respondents who have attended 7-9 conferences of national level. Only 9.2 percent respondents are those who did not attend any conference in the last five years. Only a few number of respondents had visited more than 10 national conferences.

Group-wise analysis reveals that majority of respondents of ISG (46.7%), BSG (46.6%) and ESG (44.7%) attended 1-3 national conferences during the last five years. A minor variation is reported in the respondents of PESG and CSG who participated in 1-3 national conferences; these comprise 34.0 percent and 31.6 percent respectively. On the other hand, respondents of CSG (43.9%) are those who participated in 4-6 conferences of national level, followed by PESG (37.7%) and ESG (35.1%) respondents. A little over 24 percent of respondents of BSG and ISG also reported that they have attended 4-6 national conferences during last five years. There are also such respondents from ISG (22.2%) and BSG (11.5%) who did not attend any national conference during the last five years. However, other groups contain only a few respondents who did not visit any national conference. Those who attended 7-9 conferences of national level constituted 20.8 percent respondents of PESG, followed by 14.0 percent of CSG.

It is noticed from the above analysis that majority of respondents attended only 1-3 and 4-6 national level conferences during the last five years.

Table 8.11 : Number of National Conferences Attended During the Last Five Years

Number of National Conferences Attended	*Group of Laboratories*					
	PESG	*CSG*	*BSG*	*ESG*	*ISG*	*Row Total*
0	1	2	15	7	10	35
	(1.9)	(3.5)	(11.5)	(7.4)	(22.2)	(9.2)
1 – 3	18	18	61	42	21	160
	(34.0)	(31.6)	(46.6)	(44.7)	(46.7)	(42.1)
4 – 6	20	25	33	33	11	122
	(37.7)	(43.9)	(25.2)	(35.1)	(24.4)	(32.1)
7 – 9	11	8	8	9	2	38
	(20.8)	(14.0)	(6.1)	(9.6)	(4.4)	(10.0)
10 & above	3	4	14	3	1	25
	(5.7)	(7.0)	(10.7)	(3.2)	(2.2)	(6.6)
Column Total	53	57	131	94	45	380
	(13.9)	(15.0)	(34.5)	(24.7)	(11.8)	(100.0)

8.1.8.1 Number of International Conferences Attended During the Last Five Years

The analysis of data on international conferences attended by the respondents (Table 8.12) during the last five years (1990-94) shows that 50.0 percent of the respondents did not participate in any international conference. Only 43.2 percent of respondents attended 1-3 international conferences during these years. Respondents attending 4-6 international conferences, however, constituted only 6.8 percent respondents.

Group-wise analysis reveals that except PESG, more than half of the respondents of all groups did not attend any international conference in the last five years. Again among those who participated in international conferences, majority was of those who attended 1-3 conferences. A few respondents, however, had the opportunity to attend 4-6 conferences. Group-wise analysis does not indicate much variation. PESG is the only exception where a comparatively larger proportion of respondents had participated in conferences, whereas a majority of respondents in other groups had not participated in any conference. And those who participated in conferences from these groups constitute 40-45 percent.

It is manifested from the above analysis that half of the respondents did not attend any international conference. The reasons may be the lack of financial assistance.

Table 8.12 : Number of International Conferences Attended During the Last Five Years

Number of International Conferences Attended	*Group of Laboratories*					
	PESG	*CSG*	*BSG*	*ESG*	*ISG*	*Row Total*
0	18 (34.0)	29 (50.9)	71 (54.2)	48 (51.1)	24 (53.3)	190 (50.0)
1 – 3	27 (50.9)	26 (45.6)	53 (40.5)	38 (40.4)	20 (44.4)	164 (43.2)
4 – 6	8 (15.1)	2 (3.5)	7 (5.3)	8 (8.5)	1 (2.2)	26 (6.8)
7 – 9	-	-	-	-	-	-
10 & above	-	-	-	-	-	-
Column Total	53 (13.9)	57 (15.0)	131 (34.5)	94 (24.7)	45 (11.8)	380 (100.0)

8.1.9 Papers and Articles Published

It is a common practice all over the world that the results of the researches carried out by the scientists, technologists and research scholars are published through journals etc. for wider use and appreciation. During 1991-2000, India's contribution towards research papers in world publications were 500575 that is 2.1 percent in the areas of Agricultural, Biological Sciences, Chemical Sciences, Earth Sciences, Engineering, Mathematics, Medical Sciences and Physical Sciences whereas rest of the world's contribution is 24450206 which is 97.9 percent.[2]

To fulfil the information needs of the research work, the research workers mostly depend upon the libraries of their parent organisation and other scientific and technical libraries of other research organisations to get relevant information for research works. In doing research work and writing papers for any conference/seminar or journal, the library plays an important role in supporting the research activities. In this context, significance of libraries cannot be ignored. An analysis of data regarding the contribution made by the respondents of CSIR libraries during the last five years (1990-94) is analysed in Table 8.13.

Data collected from the respondents, Table 8.13, reveals that almost all the respondents of PESG and CSG contributed papers in the conferences and research articles to the journals. Even a little over 95 percent of respondents of BSG and ESG also had made contributions. It is clear that an overwhelming majority of respondents had contributed to journals, etc.

Table 8.13 : Contribution of Respondents During the Last Five Years

Group of Laboratories	*Responses*		*Row Total*
	Yes	*No*	
PESG	53	-	53
	(100.0)		(13.9)
CSG	57	-	57
	(100.0)		(15.0)
BSG	127	4	131
	(96.9)	(3.1)	(34.5)
ESG	90	4	94
	(95.7)	(4.3)	(24.7)
ISG	37	8	45
	(82.2)	(17.8)	(11.8)
Column Total	364	16	380
	(95.8)	(4.2)	(100.0)

8.1.9.1 *Number of Contributions During the Last Five Years*

The analysis of data in Table 8.14 presents that majority of respondents, 31.1 percent, who had 6-10 articles to their credit stands at the top among all groups of CSIR Laboratories. A little variation is found in the percentage of respondents who had 1-5 and 11-20 contributions during the last five years; they constitute 26.8 percent and 25.3 percent respectively. Even 9.2 percent respondents are such who had 21-30 papers to their credit. Whereas 4.2 percent respondents from BSG, ESG and ISG, had not contributed even single paper in last five years. But there are also a few respondents in all groups of CSIR laboratories, who had 31-40, 41-50 and 51 and above contributions to their credit during the last five years.

Institution-wise analysis of data shows that an impressive percentage of respondents of ISG, i.e., 48.9 percent, have made contributions between 1 to 5 during the last five years. An equal proportion of respondents of BSG, 26.7 percent, contributed 1-5 and 11-20 contributions in the form of articles and papers in conference and seminar. A little over 24 percent respondents of CSG and ESG also reported their contributions numbering 1-5. Even 15.1 percent respondents of PESG also had 1-5 contributions during these years.

On the other hand, 37.7 percent respondents of PESG are those who had contributed 11-20 papers in the last five years, and 28.1 percent respondents of CSG and 26.7 percent of BSG, both have 11-20 papers to their credit.

The highest percentage of respondents were of ESG (37.2%) and PESG (34.0%) who had contributed 6-10 papers/articles in the last five years, followed by 32.8 percent of BSG. The percentage of 22.2 percent respondents of ISG also indicated to have made 6-10 contributions in the last five years. An equal proportion of respondents of CSG (21.1%) were found to have contributed 6-10 and 21-30 papers during the last five years. Except CSG, only a few respondents have made contribution of 21-30 papers.

Let us now have a look at the ISG response. We find that 17.8 percent of their respondents have not made any contribution during the last five years. Also we find that 4.3

percent of ESG respondents and 3.1 percent of BSG respondents having not made any contribution.

Data in regard to CSIR laboratories show that a few members of these groups have made 31-40 and 41-50 contributions in all forms during the last five years.

Table 8.14 : Number of Contributions During the Last Five Years

Number of Contributions	*Group of Laboratories*					
	PESG	*CSG*	*BSG*	*ESG*	*ISG*	*Row Total*
0	-	-	4	4	84	16
			(3.1)	(4.3)	(17.8)	(4.2)
1 – 5	8	14	35	23	22	102
	(15.1)	(24.6)	(26.7)	(24.5)	(48.9)	(26.8)
6-10	18	12	43	35	10	118
	(34.0)	(21.1)	(32.8)	(37.2)	(22.2)	(31.1)
11-20	20	16	35	22	3	96
	(37.7)	(28.1)	(26.7)	(23.4)	(6.7)	(25.3)
21-30	5	12	10	7	1	35
	(9.4)	(21.1)	(7.6)	(7.4)	(2.2)	(9.2)
31-40	1	1	1	2	-	5
	(1.9)	(1.8)	(.8)	(2.1)		(1.3)
41-50	1	-	3	-	1	5
	(1.9)		(2.3)		(2.2)	(1.3)
51 +	-	2	-	1	-	3
		(3.5)		(1.1)		(.8)

8.1.10 Purpose of Using Library

The scientists, specialists, technical staff and researchers use the libraries and their resources for different purposes to achieve the predetermined goals and objectives. These libraries and information centres are mostly used by the scientists, researchers and technical personnel for various reasons. They are requested to indicate the purpose of their usage of the libraries.

The analysis of Table 8.15 shows that 95.5 percent respondents of different disciplines used the library for research purposes whereas 90.3 percent respondents used the library for writing papers. 36.6 percent respondents were using the library for compilation of bibliographies while only 20.5 percent respondents used the library for book writing. As the library is the repository of the information particularly related to current research and developments (R&D), 38.7 percent respondents used the library to keep themselves abreast of the latest developments in the R&D fields in their respective areas and interests.

The data obtained from the users to ascertain the purposes of using the libraries reveals that the maximum use of the library is made for research purposes followed by writing papers and keeping abreast of the latest R&Ds.

Table 8.15 : Purpose of Using the Library

Purpose of Using the Library	*Responses*		
	Yes	*No*	*Total*
Research	363 (95.5)	17 (4.5)	380 (100.0)
Writing papers	343 (90.3)	37 (9.7)	380 (100.0)
Book writing	78 (20.5)	302 (79.5)	380 (100.0)
Preparation of bibliography	139 (36.6)	241 (63.4)	380 (100.0)
To keep track of latest R&Ds	147 (38.7)	233 (61.3)	380 (100.0)

8.1.10.1 Purpose of Using the Library by Group of Laboratories

The analysis of data (Table 8.16) according to group of laboratories shows that maximum use of the libraries and their resources is made only for research and writing papers by the users belonging to all the five groups of the laboratories of CSIR.

The responses in this regard indicate that the most of the respondents across the groups make use of the library for research purposes to the maximum extent. Interestingly all the respondents in the CSG used the library for research purposes. Excepting minor variation, over 95 percent respondents belonging to other groups have also responded in favour of research. However, ISG emerged as an exception where only 75.6 percent of respondents reported to have made use of the library for research purposes.

The use of the libraries for writing papers have been indicated by an overwhelming majority of respondents irrespective of group affiliation. The views of respondents reveal that the majority of ISG users (95.6%) use the library for writing papers whereas 93 percent users of CSG are using the libraries for writing papers. 90.4 percent users belonging to ESG and 89.3 percent to BSG also indicated their interest in using the library for the same purpose. The use of library by users of PESG for this purpose, however, is 84.9 percent only. The Table 8.16 reveals the objectives of using the libraries of CSIR laboratories.

Table 8.16 : Purpose of Using the Library by Group of Laboratories

Purpose of Using the Library	*Group of Laboratories*									
	PESG		*CSG*		*BSG*		*ESG*		*ISG*	
	Yes	*No*	*Yes*	*No*	*Yes*	*No*	*Yes*	*No*	*Yes*	*No*
Research	52	1	57	-	127	4	93	1	34	11
	(98.1)	(1.9)	(100.0)		(96.9)	(3.1)	(98.9)	(1.1)	(75.6)	(24.4)
Writing papers	45	8	53	4	117	14	85	9	43	2
	(84.9)	(15.1)	(93.0)	(7.0)	(89.3)	(10.7)	(90.4)	(9.6)	(95.6)	(4.4)
Book writing	11	42	4	53	29	102	13	81	21	24
	(20.8)	(79.2)	(7.0)	(93.0)	(22.1)	(77.9)	(13.8)	(86.2)	(46.7)	(53.3)
Preparation of	21	32	25	32	49	82	31	63	13	32
bibliography	(39.6)	(60.4)	(43.9)	(56.1)	(37.4)	(62.6)	(33.0)	(67.0)	(28.9)	(71.1)
Latest R&Ds	19	34	26	31	42	89	40	54	20	25
	(35.8)	(64.2)	(45.6)	(54.4)	(32.1)	(67.9)	(42.6)	(57.4)	(44.4)	(55.6)

The highest number of respondents, 46.7 percent, of ISG are using the library for writing books, followed by 22.1 percent users in BSG. The use of library for this purpose by the users belonging to PESG and BSG is not impressive. Only 20.8 percent users of PESG and 13.8 percent of BSG reported to be doing so.

Book writing seems to be an area of lesser interest amongst the scientists, specially attached to specific organisations of research laboratories. They argue that they publish their contributions in the journals because books writing is time consuming and the publication of books causes delay in making their results known. There is marginal difference in response rate in this regard. It is only ISG where 46.7 percent users reported to have made use of the library for book writing. On the other hand only 7.0 percent of users belonging to CSG have revealed using the library for this purpose.

The analysis indicates that very few scientists and researchers are using the library for preparation of bibliographies in comparison to research purposes and writing articles.

It is interesting to note that there is not much variations in the use pattern of library for the purpose of preparation of bibliographies and ascertaining the latest status of R&D. However, of all the groups, the higher percentage of users of CSG have reported to be using the library for both the purposes, i.e., preparation of bibliographies and ascertaining the status of latest R&D.

The above analysis reveals that the scientists and researchers of the CSIR laboratories are using the libraries and their resources basically for research and writing of research papers. The libraries are also used for the purposes of preparation of bibliographies and to keep themselves aware of R&D. However, the percentage of users is limited in this respect.

8.1.11 Frequency of Library Visits by Group of Laboratories

For the purpose of ascertaining the pace with which users are utilizing library resources, they were requested to indicate the frequency of their visits to the library. Keeping in view all possible frequencies of library visits, the same has been viewed into six categories as shown in different tables.

Table 8.17 : Frequency of Library Visits by Group of Laboratories

Frequency of Visits	*Group of Laboratories*					
	PESG	*CSG*	*BSG*	*ESG*	*ISG*	*Row Total*
Daily	13 (24.5)	29 (50.9)	50 (38.2)	22 (23.4)	23 (51.1)	137 (36.1)
Twice a week	25 (47.2)	19 (33.3)	56 (42.7)	42 (44.7)	13 (28.9)	155 (40.8)
Once a week	5 (9.4)	2 (3.5)	12 (9.2)	9 (9.6)	3 (6.7)	31 (8.2)
Fortnightly	2 (3.8)	1 (1.8)	2 (1.5)	5 (5.3)	-	10 (2.6)
Once a month	-	-	-	-	-	-
Whenever required	8 (15.1)	6 (10.5)	11 (8.4)	16 (17.0)	6 (13.3)	47 (12.4)
Column Total	53 (13.9)	57 (15.0)	131 (34.5)	94 (24.7)	45 (11.8)	380 (100.0)

$X^2 = 26.68861$ with 16 d.f.
$P > .01$

The analysis of Table. 8.17 shows that a comparatively higher percentage of users visit the library twice a week and at the same time a good number of users visit the library daily. The rest may be termed occasional visitors.

The analysis of data according to group of laboratories reveals that a relatively higher proportion of users belonging to CSG (50.9%) and ISG (51.1%) visits the library daily whereas users of PESG (47.2%), BSG (42.7%) and ESG (44.7%) visit only twice a week.

There is also another category of users in all the groups, who use the library once a week, fortnightly, once a month and/or whenever need arises. This group may be said to be the group of occasional users of the library. Their visit is by and large contingent upon requirement. ESG has larger concentration of occasional users (31.9%), followed by PESG with 20 percent. In other groups, there is less number of such users, but their presence is not negligible.

Chi-square test has been applied and found that Chi-square value = 26.68861 is not significant at .01 level, which does not support the difference statistically.

8.1.11.1 Frequency of the Library Visits by Sex

Table 8.18 shows that a higher proportion of females (45.8%) as compared to males (34.6%) visits the library daily. The majority of males, on the other hand, visit the library twice a week. It is found that in comparison to the male users, female users are more frequent visitors of the library. However, there is minor variation as far as occasional (i.e., fortnightly, once a week) visits to the library are concerned. Almost an equal proportion of males and females visit the library only when need arises. There seems to be no continuity on their part in this regard. However, the difference in the visit pattern of the library as explained above is not supported statistically. As Chi-square value = 3.53828 as brought out in Table 8.18 is insignificant at .01 level.

Table 8.18 : Frequency of Library Visits by Sex

Frequency of Visits	*Sex*		
	Male	*Female*	*Row Total*
Daily	115 (34.6)	22 (45.8)	137 (36.1)
Twice a week	138 (41.6)	17 (35.4)	155 (40.8)
Once a week	28 (8.4)	3 (6.3)	31 (8.2)
Fortnightly	10 (3.0)	-	10 (2.6)
Once a month	-	-	-
Whenever required	41 (12.3)	6 (12.5)	47 (12.4)
Total Column	332 (87.4)	48 (12.6)	380 (100.0)

X^2 = 3.53828 with 4 d.f.

P > .01

8.1.11.2 Frequency of the Library Visits by Different Categories of Users

Table 8.19 shows that visit of the library when analysed according to different categories of users shows that the research scholars are the most regular visitors of the library and the majority of them (57.1%) visit the library daily. Occasional ones are rare in this group. The majority of senior scientists visit the library twice a week whereas almost an equal proportion of Scientists C visit the library daily and twice a week. It is also interesting to note that almost an equal number of senior scientists visit the library daily as well as occasionally. Chi-square value = 22.60583 is insignificant at .01 level which does not support the difference between the visit pattern of the library statistically.

Table 8.19 : Frequency of Library Visits by Different Categories of Users

Frequency of Visits	*Users Category*				
	Scientist A&B	*Scientist C*	*Senior Scientists*	*Research Scholars*	*Row Total*
Daily	23 (44.2)	50 (40.7)	52 (28.3)	12 (57.1)	137 (36.1)
Twice a week	17 (32.7)	50 (40.7)	81 (44.0)	7 (33.3)	155 (40.8)
Once a week	3 (5.8)	13 (10.6)	13 (7.1)	2 (9.5)	31 (8.2)
Fortnightly	1 (1.9)	1 (.8)	8 (4.3)	-	10 (2.6)
Once a month	-	-	-	-	-
Whenever required	8 (15.4)	9 (7.3)	30 (16.3)	-	47 (12.4)
Column Total	52 (13.7)	123 (32.4)	184 (48.4)	21 (5.5)	380 (100.0)

X^2 = 22.60583 with 12 d.f.

P > .01

8.1.11.3 Frequency of Library Visits by Qualification

The analysis of the library visit according to levels of qualification in Table 8.20 indicates that those having higher qualification are comparatively more regular users of the library, as the majority of Post-Doctoral Fellows (66.7%) visit the library daily when compared to the users with Ph.D. and M.Sc. degrees.

Comparatively, a higher number of users with M.Sc. degrees (40.7%) are found to be regular user of the library than those holding Ph.D. degree, as a relatively higher percentage of users with Ph.D. degrees (41.9%) visit the library twice a week. Chi-square value = 6.07084 is insignificant at .01 level, which does not support the difference between the visit pattern of the library as per this value.

Table 8.20 : Frequency of Library Visits by Qualification

Educational Qualification	*Frequency of Visits*						
	Daily	*Twice a Week*	*Once a Week*	*Once a Fort-night*	*Once a Month*	*Whenever Required*	*Row Total*
M.Sc.	35 (40.7)	32 (37.2)	4 (4.7)	4 (4.7)	-	11 (12.8)	86 (22.6)
Ph.D.	100 (34.4)	122 (41.9)	27 (9.3)	6 (2.1)	-	36 (12.4)	291 (76.6)
Post-Doctoral Fellow	2 (66.7)	1 (33.3)	-	-	-	-	3 (.8)
Column Total	137 (36.1)	155 (40.8)	31 (8.2)	10 (2.6)	-	47 (12.4)	380 (100.0)

$X^2 = 6.07084$ with 8 d.f.

$P > .01$

8.1.12 Time Spent on Each Visit by Group of Laboratories

The analysis of time spent by users on each visit by group of laboratories (Table 8.21) reveals that ISG users spend just one hour on their each visit to the library while majority of other users of each group spend 2-3 hours in the library in their each visit. Also a good number of users of all the laboratories spend only one hour whenever they visit the library. There are also some such users, though insignificant number in each group, who spend more than 4 hours and above whenever they visit the library. Similarly, each group has such users also whose timeframe of visit to the library is not certain. Chi-square value = 30.42410 is insignificant at .01 level because this does not support the difference statistically.

Table 8.21 : Time Spent on Each Visit by Group of Laboratories

Time Spent on	*Group of Laboratories*					
Each Visit	*PESG*	*CSG*	*BSG*	*ESG*	*ISG*	*Row Total*
0 – 1 hour(s)	19 (35.8)	18 (31.6)	48 (36.6)	32 (34.0)	18 (40.0)	135 (35.5)
2 – 3 hours	29 (54.7)	38 (66.7)	76 (58.0)	53 (56.4)	17 (37.8)	213 (56.1)
4 – 5 hours	2 (3.8)	-	2 (1.5)	3 (3.2)	4 (8.9)	11 (2.9)
6 hours and above	-	-	3 (2.3)	3 (3.2)	-	6 (1.6)
Not certain (whenever required)	3 (5.7)	1 (1.8)	2 (1.5)	3 (3.2)	6 (13.3)	15 (3.9)
Column Total	53 (13.9)	57 (15.0)	131 (34.5)	94 (24.7)	45 (11.8)	380 (100.0)

X^2 = 30.42410 with 16 d.f.

P > .01

8.1.12.1 Time Spent on Each Visit by Sex

The analysis of data according to sex in Table 8.22 does not depict any difference in regard to the time spent on each visit of males (55.7%) and females (58.3%). Majority of males and females visit the library for 2-3 hours. The next large group of males and females visit the library for one hour or so. However, there is difference in the number of males and females who spend one hour in the library. Though males and females both spend more than 4 hours in the library, the proportion of females is relatively higher. However, the difference indicated above is not significant statistically as Chi-square value = 10.40137 shown in Table 8.22 is not significant at .01 level.

Table 8.22 : Time Spent on Each Visit by Sex

Time Spent on Each Visit	*Sex*		
	Male	*Female*	*Row Total*
0 – 1 hour(s)	123	12	135
	(37.0)	(25.0)	(35.5)
2 – 3 hours	185	28	213
	(55.7)	(58.3)	(56.1)
4 – 5 hours	9	2	11
	(2.7)	(4.2)	(2.9)
6 hours and above	3	3	6
	(.9)	(6.3)	(1.6)
Not certain	12	3	15
(Whenever required)	(3.6)	(6.3)	(3.9)
Total Column	332	48	380
	(87.4)	(12.6)	(100.0)

X^2 = 10.40137 with 4 d.f.

P > .01

8.1.12.2 Time Spent on Each Visit by Different Categories of Users

Table 8.23 shows that majority of Scientists C (56.1%) and senior scientists (62%) spends 2-3 hours on visit to library whereas majority of scientists A&B spend just one hour in the library. Similarly, majority of research scholars also spends 2-3 hours. Except research scholars, all other groups of users consisted of a few users who visit the library beyond 4 hours. Similarly, there are users in each group, except research scholars, whose time spent in the library is not certain. Chi-square value = 24.54133 is not significant at .01 level which does not support the difference statistically.

Table 8.23 : Time Spent on Each Visit by Different Category of Users

Time Spent on Each Visit	*Users Category*				
	Scientist A&B	*Scientist C*	*Senior Scientists*	*Research Scholars*	*Row Total*
0 – 1 hour(s)	24 (46.2)	49 (39.8)	54 (29.3)	8 (38.1)	135 (35.5)
2 – 3 hours	18 (34.6)	69 (56.1)	114 (62.0)	12 (57.1)	213 (56.1)
4 – 5 hours	3 (5.8)	2 (1.6)	6 (3.3)	-	11 (2.9)
6 hours and above	1 (1.9)	1 (.8)	3 (1.6)	1 (4.8)	6 (1.6)
Not certain (Whenever required)	6 (11.5)	2 (1.6)	7 (3.8)	-	15 (3.9)
Column Total	52 (13.7)	123 (32.4)	184 (48.4)	21 (5.5)	380 (100.0)

$X^2 = 24.54133$ with 12 d.f.
$P > .01$

8.1.12.3 Time Spent on Each Visit by Qualification

Data as analysed in Table 8.24 depicts very interesting result with regard to the amount of time being spent by the users on each of their library visits. The majority of users (56.1%) spend 2-3 hours whenever they go to the library. It can be said that this group of users are involved in serious researches which require indepth consultation of literature available. There are also users whose time of consultation of the library is beyond 4 hours. Such long hours of duration in consulting the library suggests that this group of users consist of those involved basically in serious type of reading and writing at that particular time. A good number of users (35.5%) go to the library just for an hour or so. Data when analysed according to qualification shows that almost an equal proportion of those with M.Sc. degrees spent 0-1 hour and 2-3 hours whereas majority of those with Ph.D. degrees (59.8%) spent 2-3 hours on each visit. However, the visit of Post-Doctoral Fellows is confined to one hour only. The differences, however, are not supported statistically, as Chi-square value = 13.82529 is insignificant at .01 level.

Table 8.24 : Time Spent on Each Visit by Qualification

Educational qualification	*Time Spent on Each Visit*					
	0 – 1 Hour	*2 – 3 Hours*	*4 – 5 Hours*	*6 Hours & Above*	*Not Certain*	*Row Total*
M.Sc.	39	39	1	2	5	86
	(45.3)	(45.3)	(1.2)	(2.3)	(5.8)	(22.6)
Ph.D.	93	174	10	4	10	291
	(32.0)	(59.8)	(3.4)	(1.4)	(3.4)	(76.6)
Post-Doctoral	3	-	-	-	-	3
Fellow	(100.0)					(.8)
Column Total	135	213	11	6	15	380
	(35.5)	(56.1)	(2.9)	(1.6)	(3.9)	(100.0)

$X^2 = 13.82529$ with 8 d.f.

$P > .01$

8.1.13 Stages for Consulting the Library

Scientists and research scholars of CSIR laboratories while working on different projects consult the library of their parent organisations at different stages of their work. It was found that there are five possible stages of concerning research or project work where consultations are necessary. Accordingly, users were requested to indicate the stages at which they use the library to the maximum extent.

Table 8.25 : Stages for Consulting the Library

Response of Users for Consulting the Library	*Response*		
	Yes	*No*	*Row Total*
Identify area for research	344 (90.5)	36 (9.5)	380 (100.0)
Survey of literature	378 (99.5)	2 (.5)	380 (100.0)
At the time of experiment	272 (71.6)	108 (28.4)	380 (100.0)
At the time of analysis of data	308 (81.1)	72 (18.9)	380 (100.0)
Report writing	307 (80.8)	73 (19.2)	380 (100.0)

The data presented in the Table 8.25 makes it clear that all the stages are important and with some variations, users consult the library at each stage. However, some stages are of greater importance. For example, majority of respondents i.e., 99.5 percent, consult the library at the time of survey of literature and 90.5 percent use at the stage of identification of area for research. This is, in fact, the initial stage of research problem where relevant information and sources are badly required by the researchers and specialists.

The above analysis reveals that the majority of the scientists/researchers consult the library to survey literature for identification of areas for research more in comparison to at the time of experiments and at the time of analysis of data and report writing.

8.1.13.1 Stages for Consulting the Library by Group of Laboratories

Table 8.26 shows that the analysis of data according to group of laboratories. It reveals that all the users of PESG, CSG, BSG, ESG and 95.6 percent of ISG consult the library for survey of literature. Thus it is clear that the survey of literature is the most important stage of using the library, followed by at the stage of identification of areas for research. The percentage of users consulting the library for identifying areas for research has been less in comparison to survey of literature. Nevertheless, the response is quite favourable. Some variations are, however, apparent. The majority of CSG users (89.5%) consult the library at the time of analysis of data whereas the majority of BSG users (87.0%) were consulting the library for report writing. Similarly, significant percentage of PESG users (83.0%) were consulting the library at the time of experiment while 66.4 percent BSG users were found using the library for all the above stages to get information related to their research areas. So the analysis indicates that majority of the users are using the library for survey of literature and identifying area for research.

Table 8.26 : Stages for Consulting the Library by Group of Laboratories

Stages for Consulting the Library	*Group of Laboratories*									
	PESG		*CSG*		*BSG*		*ESG*		*ISG*	
	Yes	*No*	*Yes*	*No*	*Yes*	*No*	*Yes*	*No*	*Yes*	*No*
Identifying area for research	45 (84.9)	8 (15.1)	54 (94.7)	3 (5.3)	120 (91.6)	11 (8.4)	89 (94.7)	5 (5.3)	36 (80.0)	9 (20.0)
Survey of literature	53 (100.0)	-	57 (100.0)	-	131 (100.0)	-	94 (100.0)	-	43 (95.6)	2 (4.4)
At the time of experiment	44 (83.0)	9 (17.0)	41 (71.9)	16 (28.1)	102 (77.9)	29 (22.1)	57 (60.6)	37 (39.4)	28 (62.2)	17 (37.8)
At the time of analysis of data	43 (81.1)	10 (18.9)	51 (89.5)	6 (10.5)	107 (81.7)	24 (18.3)	73 (77.7)	21 (22.3)	34 (75.6)	11 (24.4)
Report writing	39 (73.6)	14 (26.4)	41 (71.9)	16 (28.1)	114 (87.0)	17 (13.0)	77 (81.9)	17 (18.1)	36 (80.0)	9 (20.0)
All the above stages	29 (54.7)	24 (45.3)	34 (59.6)	23 (40.4)	87 (66.4)	44 (33.6)	49 (52.1)	45 (47.9)	26 (57.8)	19 (42.2)

8.1.13.2 Usefulness of the Library at Different Stages of Consultation

Table 8.27 attempts to examine the usefulness of the libraries at different stages of consultation. It is clear that at the stage of literature survey, the library is rated as very useful whereas at other stages, starting from identifying areas, for researches to report writing, it is categorised as useful. Excepting the stage of identifying areas for research and the survey of literature, a good number of respondents termed the library has not been useful for the consultation, specially at the time of experiments, analysis of report and report writing.

It can be inferred that, with exception of experimentation and analysis of the data, the consultation of the library by the users at different stages have been found useful. Thus it is evident that the library is an essential means and support for pursuing and carrying out research for various purposes.

Table 8.27 : Usefulness of the Library at Different Stages of Consultation

Stages for Consulting the Library	*Very Useful*	*Useful*	*Not Useful*	*Row Total*
Identifying area for research	159 (46.2)	170 (49.4)	15 (4.4)	344 (100.0)
Survey of literature	234 (61.9)	134 (35.4)	10 (2.6)	378 (100.0)
At the time of experiment	66 (24.3)	170 (62.5)	36 (13.2)	272 (100.0)
At the time of analysis of data	84 (27.3)	184 (59.7)	40 (13.0)	308 (100.0)
Report writing	110 (35.8)	163 (53.1)	34 (11.1)	307 (100.0)

8.2 LIBRARY COLLECTION

The library collection is one of the most valuable element of the library. The library should develop its collection in accordance with the objectives of parent organisation, then only it can help the organisation to realise its objectives. Sound collection is the very basis of effective and efficient library service. In addition to printed material, such as books, reference books, journals, theses and dissertations, technical reports, proceedings, pamphlets and reprints, translations, etc. libraries, particularly scientific and technical libraries, are diversifying to add-up a variety of non-book material, such as audio, visual, microfilms, microfiches, slides, picture transparencies/photos, CD-ROMs, etc. In order to know the extent to which the collection in CSIR libraries is satisfying the requirements of their users, an attempt has been made to obtain their reactions on four point scale, i.e. excellent, good, poor and not available.

Table 8.28 depicts the responses received from the users regarding collection of CSIR libraries. The majority of respondents seems to be extremely satisfied with the collection of books available in general category to area-specific. Over 80 percent of respondents have indicated the collection either as good or excellent. It may be mentioned that majority of respondents rate it as good. A good number of users consider the general collection on science and collection in area of specialisation as excellent. On the other hand, the proportion of such users who rated the reference collection as excellent is comparatively less than the other two categories. Nevertheless, the reference collection has been rated as good by 61.1 percent of respondents.

Contrary to users' reaction to book collection in different areas, the collection of theses and grey literature has evoked mixed response. Barring the collection of conference, seminars, workshop papers and standards, specifications, patents, the collection of theses, research project reports, government documents, pamphlets, etc. have been rated as poor by the majority of the respondents. There are also a number of respondents who have complained about non-availability of these types of collection in their libraries. It very clearly shows that CSIR libraries are not properly equipped with the collection of theses, research reports, government documents and pamphlets and reprints. In this category, only the collection of conference/workshop/seminar papers and standards, specifications, patents has been rated as good. It is surprising that CSIR libraries do not recognise the importance of these collection. However, the collection of pamphlets, reprints and government documents collection has been rated as good by the majority of respondents.

The periodicals being carrier of recent thought, are

considered to be significant part of library collection. The responses indicate that the majority of respondents are of the view that the collection of journals, including indexing journals is good. Similarly, periodicals of both the category are also rated as excellent by a good number of users. However, comparison of responses reveals little variation. An overwhelming majority of respondents have shown their satisfaction with the collection of science journals by rating it either as good or excellent but their proportion is little less in case of indexing journals.

Table 8.28 : Library Collection

Rating of Library Collection	*Response*				
	Excellent	*Good*	*Poor*	*Not Available*	*Row Total*
(a) Books					
General books on science	113 (29.7)	218 (57.4)	49 (12.9)	- -	380 (100.0)
Area of specialisation	116 (30.5)	200 (52.6)	64 (16.8)	-	380 (100.0)
Reference books	79 (20.8)	232 (61.1)	69 (18.2)		380 (100.0)
(b) Theses and Grey Literature					
Theses/ dissertations	17 (4.5)	89 (23.4)	192 (50.5)	82 (21.6)	380 (100.0)
Research/ project reports	25 (6.6)	134 (35.3)	159 (41.8)	62 (16.3)	380 (100.0)
Government documents	16 (4.2)	102 (26.8)	174 (45.8)	88 (23.2)	380 (100.0)
Conference seminar/ workshop papers	3 (8.4)	168 (44.2)	140 (36.8)	40 (10.5)	380 (100.0)
Standards, specifications and patents	32 (8.4)	161 (42.4)	133 (35.0)	54 (14.2)	380 (100.0)
Pamphlets and reprints	17 (4.5)	114 (30.0)	170 (44.7)	79 (20.8)	380 (100.0)

Rating of Library Collection	*Response*				
	Excellent	*Good*	*Poor*	*Not Available*	*Row Total*
(c) Periodicals					
Science journals and serials	127 (33.4)	229 (60.3)	24 (6.3)	- -	380 (100.0)
Indexing journals	108 (28.4)	209 (55.0)	63 (16.6)	-	380 (100.0)
Abstracting journals	107 (28.2)	195 (51.3)	78 (20.5)		380 (100.0)
(d) Non-book Material					
Microfilms/ microfiches	13 (3.4)	59 (15.5)	113 (29.7)	195 (51.3)	380 (100.0)
Audiocassettes	2 (.5)	9 (2.4)	59 (15.5)	310 (81.6)	380 (100.0)
Videocassettes	1 (.3)	14 (3.7)	57 (15.0)	308 (81.1)	380 (100.0)
Slides	4 (1.1)	22 (5.8)	55 (14.5)	299 (78.7)	380 (100.0)
CD-ROM databases	19 (5.0)	56 (14.7)	28 (7.4)	277 (72.9)	380 (100.0)
Online databases	18 (4.7)	43 (11.3)	33 (8.7)	286 (75.3)	380 (100.0)
Maps/atlases	22 (5.8)	113 (29.7)	117 (30.8)	128 (33.7)	380 (100.0)
Picture transparencies/ photos	4 (1.1)	28 (7.4)	62 (16.3)	286 (75.3)	380 (100.0)

Users' response with regard to non-book material as given in Table 8.28 reveals that none of the important items are possessed by the majority of libraries. CSIR libraries are thought to have progressed a lot in adopting latest means developed in this field. But users' response has belied the observation. An overwhelming majority of respondents have indicated that most of the non-book material as enumerated in the table is not available in their respective libraries, maps/

atlases being the only exception. Even CD-ROM databases which hold a great value for scientific and technical libraries, are not available in most of the libraries. It is evident that change in libraries is still a word of discussion and source of producing literature but certainly not a part and parcel of our libraries at least of CSIR libraries.

It is difficult to analyse reason for non-availability of such material. But it could well be that since most of the budget is spent on books and journals, there is not enough finance left to purchase and maintain several other important and costly library items. Inadequacy of infrastructure facilities also seems to be the reason behind it.

8.2.1 General Books on Science

The users response in regard to the collection of CSIR libraries of general books relating to science as given in Table 8.29 show that the majority of respondents across the group of laboratories rate the collection as good. A little over 62 percent of respondents of PESG, ESG, ISG rate the collection as good. 52.6 percent of respondents of CSG and 51.9 percent respondents of BSG termed the collection as good. In comparison a higher proportion of respondents belonging to other groups consider the collection excellent. Presence of respondents in all the groups who consider the collection as poor is a peculiar feature. It is difficult to explain the reason as to why they have categorised the collection as poor when it is being rated good and excellent overwhelmingly. May be that those who do not visit the library frequently have been unsuccessful in understanding the strength of the collection. However, minor variation in rating does not influence the result. There may be some other reasons of dissatisfaction also. Chi-square value = 12.18060 is insignificant at .01 level and does not support the difference statistically.

Table 8.29 : General Books on Science by Group of Laboratories

Group of Laboratories	*Response*				*Row Total*
	Excellent	*Good*	*Poor*	*Not Available*	
PESG	14	33	6	-	53
	(26.4)	(62.3)	(11.3)		(13.9)
CSG	19	30	8	-	57
	(33.3)	(52.6)	(14.0)		(15.0)
BSG	50	68	13	-	131
	(38.2)	(51.9)	(9.9)		(34.5)
ESG	18	59	17	-	94
	(19.1)	(62.8)	(18.1)		(24.7)
ISG	12	28	5	-	45
	(26.7)	(62.2)	(11.1)		(11.8)
Column Total	113	218	49	-	380
	(29.7)	(57.4)	(12.9)		(100.0)

X^2 = 12.18060 with 8 d.f.

P > .01

8.2.2 Area of Specialisation

Scientific community of users have specialisation in the area of their research activities. Users' views regarding resources in the area of specialisation, as recorded in Table 8.30, depicts that 64.2 percent of PESG users responded that their libraries hold good collection in the area of specialisation, whereas 58.0 percent BSG users rated the collection as good in the area of specialisation. There is minor variation in the percentage of responses of the users of ESG, ISG and CSG regarding their rating of collection as good in area of specialisation. On the other hand, 36.2 percent users of ESG indicated that their libraries hold excellent collection in their area of specialisation. Significant percentage of users termed the collection poor in their area of specialisation. There could be many reasons for their rating of collection as poor in the area of specialisation because it is reported that compared to journals, lesser amount is spent on books. Old collection of books on shelves must have lost their relevance for users. Therefore, it warrants segregation, disposal and replacement with the latest collection on the shelves in these scientific and technical libraries. However, the difference in the area of specialisation of users explained is not supported statistically, as Chi-square value (= 12.44772) is insignificant at .01 level.

Table 8.30 : Area of Specialisation by Group of Laboratories

Group of Laboratories	*Response*				
	Excellent	*Good*	*Poor*	*Not Available*	*Row Total*
PESG	15	34	4	-	53
	(28.3)	(64.2)	(7.5)		(13.9)
CSG	18	24	15	-	57
	(31.6)	(42.1)	(26.3)		(15.0)
BSG	35	76	20	-	131
	(26.7)	(58.0)	(15.3)		(34.5)
ESG	34	45	15	-	94
	(36.2)	(47.9)	(16.0)		(24.7)
ISG	14	21	10	-	45
	(31.1)	(46.7)	(22.2)		(11.8)
Column Total	116	200	64	-	380
	(30.5)	(52.6)	(16.8)		(100.0)

X^2 = 12.44772 with 8 d.f.

P > .01

8.2.3 Reference Books

The reference collection is another important area of library for providing better reference services. Reference books are considered to be the core collection of the scientific and technical libraries. The current reference collection is an essential feature of the library. The up-to-date collection of encyclopedias, directories, indexing and abstracting journals, bibliographies, etc. are useful ready reference sources to meet the information requirements of the library clients on the initial stages of their research activities.

Table 8.31 shows the users views regarding rating of reference collection. The table indicates that majority of ESG users (69.1%) termed the reference collection as good. Other groups indicated a little variation in the rating of collection of reference books. 31.1 percent users of ISG indicated the collection as excellent. Of the other groups, 30.2 percent PESG users indicated the reference collection as poor and a little over 15.3 percent users of BSG, ESG, CSG and ISG termed the reference collection as poor in their libraries.

The above analysis makes it clear that the majority of users rate the collection as good whereas a sizable number of respondents marked it as excellent collection. Chi-square value = 12.30840 is not significant at .01 level which does not support the difference statistically.

Table 8.31 : Collection of Reference Books by Group of Laboratories

Group of Laboratories	*Response*				
	Excellent	*Good*	*Poor*	*Not Available*	*Row Total*
PESG	8	29	16	-	53
	(15.1)	(54.7)	(30.2)		(13.9)
CSG	13	34	10	-	57
	(22.8)	(59.6)	(17.5)		(15.0)
BSG	30	81	20	-	131
	(22.9)	(61.8)	(15.3)		(34.5)
ESG	14	65	15	-	94
	(14.9)	(69.1)	(16.0)		(24.7)
ISG	14	23	8	-	45
	(31.1)	(51.1)	(17.8)		(11.8)
Column Total	79	232	69	-	380
	(20.8)	(61.1)	(18.2)		(100.0)

X^2 = 12.30840 with 8 d.f.

P > .01

8.2.4 Grey Literature

Grey literature, such as scientific and technical reports, conference proceedings, seminar papers, workshop papers, doctoral dissertations, reprints, pamphlets and official publications, is an indispensable part of the library collection, particularly the scientific and technical libraries and information centres. It is often difficult to identify, locate and obtain 'grey literature' because the various agencies, such as research institutes, universities, business organisations, scientific and technical organisations and government bodies, which bring out grey literature hardly distribute or publicise their research results and reports. Besides, book suppliers do not take interest in their supply due to their being non-profitable.

The transfer of scientific knowledge of the developed countries is very essential for the scientists, industries and other organisations of developing countries. Grey literature is often the key to this knowledge transfer. In United States, National Technical Information Service (NTIS) for technology reports and the UMI for doctoral dissertations are the best agencies for dissemination of such literature. But Europe has been weak in database publishing in comparison to international competitors, particularly relating to grey literature. The System for Information on Grey Literature in Europe (SIGLE) was established to tackle this problem in Europe in 1980.[3]

8.2.5 Theses/Dissertations

Theses are the primary source of information. The unpublished doctoral dissertations provide true picture of the research activities and offer quick and ready made information to those research scholars and researchers who are interested in the original research results and methodology.

The responses of users of CSIR laboratories regarding theses/dissertations are given in Table 8.32. These show that majority of users rated the collection in this area as poor. More than 67.0 percent users of ESG and PESG indicated that their libraries held poor collection on theses/dissertations, while 31.3

percent of BSG users termed the collection as good. On the other hand, percentage of users in all groups who rated the collection as excellent is very low. 51.1 percent of ISG users indicated that such type of collection is not available in these libraries. Chi-square value = 69.75548 as brought out in Table 8.32 is significant at .01 level which supports the difference statistically.

Table 8.32 : Theses/Dissertations by Group of Laboratories

Group of Laboratories	*Response*				
	Excellent	*Good*	*Poor*	*Not Available*	*Row Total*
PESG	1 (1.9)	11 (20.8)	36 (67.9)	5 (9.4)	53 (13.9)
CSG	7 (12.3)	17 (29.8)	30 (52.6)	3 (5.3)	57 (15.0)
BSG	6 (4.6)	41 (31.3)	47 (35.9)	37 (28.2)	131 (34.5)
ESG	3 (3.2)	14 (14.9)	63 (67.0)	14 (14.9)	94 (24.7)
ISG	-	6 (13.3)	16 (35.6)	23 (51.1)	45 (11.8)
Column Total	17 (4.5)	89 (23.4)	192 (50.5)	82 (21.6)	380 (100.0)

$X^2 = 69.75548$ with 12 d.f.

$P < .01$

8.2.6 Research/Project Reports

A large number of research and project reports are issued by various organisations, such as government research establishments, universities, colleges, business organisations, industries, etc. in different countries of the world. The reports produced by such organisations are very important documents for the researchers, scientists, engineers, technologists, etc. These reports have limited availability or distribution in scientific and technical organisations and industrial establishments. For easy access to such literature and for the purpose of current awareness of the patrons about such documents in each specific subject, a Technology Reports Centre must be established in each specific discipline and subject area which can be assigned the task of gathering such reports from different parts of the country as well as from abroad. The availability of these reports then must be announced in the abstracting journals or in the library. The library should make efforts to procure or collect all unrestricted reports from government establishments, learned societies, universities and business and industrial organisations.

The respondents of all groups of CSIR laboratories were asked to comment on the collection of research and project reports available in their libraries. From Table 8.33 we find that users of CSG (54.4%), ISG (51.1%) and PESG (50.9%) rated the collection of research/project reports as poor. Thus it indicates that the position of grey literature in CSIR libraries is very poor. It is only BSG whose 42.7 percent users revealed that the collection of research/project reports was good. However, the percentage of all those who rated the collection as poor is higher than those who rated the collection as good. 9.2 percent of respondents of BSG indicated the collection of reports as excellent. On the other hand, 28.9 percent of ISG users indicated non-availability of such collection. The difference is also supported by Chi-square value = 30.53646 which is significant at .01 level.

Table 8.33 : Research/Project Reports by Group of Laboratories

Group of Laboratories	*Response*				
	Excellent	*Good*	*Poor*	*Not Available*	*Row Total*
PESG	2 (3.8)	19 (35.8)	27 (50.9)	5 (9.4)	53 (13.9)
CSG	3 (5.3)	17 (29.8)	31 (54.4)	6 (10.5)	57 (15.0)
BSG	12 (9.2)	56 (42.7)	36 (27.5)	27 (20.6)	131 (34.5)
ESG	7 (7.4)	34 (36.2)	42 (44.7)	11 (11.7)	94 (24.7)
ISG	1 (2.2)	8 (17.8)	23 (51.1)	13 (28.9)	45 (11.8)
Column Total	25 (6.6)	134 (35.3)	159 (41.8)	62 (16.3)	380 (100.0)

$X^2 = 30.53646$ with 12 d.f.

$P < .01$

8.2.7 Government Documents

Users' responses regarding government documents in CSIR libraries as given in Table 8.34 show that majority of respondents termed the collection of government documents in scientific and technical libraries as poor. A high percentage of respondents of CSG (68.4%), ISG (60.0%) and PESG (54.7%) support the finding. A little over 32 percent of respondents of BSG and ESG reveal the collection in these libraries as good. But the users of BSG (33.6%), PESG (24.5%) indicated non-availability of such collection. However, a good number of users of BSG (7.6%) and CSG (7.0%) indicated the collection as excellent.

The above analysis indicates that collection of government documents is not good in these libraries, reason being non circulation of government documents. In spite of so much significance attached to government documents, CSIR laboratories pay little or no attention at all for their acquisition. The difference between response rates regarding collection of government documents is clearly supported by Chi-square value = 48.46905 which is significant at .01 level.

Table 8.34 : Government Documents by Group of Laboratories

Group of Laboratories	*Response*				*Row Total*
	Excellent	*Good*	*Poor*	*Not Available*	
PESG	-	11	29	13	53
		(20.8)	(54.7)	(24.5)	(13.9)
CSG	4	8	39	6	57
	(7.0)	(14.0)	(68.4)	(10.5)	(15.0)
BSG	10	42	35	44	131
	(7.6)	(32.1)	(26.7)	(33.6)	(34.5)
ESG	2	31	44	17	94
	(2.1)	(33.0)	(46.8)	(18.1)	(24.7)
ISG	-	10	27	8	45
		(22.2)	(60.0)	(17.8)	(11.8)
Column Total	16	102	174	88	380
	(4.2)	(26.8)	(45.8)	(23.2)	(100.0)

X^2 = 48.46905 with 12 d.f.

P < .01

8.2.8 Conference Proceedings

Conferences are unique forums for professionals to share their views and ideas on contemporary issues. As such, information generated during these conferences is brought out in the form of conference proceedings. The presence of conference proceedings in a library is necessary as these form a very important part of researchers' reading material. In order to understand usability of conference proceedings, the respondents were asked to indicate their rating, as shown in Table 8.35. All the groups are in possession of good collection of conference proceedings. The collection of conference proceedings in ESG has been rated as good by 50.0 percent of respondents, followed by 45.3 percent of PESG. The other groups which have been rated as good in terms of collection of conference proceedings include BSG 44.3 percent and CSG 40.4 percent. The difference between responses from different groups over rating of conference proceedings in laboratories is supported statistically by the Chi-square value = 26.33527 which is significant at .01 level.

Table 8.35 : Conference Proceedings by Group of Laboratóries

Group of Laboratories	*Response*				*Row Total*
	Excellent	*Good*	*Poor*	*Not Available*	
PESG	3 (5.7)	24 (45.3)	25 (47.2)	1 (1.9)	53 (13.9)
CSG	3 (5.3)	23 (40.4)	25 (43.9)	6 (10.5)	57 (15.0)
BSG	11 (8.4)	58 (44.3)	39 (29.8)	23 (17.6)	131 (34.5)
ESG	13 (13.8)	47 (50.0)	28 (29.8)	6 (6.4)	94 (24.7)
ISG	2 (4.4)	16 (35.6)	23 (51.1)	4 (8.9)	45 (11.8)
Column Total	32 (8.4)	168 (44.2)	140 (36.8)	40 (10.5)	380 (100.0)

$X^2 = 26.33527$ with 12 d.f.

$P < .01$

8.2.9 Standards, Specifications and Patents

Standards and specifications are important in scientific and technical organisations and such information must be kept and maintained in these libraries. "The orderly processes of standardisation ... have a profound and beneficial effect on industry's productive capacity and therefore on its ability to exploit trading opportunities in world markets". This statement, made in 1976 by Sir Frederick Warner's committee on 'Standards and Specifications in the Engineering Industries' to the National Economic Development Council, emphasises the importance of this kind of technological literature to the nation and the need for its effective control.[4]

On the other hand, patents are important source of scientific and technical information and constitute a distinct division of literature in scientific and technical libraries. Such information can be of tremendous use to the industrialists and entrepreneurs when they need to find out the latest and best technology in a particular field in which they are interested. The users who need such information can easily consult the vast information available in patents without wasting much time and can select the best technology suitable to them or their industrial business. Such a valuable information can also be made use of by inventors, students, researchers and authors of scientific and technical books.[5] Scientific and research organisations cannot ignore the importance of such literature because it has a greater significance for the technological developments. There should be separate section of patents collection in the library so that proper attention is paid towards its management. Such type of literature is frequently required by the users in scientific and technical libraries.

The users' response on the collection of standards, specifications and patents as shown in Table 8.36 indicates that majority of respondents think that CSIR libraries hold good collection of standards, specifications and patents. The respondents of ESG (56.4%), CSG (45.6%) and PESG (43.4%) have rated such collection as good. 34.4 percent of BSG users and 31.1 percent of ISG users have also given a good rating. 55.6 percent ISG users rated the collection of standards, specifications and patents as poor, followed by 41.5 percent PESG and 38.6 percent CSG. The percentage of users who reported non-availability of such a collection is greater in comparison to those who rated the collection as excellent. 27.5 percent users of BSG stated that such type of collection is absent in their libraries. On the other hand, 14.0 percent CSG users termed the collection of standards, specifications and patents as excellent. The difference is supported statistically by Chi-square value = 48.95964 which is significant at .01 level. This shows that there is significant difference in the collection of standards, specifications and patents in the libraries of five groups of laboratories.

The above analysis indicates that collection of standards, specifications and patents is good as marked by respondents of different groups of laboratories in comparison, as lesser number of respondent users has marked the collection as poor. The percentage of ISG users who marked the collection as poor is 55.6 percent ISG users. The reasons may be that standards, specifications and patents are used and required by research institutes. The information specialists of such libraries pay a little attention to the acquisition of such type of important literature as this is very useful and significant for scientists and research scholars of scientific and technical institutions. As analysis of collection reveals that grey literature is not procured by these libraries by paying full attention as in case of books and journals.

Table 8.36 : Standards, Specifications and Patents by Group of Laboratories

Group of Laboratories	*Response*				
	Excellent	*Good*	*Poor*	*Not Available*	*Row Total*
PESG	2 (3.8)	23 (43.4)	22 (41.5)	6 (11.3)	53 (13.9)
CSG	8 (14.0)	26 (45.6)	22 (38.6)	1 (1.8)	57 (15.0)
BSG	10 (7.6)	45 (34.4)	40 (30.5)	36 (27.5)	131 (34.5)
ESG	10 (10.6)	53 (56.4)	24 (25.5)	7 (7.4)	94 (24.7)
ISG	2 (4.4)	14 (31.1)	25 (55.6)	4 (8.9)	45 (11.8)
Column Total	32 (8.4)	161 (42.4)	133 (35.0)	54 (14.2)	380 (100.0)

X^2 = 48.95964 with 12 d.f.
P < .01

8.2.10 Pamphlets and Reprints

This specific type of publications consist of a few pages (sometimes as fewer as 64) and are called pamphlets. They are usually not as significant as books, periodicals, reprints of articles from periodicals but in scientific and technical libraries, they have their own significance. On the other hand, reprints of articles from periodicals form significant part of grey literature.

Table 8.37 shows the responses of users of five groups of CSIR laboratories on the collection of pamphlets and reprints. It indicates that CSIR libraries have poor collection of grey literature, such as pamphlets and reprints. Majority of users of PESG (60.4%) and ISG (60.0%) termed the collection of pamphlets and reprints as poor, followed by ESG (48.9%), CSG (43.9%) and BSG (30.5%), whereas users of CSG (38.6%) and BSG (35.1%) marked such collection as good. The percentage of other groups of ESG, ISG and PESG is less in comparison to CSG and BSG. Non-availability of pamphlets and reprints is also shown by the users of BSG (29.8%) and PESG (22.6%), followed by ISG (17.8%) and ESG (16.0%). A very few respondents termed the collection as excellent. These are CSG users (8.8%), ESG users (5.3%) and BSG users (4.6%).

The reasons for poor collection of pamphlets and reprints are lack of proper arrangement and mishandling of such material, lack of place for pamphlets and reprints. The difference between the responses regarding collection of pamphlets and reprints as explained above is supported by Chi-square value = 34.60432 which is significant at .01 level.

Table 8.37 : Pamphlets and Reprints by Group of Laboratories

Group of Laboratories	*Response*				
	Excellent	*Good*	*Poor*	*Not Available*	*Row Total*
PESG	1	8	32	12	53
	(1.9)	(15.1)	(60.4)	(22.6)	(13.9)
CSG	5	22	25	5	57
	(8.8)	(38.6)	(43.9)	(8.8)	(15.0)
BSG	6	46	40	39	131
	(4.6)	(35.1)	(30.5)	(29.8)	(34.5)
ESG	5	28	46	15	94
	(5.3)	(29.8)	(48.9)	(16.0)	(24.7)
ISG	-	10	27	8	45
		(22.2)	(60.0)	(17.8)	(11.8)
Column Total	17	114	170	79	380
	(4.5)	(30.0)	(44.7)	(20.8)	(100.0)

$X^2 = 34.60432$ with 12 d.f.

$P < .01$

8.2.11 Scientific Journals and Serials

Periodicals are considered to be an important part of library collection in scientific and technical libraries. Periodicals bring out the latest results of experimental research and disseminate the technical developments to the society. Importance of periodicals has been recognised in scientific and technical libraries of CSIR and a substantial portion of library budget is spent on subscription to periodicals than on acquisition of books. To meet the current research requirements, periodicals are used comprehensively by the scientific users. "Scientific and technological periodicals are indeed living organs for the transmission of information, comprising the groundwork for the advancement of human progress".[6]

Users' responses regarding scientific journals and serials

as given in Table 8.38, reveals that majority of users favour good collection of scientific journals and serials. The responses of PESG users (69.8%) and ESG (60.0%) rated availability of scientific journals and serials as good, followed by CSG (59.6%), ISG (57.8%) and BSG (53.4%). A little over 37 percent responses of BSG and ISG users revealed that their libraries have excellent collection of scientific journals and serials, followed by 36.8 percent users of CSG. The excellent responses of ESG and PESG are fewer in comparison to other groups. The significant percentage of users of BSG (9.2%) and ESG (6.4%) rated the collection poor, followed by ISG, PESG and CSG.

The above analysis indicates that majority of respondents of each group rated the scientific journals and serials good. Chi-square value = 8.34181 as brought out in Table 8.38 is insignificant at .01 level which does not support the difference statistically.

Table 8.38 : Scientific Journals and Serials by Group of Laboratories

Group of Laboratories	*Response*				
	Excellent	*Good*	*Poor*	*Not Available*	*Row Total*
PESG	14 (26.4)	37 (69.8)	2 (3.8)	-	53 (13.9)
CSG	21 (36.8)	34 (59.6)	2 (3.5)	-	57 (15.0)
BSG	49 (37.4)	70 (53.4)	12 (9.2)	-	131 (34.5)
ESG	26 (27.7)	62 (66.0)	6 (6.4)	-	94 (24.7)
ISG	17 (37.8)	26 (57.8)	2 (4.4)	-	45 (11.8)
Column Total	127 (33.4)	229 (60.3)	24 (6.3)	-	380 (100.0)

X^2 = 8.34181 with 8.d.f

P > .01

8.2.11.1 Indexing Journals

Table 8.39 shows that majority of respondents of CSIR laboratories indicated that their libraries have good collection of indexing journals. Majority of respondents of ESG (61.7%) and CSG (56.1%) specified the collection of indexing journals as good, followed by a little over 51 percent of ISG, BSG and PESG. On the other hand, 35.1 percent users of CSG pointed out the indexing journals in their libraries as excellent, followed by BSG (32.8%), ISG (31.1%) and PESG (30.2%). It is interesting to note that 16.0 percent respondents of ESG rated the collection of indexing journals excellent which is Comparatively less than the others. Indexing journals have been rated poor by 22.3 percent of ESG users, 17.8 percent ISG, 17.0 percent PESG and 15.3 percent BSG users. 8.8 percent users of CSG also indicated the indexing journals as poor. It is conspicuous from the above analysis that CSIR laboratories have good collection of indexing journals in comparison to grey literature. These libraries spend a significant amount on such material. Chi-square value = 12.43137 as shown in Table 8.39 is insignificant at .01 level, which does not support the difference statistically.

Table 8.39 : Indexing Journals by Group of Laboratories

Group of Laboratories	*Response*				*Row Total*
	Excellent	*Good*	*Poor*	*Not Available*	
PESG	16 (30.2)	28 (52.8)	9 (17.0)	-	53 (13.9)
CSG	20 (35.1)	32 (56.1)	5 (8.8)	-	57 (15.0)
BSG	43 (32.8)	68 (51.9)	20 (15.3)	-	131 (34.5)
ESG	15 (16.0)	58 (61.7)	21 (22.3)	-	94 (24.7)
ISG	14 (31.1)	23 (51.1)	8 (17.8)	-	45 (11.8)
Column Total	108 (28.4)	209 (55.0)	63 (16.6)	-	380 (100.0)

X^2 = 12.43137 with 8 d.f.
P > .01

8.2.11.2 Abstracting Journals

The responses of users of CSIR laboratories in Table 8.40 depict that majority of users indicated the abstracting journals as good. The users of PESG (58.5%) termed the abstracting journals good, followed by a little over 49 percent of CSG, ESG (50.0%) and BSG (52.7%). The percentage of ISG users is lower in comparison to other groups. On the other hand, users of CSG (36.8%) and BSG (35.1%) marked the abstracting journals as excellent, followed by 28.9 percent of ISG and a little over 18 percent of ESG and PESG. A significant number of respondents rated the abstracting journals poor which included ESG (31.9%), ISG (26.7%) and PESG (22.6%). The poor rating of abstracting journals shown by BSG and CSG is less compared to other groups. The difference between abstracting journals is clearly supported by Chi-square value = 22.33767 which is significant at .01 level.

Table 8.40 : Abstracting Journals by Group of Laboratories

Group of	*Response*				
Laboratories	*Excellent*	*Good*	*Poor*	*Not Available*	*Row Total*
PESG	10	31	12	-	53
	(18.9)	(58.5)	(22.6)		(13.9)
CSG	21	28	8	-	57
	(36.8)	(49.1)	(14.0)		(15.0)
BSG	46	69	16	-	131
	(35.1)	(52.7)	(12.2)		(34.5)
ESG	17	47	30	-	94
	(18.1)	(50.0)	(31.9)		(24.7)
ISG	13	20	12	-	45
	(28.9)	(44.4)	(26.7)		(11.8)
Column Total	107	195	78	-	380
	(28.2)	(51.3)	(20.5)		(100.0)

$X^2 = 22.33767$ with 8 d.f.

$P < .01$

8.2.12 Non-book Material

The advent of information technology has brought very rapid and drastic changes in the collection of non-book material in the libraries, particularly special libraries. Contemporary special libraries are in the forefront to acquire material, like microfilms, microfiches, audio-visual material, slides, audio-video tapes, transparencies, etc. The appearance of computer, CD-ROMs, online databases, development of networking, and multimedia have been challenging the explosion of information in the present age.

8.2.12.1 Microfilms/Microfiches

Microfilm is a continuous length of film wound onto an open spool. A microfilm reader has to magnify the reduced images so that these appear in a readable size on the machine's screen. Microfiche is a flat piece of transparent film containing images greatly reduced in size. It needs a microfiche reader to enlarge it to a readable size.

Table 8.41 shows existence of the collection of non-book material, such as microfilms/microfiches in the CSIR libraries. The majority of users of BSG (58.0%), ESG (55.3%) and ISG (51.1%) responded that their libraries do not have microfilms and microfiches, followed by CSG (42.1%) and PESG (37.7%). A little over 47 percent of users belonging to PESG and CSG marked the collection poor. Other groups, like ESG (30.9%) and ISG (26.7%) also rated the collection of microfilms/microfiches as poor, followed by 15.3 percent of BSG users. On the other hand, users of BSG (22.1%) and ISG (17.8%) rated the microfilms/microfiches as good. The collection of microfilms/microfiches rated as good by other groups include PESG (13.2%) and ESG (10.6%), followed by CSG (8.8%).

The collection was rated as excellent by lesser number of respondents of all groups. 4.6 percent users of BSG and 4.4 percent of ISG indicated the collection as excellent, followed by 3.2 percent of ESG. Other groups which rated such collection as excellent includes 1.9 percent of PESG and 1.8 percent of CSG. It is apparent from the above analysis that availability of such collection is negligible. The reasons of non-availability or poor collection of such material could be the unawareness about or unfamiliarity with such material being in the library by library staff. Lack of fund and proper place or staff for the management of such collection could be the other reasons. The difference between microfilms/microfiches in groups of CSIR libraries is supported statistically by the Chi-square value = 33.70115 which is significant at .01 level.

Table 8.41 : Microfilms/Microfiches by Group of Laboratories

Group of Laboratories	*Response*				
	Excellent	*Good*	*Poor*	*Not Available*	*Row Total*
PESG	1 (1.9)	7 (13.2)	25 (47.2)	20 (37.7)	53 (13.9)
CSG	1 (1.8)	5 (8.8)	27 (47.4)	24 (42.1)	57 (15.0)
BSG	6 (4.6)	29 (22.1)	20 (15.3)	76 (58.0)	131 (34.5)
ESG	3 (3.2)	10 (10.6)	29 (30.9)	52 (55.3)	94 (24.7)
ISG	2 (4.4)	8 (17.8)	12 (26.7)	23 (51.1)	45 (11.8)
Column Total	13 (3.4)	59 (15.5)	113 (29.7)	195 (51.3)	380 (100.0)

$X^2 = 33.70115$ with 12 d.f.

$P < .01$

8.2.12.2 Audiocassettes

Table 8.42 presents the data regarding the availability of audiocassettes in the CSIR libraries. The majority of respondents of BSG (86.3%), CSG (84.2%) and ESG (80.9%) pointed out that collection of videocassettes is not available in their libraries. Similarly, a large number of respondents of ISG

(77.8%) and PESG (71.7%) also pointed out non-availability of collection of audiocassettes. The poor collection of audiocassettes is indicated by 26.4 percent respondents of PESG and a little over 15 percent respondents of CSG, ESG and ISG. 10.7 percent respondents of BSG also rated the collection as poor. It is evident from the analysis that collection of audiocassettes is mostly missing from the libraries of CSIR laboratories. The collection of audiocassettes is rated as good only by 4.4 percent respondents of ISG, 3.2 percent of ESG, 2.3 percent of BSG and 1.9 percent of PESG. On the other hand, excellent rating of collection of audiocassettes is marked by the users of ISG (2.2%) and BSG (.8%). Those who marked the collection of audiocassettes as excellent and good constituted only a negligible proportion.

The above analysis indicates that CSIR libraries do not have facilities to acquire and manage such type of collection. Not even a single library holds such a collection which could be rated as excellent or good. Chi-square value = 13.32296 as brought out in Table 8.42 is insignificant at .01 level which shows no difference between the availability of audiocassettes in different CSIR libraries.

Table 8.42 : Audiocassettes by Group of Laboratories

Group of Laboratories	*Response*				
	Excellent	*Good*	*Poor*	*Not Available*	*Row Total*
PESG	-	1 (1.9)	14 (26.4)	38 (71.7)	53 (13.9)
CSG	-	-	9 (15.8)	48 (84.2)	57 (15.0)
BSG	1 (.8)	3 (2.3)	14 (10.7)	113 (86.3)	131 (34.5)
ESG	-	3 (3.2)	15 (16.0)	76 (80.9)	94 (24.7)
ISG	1 (2.2)	2 (4.4)	7 (15.6)	35 (77.8)	45 (11.8)
Column Total	1 (2.2)	9 (2.4)	59 (15.5)	310 (81.6)	380 (100.0)

$X^2 = 13.32296$ with 12 d.f.

$P > .01$

8.2.12.3 Videocassettes

In order to analyse the collection of videocassettes in the CSIR libraries, the respondents were asked to specify the availability of such collection in their libraries. Table 8.43 shows that a very large number of the respondents of CSG (87.7%) and BSG (86.3%) indicated the non-availability of collection of videocassettes in their libraries, followed by a little over 76 percent of ESG and ISG who also indicated non-availability of the videocassettes. Respondents of PESG (71.7%) also marked the non-availability of the collection of videocassettes in the library. 24.5 percent of respondents of PESG, 19.1 percent of ESG and a little over 12 percent of CSG and ISG indicated the collection as poor.

9.9 percent of BSG users also rated the collection as poor. 6.7 percent users of ISG, on the other hand, rated the collection of videocassettes as good. A little over 3 percent respondents of PESG, BSG and ESG rated the collection good. The 2.2 percent respondents of ISG rated the collection as excellent, the lowest percentage among the groups of users rating the collection of videocassettes.

The above analysis indicates that collection of videocassettes is negligible in all groups of CSIR libraries, as 81.1 percent respondents indicated the non-availability of such a collection. Poor collection of videocassettes was shown by 15.0 percent respondents. Only 3.7 percent of respondents expressed such collection to be good and 0.3 percent respondents indicated rated it excellent. Chi-square value = 19.23581 which is insignificant at .01 level, shows that there is no difference between the collection of videocassettes in CSIR libraries.

Table 8.43 : Videocassettes by Group of Laboratories

Group of Laboratories	*Response*				
	Excellent	*Good*	*Poor*	*Not Available*	*Row Total*
PESG	-	2	13	38	53
		(3.8)	(24.5)	(71.7)	(13.9)
CSG	-	-	7	50	57
			(12.3)	(87.7)	(15.0)
BSG	-	5	13	113	131
		(3.8)	(9.9)	(86.3)	(34.5)
ESG	-	4	18	72	94
		(4.3)	(19.1)	(76.6)	(24.7)
ISG	1	3	6	35	45
	(2.2)	(6.7)	(13.3)	(77.8)	(11.8)
Column Total	1	14	57	308	380
	(.3)	(3.7)	(15.0)	(81.1)	(100.0)

$X^2 = 19.23581$ with 12 d.f.
$P > .01$

8.2.12.4 Slides

Slides are very important item of non-print material. It is a piece of 35mm film mounted in a cardboard or plastic frame. Table 8.44 shows that scientific and technical libraries of CSIR are not in possession of slides. The majority of users of PESG (83.0%), BSG (81.7%) and CSG (80.7%) mentioned the non-availability of slides in the library. Other groups, i.e., ESG (74.5%) and ISG (71.1%) also marked the non-availability of slides in their libraries. The poor collection of slides is indicated by 18.1 percent of respondents of ESG. 13.3 percent respondents of ISG and 7.0 percent respondents of CSG also rated the collection of slides as poor. On the other hand, collection of slides is rated as good by 13.3 percent of respondents of ISG and 10.5 percent of CSG, followed by 6.4 percent ESG and 3.1 percent BSG.

The above analysis indicates non-availability of non-printed material in the CSIR libraries. The majority of respondents termed the availability of slides as poor and the reasons behind non-availability of slides may be ignorance and unawareness of usefulness of these items. The analysis reveals that except books and back volumes of periodicals, the collection of other literature, such as grey literature, non-printed material is either very poor or absent in the CSIR libraries. Chi-square value = 18.02660 as brought out in Table 8.44 is insignificant at .01 level, which shows no difference between collection of slides in individual group of CSIR libraries.

Table 8.44 : Slides by Group of Laboratories

Group of Laboratories	*Response*				
	Excellent	*Good*	*Poor*	*Not Available*	*Row Total*
PESG	1	-	8	44	53
	(1.9)		(15.1)	(83.0)	(13.9)
CSG	1	6	4	46	57
	(1.8)	(10.5)	(7.0)	(80.7)	(15.0)
BSG	-	4	20	107	131
		(3.1)	(15.3)	(81.7)	(34.5)
ESG	1	6	17	70	94
	(1.1)	(6.4)	(18.1)	(74.5)	(24.7)
ISG	1	6	6	32	45
	(2.2)	(13.3)	(13.3)	(71.1)	(11.8)
Column Total	4	22	55	299	380
	(1.1)	(5.8)	(14.5)	(78.7)	(100.0)

X^2 = 18.02660 with 12 d.f.

P > .01

8.2.12.5 CD-ROM Databases

The advent of information technology has brought a new technology in the storage and retrieval of information in a variety of ways. CD-ROM stands for compact disc-read only memory. It has revolutionised the storage and retrieval of vast quantities of information. Now the data in a hard copy, like encyclopedias, databases, etc. are available in CD format. The information contained in CD may include text, pictures or moving images as well as sound.

Respondents of CSIR libraries were asked to indicate the availability of CD-ROM databases in their libraries. Table 8.45 shows the responses regarding rating of availability of CD-ROM in CSIR libraries. The highest percentage of respondents of ESG (77.7%) termed the non-availability of CD-ROM in the library, followed by a little over 75 percent users of PESG and CSG. Almost equal percentage of respondents from ISG (68.9%) and BSG (68.7%) pointed out non-availability of CD-ROMs in their libraries. The collection of CD-ROM is rated as good by 20.6 percent of respondents of BSG, followed by 15.8 percent of CSG and 15.1 percent of PESG. The respondents of other groups, ISG (13.3%) and ESG (6.4%), also indicated the CD-ROM collection as good. The CD-ROM collection, on the other hand, is reported as excellent by 17.8 percent of ISG respondents, followed by 5.7 percent of PESG. The respondents of BSG (3.8%) rated the CD-ROM as excellent while 3.8 percent of PESG marked the CD-ROM in their libraries as poor. The lowest percentage of CSG (3.5%) and ESG (1.1%) also termed the CD-ROM as excellent. The poor collection was shown by 14.9 percent of respondents of ESG followed by 6.9 percent of BSG and 5.3 percent of CSG.

As per the above analysis the majority of respondents indicated the non-availability of CD-ROM in their libraries. This may be due to their unawareness about the availability of CD-ROM in the libraries or probably due to the lack of better knowledge of the technology as the causes for non-existence of such collection. The difference between the probability of CD-ROM in different groups of CSIR libraries as explained above is also supported by Chi-square value = 38.56282 which is significant at .01 level.

Table 8.45 : CD-ROM Databases by Group of Laboratories

Group of Laboratories	*Response*				
	Excellent	*Good*	*Poor*	*Not Available*	*Row Total*
PESG	3 (5.7)	8 (15.1)	2 (3.8)	40 (75.5)	53 (13.9)
CSG	2 (3.5)	9 (15.8)	3 (5.3)	43 (75.4)	57 (15.0)
BSG	5 (3.8)	27 (20.6)	9 (6.9)	90 (68.7)	131 (34.5)
ESG	1 (1.1)	6 (6.4)	14 (14.9)	73 (77.7)	94 (24.7)
ISG	8 (17.8)	6 (13.3)	-	31 (68.9)	45 (11.8)
Column Total	19 (5.0)	56 (14.7)	28 (7.4)	277 (72.9)	380 (100.0)

$X^2 = 38.56282$ with 12 d.f.

$P < .01$

8.2.12.6 Online Databases

Advent of computer technology has increased the capacity to store large amounts of information and decrease the costs of storage of data. This led to the development of online system. Online databases has brought a revolution in the information world to handle such a large data. Respondents of CSIR libraries were asked to indicate the online databases and their searching in their organisations; the results are shown in Table 8.46. In this way, an attempt has been made to examine accessibility of online databases in the CSIR libraries. Among the respondents of different groups of laboratories, highest percentage of respondents of ESG (81.9%) and PESG (81.1%) pointed out non-availability of online databases, followed by CSG (77.2%) and BSG (74.0%); 55.6 percent respondents of ISG also marked the non-availability of online databases. Over 22.2 percent respondents of ISG stated the online databases as excellent. The lowest percentage was of ESG (3.2%) and BSG (2.3%) who rated the online databases as excellent. On the other hand, 19.1 percent respondents of BSG rated the online databases as good as also by 15.8 percent of CSG. As equal percentage of respondents of ISG (11.1%) rated online databases good as well as poor. The percentage of respondents of ESG and PESG who stated online databases as good, was respectively 2.1 and 3.8.

From the above analysis, it is found that, like other non-printed material, online databases were also shown unavailable by the highest percentage of respondents as compared to other groups. The reasons behind the non-availability of online databases may be financial constraints to install computer and other information technologies in libraries, and lack of trained and experienced staff, etc. The difference between online databases in different groups of laboratories is clearly supported by Chi-square value = 63.62622 which is significant at .01 level.

Table 8.46 : Online Databases by Group of Laboratories

Group of Laboratories	*Response*				
	Excellent	*Good*	*Poor*	*Not Available*	*Row Total*
PESG		2	8	43	53
		(3.8)	(15.1)	(81.1)	(13.9)
CSG	2	9	2	44	57
	(3.5)	(15.8)	(3.5)	(77.2)	(15.0)
BSG	3	25	6	97	131
	(2.3)	(19.1)	(4.6)	(74.0)	(34.5)
ESG	3	2	12	77	94
	(3.2)	(2.1)	(12.8)	(81.9)	(24.7)
ISG	10	5	5	25	45
	(22.2)	(11.1)	(11.1)	(55.6)	(11.8)
Column Total	18	43	33	286	380
	(4.7)	(11.3)	(8.7)	(75.3)	(100.0)

X^2 = 63.62622 with 12 d.f.

P < .01

8.2.12.7 Maps/Atlases

From Table 8.47, it may be seen that the majority of respondents of CSG (47.4%) indicated availability of maps/atlases as poor, followed by ESG (38.3%) and PESG (34.0%). About 26.7 percent respondents of ISG marked the collection of maps and atlases in the library poor, whereas an equal percentage of respondents of ISG (26.7%) stated maps and atlases as not available in the library. On the other hand, respondents of ISG (42.2%) rated the collection of maps and atlases as good, followed by BSG (32.1%). Even 28.7 percent of ESG respondents, 24.5 percent of PESG and 21.1 percent of CSG also termed the collection of maps and atlases as good.

Respondents of BSG (41.2%) stated the non-availability of maps and atlases, followed by 35.8 percent of PESG and 31.6 percent of CSG. A little over 26 percent of respondents of ESG and ISG also termed the maps and atlases being not available. It is interesting to note that a significant percentage of respondents pointed out the collection of maps and atlases as excellent. While 8.4 percent respondents of BSG rated the maps and atlases as excellent, followed by 6.4 percent of ESG. It was found that even 4 percent to 5 percent respondents of ISG and PESG termed the collection as excellent. No responses of CSG reported the collection of maps and atlases as excellent. To find out the difference between maps and atlases in different libraries, Chi-square test has been applied. It is found that Chi-square value = 27.86061 which is significant at .01 level.

Table 8.47 : Maps/Atlases by Group of Laboratories

Group of Laboratories	*Response*				
	Excellent	*Good*	*Poor*	*Not Available*	*Row Total*
PESG	3	13	18	19	53
	(5.7)	(24.5)	(34.0)	(35.8)	(13.9)
CSG	-	12	27	18	57
		(21.1)	(47.4)	(31.6)	(15.0)
BSG	11	42	24	54	131
	(8.4)	(32.1)	(18.3)	(41.2)	(34.5)
ESG	6	27	36	25	94
	(6.4)	(28.7)	(38.3)	(26.6)	(24.7)
ISG	2	19	12	12	45
	(4.4)	(42.2)	(26.7)	(26.7)	(11.8)
Column Total	22	113	117	128	380
	(5.8)	(29.7)	(30.8)	(33.7)	(100.0)

X^2 = 27.86061 with 12 d.f.

P < .01

8.2.12.8 Picture Transparencies/Photos

Table 8.48 reveals the rating of collection of picture transparencies/photos in different groups of CSIR libraries. The majority of respondents of PESG (94.3%) have shown non-availability of picture transparencies/photos, followed by BSG (77.1%) and CSG (71.9%). Other groups of ESG (67.0%) and ISG (68.9%) marked such collection as not available. The highest percentage of respondents of ESG (26.6%) stated collection of picture transparencies/photos as poor, followed by ISG (20.0%). Even 14.5 percent respondents of BSG also termed the picture transparencies as poor, followed by 10.5 percent of CSG and 5.7 percent of PESG. The proportion of the respondents belonging to CSG (15.8%) and ISG (11.1%) who rated the collection of picture transparencies/photos as good is comparatively higher than other groups. It is interesting to note that only 2.1 percent of ESG, 1.8 percent of CSG and 0.8 percent of BSG rated picture transparencies as excellent. Other groups like PESG and ISG did not respond regarding picture transparencies to be excellent.

It is significant to note that majority of respondents (75.3%) termed the picture transparencies/photos as not available and the respondents who marked the collection as poor constituted 16.3 percent. The difference between the views of respondents regarding availability of picture transparencies/photos is clearly supported by Chi-square value = 29.31199 which is significant at .01 level.

Table 8.48 : Picture Transparencies/Photos by Group of Laboratories

Group of Laboratories	*Response*				
	Excellent	*Good*	*Poor*	*Not Available*	*Row Total*
PESG	-	-	3	50	53
			(5.7)	(94.3)	(13.9)
CSG	1	9	6	41	57
	(1.8)	(15.8)	(10.5)	(71.9)	(15.0)
BSG	1	10	19	101	131
	(.8)	(7.6)	(14.5)	(77.1)	(34.5)
ESG	2	4	25	63	94
	(2.1)	(4.3)	(26.6)	(67.0)	(24.7)
ISG	-	5	9	31	45
		(11.1)	(20.0)	(68.9)	(11.8)
Column Total	4	28	62	286	380
	(1.1)	(7.4)	(16.3)	(75.3)	(100.0)

$X^2 = 29.31199$ with 12 d.f.

$P < .01$

8.3 DOCUMENT DELIVERY SERVICES

Document delivery service was initiated for the first time by UNESCO and after that it spread all over the world. Such services are essential for the benefit of users, which include:

(a) Supply of photocopies of articles from journals required by scientists and research scholars of the laboratories.

(b) Supply of photocopies of articles from journals and documents required by researchers, scientists and research scholars of universities, learned institutes and research organisations of India and abroad on payment basis.

(c) Procurement of photocopies of articles from journals and other documents for the scientists and research scholars of the laboratories from other libraries of different organisations, university libraries of India and abroad as well on payment basis.

In the wake of the ever-escalating prices of journals and monographs, document delivery service has assumed a greater significance. Photocopies of literature available in the library could easily be provided with little efforts by the staff. But real delivery mechanism is put on the test when photocopies of required literature are obtained from other organisations located within the country and abroad. In succeeding pages an attempt has been made to analyse strength and weakness of document delivery service being arranged in this respect.

8.3.1 Provision of Document Delivery and Related Services

Respondents of CSIR laboratories were asked to comment on the provision of document delivery and related services. Table 8.49 depicts that all the users indicated that all groups of CSIR libraries are lending books to their clients. Over ninety percent of respondents of libraries termed that their libraries are also lending scientific journals to them. However, response is not the same in respect of interlibrary loan and procurement of materials from other countries. Only 69.2 percent of respondents reported that interlibrary loan facility is available in their libraries, whereas 58.9 percent respondents reported availability of such facility for obtaining materials from abroad. An overwhelming majority of respondents expressed that assistance from library staff in locating and searching library materials, guidance in using the library and obtaining required information are available to a large extent.

Table 8.49 : Provision of Document Delivery and Related Services

Document Delivery Services	*Response*		
	Yes	*No*	*Row Total*
Lending of books	380 (100.0)	-	380 (100.0)
Lending of scientific journals	348 (91.6)	32 (8.4)	380 (100.0)
Interlibrary loan	263 (69.2)	117 (30.8)	380 (100.0)
Material from other countries	224 (58.9)	156 (41.1)	380 (100.0)
Help in locating material	345 (90.8)	35 (9.2)	380 (100.0)
Guidance in using material	330 (86.8)	50 (13.2)	380 (100.0)
Requirement of specific information	320 (84.2)	60 (15.8)	380 (100.0)

8.3.1.1 Rating of Document Delivery and Related Services

Users' responses are recorded regarding the rating of document delivery and related services. Rating of document delivery and related services as given in Table 8.50, shows that majority of respondents think these service as good. Hence, a good number of respondents (35.4%) have shown their disenchantment with interlibrary loan service. Such is the case of procurement of materials from abroad. Lending facilities of books and journals are the area where a great amount of satisfaction has been expressed by respondents. The help of library staff is also a matter of appreciation as most of the users have shown their satisfaction by indicating it as good and excellent.

Table 8.50 : Rating of Document Delivery and Related Services

Document delivery	*Response*			
Services	*Excellent*	*Good*	*Poor*	*Row Total*
Lending of books	175 (46.1)	192 (50.5)	13 (3.4)	380 (100.0)
Lending of scientific journals	131 (37.6)	183 (52.6)	34 (9.8)	348 (100.0)
Interlibrary loan	41 (15.6)	129 (49.0)	93 (35.4)	263 (100.0)
Material from other countries	39 (17.4)	101 (45.1)	84 (37.5)	224 (100.0)
Help in locating material	78 (22.6)	214 (62.0)	53 (15.4)	345 (100.0)
Guidance in using material	80 (24.2)	192 (58.2)	58 (17.6)	330 (100.0)
Requirement of specific information	68 (21.3)	190 (59.4)	62 (19.4)	320 (100.0)

8.3.2 Lending of Books

Table 8.51 shows that all libraries of CSIR are providing facilities of lending books to their users. It shows that they are not meant for reference only but are available for use beyond the walls of the libraries.

Table 8.51 : Lending of Books in Group of CSIR Laboratories

Lending of	*Group of Laboratories*					
Books	*PESG*	*CSG*	*BSG*	*ESG*	*ISG*	*Row Total*
Yes	53 (100.0)	57 (100.0)	131 (100.0)	94 (100.0)	45 (100.0)	380 (100.0)
No	-	-	-	-	-	-
Column Total	53 (13.9)	57 (15.0)	131 (34.5)	94 (24.7)	45 (11.8)	380 (100.0)

8.3.2.1 Rating of Lending of Books

Table 8.52 presents the data on rating of lending of books. 50.5 percent respondents have rated this as good. A good number of respondents (46.1%) rate this service as excellent. Group-wise analysis reveals that majority of respondents belonging to CSG (50.9%) and BSG (50.4%) have rated this service as excellent, whereas the majority of respondents in case of other groups rated this service as good. However, an over all analysis suggests that an overwhelming majority of respondents across the group is very much satisfied with this service and there is no variation in this regard. Chi-square value = 12.65268 which is insignificant at .01 level shows that there is no difference between the respondents of lending of books in the groups of CSIR libraries.

Table 8.52 : Rating of Lending of Books

Group of	*Response*			
Laboratories	*Excellent*	*Good*	*Poor*	*Row Total*
PESG	20	32	1	53
	(37.7)	(60.4)	(1.9)	(13.9)
CSG	29	27	1	57
	(50.9)	(47.4)	(1.8)	(15.0)
BSG	66	62	3	131
	(50.4)	(47.3)	(2.3)	(34.5)
ESG	41	50	3	94
	(43.6)	(53.2)	(3.2)	(24.7)
ISG	19	21	5	45
	(42.2)	(46.7)	(11.1)	(11.8)
Column Total	175	192	13	380
	(46.1)	(50.5)	(3.4)	(100.0)

X^2 = 12.65268 with 8 d.f.

P > .01

8.3.3 Lending of Scientific Journals

Users' views were solicited about the facilities of lending of scientific journals in CSIR libraries. Table 8.53 shows that an overwhelming majority of BSG (95.4%) and CSG (93.0%) expressed that their libraries are having facility for lending of scientific journals in the CSIR libraries, followed by ESG (90.4%). A little over 86 percent respondents of PESG and ISG also indicated the lending of scientific journals in their libraries. The analysis of data shows that service of lending of scientific journals is being provided in almost all libraries of CSIR. However, it has been pointed out that the journals are issued over night only. Chi-square value = 5.79629 is insignificant at .01 level which shows no significant difference between the responses of lending of scientific journals in CSIR libraries.

Table 8.53 : Lending of Scientific Journals in Group of CSIR Laboratories

Lending of Scientific Journals	*Group of Laboratories*					
	PESG	*CSG*	*BSG*	*ESG*	*ISG*	*Row Total*
Yes	46	53	125	85	39	348
	(86.8)	(93.0)	(95.4)	(90.4)	(86.7)	(91.6)
No	7	4	6	9	6	32
	(13.2)	(7.0)	(4.6)	(9.6)	(13.3)	(8.4)
Column Total	53	57	131	94	45	380
	(13.9)	(15.0)	(34.5)	(24.7)	(11.8)	(100.0)

X^2 = 5.79629 with 4 d.f.

P > .01

8.3.3.1 Rating of Lending of Scientific Journals

The respondents of CSIR libraries were requested to rate lending of scientific journals as provided in their respective libraries. Table 8.54 reveals that more than 50 percent of respondents indicated lending of scientific journals as good, followed by 37.6 percent respondents who reported this service as excellent. In the group-wise analysis, not much variation is visible. The majority of users across the groups have rated this service as good, followed by those who have rated it as excellent. Chi-square value = 12.24459 is insignificant at .01 level which does not support the difference between the respondents in regard to provision of lending of scientific journals in CSIR libraries.

Table 8.54 : Rating of Lending of Scientific Journals

Group of Laboratories	*Response*			
	Excellent	*Good*	*Poor*	*Row Total*
PESG	15 (32.6)	28 (60.9)	3 (6.5)	46 (13.2)
CSG	20 (37.7)	28 (52.8)	5 (9.4)	53 (15.2)
BSG	57 (45.6)	60 (48.0)	8 (6.4)	125 (35.9)
ESG	29 (34.1)	46 (54.1)	10 (11.8)	85 (24.4)
ISG	10 (25.6)	21 (53.8)	8 (20.5)	39 (11.2)
Column Total	131 (37.6)	183 (52.6)	34 (9.8)	348 (100.0)

X^2 = 12.24459 with 8 d.f.

P > .01

8.3.4 Interlibrary Loan

Interlibrary loan is an old arrangement of resource sharing among libraries. Even after the advent of technology this practice of resource sharing continues to be followed in the libraries. It is extended out of necessity to supplement resources of libraries and serve the users of other places of different libraries.

An analysis of Table 8.55 reveals that majority of respondents, 69.2 percent, across the group of laboratories indicated that CSIR libraries are providing interlibrary loan services. Group-wise analysis of CSIR libraries shows that an overwhelming majority of respondents of ISG (97.8%) indicated availability of the provision to provide interlibrary loan service. Though the response rate is not the same in case of PESG and ESG, an overwhelming majority of respondents of both the groups have indicated provision of such services. However, BSG and CSG have only 58.8 percent and 52.6 percent of respondents respectively, who have indicated provision of interlibrary loan service in their libraries. This is such a service that unless one personally avails of it, he/she cannot be aware of its being in vogue. It can, therefore, be said that all those who have indicated non-availability of such a service would not have used this service, or they were not aware of such arrangement. Chi-square value = 35.58630, which is significant at .01 level shows the difference between the respondents in regard to provision of interlibrary loan service in CSIR libraries.

Table 8.55 : Interlibrary Loan in Group of CSIR Laboratories

Interlibrary	*Group of Laboratories*					
Loan	*PESG*	*CSG*	*BSG*	*ESG*	*ISG*	*Row Total*
Yes	43	30	77	69	44	263
	(81.1)	(52.6)	(58.8)	(73.4)	(97.8)	(69.2)
No	10	27	54	25	1	117
	(18.9)	(47.4)	(41.2)	(26.6)	(2.2)	(30.8)
Column Total	53	57	131	94	45	380
	(13.9)	(15.0)	(34.5)	(24.7)	(11.8)	(100.0)

X^2 = 35.58630 with 4 d.f.

P > .01

8.3.4.1 Rating of Interlibrary Loan

Table 8.56 shows the responses relating to rating of interlibrary loan service provided in CSIR libraries. The noticeable feature of rating of this service has been poor. A large number of respondents (35.4%) rate this service as poor. However, number of such respondents is predominant in CSG (53.3%) and ESG (43.5%). Among the groups where this service has been rated as good are BSG (58.4%) and ISG (56.8%). The number of those respondents who have rated this service as excellent is noteworthy in each group. The reasons behind poor rating of interlibrary loan service is most probably due to lack of effective channel of exchange of resources. This service can be offered properly only when more personal attention is paid to the demand of users. This service can be arranged to the maximum extent these days by using modern technologies such as E-mail etc. Chi-square value = 13.86206 is insignificant at .01 level which shows that there is no significant difference between the respondents of interlibrary loan in different groups of CSIR.

Table 8.56 : Rating of Interlibrary Loan

Group of	*Response*			
Laboratories	*Excellent*	*Good*	*Poor*	*Row Total*
PESG	5	21	17	43
	(11.6)	(48.8)	(39.5)	(16.3)
CSG	5	9	16	30
	(16.7)	(30.0)	(53.3)	(11.4)
BSG	14	45	18	77
	(18.2)	(58.4)	(23.4)	(29.3)
ESG	10	29	30	69
	(14.5)	(42.0)	(43.5)	(26.2)
ISG	7	25	12	44
	(15.9)	(56.8)	(27.3)	(16.7)
Column Total	41	129	93	263
	(15.6)	(49.0)	(35.4)	(100.0)

X^2 = 13 86206 with 8 d.f.

P > .01

8.3.5 Procuring/Acquiring Specific Material from Other Countries on Request

In order to ascertain the provision of procurement of specific material from other countries, users were asked to indicate the arrangement of such provisions in their respective organisations. Table 8.57 reveals that more than 50 percent of respondents of different CSIR libraries expressed that their respective libraries have arrangement of procuring reading material from abroad. It seems from the group-wise analysis that except PESG the majority of respondents of different groups have indicated that their libraries are providing such service. 71.1 percent respondents of ISG indicated that their libraries procure the specific material on the request of users, followed by CSG (63.2%) and BSG (61.1%). It is clear that except PESG, all other groups have the arrangement of procuring specific material from other countries. Chi-square value = 8.96452 is insignificant at .01 level which shows no significant difference between the procuring specific material from other countries on the request of users.

Table 8.57 : Procuring/Acquiring Specific Material from Other Countries on Request in Groups of CSIR Laboratories

Procuring/ Acquiring Specific Material from Other Countries on Request	*Group of Laboratories*					
	PESG	*CSG*	*BSG*	*ESG*	*ISG*	*Row Total*
Yes	23 (43.4)	36 (63.2)	80 (61.1)	53 (56.4)	32 (71.1)	224 (58.9)
No	30 (56.6)	21 (36.8)	51 (38.9)	41 (43.6)	13 (28.9)	156 (41.1)
Column Total	53 (13.9)	57 (15.0)	131 (34.5)	94 (24.7)	45 (11.8)	380 (100.0)

X^2 = 8.96452 with 4 d.f.
P > .01

8.3.5.1 *Rating of Procuring/Acquiring Specific Material from Other Countries on Request*

The views of respondents' on procurement of specific materials from other countries on request is rated in Table

8.58. Though most of the respondents have rated this service as good, a larger group of users considered this service as poor. Only 17.4 percent respondents have considered this service as excellent. Group-wise analysis of data reveals that the majority of respondents of PESG (60.9%) rated the acquisition of specific material on demand as poor, followed by CSG (50.0%). Equal proportions of respondents of ISG (34.4%) have indicated the service as good as well as poor. While over 50 percent respondents both of ESG and BSG rated the procurement of specific material from abroad as good, so was by 38.9 percent CSG. 31.3 percent respondents of ISG and BSG are those who rated such provision as excellent and also poor respectively. A little over 15 percent respondents of PESG, BSG and ESG also indicated procurement of such material from abroad as excellent. However, the delay in the process of procurement of specific materials from abroad could be the reason in rating it as poor. Chi-square value = 17.05458 being insignificant at .01 level, does not support the difference between procurement of specific information from abroad in CSIR libraries.

Table 8.58 : Rating of Procuring/Acquiring Specific Material from Other Countries on Request

Group of Laboratories	*Response*			*Row Total*
	Excellent	*Good*	*Poor*	
PESG	4 (17.4)	5 (21.7)	14 (60.9)	23 (10.3)
CSG	4 (11.1)	14 (38.9)	18 (50.0)	36 (16.1)
BSG	13 (16.3)	42 (52.5)	25 (31.3)	80 (35.7)
ESG	8 (15.1)	29 (54.7)	16 (30.2)	53 (23.7)
ISG	10 (31.3)	11 (34.4)	11 (34.4)	32 (14.3)
Column Total	39 (17.4)	101 (45.1)	84 (37.5)	224 (100.0)

X^2 = 17.05458 with 8 d.f.
P > .01

8.3.6 Assistance and Guidance in Searching/Locaung of the Material

The sincere and committed library staff add a great value to the services and management of the library. In order to evaluate the cooperation and assistance provided by the library staff in locating reading material, users of CSIR libraries were advised to indicate the attitude and helpfulness of their library staff. Over 90 percent of respondents are of the view that library staff of their libraries is very co-operative and help in locating particular material for them. It has been found from the analysis that cooperation of library staff of CSIR libraries is very appreciatable and satisfactory.

It is clear from the Table 8.59 that the library staff in CSIR laboratories is helpful to the users, as an overwhelming majority of users across the libraries have shown satisfaction in this respect. However, the difference between provision of assistance in searching/locating of the material is not significant statistically as Chi-square value = 9.72155 is not significant at .01 level.

Table 8.59 : Assistance and Guidance in Searching/Locating of the Material in Group of CSIR Laboratories

Assistance in Searching/ Locating of the Material	*Group of Laboratories*					
	PESG	*CSG*	*BSG*	*ESG*	*ISG*	*Row Total*
Yes	48 (90.6)	54 (94.7)	112 (85.5)	91 (96.8)	40 (88.9)	345 (90.8)
No	5 (9.4)	3 (5.3)	19 (14.5)	3 (3.2)	5 (11.1)	35 (9.2)
Column Total	53 (13.9)	57 (15.0)	131 (34.5)	94 (24.7)	45 (11.8)	380 (100.0)

X^2 = 9.72155 with 4 d.f.

P > .01

8.3.6.1 Rating of the Assistance in Searching/Locating Required Material

The Table 8.60 shows rating of the help of the library staff in searching and locating the desired material and specific information. Over 80 percent of respondents rated this service either as excellent or good. It means that respondents are satisfied with the help extended to them by the staff. Group-wise analysis of data also doesn't indicate any noticeable variation in response rate. Chi-square value = 10.06405 is insignificant at .01 level, which shows no significant difference between the help in searching/locating the material in CSIR libraries.

Table 8.60 : Rating of Assistance in Searching/Locating Required Material

Group of Laboratories	*Response*			
	Excellent	*Good*	*Poor*	*Row Total*
PESG	10	25	13	48
	(20.8)	(52.1)	(27.1)	(13.9)
CSG	8	37	9	54
	(14.8)	(68.5)	(16.7)	(15.7)
BSG	29	71	12	112
	(25.9)	(63.4)	(10.7)	(32.5)
ESG	23	54	14	91
	(25.3)	(59.3)	(15.4)	(26.4)
ISG	8	27	5	40
	(20.0)	(67.5)	(12.5)	(11.6)
Column Total	78	214	53	345
	(22.6)	(62.0)	(15.4)	(100.0)

$X^2 = 10.06405$ with 8 d.f.

$P > .01$

8.3.7 Guidance in Using Library and Its Resources

In addition to building the collection in the library, the guidance of the library staff for using the library creates an atmosphere conducive for the users to make the maximum use of the library and it establishes good relation between the staff and the users. The majority of users (86.8%) in Table 8.61 expressed that the library staff of CSIR libraries provide them guidance in using library. More than 85 percent respondents of CSG, ESG, PESG and BSG have indicated to have received guidance from library staff whenever the same is required. The pattern of overall response is almost visible across the groups, except ISG where 77.8 percent of respondents reported to be receiving guidance in using the library. Chi-square test has been applied and found that Chi-square value = 4.29884 is insignificant at .01 level, does not support the difference between guidance in using library in groups of CSIR libraries.

Table 8.61 : Guidance in Using Library and Its Resources

Guidance in Using the Library	*Group of Laboratories*					
	PESG	*CSG*	*BSG*	*ESG*	*ISG*	*Row Total*
Yes	47 (88.7)	51 (89.5)	113 (86.3)	84 (89.4)	35 (77.8)	330 (86.8)
No	6 (11.3)	6 (10.5)	18 (13.7)	10 (10.6)	10 (22.2)	50 (13.2)
Column Total	53 (13.9)	57 (15.0)	131 (34.5)	94 (24.7)	45 (11.8)	380 (100.0)

X^2 = 4.29884 with 4 d.f.

P > .01

8.3.7.1 Rating of Guidance in Using Library and its Resources

Table 8.62 indicates that the guidance as given by the library staff to the respondents is good. It means that the library staff makes efforts to meet the information needs of their users. Over 80 percent of the respondents of all other groups, except PESG and ESG, rate the guidance as good. Minor variation is evident when, barring PESG and CSG, over 25 percent of respondents of the other three groups rate this as excellent also. Chi-square test has been applied and found that Chi-square value = 11.02359 is not significant at .01 level. There is no significant difference between respondents of rating of guidance available in making use of the library.

Table 8.62 : Rating of Guidance in Using Library and its Resources

Group of Laboratories	*Response* Excellent	*Good*	*Poor*	*Row Total*
PESG	8	26	13	47
	(17.0)	(55.3)	(27.7)	(14.2)
CSG	11	30	10	51
	(21.6)	(58.8)	(19.6)	(15.5)
BSG	29	71	13	113
	(25.7)	(62.8)	(11.5)	(34.2)
ESG	22	43	19	84
	(26.2)	(51.2)	(22.6)	(25.5)
ISG	10	22	3	35
	(28.6)	(62.9)	(8.6)	(10.6)
Column Total	80	192	58	330
	(24.2)	(58.2)	(17.6)	(100.0)

X^2 = 11.02359 with 8 d.f.

P > .01

8.3.8 Provision of Specific Information When Required

Users of CSIR libraries were requested to indicate whether their library staff provides them specific information when asked for. Table 8.63 shows that an overwhelming majority of respondents (84.2%) expressed that their respective organisations have arrangement to provide specific information as and when required by the users. The majority of respondents of each group have indicated the provision of such services in their organisations. However, the proportion of such respondents is higher in CSG (93.0%) and ESG (91.5%) as compared to other groups. Chi-square value = 11.89507 is insignificant at .01 level shows no difference between the respondents of fulfilling requirement of specific information.

Table 8.63 : Provision of Specific Information When Required in Group of CSIR Laboratories

Provision of Specific Information	*Group of Laboratories*					
	PESG	*CSG*	*BSG*	*ESG*	*ISG*	*Row Total*
Yes	43 (81.1)	53 (93.0)	103 (78.6)	86 (91.5)	35 (77.8)	320 (84.2)
No	10 (18.9)	4 (7.0)	28 (21.4)	8 (8.5)	10 (22.2)	60 (15.8)
Column Total	53 (13.9)	57 (15.0)	131 (34.5)	94 (24.7)	45 (11.8)	380 (100.0)

$X^2 = 11.89507$ with 4 d.f.

$P > .01$

8.3.8.1 Rating of Provision of Specific Information When Required

Rating of provision of providing specific information has been shown in Table 8.64. It reveals that an overwhelming majority of respondents (80.7%) are satisfied with this service. Out of this, 21.3 percent of respondents have rated this service as excellent and the rest as good. Interestingly, there is not much variation in response rate. The difference between rating of provision of specific information when required by the respondents is supported by Chi-square value = 20.09797 which is significant at .01 level.

Table 8.64 : Rating of Provision of Specific Information When Required

Group of Laboratories	*Response* Excellent	Good	Poor	*Row Total*
PESG	8	18	17	43
	(18.6)	(41.9)	(39.5)	(13.4)
CSG	9	33	11	53
	(17.0)	(62.3)	(20.8)	(16.6)
BSG	26	66	11	103
	(25.2)	(64.1)	(10.7)	(32.2)
ESG	15	52	19	86
	(17.4)	(60.5)	(22.1)	(26.9)
ISG	10	21	4	35
	(28.6)	(60.0)	(11.4)	(10.9)
Column Total	68	190	62	320
	(21.3)	(59.4)	(19.4)	(100.0)

$X^2 = 20.09797$ with 8 d.f.

$P < .01$

8.4 REFERENCE AND INFORMATION SERVICES

Reference service is perceived as very effective mechanism to build up personal rapport with the users by way of providing various helps. This is backbone of library services. In the age of greater use of information technology, only nature of rendering service has changed but certainly not the contents. It is in this context an effort has been made to find out whether there is provision of reference service in CSIR libraries or not and also as to how these services are perceived.

The respondents of CSIR libraries were advised to specify the availability of reference services in their libraries. Table 8.65 shows that over 80 percent respondents have stated that CSIR libraries have the provision of reference services and the lists of new books acquired and journals subscribed and discontinued in their libraries are displayed and circulated for awareness of the users. Except list of new books and journals subscribed/discontinued, responses vary significantly in all other services. 59.5 percent respondents indicated that they are getting the benefit of literature search whereas 55.5 percent respondents stated the provision of contents of periodicals being made available. Availability of indexing and abstracting services are also shown by 52.4 percent respondents. However, there is a little difference in the responses of preparation of bibliographies on demand and bibliographic services. Provision of preparation of bibliographies on demand is stated by 47.6 percent respondents, while availability of bibliographic services is shown by 45.8 percent respondents. In addition to digest of scientific, technical and industrial information, provision of SDI service is also negligible in CSIR libraries.

It is evident from the above analysis that less number of respondents have indicated provision of preparation of bibliographies on demand, bibliographic services, digest of scientific, technical and industrial information and SDI services in their libraries. It means that libraries are offering only elementary reference service. Advanced type of reference service, i.e., highly developed information services are not arranged so extensively.

Table 8.65 : Provision of Reference and Information Services

Provision of Reference and Information Services	*Response*			
	Yes	*No*	*Not Stated*	*Row Total*
List of new books acquired	306 (80.5)	74 (19.5)	-	380 (100.0)
List of journals subscribed/ discontinued	320 (84.2)	60 (15.8)	-	380 (100.0)
Preparation and supply of bibliographies on demand	181 (47.6)	199 (52.4)	-	380 (100.0)
Indexing and abstracting services	199 (52.4)	181 (47.6)	-	380 (100.0)

Bibliographical services	174 (45.8)	206 (54.2)	-	380 (100.0)
Literature search	226 (59.5)	154 (40.5)	-	380 (100.0)
Contents pages of periodicals	211 (55.5)	169 (44.5)	-	380 (100.0)
SDI service	58 (15.3)	296 (77.9)	26 (6.8)	380 (100.0)
Digest of scientific, technical and industrial information	97 (25.5)	271 (71.3)	12 (3.2)	380 (100.0)

8.4.1 Rating of Reference and Information Services

Table 8.66 presents data regarding rating of reference and information services reported by the respondents of CSIR libraries. More than 60 percent respondents rated the contents of periodicals, list of journals subscribed/discontinued, list of new books acquired and the digest of scientific, technical and industrial information as good. Rest of over 50 percent respondents are those who rated literature search, preparation of bibliography on demand, bibliographic services and indexing and abstracting services as good. Over 25 percent respondents in regard to indexing and abstracting services, list of new books acquired, bibliographic services and list of journals subscribed/discontinued have rated such services as excellent for keeping users abreast of the materials of their interests. Whereas SDI services and digest of scientific, technical and industrial information have been rated as excellent by insignificant number of respondents. On the other hand, preparation of bibliography on demand, digest of scientific, technical and industrial information and bibliographic services are placed as poor across the groups of CSIR libraries. Even indexing and abstracting services and literature search are also rated as poor by 20.6 percent and 18.6 percent of respondents respectively.

It is apparent from the above analysis that majority of users are satisfied with the services provided by their libraries. However, some variation is visible in the rating of these services. It may be said that lack of professional, trained and experienced staff may be responsible for the poor services of these libraries. The computer facilities are another factor that is badly hampering such facilities. In addition to this, the lack of dedication towards services has also been noticed.

Table 8.66 : Rating of Reference and Information Services

Group of Laboratories	*Response*			
	Excellent	*Good*	*Poor*	*Row Total*
List of new books acquired	86 (28.1)	190 (62.1)	30 (9.8)	306 (100.0)
List of journals subscribed/ discontinued	82 (25.6)	202 (63.1)	36 (11.3)	320 (100.0)
Preparation and supply of bibliographies on demand	38 (21.0)	98 (54.1)	45 (24.9)	181 (100.0)
Indexing and abstracting services	57 (28.6)	101 (50.8)	41 (20.6)	199 (100.0)
Bibliographical services	47 (27.0)	89 (51.1)	38 (21.8)	174 (100.0)
Literature search	53 (23.5)	131 (58.0)	42 (18.6)	226 (100.0)
Contents pages of periodicals	45 (21.3)	140 (66.4)	26 (12.3)	211 (100.0)
SDI service	10 (17.2)	45 (77.6)	3 (5.2)	58 (100.0)
Digest of scientific, technical and industrial information	15 (15.5)	59 (60.8)	23 (23.7)	97 (100.0)

8.4.2 Lists of New Books Acquired

Circulation of the lists of new additions is a very important means and technique of Current Awareness Service (CAS) which assists the users community to identify the latest literature pertaining to their research fields acquired by their respective libraries. In Table 8.67 respondents of different disciplines were asked to indicate whether or not there is the provision of CAS such as list of new books acquired in their libraries are circulated. An overwhelming majority of respondents of CSG (94.7%) stated that their libraries have the provision of such services. But the percentage of such respondents is a little less in case of BSG (81.7%) and ESG (78.7%). The provision of such service has also been indicated by the respondents of ISG (73.3%) and PESG (71.7%). The above analysis reveals that the majority of the respondents are availing of CAS of this type. Chi-square value = 11.76497, which is insignificant at .01 level, shows that there is no significant difference between the respondents in regard to provision of providing list of new books acquired.

Table 8.67 : Lists of New Books Acquired

List of New Books Acquired	*Group of Laboratories*					
	PESG	*CSG*	*BSG*	*ESG*	*ISG*	*Row Total*
Yes	38	54	107	74	33	306
	(71.7)	(94.7)	(81.7)	(78.7)	(73.3)	(80.5)
No	15	3	24	20	12	74
	(28.3)	(5.3)	(18.3)	(21.3)	(26.7)	(19.5)
Column Total	53	57	131	94	45	380
	(13.9)	(15.0)	(34.5)	(24.7)	(11.8)	(100.0)

X^2 = 11.76497 with 4 d.f.
P > .01

8.4.2.1 Rating of the Lists of New Books Acquired

Table 8.68 shows the rating of reference services, such as list of new books acquired. This rating helps to measure the usefulness of current awareness services. Mode of receiving information about the latest additions to the library in the form of lists of new books was rated as a good service by a majority of respondents of PESG (71.1%), followed by CSG (64.8%). Over 59 percent respondents of ESG and BSG also indicated this service as good. Even 51.5 percent respondents of ISG also stated the list of new additions as good.

On the other hand, a good number of respondents in almost all the groups have rated this service as excellent. ESG has the largest number, i.e., 35.1 percent, followed by BSG-29.9

percent and ISG-27.3 percent, who appreciate and value this sort of service.

However, there are some respondents in each group who are not satisfied with this service and rated it as poor. The largest number of such members are in ISG (21.2%), followed by PESG (13.2%) and CSG (11.1%).

Overall the analysis suggests that this service has been rated as good by CSIR laboratories (62.1%), followed by 28.1 percent of respondents who have rated it as excellent one. Chi-square value = 11.99605, which is insignificant at .01 level. This does not support the difference statistically.

Table 8.68 : Rating of Lists of New Books Acquired

Group of Laboratories	*Response*			
	Excellent	*Good*	*Poor*	*Row Total*
PESG	6	27	5	38
	(15.8)	(71.1)	(13.2)	(12.4)
CSG	13	35	6	54
	(24.1)	(64.8)	(11.1)	(17.6)
BSG	32	67	8	107
	(29.9)	(62.6)	(7.5)	(35.0)
ESG	26	44	4	74
	(35.1)	(59.5)	(5.4)	(24.2)
ISG	9	17	7	33
	(27.3)	(51.5)	(21.2)	(10.8)
Column Total	86	190	30	306
	(28.1)	(62.1)	(9.8)	(100.0)

X^2 = 11.99605 with 8 d.f.

P > .01

8.4.3 List of Journals Subscribed and Discontinued

Through CAS such libraries announce their in-house activities for keeping users up-to-date by publishing bulletins and using other media also for the same. The list of journals subscribed/discontinued is also an attempt to alert the users about the status of journals in the library. Table 8.69 reveals that majority of the respondents of CSG (87.7%) were of the opinion that their libraries have the arrangement to bring out such lists of journals subscribed or discontinued for their benefit. Comparatively, a higher proportion of respondents of CSG, BSG and ESG than ISG and PESG indicated the presence of provision of circulating the list of journals subscribed and discontinued in their libraries.

Chi-square value = 2.75262, which is highly non-significant at .01 level, shows that there is no significant difference between the provision of this service being offered by various libraries.

Table 8.69 : List of Journals Subscribed and Discontinued

List of Journals Subscribed/ Discontinued	*Group of Laboratories*					
	PESG	*CSG*	*BSG*	*ESG*	*ISG*	*Row Total*
Yes	41	50	112	80	37	320
	(77.4)	(87.7)	(85.5)	(85.1)	(82.2)	(84.2)
No	12	7	19	14	8	60
	(22.6)	(12.3)	(14.5)	(14.9)	(17.8)	(15.8)
Column Total	53	57	131	94	45	380
	(13.9)	(15.0)	(34.5)	(24.7)	(11.8)	(100.0)

$X^2 = 2.75262$ with 4 d.f.

$P < .01$

8.4.3.1 Rating of List of Journals Subscribed and Discontinued

An attempt has been made in Table 8.70 to show the rating of this service. Data as presented reveals the views of the respondents about the list of journals subscribed and discontinued. This service is rated as good by the majority of respondents of PESG (70.7%), followed by ESG (66.3%). A little over 61 percent respondents of BSG and CSG also indicated this service as being good. However, the provision of this service is rated good by a comparatively less number of respondents of ISG (54.1%). A good number of respondents of BSG and ISG also rate the service as excellent. There are also some respondents in each group who rate the service as poor. However, percentage of such respondents is higher in CSG, ISG and PESG only. Chi-square value = 8.39623 as brought out in Table 8.70, is insignificant at .01 level. This shows no difference between list of journals subscribed and discontinued among the respondents of five groups of CSIR libraries.

Table 8.70 : Rating of List of Journals Subscribed and Discontinued

Group of Laboratories	*Response*			*Row Total*
	Excellent	*Good*	*Poor*	
PESG	7 (17.1)	29 (70.7)	5 (12.2)	41 (12.8)
CSG	10 (20.0)	31 (62.0)	9 (18.0)	50 (15.6)
BSG	34 (30.4)	69 (61.6)	9 (8.0)	112 (35.0)
ESG	20 (25.0)	53 (66.3)	7 (8.8)	80 (25.0)
ISG	11 (29.7)	20 (54.1)	6 (16.2)	37 (11.6)
Column Total	82 (25.6)	202 (63.1)	36 (11.3)	320 (100.0)

X^2 = 8.39623 with 8 d.f.

P > .01

8.4.4 Preparation and Supply of Bibliographies on Demand

Preparation and supply of bibliographies are carried out either on the request of the users or on anticipatory requirements of them. Such service is of great assistance to the research community in saving their valuable time in ascertaining and identifying the documents of their interests.

In Table 8.71 respondents were asked to indicate their views regarding the provision of making available bibliographies on demand. The majority of respondents of PESG (60.4%) and ISG (53.3%) indicated that there exists the provision for preparation of bibliography on demand in their libraries. Facilities for preparation and supply of bibliographies on demand are also indicated by the respondents of CSG (47.4%) and ESG (46.8%).

However, the percentage of those who indicated availability of such facility in BSG is less than in other groups. Although the majority of respondents indicated non-availability of such service in all the libraries, it is quite likely that there exists such service but due to poor publicity a large number of users are not aware of the service.

Chi-square value = 6.22339 which is not significant at .01 level shows that there is no significant difference between the provision of preparation and supply of bibliographies on demand in different groups of CSIR libraries.

Table 8.71 : Preparation and Supply of Bibliographies on Demand

Preparation and Supply of Bibliographies on Demand	*Group of Laboratories*					
	PESG	*CSG*	*BSG*	*ESG*	*ISG*	*Row Total*
Yes	32 (60.4)	27 (47.4)	54 (41.2)	44 (46.8)	24 (53.3)	181 (47.6)
No	21 (39.6)	30 (52.6)	77 (58.8)	50 (53.2)	21 (46.7)	199 (52.4)
Column Total	53 (13.9)	57 (15.0)	131 (34.5)	94 (24.7)	45 (11.8)	380 (100.0)

$X^2 = 6.22339$ with 4 d.f.

$P > .01$

8.4.4.1 Rating of Preparation and Supply of Bibliographies on Demand

Respondents of CSIR libraries were asked to give their comments on the preparation and supply of bibliographies on demand. Their response has been analysed in Table 8.72. It is based on the responses of 181 respondents who have indicated about provision and facilities in their respective libraries. The majority of respondents (54.1%) found it as a good.

Preparation and supply of bibliographies on demand is rated as good by the majority of respondents of ESG (63.6%) and PESG (62.5%) followed by BSG (53.7%). Even respondents of ISG (45.8%) and CSG (37.0%) also rated this service as good. Poor rating of preparation and supply of bibliographies on demand is shown by respondents of CSG (48.1%) and PESG (25.0%). A little over 20 percent respondents of BSG and ESG have also shown preparation of bibliographies on demand as poor followed by ISG (16.7%). On the other hand, 37.5 percent of respondents of ISG and 25.9 percent respondents of BSG rated the preparation and supply of bibliographies on demand as excellent. Chi-square value = 16.10449 as brought out in Table 8.72 is insignificant at .01 level which shows no difference between the preparation and supply of bibliographies on demand among the respondents of CSIR libraries.

Table 8.72 : Rating of Preparation and Supply of Bibliographies on Demand

Group of	*Response*			
Laboratories	*Excellent*	*Good*	*Poor*	*Row Total*
PESG	4	20	8	32
	(12.5)	(62.5)	(25.0)	(17.7)
CSG	4	10	13	27
	(14.8)	(37.0)	(48.1)	(14.9)
BSG	14	29	11	54
	(25.9)	(53.7)	(20.4)	(29.8)
ESG	7	28	9	44
	(15.9)	(63.6)	(20.5)	(24.3)
ISG	9	11	4	24
	(37.5)	(45.8)	(16.7)	(13.3)
Column Total	38	98	45	181
	(21.0)	(54.1)	(24.9)	(100.0)

X^2 = 16.10449 with 8 d.f.

P > .01

8.4.5 Indexing and Abstracting Services

Table 8.73 shows that majority of respondents of BSG (55.7%), PESG (54.7%) and ESG (54.3%) were of the opinion that their libraries have made the provision for such services. The availability of indexing and abstracting services is also stated by 51.1 percent of respondents of ISG. However, CSG has a less number of such respondents who are aware of these services.

The reasons behind the non-availability of such services may be due to the lack of professional, trained and experienced staff who can perform indexing and abstracting of selected articles of journals in the area of specialisation of laboratories. Absence of computer and other information technologies can be the other problem. Chi-square value = 4.17187 as brought out in Table 8.73, is not significant at .01 level which shows no significant difference between the views expressed by the respondents in regard to indexing and abstracting services as offered by different groups of laboratories.

Table 8.73 : Indexing and Abstracting Services

Indexing and Abstracting Services	*Group of Laboratories*					
	PESG	*CSG*	*BSG*	*ESG*	*ISG*	*Row Total*
Yes	29	23	73	51	23	199
	(54.7)	(40.4)	(55.7)	(54.3)	(51.1)	(52.4)
No	24	34	58	43	22	181
	(45.3)	(59.6)	(44.3)	(45.7)	(48.9)	(47.6)
Column Total	53	57	131	94	45	380
	(13.9)	(15.0)	(34.5)	(24.7)	(11.8)	(100.0)

X^2 = 4.17187 with 4 d.f.

P > .01

8.4.5.1 Rating of Indexing and Abstracting Service

In order to find out the efficacy and importance of indexing and abstracting services offered by CSIR libraries, respondents were asked to state their views about such services. Table 8.74 shows that the majority of respondents of BSG (54.8%) and PESG (51.7%) pointed out the indexing and abstracting services as good. Even 47 percent to 49 percent respondents of CSG and ESG also rated this service as good. 43.5 percent respondents of ISG considered the indexing and abstracting services as good as well as excellent. Indexing and abstracting services are also pointed out by BSG (34.2%) as excellent. Though the respondents of each group have expressed dissatisfaction by rating these services as poor, the percentage of such respondents is comparatively higher in ESG (31.4%) and CSG (30.4%) who consider these services as poor. This is because such services in certain libraries could be lacking. Chi-square value = 13.21779 is insignificant at .01 level, which shows no significant difference between indexing and abstracting services in CSIR libraries in India.

Table 8.74 : Rating of Indexing and Abstracting Services

Group of Laboratories	*Response*			
	Excellent	*Good*	*Poor*	*Row Total*
PESG	7 (24.1)	15 (51.7)	7 (24.1)	29 (14.6)
CSG	5 (21.7)	11 (47.8)	7 (30.4)	23 (11.6)
BSG	25 (34.2)	40 (54.8)	8 (11.0)	73 (36.7)
ESG	10 (19.6)	25 (49.0)	16 (31.4)	51 (25.6)
ISG	10 (43.5)	10 (43.5)	3 (13.0)	23 (11.6)
Column Total	57 (28.6)	101 (50.8)	41 (20.6)	199 (100.0)

X^2 = 13.21779 with 8 d.f.

P > .01

8.4.6 Bibliographical Services

The analysis of data regarding bibliographical services in Table 8.75 depicts that more than half of the two groups of respondents of CSIR libraries namely ISG (55.6%) and PESG (54.7%) indicated availability of bibliographical services. However, a relatively less number of respondents of BSG, CSG and ESG have indicated availability of such services in the library.

Chi-square value = 4.68512 is insignificant at .01 level, which shows no significant difference between views expressed by respondents regarding availability of bibliographical services in different groups of CSIR libraries.

Table 8.75 : Bibliographical Services

Bibliographical	*Group of Laboratories*					
Services	*PESG*	*CSG*	*BSG*	*ESG*	*ISG*	*Row Total*
Yes	29	24	55	41	25	174
	(54.7)	(42.1)	(42.0)	(43.6)	(55.6)	(45.8)
No	24	33	76	53	20	206
	(45.3)	(57.9)	(58.0)	(56.4)	(44.4)	(54.2)
Column Total	53	57	131	94	45	380
	(13.9)	(15.0)	(34.5)	(24.7)	(11.8)	(100.0)

X^2 = 4.68512 with 4 d.f.

P > .01

8.4.6.1 Rating of Bibliographical Services

In order to measure the effectiveness of bibliographical services offered in CSIR libraries, users' remarks were obtained. From Table 8.76, it is evident that the majority of respondents (51.1%) of CSIR libraries are of the opinion that their libraries are providing good bibliographical services, whereas 27.0 percent respondents rate such services as excellent. Only 21.8 percent of respondents did not respond in favour of bibliographic service. They indicated bibliographical service as poor in their libraries. Analysis of bibliographical services in this study is shown in Table 8.76 which reveals that the majority of respondents of PESG (62.1%) found bibliographical services as good, followed by respondents of BSG (52.7%), CSG (50.0%) and ESG (48.8%). It is interesting to note that almost an equal number of respondents of ISG have reported these services as good and excellent. BSG is found to be another group where a good number of respondents have rated this service as excellent. It is interesting feature that there are noticeable presence of a good number of users in all the groups who describe this service as poor. This may be a fact in certain libraries.

But overall the analysis suggests that the majority of users belonging to each group found this service satisfactory. Chi-square value = 5.59734, which is insignificant at .01 level does not support the difference statistically.

Table 8.76 : Rating of Bibliographical Services

Group of Laboratories	*Response*			*Row Total*
	Excellent	*Good*	*Poor*	
PESG	6 (20.7)	18 (62.1)	5 (17.2)	29 (16.7)
CSG	5 (20.8)	12 (50.0)	7 (29.2)	24 (13.8)
BSG	16 (29.1)	29 (52.7)	10 (18.2)	55 (31.6)
ESG	10 (24.4)	20 (48.8)	11 (26.8)	41 (23.6)
ISG	10 (40.0)	10 (40.0)	5 (20.0)	25 (14.4)
Column Total	47 (27.0)	89 (51.1)	38 (21.8)	174 (100.0)

X^2 = 5.59734 with 8 d.f.

P > .01

8.4.7 Literature Search Services

In order to ascertain the arrangement of the services for literature search in CSIR libraries (Table 8.77), the users were asked to shed light on the availability of literature search services in their libraries. It was found that the majority of respondents responded affirmatively in regard to availability of literature search facilities in their libraries. However, there a sizable number of respondents who reported non-availability of such services. It is difficult to trace out the reason behind such a variation. But it seems to be matter of indifferent attitude of the library staff in creating awareness about their activities for wider use and appreciation. At the same time it could also be possible that this group of users might have not felt any need to utilise such services. Hence, they are not familiar with such facilities. It may be pointed out that of all the groups, a proportion of users of PESG (67.9%) who indicated existence of such service is higher than others. The users of BSG are equally divided in expressing their opinion in regard to literature search facilities in their respective libraries. It is surprising to note that half of the respondents have expressed in favour of availability of such facility and half of them point out that this facility is not available. However, these variations are not supported statistically, because Chi-square value = 6.29488 is insignificant at .01 level.

Table 8.77 : Literature Search Services

Literature Search	*Group of Laboratories*					
	PESG	*CSG*	*BSG*	*ESG*	*ISG*	*Row Total*
Yes	36 (67.9)	32 (56.1)	83 (63.4)	47 (50.0)	28 (62.2)	226 (59.5)
No	17 (32.1)	25 (43.9)	48 (36.6)	47 (50.0)	17 (37.8)	154 (40.5)
Column Total	53 (13.9)	57 (15.0)	131 (34.5)	94 (24.7)	45 (11.8)	380 (100.0)

X^2 = 6.29488 with 4 d.f.
P > .01

8.4.7.1 Rating of Literature Search Facilities

The respondents were asked to indicate their views about literature search facilities presently being provided by their libraries. Analysis is based on the responses of those who indicated provision of this service in their organisations. The results of literature search as shown in Table 8.78 indicate that the majority of respondents of BSG (67.5%) and ESG (57.4%) termed the literature search as good, followed by CSG (53.1%). However, the number of such respondents is little less in PESG and ISG. Though the number of such respondents who considered this service as excellent could be seen in all the groups. Comparatively their number is higher in ISG and BSG. Thus more respondents in these groups than other group consider this service as excellent. Chi-square value = 15.92418, which is insignificant at .01 level, shows that there is no significant difference between the literature search among the respondents of groups of CSIR libraries.

Table 8.78 : Rating of Literature Search Facilities

Group of Laboratories	*Response* *Excellent*	*Good*	*Poor*	*Row Total*
PESG	9	18	9	36
	(25.0)	(50.0)	(25.0)	(15.9)
CSG	4	17	11	32
	(12.5)	(53.1)	(34.4)	(14.2)
BSG	20	56	7	83
	(24.1)	(67.5)	(8.4)	(36.7)
ESG	10	27	10	47
	(21.3)	(57.4)	(21.3)	(20.8)
ISG	10	13	5	28
	(35.7)	(46.4)	(17.9)	(12.4)
Column Total	53	131	42	226
	(23.5)	(58.0)	(18.6)	(100.0)

X^2 = 15.92418 with 8 d.f.
P > .01

8.4.8 Contents Pages of Periodicals Services

Contents of periodicals is the compiled lists of contents pages of the journals subscribed to in the library. It saves the time of users as articles of their interest are contained in these lists and they can have a look at the titles without scanning several journals. In scientific and technical libraries journals are heavily used and subscribed to by the library. Users' views were recorded in Table 8.79 regarding provision of the services of the list of contents of periodicals received in their libraries. The majority of users belonging to ISG (66.7%) and ESG (60.6%) remarked that their libraries are arranging such services on regular basis. Response is almost similar of the respondents belonging to BSG. However, the majority of users of PESG and CSG indicated that there is no provision of such facilities in their libraries. Chi-square value = 7.82521 is not significant at .01 level, which shows no significant difference between respondents of contents of periodicals in different groups of libraries.

Table 8.79 : Contents Pages of Periodicals Services

Contents of	*Group of Laboratories*					
Periodicals	*PESG*	*CSG*	*BSG*	*ESG*	*ISG*	*Row Total*
Yes	24	26	74	57	30	211
	(45.3)	(45.6)	(56.5)	(60.6)	(66.7)	(55.5)
No	29	31	57	37	15	169
	(54.7)	(54.4)	(43.5)	(39.4)	(33.3)	(44.5)
Column Total	53	57	131	94	45	380
	(13.9)	(15.0)	(34.5)	(24.7)	(11.8)	(100.0)

$X^2 = 7.82521$ with 4 d.f.

$P > .01$

8.4.8.1 Rating of the Services of Contents Pages of Periodicals

The users of CSIR libraries were asked to rate the circulation of content pages of periodicals among them. Table 8.80 analyses the data on contents of periodicals which shows that the majority of respondents, 66.4 percent, found this service to be good. However, in some groups percentage is higher. A large number of respondents of ESG (80.7%) rated the contents of periodicals as good. Over 60 percent respondents of BSG, PESG and CSG also rated contents of periodicals as good. However, the percentage of those who rated the service as good is just 46.7 percent in ISG. There is comparatively a larger number of respondents in ISG (36.7%) and CSG (23.1%) who rated this service as excellent. This service has also been considered as poor by 25.0 percent of respondents of PESG. Chi-square value = 16.09495 is insignificant at .01 level which shows no difference between the contents of periodicals in CSIR libraries.

Table 8.80 : Rating of the Services of Contents Pages of Periodicals

Group of Laboratories	*Response* Excellent	Good	Poor	*Row Total*
PESG	3	15	6	24
	(12.5)	(62.5)	(25.0)	(11.4)
CSG	6	16	4	26
	(23.1)	(61.5)	(15.4)	(12.3)
BSG	16	49	9	74
	(21.6)	(66.2)	(12.2)	(35.1)
ESG	9	46	2	57
	(15.8)	(80.7)	(3.5)	(27.0)
ISG	11	14	5	30
	(36.7)	(46.7)	(16.7)	(14.2)
Column Total	45	140	26	211
	(21.3)	(66.4)	(12.3)	(100.0)

X^2 = 16.09495 with 8 d.f.

P > .01

8.4.9 SDI Services

In special libraries, particularly scientific and technical libraries, Selective Dissemination of Information (SDI) services have their own significance and usefulness. An attempt has been made to ascertain whether or not this type of service is being offered in CSIR libraries. It is evident from the Table 8.81 that an overwhelming majority of respondents have stated that there is no provision of such services. It is unpleasant to observe that inspite of the utility of these services, particularly in CSIR libraries, no importance is being attached to it. However, the fact remains that it is most useful service for scientists and specialists. Chi-square value = 13.51493 which is insignificant at .01 level shows that there is no significant difference between the respondents of SDI services in different groups of CSIR libraries.

Table 8.81 : SDI Services

SDI Services	*Group of Laboratories*					
	PESG	*CSG*	*BSG*	*ESG*	*ISG*	*Row Total*
Yes	8	10	23	9	8	58
	(15.1)	(17.5)	(17.6)	(9.6)	(17.8)	(15.3)
No	37	42	102	78	37	296
	(69.8)	(73.7)	(77.9)	(83.0)	(82.2)	(77.9)
Not stated	8	5	6	7	-	26
	(15.1)	(8.8)	(4.6)	(7.4)		(6.8)
Column Total	53	57	131	94	45	380
	(13.9)	(15.0)	(34.5)	(24.7)	(11.8)	(100.0)

X^2 = 13.51493 with 8 d.f.

P > .01

8.4.9.1 Rating of SDI Services

As seen in Table 8.82, the provision of SDI services is restricted to a very limited number of libraries. It is beyond doubt that benefits of services such as SDI are not being provided by a very significant proportion of CSIR laboratories. However, wherever it is being given, it has been found to the satisfaction of users. The data in Table 8.82 reveals that an overwhelming majority of respondents have rated this service as good. Also there is representation of some respondents who have rated this service as excellent. It is to clarify that their rating was invited on the provision of SDI services as made out by the different laboratories.

Table 8.82 : Rating of SDI Services

Group of Laboratories	*Response* Excellent	Good	Poor	*Row Total*
PESG	2	5	1	8
	(25.0)	(62.5)	(12.5)	(13.8)
CSG	-	10	-	10
		(100.0)		(17.2)
BSG	3	19	1	23
	(13.0)	(82.6)	(4.3)	(39.7)
ESG	-	9	-	9
		(100.0)		(15.5)
ISG	5	2	1	8
	(62.5)	(25.0)	(12.5)	(13.8)
Column Total	10	45	3	58
	(17.2)	(77.6)	(5.2)	(100.0)

8.4.10 Digest of Scientific, Technical and Industrial Information

Table 8.83 shows respondents' reaction on provision of service such as digest of scientific, technical and industrial information to their users. Only 25.5 percent respondents of CSIR libraries indicated that their libraries are providing digest of scientific, technical and industrial information. Surprisingly an overwhelming majority of respondents across the libraries indicated non-availability of such services. Chi-square value = 27.47023 which is significant at .01 level shows that there is a significant difference between the respondents of digest of scientific, technical and industrial information in different groups of CSIR libraries, although this type of service is considered to be an essential service in such libraries of research laboratories.

Table 8.83 : Digest of Scientific, Technical and Industrial Information

Digest of Scientific, Technical and Industrial Information	*Group of Laboratories*					
	PESG	*CSG*	*BSG*	*ESG*	*ISG*	*Row Total*
Yes	9	13	48	21	6	97
	(17.0)	(22.8)	(36.6)	(22.3)	(13.3)	(25.5)
No	40	39	81	72	39	271
	(75.5)	(68.4)	(61.8)	(76.6)	(86.7)	(71.3)
Not stated	4	5	2	1	-	12
	(7.5)	(8.8)	(1.5)	(1.1)		(3.2)
Column Total	53	57	131	94	45	380
	(13.9)	(15.0)	(34.5)	(24.7)	(11.8)	(100.0)

X^2 = 27.47023 with 8 d.f.

$P < .01$

8.4.10.1 Rating of Digest of Scientific, Technical and Industrial Information

As shown in the previous analysis, the preparation of digest of scientific, technical and industrial information is not common practice in libraries attached to CSIR laboratories. But provision of providing digest wherever available, is of a great satisfaction, as an overwhelming majority of respondents in each group has rated this service as good. The only exception is PESG where a sizable proportion of respondents have termed this service as poor.

Table 8.84 : Rating of Digest of Scientific, Technical and Industrial Information

Group of Laboratories	*Response*			*Row Total*
	Excellent	*Good*	*Poor*	
PESG	2	3	4	9
	(22.2)	(33.3)	(44.4)	(9.3)
CSG	3	7	3	13
	(23.1)	(53.8)	(23.1)	(13.4)
BSG	4	36	8	48
	(8.3)	(75.0)	(16.7)	(49.5)
ESG	2	12	7	21
	(9.5)	(57.1)	(33.3)	(21.6)
ISG	4	1	1	6
	(66.7)	(16.7)	(16.7)	(6.2)
Column Total	15	59	23	97
	(15.5)	(60.8)	(23.7)	(100.0)

8.4.11 Indexing Journals Subscribed in the Area of Specialisation

The respondents of groups of CSIR libraries were asked to state the status of indexing journals subscribed to in the area of their specialisations. Table 8.85 shows that an overwhelming majority of respondents across the group indicated that indexing journals were being subscribed to in their respective libraries. Only variation that comes to notice is the response of ISG which is not in tune with the other groups.

The above analysis suggests that position of indexing journals subscribed to in the area of specialisation is satisfactory. Chi-square value = 22.48122 which is significant at .01 level. This shows that the subscription of indexing journals differ from group to group.

Table 8.85 : Indexing Journals Subscribed to in the Area of Specialisation

Indexing Journals	*Group of Laboratories*					
	PESG	*CSG*	*BSG*	*ESG*	*ISG*	*Row Total*
Yes	48	55	111	85	30	329
	(90.6)	(96.5)	(84.7)	(90.4)	(66.7)	(86.6)
No	5	2	20	9	15	51
	(9.4)	(3.5)	(15.3)	(9.6)	(33.3)	(13.4)
Column Total	53	57	131	94	45	380
	(13.9)	(15.0)	(34.5)	(24.7)	(11.8)	(100.0)

$X^2 = 22.48122$ with 4 d.f.
$P < .01$

8.4.11.1 Rating of Indexing Journals Subscribed to in the Area of Specialisation

Respondents of CSIR libraries were requested to rate the indexing journals subscribed to in the area of their specialisation. In this connection, majority of respondents of CSG (67.3%) and ISG (63.3%) (Table 8.86) rated the indexing journals in the area of specialisation as good. On the other hand, there were respondents of other groups, i.e., ESG (57.6%) and BSG (55.9%) who also rated such journals as good. However, a little less number of respondents of PESG (50.0%) as compared to other groups, rated indexing journals in the area of specialisation as good. Also a good number of respondents in each group rated availability of indexing journals as excellent.

The above analysis indicates that the majority of respondents (58.1%) of CSIR libraries rated the indexing journals as good, whereas 31.3 percent respondents valued the indexing journals as excellent. Only a negligible percentage of respondents (10.6%) stated the indexing journals as poor. It is manifested from the analysis that those users who have indicated the position of indexing journals as poor may not be fully aware of such items. It is also possible that they do not make use of those journals.

Table 8.86 : Rating of Indexing Journals Subscribed to in the Area of Specialisation

Group of Laboratories	*Response* Excellent	Good	*Poor*	*Row Total*
PESG	13	24	11	48
	(27.1)	(50.0)	(22.9)	(14.6)
CSG	16	37	2	55
	(29.1)	(67.3)	(3.6)	(16.7)
BSG	42	62	7	111
	(37.8)	(55.9)	(6.3)	(33.7)
ESG	21	49	15	85
	(24.7)	(57.6)	(17.6)	(25.8)
ISG	11	19	-	30
	(36.7)	(63.3)		(9.1)
Column Total	103	191	35	329
	(31.3)	(58.1)	(10.6)	(100.0)

$X^2 = 23.32203$ with 8 d.f.

$P < .01$

8.4.12 Abstracting Journals Subscribed to in the Area of Specialisation

Table 8.87 shows that a little over 90 percent respondents belonging to ESG, CSG and PESG have expressed that their libraries have provisions to subscribe to abstracting journals in the area of specialisation. The percentage of respondents of BSG (81.7%) and ISG (73.3%) is comparatively less who indicated provision of abstracting journals in their libraries.

It is apparent from the analysis that the majority of all the groups of CSIR libraries have provision of such services. Chi-square value = 12.42221 is insignificant at .01 level which shows that there is no significant difference between the subscription of abstracting journals in different groups of CSIR libraries.

Table 8.87 : Abstracting Journals Subscribed to in the Area of Specialisation

Abstracting Journals	*Group of Laboratories*					
	PESG	*CSG*	*BSG*	*ESG*	*ISG*	*Row Total*
Yes	48 (90.6)	52 (91.2)	107 (81.7)	86 (91.5)	33 (73.3)	326 (85.8)
No	5 (9.4)	5 (8.8)	24 (18.3)	8 (8.5)	12 (26.7)	54 (14.2)
Column Total	53 (13.9)	57 (15.0)	131 (34.5)	94 (24.7)	45 (11.8)	380 (100.0)

$X^2 = 12.42221$ with 4 d.f.

$P < .01$

8.4.12.1 Rating of Abstracting Journals Subscribed to in the Area of Specialisation

In Table 8.88, responses regarding abstracting journals subscribed to in the area of specialisation have been analysed. It is satisfying to note that subscription to abstracting journals in all the groups has been rated as either good or excellent. Similarity, the response rate is also supported statistically as Chi-square value = 12.53597 is insignificant at .01 level.

Table 8.88 : Rating of Abstracting Journals Subscribed to in the Area of Specialisation

Group of Laboratories	*Response*			
	Excellent	*Good*	*Poor*	*Row Total*
PESG	10 (20.8)	31 (64.6)	7 (14.6)	48 (14.7)
CSG	14 (26.9)	32 (61.5)	6 (11.5)	52 (16.0)
BSG	38 (35.5)	64 (59.8)	5 (4.7)	107 (32.8)
ESG	26 (30.2)	45 (52.3)	15 (17.4)	86 (26.4)
ISG	12 (36.4)	19 (57.6)	2 (6.1)	33 (10.1)
Column Total	100 (30.7)	191 (58.6)	35 (10.7)	326 (100.0)

$X^2 = 12.53597$ with 8 d.f.

$P > .01$

8.4.13 Translation Service

Findings of researchers, their views and ideas, and results are quite often are published/brought out in those languages of which the users of the library may be unfamiliar. Therefore, there is always a need to get the translation done in languages known to the users. Quite often those articles contain such vital information that their consultation becomes essential and unavoidable. This necessitates the provision of translation service in the libraries. This could be organised in-house or through necessary networking arrangement with other organisations. An attempt has been made to find out whether this facility is available in CSIR libraries or not.

Table 8.89 shows that majority of users (86.8%) are of the view that there is no arrangement to provide translation service in their organisation. After having responses from such a large number of users, there remain no scope to emphasise on a minority view of 13.2 percent in regard to availability of such service. However, comparison between various groups reveals that a good number of users of CSG (40.4%) and ISG (31.1%) indicated that this facility is available in their libraries. The difference between translation service in the group of laboratories is also supported by Chi-square value = 68.66302 which is significant at .01 level.

Table 8.89 : Translation Service Offered by CSIR Libraries

Group of Laboratories	*Response*		
	Yes	*No*	*Row Total*
PESG	-	53	53
		(100.0)	(13.9)
CSG	23	34	57
	(40.4)	(59.6)	(15.0)
BSG	9	122	131
	(6.9)	(93.1)	(34.5)
ESG	4	90	94
	(4.3)	(95.7)	(24.7)
ISG	14	31	45
	(31.1)	(68.9)	(11.8)
Column Total	50	330	380
	(13.2)	(86.8)	(100.0)

$X^2 = 68.66302$ with 4 d.f.

$P < .01$

8.4.13.1 Rating of Translation Service

Table 8.90 shows the respondents' views regarding rating of translation service in the CSIR libraries. It is surprising that such an important service is not available in such organisations where it is a must. In view of the fewer responses in regard to availability of this service, rating was thought inappropriate to be sought, because the response rate has created doubts as to the very existence of this service. Chi-square value = 7.91550 as brought out in Table 8.90 is insignificant at .01 level. It shows no difference between translation service in the group of CSIR libraries.

Table 8.90 : Rating of Translation Service

Group of Laboratories	*Response*			
	Excellent	*Good*	*Poor*	*Row Total*
CSG	3	16	4	23
	(13.0)	(69.6)	(17.4)	(46.0)
BSG	-	7	2	9
		(77.8)	(22.2)	(18.0)
ESG	-	4	-	4
		(100.0)		(8.0)
ISG	4	10	-	14
	(28.6)	(71.4)		(28.0)
Column Total	7	37	6	50
	(14.0)	(74.0)	(12.0)	(100.0)

X^2 = 7.91550 with 6 d.f.

P > .01

8.4.14 Reprographic Services

Invention of technologies has brought about various techniques and means in the information world conducive to making available any piece of information without loss of time. Photocopying is one of them which has extended a facility to users to obtain a copy of even a smallest part of information from a document or even reference sources. The electrostatic processes were invented and developed in 1938 in the USA. Previously it was known as xerography. Since then several latest technologies have been developed for photocopying. Reprographic section of scientific and technical libraries are equipped with the latest technologies and tools for reprographic services.

The availability of photocopying service in the CSIR libraries as indicated in Table 8.91 reveals that this facility is available in almost all the libraries of CSIR. At least in the three groups, i.e., PESG, BSG and ISG, the response is 100 percent. It shows that all the libraries in these groups are in the possession of photocopying equipment. However, response in the group of CSG and BSG is not the same. It meant some of the libraries don't have this facility. It is, indeed, a matter of great concern that such a common and useful facility is not available in scientific and technical libraries of CSIR laboratories. Chi-square value = 50.27028 which is significant at .01 level supports the difference statistically.

Table 8.91 : Reprographic Services Offered by CSIR Libraries

Group of Laboratories	*Response*		
	Yes	*No*	*Row Total*
PESG	53	-	53
	(100.0)		(13.9)
CSG	43	14	57
	(75.4)	(24.6)	(15.0)
BSG	131	-	131
	(100.0)		(34.5)
ESG	81	13	94
	(86.2)	(13.8)	(24.7)
ISG	45	-	45
	(100.0)		(11.8)
Column Total	353	27	380
	(92.9)	(7.1)	(100.0)

$X^2 = 50.27028$ with 4 d.f.

$P < .01$

8.4.14.1 Rating of Reprographic Services

The responses with regard to the efficiency of reprographic services in CSIR libraries have been shown in Table 8.92. These reveal that the majority of respondents of BSG (58.0%) indicated the photocopying service as good, followed by CSG (55.8%) and ESG (55.6%). Photocopying facilities have also been rated as good by PESG (47.2%) and ISG (42.2%) which is obviously low as compared to other groups. It is surprising to note that some of the libraries offer poor quality of photocopying facilities despite the availability of modern tools and machines thereof. The users of PESG (47.2%) rated the photocopy service as poor in their group which is followed by a little over (31%) by ISG and ESG.

The lowest percentage of poor service was also shown by CSG (25.6%) and BSG (17.6%). On the other hand, the users of ISG (26.7%) and BSG (24.4%) indicated the service as being excellent, followed by CSG (18.6%). Other groups such as ESG (9.9%) and PESG (5.7%) also indicated this service as excellent. Chi-square value = 27.73382 which is significant at .01 level, shows difference between photocopying service in groups of CSIR libraries.

Table 8.92 : Rating of Reprographic Services

Group of	*Response*			
Laboratories	*Excellent*	*Good*	*Poor*	*Row Total*
PESG	3	25	25	53
	(5.7)	(47.2)	(47.2)	(15.0)
CSG	8	24	11	43
	(18.6)	(55.8)	(25.6)	(12.2)
BSG	32	76	23	131
	(24.4)	(58.0)	(17.6)	(37.1)
ESG	8	45	28	81
	(9.9)	(55.6)	(34.6)	(22.9)
ISG	12	19	14	45
	(26.7)	(42.2)	(31.1)	(12.7)
Column Total	63	189	101	353
	(17.8)	(53.5)	(28.6)	(100.0)

$X^2 = 27.73382$ with 8 d.f.

$P < .01$

8.4.15 Provision of Obtaining Photocopy Material from Other Libraries

Responses of users regarding provision of making photocopy material available from other libraries has been analysed in Table 8.93. The majority of users (51.1%) indicated that their libraries do not have such provision to procure photocopy material from other libraries. But the preponderance of such respondents is evident in ESG (67.0%) followed by CSG (56.1%). Over 45 percent respondents of BSG and ISG are of the view that their libraries also do not have such facility.

The above analysis clearly shows that half of the respondents of PESG, BSG and ISG are of the view that CSIR libraries have the arrangement of obtaining the photocopy material from other libraries. Chi-square value = 18.16939 which is significant at .01 level, shows significant difference between the responses regarding arrangement of photocopy material from other libraries.

Table 8.93 : Provision of Obtaining Photocopy Material from Other Libraries

Provision of Photocopy Material	*Group of Laboratories*					
	PESG	*CSG*	*BSG*	*ESG*	*ISG*	*Row Total*
Yes	35	25	71	31	24	186
	(66.0)	(43.9)	(54.2)	(33.0)	(53.3)	(48.9)
No	18	32	60	63	21	194
	(34.0)	(56.1)	(45.8)	(67.0)	(46.7)	(51.1)
Column Total	53	57	131	94	45	380
	(13.9)	(15.0)	(34.5)	(24.7)	(11.8)	(100.0)

$X^2 = 18.16939$ with 4 d.f.

$P < .01$

8.4.15.1 Need for Obtaining Photocopy Material from Other Libraries

Table 8.94 presents the responses of those users who have indicated about non-availability of facility for obtaining photocopy material from other libraries. Data as presented in this table shows that every user feels the need for such facilities. This supports the view that no library is self-sufficient.

Hence, resource sharing is essential for augmenting their services for others.

Table 8.94 : Need for Obtaining Photocopy Material from Other Libraries

Need of Photocopy Materials	*Group of Laboratories*					
	PESG	*CSG*	*BSG*	*ESG*	*ISG*	*Row Total*
Yes	18 (34.0)	32 (56.1)	60 (45.8)	63 (67.0)	21 (46.7)	194 (51.1)

8.5 THE PROVISION OF COMPUTERISED INFORMATION SERVICES

An attempt has been made to ascertain whether the application of computers is vogue in CSIR libraries for extending and managing library services. The data in the Table 8.95 reveals that majority of respondents, 61.1 percent, were of the opinion that their libraries don't have computerised services. Only about 40 percent respondents indicated as to such being facilities in their libraries.

Data when analysed institution-wise depicts a similar situation. Excepting PESG, majority of the respondents belonging to the rest of the groups reports that provision of computerised services are not available in their organisation.

Table 8.95 : Provision of Computerised Information Services

Provision of Computerised Information Services	*Group of Laboratories*					
	PESG	*CSG*	*BSG*	*ESG*	*ISG*	*Row Total*
Yes	33 (62.3)	20 (35.1)	46 (35.1)	29 (30.9)	20 (44.4)	148 (38.9)
No	20 (37.7)	37 (64.9)	85 (64.9)	65 (69.1)	25 (55.6)	232 (61.1)
Column Total	53 (13.9)	57 (15.0)	131 (34.5)	94 (24.7)	45 (11.8)	380 (100.0)

8.5.1 Provision of Computerised Literature Search

Table 8.96 shows that out of 148 respondents who indicated provision of computerised services in their organisations, 131 (88.5%) indicated that their organisations offer computerised literature search facilities to them. The response rate is almost similar across the group. Looking at the overwhelming responses with regard to availability of facility for literature search, it can be said that all the libraries are offering such advanced services to their users. Chi-square value = 6.66607 which is insignificant at .01 level shows no significant difference between the responses of computerised literature search in CSIR libraries.

Table 8.96 : Provision of Computerised Literature Search

Computerised	*Group of Laboratories*					
Literature Search	*PESG*	*CSG*	*BSG*	*ESG*	*ISG*	*Row Total*
Yes	30	15	43	24	19	131
	(90.9)	(75.0)	(93.5)	(82.8)	(95.0)	(88.5)
No	3	5	3	5	1	17
	(9.1)	(25.0)	(6.5)	(17.2)	(5.0)	(11.5)
Column Total	33	20	46	29	20	148
	(22.3)	(13.5)	(31.1)	(19.6)	(13.5)	(100.0)

$X^2 = 6.66607$ with 4 d.f.

$P > .01$

8.5.1.1 Rating of Computerised Literature Search

Table 8.97 reveals that highest percentage of respondents of both CSG and ESG (66.7%) marked the computerised service of literature search as good, followed by BSG (62.8%). About 42 percent respondents of ISG and 37 percent PESG also rated the computerised literature search as good. On the other hand, 57.9 percent respondents of ISG and 37.2 percent of BSG indicated computerised service of literature search as excellent, followed by 33.3 percent of PESG. However, the percentage of the respondents belonging to CSG (20.0%) and ESG (16.7%) is comparatively lower. The literature search facilities have been rated to be poor by other groups also, but their percentage is higher in PESG.

The difference between literature search among the respondents of groups of CSIR libraries is clearly supported by Chi-square value = 26.96230 which is significant at .01 level.

Table 8.97 : Rating of Computerised Literature Search

Group of Laboratories	*Response* Excellent	Good	Poor	*Row Total*
PESG	10	11	9	30
	(33.3)	(36.7)	(30.0)	(22.9)
CSG	3	10	2	15
	(20.0)	(66.7)	(13.3)	(11.5)
BSG	16	27	-	43
	(37.2)	(62.8)		(32.8)
ESG	4	16	4	24
	(16.7)	(66.7)	(16.7)	(18.3)
ISG	11	8	-	19
	(57.9)	(42.1)		(14.5)
Column Total	44	72	15	131
	(33.6)	(55.0)	(11.5)	(100.0)

$X^2 = 26.96230$ with 8 d.f.

$P < .01$

8.5.2 Provision of Computerised Indexing of Periodicals

The data about computerised indexing of periodicals in CSIR libraries given in Table 8.98 indicates that majority of respondents (78.4%) are of the opinion that their libraries have computerised indexing of periodicals. On the other hand, over 80 percent respondents of PESG, ESG and BSG indicated to have provision of such computerised services in their libraries. Chi-square value = 4.19903 is insignificant at .01 level which does not support the difference statistically.

Table 8.98 : Provision of Computerised Indexing of Periodicals

Computerised Indexing of Periodicals	*Group of Laboratories*					
	PESG	*CSG*	*BSG*	*ESG*	*ISG*	*Row Total*
Yes	28	13	37	24	14	116
	(84.8)	(65.0)	(80.4)	(82.8)	(70.0)	(78.4)
No	5	7	9	5	6	32
	(15.2)	(35.0)	(19.6)	(17.2)	(30.0)	(21.6)
Column Total	33	20	46	29	20	148
	(22.3)	(13.5)	(31.1)	(19.6)	(13.5)	(100.0)

X^2 = 4.19903 with 4 d.f.

P > .01

8.5.2.1 Rating of Computerised Indexing of Periodicals

Analysis of provision of computerised indexing of periodicals as given in Table 8.99 shows that computerised indexing of periodicals as offered by CSIR libraries is rated good by the majority of respondents (63.8%). Also a good number of respondents (24.1%) have found this service as excellent. The proportion of those who considered this service as poor is 12.1 percent. Variation in response at each level is noticeable. A higher proportion of respondents of CSG (69.2%), BSG (70.3%) and ESG (70.8%) have rated this service as good as compared to PESG (50.0%) and ISG (57.1%). Among those organisations service of which have been rated as excellent, ISG stood at the top with 42.9 percent of respondents followed by PESG (28.6%) and BSG (27.0%).

However, whatever variation is found have not been supported statistically because chi-square value = 14.76412 as brought out in Table 8.99 is insignificant at .01 level.

Table 8.99 : Rating of Computerised Indexing of Periodicals

Group of Laboratories	*Response* Excellent	Good	Poor	*Row Total*
PESG	8 (28.6)	14 (50.0)	6 (21.4)	28 (24.1)
CSG	2 (15.4)	9 (69.2)	2 (15.4)	13 (11.2)
BSG	10 (27.0)	26 (70.3)	1 (2.7)	37 (31.9)
ESG	2 (8.3)	17 (70.8)	5 (20.8)	24 (20.7)
ISG	6 (42.9)	8 (57.1)	-	14 (12.1)
Column Total	28 (24.1)	74 (63.8)	14 (12.1)	116 (100.0)

X^2 = 14.76412 with 8 d.f.

P > .01

8.5.3 Provision of Computerised Compilation of Bibliographies

The majority of respondents (76.4%) in Table 8.100 indicated that computerised compilation of bibliographies facilities are available in their libraries. 85.0 percent respondents belonging to ISG indicated that their libraries are providing computerised bibliographical services, followed by 82.8 percent of respondents of BSG. Other groups belonging to PESG, BSG and CSG also indicated provision of such services in their libraries but percentage of these groups is lesser in comparison to ISG and ESG. Chi-square value = 3.56558 which is insignificant at .01 level does not support the difference between responses of computerised compilation of bibliographies in CSIR libraries.

Table 8.100 : Provision of Computerised Compilation of Bibliographies

Computerised Compilation of Bibliographies	*Group of Laboratories*					
	PESG	*CSG*	*BSG*	*ESG*	*ISG*	*Row Total*
Yes	26 (78.8)	13 (65.0)	33 (71.7)	24 (82.8)	17 (85.0)	113 (76.4)
No	7 (21.2)	7 (35.0)	13 (28.3)	5 (17.2)	3 (15.0)	35 (23.6)
Total	33 (22.3)	20 (13.5)	46 (31.1)	29 (19.6)	20 (13.5)	148 (100.0)

X^2 = 3.56558 with 4 d.f.

P > .01

8.5.3.1 Rating of Computerised Compilation of Bibliographies

The data about compilation of bibliographies (Table 8.101) using computer facilities reveal that majority of respondents across the group termed it as good. When responses at excellent and good are taken into consideration it becomes all the more clear that CSIR libraries are providing good computerised bibliographical services. When we look at groups of laboratories individually, we find that BSG has the largest number of respondents who rated this service as good. Except PESG, over 50 percent of respondents in other groups rate this service as good. However, among the groups, services of which has been rated as excellent, ISG stand at the top with 47.1 percent of respondents terming the facility as excellent, followed by PESG (23.1%). Chi-square value = 19.58699 is insignificant at .01 level which does not support the difference statistically.

Table 8.101 : Rating of Computerised Compilation of Bibliographies

Group of Laboratories	*Response* Excellent	Good	Poor	*Row Total*
PESG	6	11	9	26
	(23.1)	(42.3)	(34.6)	(23.0)
CSG	1	7	5	13
	(7.7)	(53.8)	(38.5)	(11.5)
BSG	7	22	4	33
	(21.2)	(66.7)	(12.1)	(29.2)
ESG	2	14	8	24
	(8.3)	(58.3)	(33.3)	(21.2)
ISG	8	9	-	17
	(47.1)	(52.9)		(15.0)
Column Total	24	63	26	113
	(21.2)	(55.8)	(23.0)	(100.0)

$X^2 = 19.58699$ with 8 d.f.

$P > .01$

8.5.4 Need for the Computerised Information Services

The views of respondents with regard to the need of computerised services have been obtained from those libraries where computerised facility is not available in the CSIR libraries. The analysis of data in Table 8.102 shows that the majority of respondents (61.1%) reported that they feel the necessity of computerised facilities in their libraries. In group-wise analysis of data, 69.1 percent respondents of ESG reported that they would like that their libraries also provide computerised services. Equal proportion of respondents in CSG and BSG (64.9%) are also in favour of such a service. Respondents of ISG (55.6%) and PESG (37.7%) also wish to avail of the benefit of computerised services in their libraries.

Table 8.102 : Need of Computerised Information Services

Need of Computerised Information Services	*Group of Laboratories*					
	PESG	*CSG*	*BSG*	*ESG*	*ISG*	*Row Total*
Yes	20 (37.7)	37 (64.9)	85 (64.9)	65 (69.1)	25 (55.6)	232 (61.1)

8.5.5 Access to National and International Online Searching

In Table 8.103, users' comments are recorded to find out whether CSIR libraries are providing online searching to national and international databases. 80.8 percent respondents indicated that there is no such facilities of online searches of national and international databases in CSIR libraries. An overwhelming majority of respondents 92.5 percent of PESG revealed that their libraries do not have facility of online searching, followed by ESG 89.4 percent and CSG 82.5 percent. Similarly, 74.8 percent respondents belonging to BSG and 64.4 percent of ISG indicated absence of such services in their libraries. A little higher proportion of respondents of ISG and BSG indicated that online search facilities are available, but it makes no material difference as the largest section of respondents have indicated non-availability of such a facility. Chi-square value = 19.96307 which is significant at .01 level, supports the difference in response.

Table 8.103 : Access to National and International Online Searching

Access to On-line Searching	*Group of Laboratories*					
	PESG	*CSG*	*BSG*	*ESG*	*ISG*	*Row Total*
Yes	4 (7.5)	10 (17.5)	33 (25.2)	10 (10.6)	16 (35.6)	73 (19.2)
No	49 (92.5)	47 (82.5)	98 (74.8)	84 (89.4)	29 (64.4)	307 (80.8)
Column Total	53 (13.9)	57 (15.0)	131 (34.5)	94 (24.7)	45 (11.8)	380 (100.0)

$X^2 = 19.96307$ with 4 d.f.

$P < .01$

8.5.5.1 Access to Number of Online Databases

Users of CSIR libraries were asked to comment on the availability of number of online databases. Table 8.104 shows that the majority of respondents, 80.8 percent, do not have online databases. This seems to be the fact as query of this service remains unreplied in the majority of cases. This is surprising that such a provision these days is not available in CSIR libraries in the country which are highly scientific and technical.

Table 8.104 : Access to Number of Online Databases by Group of Laboratories

Group of Laboratories	*Number of Online Databases*						
	1	*2*	*3*	*4*	*Not Stated*	*Not Applicable*	*Row Total*
PESG	3	-	1	-	-	49	53
	(5.7)		(1.9)			(92.5)	(13.9)
CSG	2	-	-	-	8	47	57
	(3.5)				(14.0)	(82.5)	(15.0)
BSG	7	4	4	-	18	98	131
	(5.3)	(3.1)	(3.1)		(13.7)	(74.8)	(34.5)
ESG	3	1	1	-	5	84	94
	(3.2)	(1.1)	(1.1)		(5.3)	(89.4)	(24.7)
ISG	5	3	3	3	2	29	45
	(11.1)	(6.7)	(6.7)	(6.7)	(4.4)	(64.4)	(11.8)
Column Total	20	8	9	3	33	307	380
	(5.3)	(2.1)	(2.4)	(.8)	(8.7)	(80.8)	(100.0)

8.6 RATING OF ARRANGEMENT OF BOOKS ON SHELVES

The strength of library services does not depend only on number of the library collection but several other factors are also important. Proper and systematic arrangement on shelves is one of the very important factors. It provides easy access to valuable collection of the library. It could be ensured only through very well co-ordinated processing section and vigilant library staff.

In view of the importance attached to arrangement of books on shelves, the responses from users were solicited. The data collected on arrangement of books (Table 8.105) reveals that the majority of respondents of ISG (66.7%) and PESG (66.0%) regarded the arrangement of books on shelves as good, followed by 62.6 percent of respondents of BSG. The number of such respondents in CSG and ESG is comparatively less. On the other hand, comparatively larger number of respondents belonging to CSG rate this service as excellent. There are also respondents in other groups who consider the service as excellent. However, it is significant only in CSG and ESG. The difference in responses regarding arrangement of books on shelves is clearly supported by Chi-square value = 25.03516 which is significant at .01 level.

Table 8.105 : Rating of Arrangement of Books on Shelves

Group of Laboratories	*Response*			
	Excellent	*Good*	*Poor*	*Row Total*
PESG	11	35	7	53
	(20.8)	(66.0)	(13.2)	(13.9)
CSG	27	29	1	57
	(47.4)	(50.9)	(1.8)	(15.0)
BSG	27	82	22	131
	(20.6)	(62.6)	(16.8)	(34.5)
ESG	27	54	13	94
	(28.7)	(57.4)	(13.8)	(24.7)
ISG	6	30	9	45
	(13.3)	(66.7)	(20.0)	(11.8)
Column Total	98	230	52	380
	(25.8)	(60.5)	(13.7)	(100.0)

$X^2 = 25.03516$ with 8 d.f.

$P < .01$

8.7 RATING OF ARRANGEMENT OF JOURNALS ON SHELVES

The arrangement of journals on shelves has been rated by a majority of respondents in each group as good (Table 8.106). Interesting feature of the responses is that the arrangement has been rated as excellent by 31.3 percent of respondents. Also when we look at the responses individually, we find that all are on similar pattern. In this case also, if we consider the responses rating the arrangement as good and excellent, we find that over 80 percent of respondents in each group have shown their appreciation of the service. Chi-square test has been applied for to find out the differences. Chi-square value = 6.16425 is insignificant at .01 level which does not support the difference statistically.

The above analysis indicates that arrangement of journals on shelves is rated as good and excellent by majority of users. The reasons behind good arrangement of documents on shelves may be the result of proper technical processing and supported by efficient shelving system. It is clear that in all CSIR libraries, arrangement of books and journals on shelves is good.

Table 8.106 : Rating of Arrangement of Journals on Shelves

Group of Laboratories	*Response*			
	Excellent	*Good*	*Poor*	*Row Total*
PESG	14 (26.4)	35 (66.0)	4 (7.5)	53 (13.9)
CSG	21 (36.8)	31 (54.4)	5 (8.8)	57 (15.0)
BSG	42 (32.1)	75 (57.3)	14 (10.7)	131 (34.5)
ESG	27 (28.7)	51 (54.3)	16 (17.0)	94 (24.7)
ISG	15 (33.3)	26 (57.8)	4 (8.9)	45 (11.8)
Column Total	119 (31.3)	218 (57.4)	43 (11.3)	380 (100.0)

X^2 = 6.16425 with 8 d.f.

P > .01

8.8 RATING OF ARRANGEMENT OF RESEARCH/PROJECT REPORTS ON SHELVES

The analysis of data in Table 8.107 has been carried out to find out the arrangement of reports on shelves in different groups of CSIR libraries. Responses, as given in the table, show that the arrangement has been indicated by a fairly large number of respondents as poor. Though the respondents are appreciative of the arrangement, their percentage is much less than the responses we have in case of journals and books. The arrangement is rated as good by over 45 percent of respondents belonging to CSG and BSG, whereas only over 35 percent of respondents PESG found the arrangement good. There are also respondents in each group who have considered this service as excellent. But their proportion is insignificant. Those who considered this service as poor are more in number in ISG (51.1%) and PESG (52.8%) than in other groups.

Chi-square value = 6.86081, which is insignificant at .01 level, shows that there is no difference between the arrangement of reports as indicated by respondents of CSIR libraries.

Table 8.107 : Rating of Arrangement of Research/Project Reports on Shelves

Group of Laboratories	*Response*			
	Excellent	*Good*	*Poor*	*Row Total*
PESG	6 (11.3)	19 (35.8)	28 (52.8)	53 (13.9)
CSG	9 (15.8)	27 (47.4)	21 (36.8)	57 (15.0)
BSG	13 (9.9)	63 (48.1)	55 (42.0)	131 (34.5)
ESG	15 (16.0)	36 (38.3)	43 (45.7)	94 (24.7)
ISG	5 (11.1)	17 (37.8)	23 (51.1)	45 (11.8)
Column Total	48 (12.6)	162 (42.6)	170 (44.7)	380 (100.0)

X^2 = 6.86081 with 8 d.f.

$P > .01$

8.9 AVAILABILITY OF READING ROOM FACILITIES

Reading room facility is another important factor which affects the use of the library and information services. Reading room facilities like individual study carrels, comfortability in reading and study, adequate lighting, emergency light during light failure, and seminar/conference room to organise the meetings, discussion among the librarians and professionals of other libraries, are the crucial links between users and reading materials. Their availability and updating have an impact on library use. It is, therefore, important to examine the provision of such facilities in the libraries.

An overwhelming majority of respondents 91.6 percent (Table 8.108) indicated that there is provision of adequate lighting facilities in their libraries. Similarly, an overwhelming majority of respondents (77.1%) indicated availability of comfortability of place for reading and study. However, the availability of seminar/conference room has been shown by only 50.8 percent of the respondents. Availability of emergency light and individuals study carrels which constitute major components of good infrastructural facilities, seem to have received no attention in CSIR libraries.

It is obvious from the above analysis that except emergency light and individual study carrels, CSIR libraries are equipped with adequate lighting, reading room and seminar halls.

Table 8.108 : Availability of Reading Room Facilities

Reading Room Facilities	*Response*		
	Yes	*No*	*Row Total*
Individual study carrels	73 (19.2)	307 (80.8)	380 (100.0)
Comfortability in reading and study	293 (77.1)	87 (22.9)	380 (100.0)
Adequate lighting	348 (91.6)	32 (8.4)	380 (100.0)
Emergency light	136 (35.8)	244 (64.2)	380 (100.0)
Seminar/conference room	193 (50.8)	187 (49.2)	380 (100.0)

8.9.1 Rating of Reading Room Facilities

Table 8.109 shows variations in relation to the preferences given to the various reading room facilities. The majority of respondents rated almost all the facilities as good. However, a higher proportion of respondents rated the facility of seminar/conference and adequate lighting as good. Some facilities, such as comfortability of place in reading and study, individual study carrels, seminar/conference room, have been rated excellent by a relatively higher proportion of respondents.

Table 8,109 : Rating of Reading Room Facilities

Rating of Reading Room Facilities	*Response*			
	Excellent	*Good*	*Poor*	*Row Total*
Individual study carrels	23 (31.5)	42 (57.5)	8 (11.0)	73 (100.0)
Comfortability in reading and study	71 (24.2)	183 (62.5)	39 (13.3)	293 (100.0)
Adequate lighting	74 (21.3)	230 (66.1)	44 (12.6)	348 (100.0)
Emergency light	26 (19.1)	82 (60.3)	28 (20.6)	136 (100.0)
Seminar/Conference room	50 (25.9)	125 (64.8)	18 (9.3)	193 (100.0)

8.9.2 Individual Study Carrels

Table 8.110 reveals that an overwhelming majority of respondents of all the groups indicated non-availability of individual study carrels in their respective organisations. Since each group is a cluster of many laboratories, it is possible that availability of such facility as shown by a few must be available in some cases. However, Chi-square test has been applied and found that difference between respondents of individual study carrels is also supported by Chi-square value = 30.91055 which is significant at .01 level.

Table 8.110 : Individual Study Carrels by Group of Laboratories

Individual	*Group of Laboratories*					
Study Carrels	*PESG*	*CSG*	*BSG*	*ESG*	*ISG*	*Row Total*
Yes	18 (34.0)	10 (17.5)	13 (9.9)	30 (31.9)	2 (4.4)	73 (19.2)
No	35 (66.0)	47 (82.5)	118 (90.1)	64 (68.1)	43 (95.6)	307 (80.8)
Column Total	53 (13.9)	57 (15.0)	131 (34.5)	94 (24.7)	45 (11.8)	380 (100.0)

X^2 = 30.91055 with 4 d.f.

P < .01

8.9.2.1 Rating of Individual Study Carrels

Rating of individual study carrels as given in Table 8.111 shows that by and large there availability has been rated good in almost all the laboratories. A minor variation, however, does not affect major change. This facility has also been rated as excellent by the majority of respondents belonging to ISG. Also a good number of respondents of CSG and BSG have termed this facility as excellent.

Chi-square value = 6.37071 is insignificant at .01 level which shows that there is no significant difference between the respondents of individual study carrels in CSIR libraries.

Table 8.111 : Rating of Individual Study Carrels

Group of Laboratories	*Response*			
	Excellent	*Good*	*Poor*	*Row Total*
PESG	5	11	2	18
	(27.8)	(61.1)	(11.1)	(24.7)
CSG	4	6	-	10
	(40.0)	(60.0)		(13.7)
BSG	5	7	1	13
	(38.5)	(53.8)	(7.7)	(17.8)
ESG	8	18	4	30
	(26.7)	(60.0)	(13.3)	(41.1)
ISG	1	-	1	2
	(50.0)		(50.0)	(2.7)
Column Total	23	42	8	73
	(31.5)	(57.5)	(11.0)	(100.0)

$X^2 = 6.37071$ with 8 d.f.

$P > .01$

8.9.3 Comfortability in Reading and Study

In order to make library attractive and comfortable place for reading and study, convenience, comfort and congenial atmosphere for reading are considered very important factors. A large number of CSIR libraries came into existence in the beginning of 50s and 60s. With this in view, respondents of CSIR libraries were asked to comment on the present arrangement for reading room facilities. In this regard an overwhelming majority of respondents indicated that their libraries have comfortable place for reading whereas 22.9 percent responded negatively.

Group-wise analysis on the other hand (Table 8.112) indicates that the majority of respondents of CSG (93.0%) have comfortability of place for reading and study, followed by 77 percent respondents of ESG and PESG. Similar response with slight variation has been received from respondents of BSG (72.5%) and ISG (68.9%). Chi-square value = 11.43959 is not significant at .01 level which shows that there is no significant difference between respondents of comfortability of place for reading and study in CSIR libraries.

Table 8.112 : Comfortability in Reading and Study

Comfortability in Reading and Study	*Group of Laboratories*					
	PESG	*CSG*	*BSG*	*ESG*	*ISG*	*Row Total*
Yes	41	53	95	73	31	293
	(77.4)	(93.0)	(72.5)	(77.7)	(68.9)	(77.1)
No	12	4	36	21	14	87
	(22.6)	(7.0)	(27.5)	(22.3)	(31.1)	(22.9)
Column Total	53	57	131	94	45	380
	(13.9)	(15.0)	(34.5)	(24.7)	(11.8)	(100.0)

$X^2 = 11.43959$ with 4 d.f.

$P > .01$

8.9.3.1 *Rating of Comfortability in Reading and Study*

Response regarding the rating of comfortability of place for reading and study as given in Table 8.113 reveals that an overwhelming majority of respondents (62.5%) are of the opinion that comfortability of place for reading and study in their libraries is good. Even a good number of respondents, 24.2 percent, indicated this facility as excellent.

Group-wise analysis of data regarding comfortability of place for reading and study indicates that the highest percentage of respondents of CSG (69.8%) rated this facility as good, followed by BSG (68.4%). There seems to be some variation in response pattern of respondents across the group. As majority of respondents in each group rated this facility as good but the percentage of those who rated this facility as excellent varies from group to group. Only noticeable variation is that a good number of respondents belonging to PESG have rated provision of such facility as poor.

The difference is also supported by Chi-square value = 22.42372 which is significant at .01 level.

Table 8.113 : Rating of Comfortability in Reading and Study

Group of Laboratories	*Response* Excellent	Good	Poor	*Row Total*
PESG	10	18	13	41
	(24.4)	(43.9)	(31.7)	(14.0)
CSG	7	37	9	53
	(13.2)	(69.8)	(17.0)	(18.1)
BSG	22	65	8	95
	(23.2)	(68.4)	(8.4)	(32.4)
ESG	22	44	7	73
	(30.1)	(60.3)	(9.6)	(24.9)
ISG	10	19	2	31
	(32.3)	(61.3)	(6.5)	(10.6)
Column Total	71	183	39	293
	(24.2)	(62.5)	(13.3)	(100.0)

X^2 = 22.42372 with 8 d.f.

P < .01

8.9.4 Adequate Lighting

The analysis of data on availability of adequate lighting reveals that an overwhelming majority of respondents of ESG (94.7%) indicated that their libraries have adequate lighting arrangement in their libraries, followed by CSG (93.0%). It can be seen from the Table 8.114 that even 90.8 percent respondents of BSG have also stated the availability of such facility. Similarly, the respondents of ISG (88.9%) and PESG (88.7%) also reported that their libraries have facility of adequate lighting for study.

The difference between the provision of adequate lighting is not significant as Chi-square value = 2.41133 which is insignificant at .01 level.

Table 8.114 : Adequate Lighting

Adequate Lighting	*Group of Laboratories*					
	PESG	*CSG*	*BSG*	*ESG*	*ISG*	*Row Total*
Yes	47 (88.7)	53 (93.0)	119 (90.8)	89 (94.7)	40 (88.9)	348 (91.6)
No	6 (11.3)	4 (7.0)	12 (9.2)	5 (5.3)	5 (11.1)	32 (8.4)
Column Total	53 (13.9)	57 (15.0)	131 (34.5)	94 (24.7)	45 (11.8)	380 (100.0)

X^2 = 2.41133 with 4 d.f.

P > .01

8.9.4.1 Rating of Adequate Lighting

The respondents' satisfaction regarding adequate lighting arrangement has been rated in Table 8.115. An impressive percentage of respondents in BSG (76.5%) are satisfied with lighting arrangement as they rated this facility as good, followed by ISG (70.0%). Even respondents of ESG and CSG also indicated their satisfaction regarding adequate lighting by terming it as good. Though less in number as compared to other groups, a good number of respondents of PESG (46.8%) also reported such facility as good.

It is strange to note that the lighting facility has been rated as poor by the respondents of the two groups, namely PESG and CSG. Contrary to this, lighting facility has been rated as excellent by some of the respondents in each group.

Adequate lighting arrangement is the basic minimum that cannot be done away with. Without proper lighting, not only consulting literature and other documents within the premises of library is obstructed, but operation of other activities also become difficult.

The difference as stated above is supported statistically, as Chi-square value = 39.01555 is found significant at .01 level.

Table 8.115 : Rating of Adequate Lighting

Group of Laboratories	*Response*			
	Excellent	*Good*	*Poor*	*Row Total*
PESG	12 (25.5)	22 (46.8)	13 (27.7)	47 (13.5)
CSG	10 (18.9)	27 (50.9)	16 (30.2)	53 (15.2)
BSG	20 (16.8)	91 (76.5)	8 (6.7)	119 (34.2)
ESG	22 (24.7)	62 (69.7)	5 (5.6)	89 (25.6)
ISG	10 (25.0)	28 (70.0)	2 (5.0)	40 (11.5)
Column Total	74 (21.3)	230 (66.1)	44 (12.6)	348 (100.0)

$X^2 = 39.01555$ with 8 d.f.

$P < .01$

8.9.5 Emergency Light

In order to find out the provision of emergency light during frequent failure of power in CSIR libraries, the respondents of the laboratories were requested to indicate the availability of such a facility. In this context, Table 8.116 indicates that over 70 percent respondents of ISG and BSG stated that their libraries do not have emergency light that could be put in use during light failure in their libraries.

It is obvious from the above analysis that non-availability of emergency light is indicated by the majority of respondents (64.2%). It is interesting to notice that in majority of cases emergency light is absent. It is surprising to note that scientific and technical libraries of such large scientific and technical organisations of national importance do not have facility of generator or emergency light during frequent lighting failure. However, Chi-square value = 12.35775 is not significant at .01 level.

Table 8.116 : Emergency Light

Emergency Light	*Group of Laboratories*					
	PESG	*CSG*	*BSG*	*ESG*	*ISG*	*Row Total*
Yes	19	31	39	35	12	136
	(35.8)	(54.4)	(29.8)	(37.2)	(26.7)	(35.8)
No	34	26	92	59	33	244
	(64.2)	(45.6)	(70.2)	(62.8)	(73.3)	(64.2)
Column Total	53	57	131	94	45	380
	(13.9)	(15.0)	(34.5)	(24.7)	(11.8)	(100.0)

X^2 = 12.35775 with 4 d.f.

P > .01

8.9.5.1 Rating of Emergency Light

Provision of emergency light is a good facility but the provision alone is not enough in itself. Therefore, it was necessary to evaluate the functional aspect of this facility.

Analysis as given in Table 8.117, shows that users across the groups are satisfied with this facility. Their response is further indication of the fact that at the time when light is not operational, the emergency light is put into use. There is also a marked similarity in the pattern of response. Chi-square test has been applied and found that the Chi-square value = 8.25361 is not significant at .01 level. There is no significant difference between the respondents of rating of emergency light.

Table 8.117 : Rating of Emergency Light

Group of Laboratories	*Response*			
	Excellent	*Good*	*Poor*	*Row Total*
PESG	2	13	4	19
	(10.5)	(68.4)	(21.1)	(14.0)
CSG	6	16	9	31
	(19.4)	(51.6)	(29.0)	(22.8)
BSG	5	26	8	39
	(12.8)	(66.7)	(20.5)	(28.7)
ESG	11	18	6	35
	(31.4)	(51.4)	(17.1)	(25.7)
ISG	2	9	1	12
	(16.7)	(75.0)	(8.3)	(8.8)
Column Total	26	82	28	136
	(19.1)	(60.3)	(20.6)	(100.0)

X^2 = 8.25361 with 8 d.f.

P > .01

8.9.6 Seminar/Conference Room

Availability of seminar/conference room in the libraries serves multiple purposes. Basically, it is used for imparting orientation programmes to the users. Also it is required for arranging professional meetings, get togethers of library staff. Needless to say that such facilities do not have direct impact on library services, but they certainly add value to the library. Data in Table 8.118 shows that half of the respondents have indicated availability of seminar/conference room in their respective libraries. The difference between the respondents of seminar/conference room is supported by Chi-square value = 20.74841 which is significant at .01 level.

Table 8.118 : Seminar/Conference Room in Group of Laboratories

Seminar/ Conference Room	*Group of Laboratories*					
	PESG	*CSG*	*BSG*	*ESG*	*ISG*	*Row Total*
Yes	20	33	52	62	26	193
	(37.7)	(57.9)	(39.7)	(66.0)	(57.8)	(50.8)
No	33	24	79	32	19	187
	(62.3)	(42.1)	(60.3)	(34.0)	(42.2)	(49.2)
Column Total	53	57	131	94	45	380
	(13.9)	(15.0)	(34.5)	(24.7)	(11.8)	(100.0)

X^2 = 20.74841 with 4 d.f.

P < .01

8.9.6.1 Rating of Seminar/Conference Room

Of those who have indicated availability of such facilities, an overwhelming majority of respondents have rated this facility as good. There are also such respondents who have rated this service as excellent. Some of the respondents found this facility as poor but the response rate is not significant enough to arrive at the definite conclusion. Chi-square value = 10.27828 is significant at .01 level, which shows significant difference between the respondents of seminar/conference room of CSIR libraries.[7]

Table 8.119 : Rating of Seminar/Conference Room

Group of Laboratories	*Response* Excellent	Good	Poor	*Row Total*
PESG	5	14	2	21
	(23.8)	(66.7)	(9.5)	(10.9)
CSG	6	22	5	33
	(18.2)	(66.7)	(15.2)	(17.1)
BSG	16	36	-	52
	(30.8)	(69.2)		(26.9)
ESG	17	35	9	61
	(27.9)	(57.4)	(14.8)	(31.6)
ISG	6	18	2	26
	(23.1)	(69.2)	(7.7)	(13.5)
Column Total	50	125	18	193
	(25.9)	(64.8)	(9.3)	(100.0)

$X^2 = 10.27828$ with 8 d.f.

$P < .01$

8.10 DISCUSSIONS AND CONCLUSIONS

In order to assess the efficiency of services and users' satisfaction, it is necessary to examine the effectiveness and use of existing services in the CSIR libraries. The present study was undertaken to explore, analyze and describe the important aspects in the provision and use of services rendered by the CSIR libraries.

8.10.1 Respondents' Profile

Out of 380 scientists and research scholars in the survey sample, 87.4 percent are males and the rest are females. The majority of users of ESG (98.9%), CSG (96.5%) and PESG (96.2%) are male scientists. Designation-wise analysis reveals that 94.5 percent of respondents are scientists who constitute the majority of the users of CSIR libraries. Only 5.5 percent of the respondents are research scholars. All respondents in ESG are scientists, whereas 13.0 percent respondents of BSG are research scholars. Senior scientists constitute 48.4 percent of respondents, followed by 32.4 percent of scientists C. The majority of respondents consists of senior scientists in all the groups except in ISG which has relatively younger scientists A&B (53.3%). The majority of respondents (76.6%) in all the groups have Ph.D. degrees in their respective areas. In the CSG, 89.5 percent respondents have Ph.D. degree, whereas 46.7 percent respondents of ISG had only M.Sc. at the time of the survey.

Out of nine specialized areas, 28.9 percent of the respondents have their specialization in chemistry and chemical technology, whereas 17.1 percent respondents have specialisation in engineering sciences. All respondents in ISG have their specialisation in information science and technology. About 90 percent respondents belonging to CSG have specialised in chemistry and chemical technology.

Majority of the respondents (82.9%) are members of multiple professional bodies at state, national and international levels. Interestingly, 17.1 percent of respondents do not have membership of any professional body, society, etc. About 29 percent of the respondents are members of at least two national level associations, whereas 24.7 percent respondents have membership of national level associations. Only a small percentage of respondents (3.2) are members of at least five national level associations. About 73 percent of respondents do not have membership of any international association. Around one-fifth respondents have membership with at least one international association.

Majority of scientists have experience of attending national as well as international conferences. Around 42 percent of respondents have attended one to three and, 32.1 percent have participated in four to six national conferences. Around one-tenth of scientists have not participated in any national conference during the last five years. About 47 percent scientists of BSG and ISG have participated in one to three national conferences. Fairly large number of respondents (43.2%) has the experience of attending at least one international conference during the last five years. These respondents are found to be the frequent visitors of libraries of their respective laboratories.

All respondents of PESG and CSG have contributed working papers in conferences and research articles to journals. The respondents of BSG (96.9%) and ESG (95.7%) also have contributed research papers and articles, which indicate that an overwhelming majority of respondents had published papers/articles in journals for which they have made the use of the library to the maximum extent. 'Publish or perish' syndrome can be seen clearly amongst the CSIR scientists, and we can categorize them into four groups: ritualistic contributors (26.8%) with one to five publications; regular contributors (31.1%) with six to ten publications; extensive contributors (25.3%) with eleven to twenty publications; and a small group of prolific contributors (0.8%) with more than 51 publications in the last five years. Only 4.2 percent have not contributed any paper in the last five years. It has been revealed that 48.9 percent respondents belonging to ISG have published one to five research papers, whereas 37 percent respondents of ESG and PESG have contributed six to ten and eleven to twenty papers. Interestingly, 17.8 percent respondents belonging to ISG did not publish any paper during the last five years. Such persons are those who attach little importance to libraries and do not make use of them regularly.

8.10.2 Purpose of Visiting the Library

About 96 percent respondents of different specialization have made use of the library for research purposes, whereas 90.3 percent have used the library for writing papers. There are a substantial number of users (38.7%) who keep themselves abreast of the latest happenings in their area of interest, while 36.6 percent respondents have been using the library for preparation of bibliographies. On the other hand, 20.5 percent respondents use the library for book writing. Scientists and research scholars are using libraries for research and writing papers. They also use libraries for preparation of bibliographies and to keep track with the R&D. However, the number of this category of users is relatively very small. The CSIR libraries are mostly used effectively in conducting research and writing papers.

8.10.3 Frequency of Library Visits

About 41 percent respondents visited the library twice a week and 36.1 percent consult the library daily. The majority of respondents of ISG (51.1%) and CSG (50.9%) visit the library daily. There are some respondents (47.2%) in PESG who visit the library twice a week.

The majority of research scholars (57.1%), as compared to scientists, visit the library daily to keep themselves abreast of research and development in the field of their specialization. A large number of senior scientists (44.0%) have been found to be frequently visiting the library, at least twice a week, compared to scientists A&B, scientists C and research scholars. Mostly Post-doctoral Fellows (66.7%) and respondents having M.Sc. degree (40.7%) are daily visitors to the CSIR libraries. About 42 percent respondents having Ph.D. degree visit the library twice a week.

8.10.4 Time Spent on Each Visit

About 56 percent respondents spend 2-3 hours in the library on each visit, whereas 35.5 percent respondents normally spend just an hour on their visit to the library. The majority of respondents 66.7 percent of CSG spend 2-3 hours, followed by BSG (58.0%), ESG (56.4%) and PESG (54.7%).

It has been found from the analysis that the majority of scientists and research scholars, except scientist A&B, spend 2-3 hours on each visit. The majority of senior scientists (62.0%) spent 2-3 hours during their visit in the library, whereas 57.1 percent of research scholars and 56.1 percent of scientists C also spend 2-3 hours in the library on each visit. The majority of scientists A&B are those who spent 0-1 hour followed by scientist C (39.8%) and research scholars (38.1%).

8.10.5 Stages for Consulting the Library

The majority of scientists and research scholars consult the library for survey of literature and to identify the area for research as compared to at the stages of experiment, analysis of data and report writing. An overwhelming majority of respondents (99.5%) consult the library at the time of survey of literature and 90.5% of the respondents use the library to identify areas for research.

All respondents of PESG, CSG, BSG, ESG and ISG (95.6%) consult the library for survey of literature, whereas an equal number of respondents of CSG and ESG (94.7%) consult the library for identifying area for research. 83.0 percent of the respondents of PESG consult the library at the time of experiment, whereas 89.5 percent of the respondents of CSG consult the library at the time of analysis of data. There are 87.0 percent of the respondents of BSG that consult the library at the stage of report writing, followed by ESG (81.9%) and ISG (80.0%).

8.10.6 Usefulness of the Library at Different Stages of Consultation

The majority of respondents (62.5%) rated the library as useful at the time of experiment, whereas 61.9 percent of the respondents expressed that the library is very useful at the time of survey of literature. About 49 percent of the respondents indicated usefulness of the library in identifying the area for research. Usefulness of the library has also been indicated at the time of analysis of data and report writing. This indicates the effectiveness of the library and its efficacy at different stages of research and advanced studies and thus, the library plays an effective role as a centre of information.

8.10.7 Library Collection

8.10.7.1 General Books on Science

Analysis revealed that 57.4 percent of the respondents indicated the general collection of books on science as good, whereas 29.7 percent of the respondents categorised the collection as excellent. Only 12.9 percent of the respondents remarked the collection as poor. More than 62 percent of the respondents of PESG, ESG and ISG indicated such collection as good, whereas excellent rating of such collection is indicated by 38.2 percent respondents of BSG, followed by 33.3 percent of CSG. About 18 percent of the respondents of ESG expressed rating of general books on science as poor.

8.10.7.2 Area of Specialisation

As regards the area of specialisation, 52.6 percent of the respondents indicated the collection as good. Only 30.5 percent of the respondents rated the collection as excellent, whereas 16.8 percent of the respondents stated such collection as poor. Group-wise analysis revealed that 64.2 percent respondents of PESG and 58.0 percent of BSG indicated the collection of books on area of specialisation as good. Respondents of ESG (36.2%), CSG (31.6%) and ISG (31.1%) indicated such collection as excellent. About 26 percent respondents of CSG and 22.2 percent of ISG stated books on their area of specialisation as poor. Almost one in every five respondents indicating the specialised collection as 'poor' should be considered an indicator that the area needs further development, and requires the participation of the users in collection development.

8.10.7.3 Reference Books

About 61 percent respondents rated reference books as good, whereas 20.8 percent of the respondents stated such collection as excellent. The majority of respondents of ESG (69.1%) and BSG (61.8%) indicated the reference collection as good. Respondents of ISG (31.1%), BSG (22.9%) and CSG (22.8%) stated the same as excellent. This indicates that the libraries of CSIR are in possession of good reference collection, but 30.2 percent of PESG respondents indicated reference collection in their area as poor. It should be taken as an indicator of the need for improvements.

8.10.7.4 Theses/Dissertations

As regards theses/dissertations, 50.5 percent of respondents indicated the collection of theses/dissertations as poor, whereas 23.4 percent of the respondents stated the same as good. About 22 percent of the respondents indicated that their libraries do not have such type of collection. More than 67 percent of the respondents of PESG and ESG stated this collection as poor. Respondents of BSG (61.8%) pointed out the collection of theses/dissertation as good, whereas 22.9 percent respondents of BSG rated such collection as excellent. There are some respondents in each group, i.e. ISG (51.1%) and BSG (28.2%) who stated that their libraries do not have this type of collection. It is evident that such works are not available in those libraries. CSIR libraries should consider (based on the needs) increasing their collections in this area.

8.10.7.5 Research/Project Reports

About 42 percent of the respondents across the five groups of CSIR laboratories rated the research/project reports as poor, whereas 35.3 percent of the respondents indicated such collection as good. There are 16.3 percent of the respondents who termed the non-availability of such material in their libraries. Only 6.6 percent of the respondents marked the availability of such collection as excellent. The data analysis revealed that 54.4 percent respondents of CSG and 51.1 percent of ISG stated the position of such material as poor. This material was also indicated to be poor by 50.9 percent respondents of PESG and 44.7 percent of ESG. Only 42.7 percent of the respondents of BSG rated such collection as good. About 9 percent of the respondents of BSG rated the same as excellent. This is also a grey area in the CSIR collections, and should be strengthen on priority bases.

8.10.7.6 Government Documents

About 46 percent of the respondents among five groups of CSIR laboratories rated availability of government documents in their libraries as poor, whereas 26.8 percent of the respondents termed such collection as good. 23.2 percent of the users indicated that their libraries do not have such type of material. Only 4.2 percent of the respondents marked it as excellent. Respondents of CSG (68.4%), ISG (60.0%) and PESG (54.7%) rated this collection as poor. 33.0 percent respondents of ESG and 32.1 percent of BSG rated such collection as good. Only 33.6 percent respondents of BSG termed the non-availability of government documents in their libraries. It is evident that grey literature, despite its being valuable, is not sufficiently available.

8.10.7.7 Conference Proceedings

This collection was rated as good by 44.2 percent of the respondents, and 36.8 percent of the respondents indicated the same as poor and 10.5 percent of the respondents remarked the non-availability of such collection. Only 8.4 percent of the respondents rated such collection as excellent. Respondents of ISG (51.1%), PESG (47.2%) and CSG (43.9%) rated the same as poor, followed by an equal number of respondents, i.e. 29.8 percent of BSG and ESG. 50.0 percent respondents of ESG and 45.3 percent of PESG indicated this collection as good, followed by 44.3 percent respondents of BSG. 17.6 percent of the respondents of BSG termed non-availability of such collection.

8.10.7.8 Standards, Specifications and Patents

The collection of standards, specifications and patents was rated as good by 42.2 percent of the respondents, whereas 35.0 percent of the respondents marked such collection as poor. 14.2 percent respondents indicated non-availability of such collection. Group-wise analysis revealed that 56.4 percent respondents of ESG, 45.6 percent of CSG and 43.4 percent of PESG, rated such collection as good. On the other hand, 55.6 percent of the respondents of ISG and 41.5 percent of the respondents of PESG indicated such collection as poor, whereas 27.5 percent of the respondents of BSG stated that such collection is not available in their libraries.

8.10.7.9 Pamphlets and Reprints

The data analysis revealed that 44.7 percent of the respondents rated such collection as poor, whereas 30.0 percent of the respondents marked it as good. About 21 percent of the respondents indicated the non-availability of pamphlets and reprints in their libraries. A little over 60 percent of the respondents of PESG and ISG rated such material as poor, followed by ESG (48.9%) and CSG (43.9%). Respondents of CSG (38.6%) and BSG (35.1%) rated pamphlets and reprints as good, whereas 29.8 percent of the respondents of BSG and 22.6 percent of PESG stated that their libraries do not have this type of collection.

8.10.7.10 Scientific Journals and Serials

The majority of respondents, 60.3 percent, rated the availability of scientific journals and serials as good, whereas 33.4 percent of the respondents indicated that their libraries have excellent collection of this type of literature. More than 66 percent of the respondents of PESG and ESG rated scientific journals and serials as good, whereas over 36 percent of the respondents of BSG, CSG and ISG termed the availability of such material as excellent.

8.10.7.11 Indexing Journals

Analysis revealed that 55.0 percent of respondents indicated the availability of the indexing journals as good, whereas 28.4 percent of the respondents pointed out indexing journals as excellent. Only 16.6 percent of the respondents marked indexing journals as poor. The respondents of ESG (61.7%) rated the same as good, followed by CSG (56.1%). More than 50.0 percent of the respondents of PESG, BSG and ISG also rated availability of indexing journals as good, whereas 35.1 percent respondents of CSG indicated such collection as excellent, followed by over 30 percent of the respondents of PESG, BSG and ISG. Availability of indexing journals has been rated poor by 22.3 percent of the respondents of ESG followed by ISG (17.8%) and PESG (17.0%). As such it is essential that those libraries should pay more attention where such tools are not so sufficient.

8.10.7.12 Abstracting Journals

About 51 percent of the respondents among five groups of laboratories rated the abstracting journals as good, whereas 28.2 percent of the respondents rated these journals as excellent. On the other hand, 20.5 percent of the respondents stated the availability of abstracting journals as poor. The respondents of PESG (58.5%), BSG (52.7%) and ESG (50.0%) indicated the abstracting journals as good. Respondents of CSG (36.8%) and BSG (35.1%) pointed out availability of such material as excellent, whereas 31.9 percent of the respondents of ESG and 26.7 percent of ISG indicated the availability of abstracting journals as poor.

One of the major activities of the library is to develop usable collection that meets the information requirements of the users. The performance of the library as a service organisation depends to a very large extent on the quality, quantity and value-based print and non-print collection. CSIR libraries need more attention in the area of grey literature, theses/dissertations, research/project reports, conference proceedings, government documents, standards, specifications and patents, and abstracting journals, etc.

8.10.8 Non-Book Material

8.10.8.1 Microfilms/Microfiches

About 51 percent of respondents responded that their libraries do not have microfilms/microfiches, whereas 29.7 percent respondents indicated the availability of such materials as poor. Only 15.5 percent respondents pointed out the collection of such type of material as good. The respondents of BSG (58.0%), ESG (55.3%) and ISG (51.1%) indicated the non-availability of such items followed by CSG (42.1%) and PESG (37.7%). A little over 47 percent respondents of PESG and CSG rated the availability of microfilms/microfiches as poor, whereas 22.1 percent of respondents of BSG and 17.8 percent users of ISG rated such collection as good.

8.10.8.2 Audiocassettes

It is evident from the analysis that 81.6 percent of the respondents rated the non-availability of audiocassettes in their libraries. The respondents of BSG (86.3%), CSG (84.2%), ESG (80.9%) indicated that their libraries do not have the audiocassettes, followed by ISG (77.8%) and PESG (71.7%). 26 percent of the respondents of PESG indicated this collection as poor followed by over 15 percent of the respondents of CSG, ESG and ISG.

8.10.8.3 Videocassettes

Like the audiocassettes, it has been found that 81.1 percent of the respondents across the five groups of laboratories expressed that their libraries do not have the collection of videocassettes, whereas 15.0 percent of the respondents termed such collection as poor. Over 86 percent of the respondents of CSG and BSG indicated that their libraries do not possess such type of material, followed by ISG (77.8%), ESG (76.6%) and PESG (71.7%). There are some respondents in PESG (24.5%) and ESG (19.1%) who indicated this collection as poor.

8.10.8.4 Slides

About 79 percent of the respondents indicated that their libraries do not possess this type of collection, whereas 14.5 percent of the respondents rated this collection as poor. More than 80 percent of the respondents of PESG, CSG and BSG indicated that their libraries, do not have the slides in their libraries, followed by ESG (74.5%) and ISG (71.1%). Out of those 13.3 percent respondents of ISG and 10.5 percent of CSG rated slide collection as good.

8.10.8.5 CD-ROM Databases

As regards CD-ROM, 72.9 percent respondents pointed out that their libraries do not possess the CD-ROM databases, whereas 14.7 percent respondents indicated the availability of CD-ROM databases as good. More than 75 percent respondents of PESG, CSG and ESG expressed that their libraries do not possess CD-ROM databases, followed by a little over 68 percent of the respondents of BSG and ISG. Whereas 20.6 percent respondents of BSG termed the availability of CD-ROM databases as good, followed by over 15 percent respondents of PESG and CSG. However, 17.8 percent respondents of ISG indicated the availability of CD-ROMs in their libraries as excellent. This means that this type of material is in use in some CSIR libraries.

8.10.8.6 Online Databases

Analysis revealed that 75.3 percent of respondents indicated non-availability of online databases in their libraries, whereas 11.3 percent respondents indicated availability of online databases as good. Group-wise analysis indicates that over 81 percent respondents of PESG and ESG indicated the non-availability of these databases, followed by CSG (77.2%) and BSG (74.0%). Even 55.6 percent of the respondents of ISG stated that their libraries do not possess the online databases. The availability of online databases was rated as excellent by 22.2 percent of the respondents of ISG. About 19 percent of the respondents of BSG and 15.8 percent of CSG rated the online databases as good.

8.10.8.7 Maps/Atlases

About 33 percent respondents belonging to five groups of CSIR laboratories pointed out the non-existence of maps/ atlases in their libraries, whereas 30.8 percent of respondents rated such collection as poor. Only 29.7 percent of the respondents indicated this collection as good. Respondents of BSG (41.2%) and PESG (35.8%) indicated that their libraries do not have this collection, followed by CSG (31.6%) and ESG and ISG (27%), whereas 42.2 percent respondents of ISG and 32.1 percent of BSG rated such collection as good.

8.10.8.8 Picture Transparencies/Photos

About 75 percent of respondents have shown non-availability of picture transparencies/photos, whereas 16.3 percent of the respondents rated such collection as poor. Only 7.4 percent respondents rated such collection as good. An overwhelming majority of respondents of PESG (94.3%) pointed out that such type of collection does not exist in their libraries, followed by BSG, CSG, ISG and ESG. 15.8 percent respondents of CSG and 11.1 percent of ISG pointed out such collection as good.

It is clear from the analysis that availability of non-book material is negligible in CSIR libraries. The libraries should allocate their budget to procure electronic resources in the form of CD-ROMs/DVDs and online databases. It is also interesting to note that lack of information about availability of a particular type of resource is quite significant across the libraries. For example 75 percent respondents in PESG, CSG and ESG indicated that CD-ROM databases are not available but 15 percent say that their collection is good. In essence, the library users are not aware of the nature of collection and the libraries should take appropriate steps to market the already existing products and services.

8.10.9 Document Delivery and Related Services

Respondents belonging to five groups of CSIR laboratories indicated that their libraries are providing the service of lending books, scientific journals, interlibrary loan, material from other countries and assistance in locating material. 62.0 percent respondents stated the help of locating material as good, whereas 59.4 percent respondents stated the requirement of specific information as provided by their libraries as good. A little over 50.0 percent of scientists and research scholars indicated the services like lending of books and lending of scientific journals as good, whereas services like lending of books and lending of scientific journals are marked as excellent by 46.1 percent and 37.6 percent respondents. Interlibrary loan and procuring reading material from other countries on the request of users indicated as poor by 35.4 percent and 37.5 percent respondents respectively. On the other hand, 15.4 percent, 17.6 percent and 19.4 percent respondents rated assistance in locating material, guidance in using material and requirement of specific information, as poor, respectively.

8.10.10 Reference and Information Services

About 84 percent of respondents have indicated that CSIR libraries have the provision of supplying the list of journals subscribed/discontinued, whereas 80.5 percent respondents indicated the provision of list of new books acquired. The availability of literature search facilities has been indicated by 59.5 percent of respondents. About 56 percent respondents pointed out that their libraries have the provision to provide contents pages of periodicals on regular basis. Only 52.4 percent respondents indicated the availability of indexing and abstracting services. The analysis revealed that the provision of preparation and supply of bibliographies on demand and bibliographical services indicated by 47.6 percent and 45.8 percent respondents respectively, whereas digest of scientific, technical and industrial information and SDI services are indicated by 25.5 percent and 15.3 percent respondents respectively. It clarifies that CSIR libraries are offering only elementary reference and information services. Advanced type of reference and information services are not being provided in these libraries.

8.10.10.1 List of New Books Acquired

Analysis indicated that an overwhelming majority of respondents of CSG (94.7%) pointed out that their libraries are providing list of new books acquired, followed by 81.7 percent of respondents of BSG. This service is rated as good by the majority of respondents of PESG (71.1%), followed by CSG (64.8%) and BSG (62.6%) respectively. Even a good number of respondents of ESG (35.1%) rated this service as excellent, followed by BSG (29.9%). Only 21.2 percent of the respondents of ISG pointed out the provision of this service in their libraries as poor.

8.10.10.2 List of Journals Subscribed/Discontinued

The majority of respondents of CSG (87.7%) have indicated the availability of this service, followed by a little over 85 percent of BSG and ESG respondents. This service has been rated as good by 70.7 percent of the respondents of PESG while 29.7 percent of the respondents of ISG pointed out list of journals subscribed/discontinued as excellent. Only 18.0 percent respondents of CSG rate this service as poor.

8.10.10.3 Preparation and Supply of Bibliographies on Demand

Respondents of PESG (60.4%) and ISG (53.3%) indicated that there is provision of preparation and supply of bibliographies on demand. Respondents belonging to three groups, BSG (58.8%), ESG (53.2%) and CSG (52.6%), expressed the non-availability of such services. It is due to poor publicity that a large number of users are not aware of them. The majority of respondents of ESG (63.6%) rated this service as good, followed by PESG (62.5%). On the other hand, 48.1 percent of the respondents of CSG pointed out such service as poor. Preparation and supply of bibliographies on demand is rated as excellent by 37.5 percent of the respondents of ISG.

8.10.10.4 Indexing and Abstracting Services

The respondents of BSG (55.7%), PESG (54.7%), ESG (54.3%) and ISG (51.1%) stated that their libraries have made the provision of indexing and abstracting services, whereas 59.6 percent of respondents of CSG were of the opinion that their libraries do not have the provision to provide such services. Respondents belonging to BSG (54.8%) and PESG (51.7%) have rated this service as good, whereas 43.5 percent of the respondents of ISG termed this service as excellent. The respondents of ESG (31.4%) have rated indexing and abstracting services as poor, followed by CSG (30.4%).

8.10.10.5 Bibliographical Services

Respondents of ISG (55.6%) and PESG (54.7%) indicated that their libraries have provision of bibliographical services, whereas a little over 56 percent respondents of BSG, CSG and ESG stated that there is no provision of bibliographical services in their libraries. About 51 percent of the respondents rated the bibliographical services as good. Respondents belonging to PESG (62.1%) rated this service as good, whereas 40.0 percent of the respondents of ISG termed the bibliographical services as excellent. There are 29.2 percent of the respondents of CSG who pointed out this service as poor.

8.10.10.6 Literature Search

Availability of literature search services was indicated by 59.5 percent of the respondents of the CSIR laboratories. A higher proportion of respondents of PESG, 67.9 percent, stated the availability of such services in their libraries, followed by BSG, ISG and ESG. The respondents belonging to BSG (67.5%)

and ESG (57.4%) indicated such services as good, followed by CSG (53.1%). These services were rated as excellent by 35.7 percent of the respondents of ISG and 25.0 percent of the respondents of PESG. However, 25.0 percent respondents of PESG opined the literature search services to be poor.

8.10.10.7 Contents Pages of Periodicals Services

About 67 percent of the respondents of ISG and 60.6 percent of ESG indicated that their libraries are providing the services of contents pages of periodicals on regular basis, whereas a little over 54 percent respondents of PESG and CSG reported that their libraries are not providing such services. The higher proportion of respondents of ESG (80.7%) rated these services as good. More than 66 percent of the respondents of PESG, CSG and BSG rated such services as good, whereas 36.7 percent of the respondents of ISG indicated such services as excellent. Only 25.0 percent of the respondents of PESG rated such services as poor.

8.10.10.8 SDI Services

About 78 percent of the respondents belonging to five groups of CSIR laboratories have indicated that their libraries are not providing SDI services. Only 15.3 percent of the respondents indicated that such services are available in their libraries. Majority of respondents of ESG (83.0%) and ISG (82.2%) expressed that SDI services are not being provided in their libraries, followed by BSG (77.9%), CSG (73.7%) and PESG (69.8%). More than 17 percent respondents belonging to CSG, BSG and ISG indicated the availability of SDI services.

8.10.10.9 Digest of Scientific, Technical and Industrial Information

About 71 percent respondents expressed that their libraries do not have provision of digest of scientific, technical & industrial information. Only 25.5 percent of the respondents stated the availability of such services in their libraries. 86.7 percent respondents of ISG stated the non-availability of such services in their libraries, followed by over 75 percent respondents of PESG and ESG. Only 36.6 percent respondents of BSG indicated the availability such services in their libraries.

8.10.11 Translation Services

Majority of respondents (86.8%) expressed that their libraries do not have the arrangement to provide translation service. Only 13.2 percent of respondents indicated the provision of translation service in their libraries. Almost all respondents of PESG remarked non-availability of translation service, followed by over 93 percent of the respondents of BSG and ESG. The availability of translation service was indicated by only 40.4 percent respondents of CSG and 31.1 percent of ISG.

8.10.12 Reprographic Services

Photocopying services are available in almost all the libraries of PESG, BSG and ISG. Only 24.6 percent respondents belonging to CSG and 13.8 percent of ESG indicated the non-availability of photocopying services in their libraries. More than 55 percent respondents belonging to BSG, CSG and ESG stated photocopying services as good, whereas respondents of PESG (47.2%), ESG (34.6%) and ISG (31.1%) indicated such facilities as poor.

8.10.13 Provision of Obtaining Photocopy of Material from Other Libraries

About 51 percent respondents expressed that their libraries do not have the facilities to obtain photocopy material from other libraries. A higher proportion of respondents of ESG (67.0%) and CSG (56.1%) indicated the non-availability of such facilities. Whereas, majority of respondents of PESG (66.0%) indicated that such facilities are available in their libraries followed by BSG (54.2%) and ISG (56.1%).

8.10.14 Indexing Journals Subscribed in the Area of Specialisation

An overwhelming majority of respondents of CSG (96.5%), PESG (90.6%) and ESG (90.4%) indicated that indexing journals related to the area of their specialisation are being subscribed to by their libraries, followed by BSG (84.7%). About

67 percent respondents of CSG and 63.3 percent of ISG rated the provision to subscribe to indexing journals in their area of specialisation as good, followed by over 55 percent respondents of BSG and ESG. More than 36 percent respondents of BSG and ISG stated such provision as excellent. On the other hand, 22.9 percent respondents of PESG rated such facility as poor.

8.10.15 Abstracting Journals Subscribed in the Area of Specialisation

About 86 percent respondents of CSIR laboratories expressed that abstracting journals in the area of their specialisation are being subscribed to by their libraries. An overwhelming majority of respondents of CSG (96.5%), PESG (90.6%) and ESG (90.4%) indicated that their libraries are subscribing to such journals, followed by ISG (66.7%). It is evident that majority of CSIR libraries of all groups have provision of such services. The majority of respondents of PESG (64.6%) and CSG (61.5%) rated such provision as good followed by BSG (59.8%). Whereas such provision rated as excellent by the respondents of ISG (36.4%), BSG (35.5%) and ESG (30.2%). Only 17.4 percent respondents of ESG termed it as poor.

On the whole, it has been observed that majority of the CSIR libraries are not providing satisfactory services except some traditional services. As such, it is desirable that they should provide all sorts of SDI and CAS, digest of scientific, technical and industrial information, state-of-art services and review of literature so as to keep their client up-to-date and aware of the developments in their own fields which are considered to be most important functions of the special libraries, specially technical and research libraries under which CSIR libraries come.

8.10.16 Computerised Information Services

About 60 percent of the respondents indicated that their libraries do not have the computerised facilities. On the other hand, 62.3 percent of the respondents belonging to PESG indicated that their libraries are providing the computerised information services. 69.1 percent of the respondents of ESG stated that such services are not available in their libraries, followed by an equal number of respondents of CSG and BSG (64.9%). Out of five groups, 38.9 percent of the respondents have indicated that they are availing this facility.

8.10.16.1 Computerised Literature Search

Out of 148 respondents of the five groups of CSIR laboratories have indicated that computerised library services are available in their libraries. About 89 percent (131) respondents stated their libraries are providing the computerised literature search. Over 90 percent of respondents of ISG, BSG and PESG indicated provision of literature search services in their libraries. 82.8 percent of the respondents of ESG and CSG also indicated such provision in their libraries. An equal number of respondents of CSG and ESG (66.7%) rated the computerised literature search as good, followed by 62.8 percent of the respondents of BSG and 57.9 percent of the respondents of ISG.

8.10.16.2 Computerised Indexing of Periodicals

About 78 percent (116) respondents stated that their libraries are providing computerised indexing of periodicals. Over 80 percent respondents of PESG, ESG and BSG have stated that such provision is available in their libraries, followed by ISG (70.0%) and CSG (65.0%). About 70 percent of the respondents of ESG, BSG and CSG rated indexing of periodicals as good, whereas 42.9 percent of the respondents of ISG rated indexing of periodicals as excellent.

8.10.16.3 Computerised Compilation of Bibliographies

The majority of respondents 113 (76.4%) indicated the provision of the facility of computerised compilation of bibliographies available in their libraries. Majority of respondents of ISG (85.0%) stated that their libraries are providing computerized bibliographical services, followed by 82.8 percent respondents of ESG. 66.7 percent respondents of BSG termed this facility as good, followed by 58.3 percent of the respondents of ESG. About 53 percent of the respondents of CSG and ISG also rated computerised compilation of bibliographies as good. There are over 33 percent of the respondents of ESG, CSG and PESG who indicated the provision of such services as poor. About 61 percent respondents feel the necessity of computerised facilities in their libraries. A higher number of the respondents, 69.1 percent, of ESG are in favour of computerised facilities, followed by an equal number of respondents of CSG and BSG (64.9%).

8.10.17 Access to National and International Online Searching

About 81 percent of the respondents of CSIR laboratories indicated that there are no facilities of online searching of national and international databases in CSIR libraries. The majority of respondents across all groups stated that online searching of national and international databases is not available in their libraries. Only 35.6 percent respondents of ISG termed that their libraries are having this facility.

In order to link the libraries of all the CSIR laboratories to the network of their own as well as other networking systems functioning on various levels. It is essential that these libraries should have their own networking system and should be brought under the scheme so that they could use the resources of each other as well as the libraries of other institutions through networks.

8.10.18 Arrangement of Reading Materials

As regards arrangement of reading materials on shelves, the data revealed that majority of respondents (60.5%) indicated the arrangement of reading materials on shelves as good. Only 25.8 percent of the respondents termed such arrangement as excellent. A higher number of the respondents of ISG (66.7%) and PESG (66.0%) pointed out that arrangement of books on shelves was good, followed by 62.6 percent of the respondents of BSG. There are 47.4 percent of the respondents of CSG who rated the arrangement of books on shelves as excellent. Only 20.0 percent of the respondents of ISG are those who rated the arrangement of books on shelves as poor.

About 57 percent of the respondents indicated the arrangement of journals on shelves as good. There is some respondents who rated such arrangement as excellent; they constitute 31.3 percent of respondents. Only 11.3 percent of the respondents rated this arrangement as poor. The majority of respondents of PESG (66.0%) rated the arrangement of journals on shelves as good, followed by 57 percent of the respondents of BSG and ISG. Even 54 percent of the respondents of CSG and ESG also termed such arrangement as good. However, 36.8 percent respondents of CSG rated the arrangement of journals on shelves as excellent followed by ISG (33.3%) and BSG (32.1%).

The arrangement of research/project reports on the shelves was rated as poor by the majority of respondents (44.7%), whereas 42.6 percent of the respondents found the arrangement of research/project reports as good. The majority of respondents belonging to PESG (52.8%) and ISG (51.1%) rated the arrangement of research/project reports on shelves as poor, followed by 45.7 percent respondents of ESG and 42.0 percent of the respondents of BSG. The arrangement of research/project reports on shelves was rated as good by a little over 47 percent of the respondents of CSG and BSG. Even over 36 percent of the respondents of PESG, ESG and ISG also stated such arrangements as good.

8.10.19 Reading Facilities

The responses in this regard received from scientists and research scholars of CSIR laboratories indicated that reading facilities like individual study carrels, emergency light and seminar/conference room are not available in all libraries. About 92 percent of the respondents stated that their libraries have adequate lighting facilities, followed by 77.1 percent of the respondents, who indicated provision of comfortable place for reading and study. On the other hand, 80.8 percent of the respondents find that individual study carrels are not available in their libraries. There are 64.2 percent respondents who indicated that their libraries do not have emergency light, followed by seminar/conference room by 49.2 percent of the respondents.

8.10.19.1 Individual Study Carrels

Respondents' views regarding individual study carrels shows that an overwhelming majority of respondents of ISG

(95.6%) and BSG (90.1%) stated that they do not have such facilities. Even 80.5 percent of the respondents of CSG also indicated the lack of individual study carrels in their libraries. Same trend is observed in PESG and ESG.

8.10.19.2 Comfortability in Reading and Study

The majority of respondents (93.0%) of CSG indicated that comfortability in reading and study is not available in their libraries. A little over 77 percent of the respondents of ESG and PESG also find that such facility is also not available in their libraries. Same is the case with ISG also.

8.10.19.3 Adequate Lighting

The majority of respondents of ESG (94.7%) and CSG (93.0%) indicated that their libraries have provision for adequate lighting, followed by 90.8 percent respondents of BSG. A little over 88 percent of the respondents also stated provision of adequate lighting being there in their libraries. The majority of respondents of BSG (76.5%), ISG (70.0%) and ESG (69.7%) rated the lighting adequate and good. Only 30.2 percent of the respondents of CSG and 27.7 percent of PESG rated such facilities as poor.

8.10.19.4 Emergency Light

Over 70 percent of the respondents of ISG and BSG rated that their libraries do not have the facility of emergency light. It is noticed that majority of respondents of all groups indicated non-availability of emergency light during frequent lighting failure, except CSG where 54.4 percent of the respondents indicated that their libraries have the emergency light during frequent lighting failure. Out of 35.8 percent respondents who indicated the availability of facility of emergency light in their libraries, 75 percent of the respondents of ISG rated the provision of emergency light as good, which is followed by ESG (68.4%) and BSG (66.7%), who rated it as good. Emergency light was rated as excellent by 31.4 percent of the respondents of ESG, whereas, 29.0 percent of the respondents of CSG rated emergency light as poor.

8.10.19.5 Seminar/Conference Room

Data analysis regarding seminar/conference room revealed that majority of respondents of ESG (66.0%) indicated that their libraries have the conference/seminar room facility to arrange professional meetings, discussions and get-togethers of the library staff. A little over 57 percent of the respondents of CSG and ISG stated that the facility of seminar/conference room is available in their libraries, whereas respondents of PESG (62.3%) and BSG (60.3%) stated the non-availability of conference/seminar room in their libraries. Rating of 50.8 percent of the respondents of five groups indicate that an equal number of respondents of BSG and ISG stated such facility of seminar/conference room as good, which is followed by an equal percentage of PESG and CSG (66.7%). Only 30.8 percent of the respondents of BSG rated such facility as excellent.

This chapter briefly reported the perceptions of 380 users about the purpose of using the library, library collection (print and non-book material), document delivery and related services, reference services, computerised services, access to online national and international databases, organisation of reading materials, reading facilities, etc. Users views about the usefulness of library collection, helpful attitude of staff and services provided by the library are used to evaluate the resources, services and facilities offered by CSIR libraries. Conducive environment for study and reading facilities in these libraries also attract the scientists to study and consult the library on regular basis. Innovations in information and communication technology have opened new vistas to apply information technology to accumulate, store, retrieve, share and disseminate information across the organisations. Online reference and current awareness services generated by a library can be useful to the scientists of other libraries of CSIR and it can be disseminated to other organisations as well. Procurement of electronic publications and online databases can be helpful to provide rapid access to information. Online reference services generated by one library can be helpful and useful to the scientists of other laboratories too.

REFERENCES

1. Singh, Dev Raj. University library professionals: Some sociological aspects. *Journal of Library and Information Science,* 17(2), 1992, 2.
2. Research and Development Statistics 2000-01. New Delhi: Department of Science and Technology, 2002. 108p.
3. Information sources: Tracking down 'Grey Literature'. *Information Today & Tomorrow,* 14(2/3), 1995, 11.
4. Burkett, Jack. Library and information networks in the United Kingdom. London: Aslib, 1979. P.100.
5. Kuruvilla, P. K. Legal aspects of patenting and information support. *Library Science with a Slant to Documentation,* 18(1), 1981, 37-53.
6. Strauss, Lucilla J., Strieby, Irene M. and Brown, Alberta L. Scientific and technical libraries: Their organisation and administration. New York: Interscience Publishers, 1964. P.125
7. Thakur, D. S. Effectiveness and use of library and information services of the laboratories of Council of Scientific and Industrial Research in India. Ph. D. Thesis. Gwalior: Jiwaji University, 1997. 540p.

9
Findings and Suggestions for Improvement

Special library and information centre exists to subserve scientists, engineers and research scholars. On the basis of the study, it has been revealed that the libraries of CSIR laboratories are playing a significant role in the promotion of R&D programmes of the laboratories and research institutions of the country. They are serving scientists, engineers, technologists and research scholars as well as specialists of different fields of applied sciences. The present study is an endeavour to critically examine how effective are the libraries and information centres of the CSIR laboratories in India in the delivery of services. Against this background, the study has been carried out to see how effective are the libraries of CSIR laboratories in the present day set-up and whether such libraries can be revamped to serve the users more beneficially. The study recommends measures to enhance effectiveness of such libraries. This chapter states the findings, on which suggestions have been made, which can go on to enhance in a big way the effectiveness of CSIR libraries and information centres.

The major findings are described in the following sections.

9.1 FINDINGS OF THE STUDY

The conclusion highlighted in the previous chapter, puts forth important findings which deserves urgent attention if the CSIR libraries have to provide better and improved services to the users in particular, and to the nation at large. The findings are:

1. The collection of the library resources, such as theses/dissertations, grey literature, and research/project reports, conference proceedings, standards, specifications and patents, etc. is poor in most of the libraries.
2. The collection of non-book material, such as microfilms/microfiches, audiocassettes, videocassettes, slides, CD-ROM databases, online databases, etc. is poor and not available in a large number of libraries.
3. Library and information services like indexing and abstracting services, SDI services, digest of scientific, technical and industrial information are not available in the CSIR libraries.
4. Translation service and reprographic services need to be introduced as the prevailing ones are not so satisfactory.
5. Most of CSIR libraries have not yet introduced computer and other information technologies toward modernisation.
6. It has been observed that SIRNET facility is available in most of the CSIR laboratories, but libraries are not availing this facility.
7. Reading facilities, like individual study carrels, comfortability of place for reading and study, adequate space for reading, emergency light, conference room, etc. are not available in most of the libraries.
8. The present budgetary allocation in CSIR libraries is reported to be inadequate and there is demand to increase it substantially.

9.2 RECOMMENDATIONS AND SUGGESTIONS

CSIR libraries are facing many problems in the organisation and management of libraries, such as budget, library staff, collection development, i.e. books, journals and non-book material, interlibrary loan and resource sharing, procurement of material from other countries on request of users, library services and facilities like CAS and SDI services, translation service and air-conditioning facilities, application of automation in libraries, CD-ROM databases and absence of participation of national and international databases and networks, organisation of reading materials and reading facilities. The lack of these facilities creates many problems in terms of access to, use and optimum utilization of library resources. This requires organisational support and proper atmosphere which must be created to meet the information needs of the readers more efficiently and effectively.

To make the library system of the multi-disciplinary laboratories of CSIR more efficient and effective, it is necessary to establish information network of CSIR laboratories and consortia based access to electronic journals and other online resources. This can provide information services in more effective way to their related research and development areas. CSIR libraries need to be developed and improved in a systematic and planned way.

On the basis of this study, some suggestions and recommendations on different aspects of CSIR laboratories are made which will go on to help in solving the problems of their readers and making the information system more effective. The following recommendations, if implemented, will provide effective and efficient library services to the CSIR laboratories.

9.2.1 Strengthening of the Library Resources

The collection of scientific and technical library must meet the information requirements of their users. The present study revealed that except for general collection, material in the area of specialisation, such as grey literature, conference proceedings, standards, specifications and patents, etc. are not sufficient to meet the research requirements of the users. The grey literature, standards, patents, etc. are important items for the research work of scientists and research scholars especially in CSIR libraries. Adequate attention should be given to scientists and research scholars in core areas of the research organisation. It is recommended that the CSIR library authorities should be careful in this respect.

Scientists and research scholars of scientific and technical organisations are more interested in journals and grey literature than books. The availability of microform literature is negligible in many CSIR libraries. Like other developed countries, there is an urgent necessity for setting up an online National Resource Centre of grey literature for which CSIR should take initiatives. More and more emphasis should be laid on the acquisition of electronic and online resources in the libraries.

Scientists and research scholars pointed out that some important journals subscribed earlier in their libraries were discontinued due to financial stringency. Potential users have suggested that the discontinued journals should be renewed and more useful journals should be added and subscribed to meet the research requirements.

A Library Committee of scientists working in different areas of specialisation must be constituted to chart out well thought of policy for selection of books, journals and other documents. In addition, librarians should present the new ideas in order to plan for improved and effective functioning of the libraries. Such provision does not exist in this specialised and highest organisation of applied research.

9.2.2 Consortia-Based Subscription to Electronic Journals

No single library, including a research library, can singularly have the library materials on all disciplines to meet the needs of all types of readers. There should be definite consortia-based subscription of e-journals and cooperative acquisition policy in CSIR laboratories. Tremendous growth of electronic reference sources and online journals has opened new avenues to libraries to buy the consortia-based subscription of e-journals. All well-established publishers of developed world have launched their products online which can be accessed through Internet. Consortia-based access to e-journals will not only solve the problems of paucity of the library funds, escalating costs of the journals and problem of space but also increase the number of subscription of journals, round-the-clock access, and enhance the utility and effectiveness of the libraries.

In this regard, Ministry of Human Resource Development has announced the formation of a consortium of Indian

National Digital Library in Engineering, Science and Technology (INDEST) of Indian Institutes of Technology (IITs), Indian Institute of Science (IISc), National Institutes of Technology (NITs), Indian Institutes of Management (IIMs) and few other organisations and funded the subscription for online journals databases. If the libraries of CSIR laboratories constitute or join the consortium of the online journals, such as INDEST, and UGC-Infonet E-journals consortium, the problems of escalating costs of journals, budget constraints, lesser number of journals coming in these libraries and problem of space will be solved.

9.2.3 Trained Staff

The libraries and information centres are the pool of knowledge and without trained and experienced staff, it is not possible to maximize the use of the library. Trained and qualified staff can provide adequate, relevant and timely information through effective services. Special training courses should be given to the staff to provide fast, adequate, exact, and timely information to the users. Training for the library professionals and supporting staff should be arranged regularly to generate qualitative services from time to time. There is a lack of training facilities. Short-term training courses and professional training related to information and communication technologies will be very helpful in providing and improving the effective and efficient library services.

9.2.4 Library and Documentation Services

The CASs, like list of new additions, list of journals subscribed, indexing and abstracting of journal articles and documents, compilation of bibliography and bibliographic services, contents of periodicals, literature search and SDI services, should be offered online where they do not exist. All these services can be extended among all libraries of CSIR laboratories through the networking system. These services will force the librarians of other laboratories to strengthen the resource sharing and exchange of proceedings, technical reports and other published and unpublished resources.

All CSIR laboratories are multi-disciplinary in nature and requirements of scientists and research scholars and libraries are similar to some extent. Some libraries are providing documentation activities, i.e., list of new additions in the library, list of journals subscribed and discontinued, indexing and abstracting services, bibliographical services, contents pages of periodicals and translation of articles and other reports to the users of the parent bodies. These libraries should circulate the copies of their documentation work and other activities related to library services among the all CSIR libraries to make the sharing of documentation services and library resources very effective. It will enhance the effectiveness and use of library services among CSIR libraries.

9.2.5 User Education

To educate the users of the library is very essential for proper use of the library and to facilitate their access to reading materials. Users education involves orientation to the library regarding use of the library and its resources so that the users can explore the available library resources at the optimum level. Accelerated growth of information technology and electronic resources have posed challenges to users in the access and use of resources. Orientation programmes towards the use of new electronic resources are required for optimal library utilization. Library professionals should assist the users regarding use of OPAC, online resources, Internet, access of Intranet and extranet, electronic databases and online databases. Moreover, some training programmes should be initiated in scientific and technical libraries to make the users aware about the library activities and services. UNESCO lays much emphasis on users' training and CSIR should make some arrangement for this programme.

9.2.6 Emphasis on the Adoption of Information Technology

The computerisation of library activities and services should be introduced in these libraries to harness the advantages of information technology. Moreover, greater emphasis should be laid on the introduction of information and communication technologies for the various library operations and information services in the CSIR laboratories. The major changes in scientific and technical libraries are caused by the application of new information technologies. The application of ICT, barcode system for circulation, intranet and extranet technology has brought a revolution in the special libraries. These modernised technologies have improved information service and have made the library operations efficient and effective. In special libraries the use of barcode system for circulation, computer networks, online databases searching on national and international level, electronic document delivery, transmission of documents, electronic publishing, telecommunications and CD-ROM technology are very effective but they lack in CSIR laboratories' libraries. Moreover, adequate space to the library and information centres of CSIR Laboratories must be provided on the Website to launch their products, such as online documentation services, electronic documents, full-text articles of the scientists of the laboratories and other technical reports.

9.2.7 Networking and Resource Sharing

In the modern age of information world, no single library can have all the materials on research and development and cannot be self-sufficient in meeting the needs of readers. The CSIR libraries should make efforts to establish cooperative activities in sharing library resources. This is possible only if CSIR libraries join networking. The library network is the most important and modern technique of resource sharing. Through the networks, the library resources of other scientific and technical libraries can be fully utilized. The computerised networks have widened the coverage and scope of access to library materials. These research libraries cooperate in various consortia and networks. Most research libraries belong to one of the local area library networks, DELNET, CALIBNET, INFLIBNET, MYLIBNET, ADINET, etc. Active participation in such programmes is essential. INFLIBNET is a very wide library network and can be very helpful for the exchange of information among universities and research organisations, if CSIR libraries are connected with this network. Since CSIR is a multidisciplinary network of laboratories so it is imperative that all S&T organisations such as CSIR, DRDO, DST, DAE, DBT, DOD, DOS, ICAR, ICMR and Ministry of Information

Technology should join the consortia based subscription of journals and develop a network to meet their information needs of multidisciplinary R&D programmes.

9.2.8 Adequate Facilities to Make Effective Use of the Library

Adequate facilities like book reservation, interlibrary loan and resource sharing also must be strengthened to make the effective use of the library and information resources. The physical facilities like space, study carrels, good lighting, generator system facility, air-conditioning facilities and drinking water must be provided to make environment conducive for research programmes. The space problem is also being faced in these libraries. Moreover, attractive furnishings are also essential that encourage the users to use the library. Cubicles are must for the researchers and senior faculty for their serious research and project works. To provide the effective information service to the users, information specialists should ascertain the physical facilities of the library and information centres according to the requirements of the users.

CSIR libraries are used by specialists and scientists and it is necessary to create such an atmosphere which can attract the users. The comfortable atmosphere is essential to make greater use of the library resources. There should be air-conditioned facility in the CSIR libraries for users and for the conservation and preservation of traditional as well as untraditional materials so that important items are not spoiled. The Online Public Access Catalogue (OPAC), electronic databases and access to Internet and intranet provide library users with a wide variety of information resources. These services are augmented with traditional as well as modern electronic reference sources and services to strengthen the needs of users.

9.2.9 Co-operation of Professionals

It was found from the survey that the library staff in some libraries is very helpful and cooperative in their duties. Some scientists expressed their satisfaction with the work of the library staff. Those who were found dissatisfied with the library staff indicated some reasons. The library staff of these libraries are not professionally qualified, trained and experienced. Some indicated that qualified and specialised staff in the area of their specialisation could arrange the multifarious information requirements of scientists and research scholars. Some scientists and research scholars felt that the library staff of their libraries renders specific services to only the senior scientists and their close persons. Such atmosphere should not exist in such libraries of highly specialised field.

9.2.10 Space Problem

The maximum CSIR libraries were established during 50s and 60s. At present these libraries are facing the acute shortage of space for proper display of the materials acquired. Attention should be paid to this problem. Where such libraries are starving for space - non-print material such as online journals and reference sources on CD-ROM and DVDs should be acquired more as it involves significantly low requirement of space.

9.2.11 Organisation and Management of CSIR Libraries

A good organisation and effective management of the special libraries can provide better services and manage the library in a good manner. Many CSIR libraries have Incharges who are not professional. Librarians or Information Officers or Documentation Officers who are professionals work under the Incharges and their professional opinions are not used for library management.

The scale of librarians and other staff members is different from laboratory to laboratory. Inequality in the remuneration of the library staff hinders the professional work of the library on account of dissatisfaction.

A common policy on all CSIR libraries should be maintained which will help in reducing the variations. There should be certain norms and standards between organisation and management of the institution and the library for the development and effective organisation and management of the library.

The CSIR libraries should formulate a plan in accordance with the aims of the laboratory. The following aspects are necessary which may be included in this plan:

1. Objective of the library
2. Budgetary provision
3. Staffing structure of the library
4. Acquisition and collection development, including books, journals, grey literature and electronic resources.
5. Service requirements
6. Administrative hierarchy of the librarian
7. Networking and Resource Sharing
8. Online resources

9.2.12 Digitisation

Digital information is the need of the 21st century libraries and every library should aim to digitise its physical collection and huge amount of paper-based information into electronic format. All libraries of CSIR laboratories should take initiative to digitise their own publications published and unpublished resources, such as current research studies, occasional papers, training programmes reports, articles of scientists, books, journals, dissertations and theses to bring online to offer round-the-clock access to users doing research in other laboratories. Digitisation of research studies and other publications and easy access to those resources on Web is an invaluable contribution to the academic and research community. Before digitisation, it must be ensured that quality of digitised product should meet the national and international standards. It must be the motive of the non-profit making organisations to disseminate its published and unpublished resources and research results to the wide spectrum of scholars engaged in the area of higher education and S&T research and development programmes.

9.2.13 Intranet and Extranet

Libraries of CSIR laboratories must lay down emphasis to develop and strengthen the intranet activities of the organisation to handle various types of internal information among scientists, research scholars and technical officers. The role of intranet enhances the utility and effectiveness of sharing of ideas between two or more than two users. Electronic resources can be shared and better utilized through intranet. Easy access to the information system is important for timely and effective decision making during meetings. Major goal of any information system is to structure the unstructured information scattered in the organisational units in such a fashion that can be easily leveraged and shared in the organisation. Further, it will assist the management and decision-making body to make decisions, evaluation of scientists and observe to what extent the organisation has achieved its goals. Scientists, research scholars and other technical officers must furnish the electronic files of their works, such as books, research works, articles, and proceedings without any hesitation to strengthen the knowledge pool of the organisation. Moreover, all kinds of forms used in the organisation and library can be uploaded on intranet for official use. Through this the management and decision making body can take decision regarding recruitment of scientists and staff for research, training, group meetings, research technology and web development. Beside this decision making body can take instant decisions in the area of scientists assessment, financial stability, infrastructure and growth and development of the organisation. Moreover, other documentation activities can be generated and updated from time to time. National and international links of full text scientific and technical reports, etc. can be given on the intranet to take advantage of immediate and round-the-clock access.

CSIR laboratories must emphasize to build a system which could capture all the organisation's internal knowledge and integrate the same with useful outside knowledge such as scientific and technical news from the Web and e-mail communications with intellectual groups, discussions, talks, etc. The main purpose of the intranet is to create one-stop-pool for knowledge rather than having to go to several places for the information you need. The site can also feature other organisational information such as budget information, financial benefits, work-in-progress documents, sale of documents, archived e-mail discussions of internal and external intellectuals, data and manpower directory, etc. Outdated, irrelevant and inaccurate data and information can be removed from the intranet on the feedback of the internal as well as online users.

Moreover, other information which cannot be uploaded on the Web site must be accessible and shared on intranet, e.g. online databases and information about official circulation. Sharing of ideas on intranet radically improves an organisation's development and breaks communication barrier across the organisation. Indeed, an intranet is one step closer to the paperless office and probably it is a one of the major benefit to the entire organisation as it can reduce paper expenses, increase the productivity and morale, save the time of the staff and bring them closer to each other. To disseminate or access the information beyond the firewall, a password-protected extranet enables the scientists, research scholars and decision makers to share the internal and external pool of information and knowledge with the colleagues all over the world. They can contribute information to the knowledge pool from any part of the world.

9.2.14 Development of Knowledge Management System

Knowledge Management System (KMS) must be developed to capture tacit and explicit knowledge of the scientists, engineers and intellectuals and bring a platform of sharing of ideas and insights. It will develop human competencies and nurture innovative culture to share the ideas embedded in the few minds across the organization. Knowledge is contributed and shared through research papers, technical briefings, good practices, product evaluations and reports. Scientists and intellectuals can share experiences, locate people with expertise in their field. Knowledge management system is a process to integrate various databases and processes of the organisation in order to bring efficiency, effectiveness, productivity, quality and qualitative change in the working of entire organisation. It will assist the decision makers, policy makers and administrators in making decisions and strengthen decision support system, document management, communication, and dissemination of information and develop knowledge products.

Besides this, KMS will encompass activities of all units across the organisation. Financial information, publications, document management, knowledgeable products and all kinds of forms used in the organisation would also assist the administrators to take quick decisions. Directory of scientists, training participants, resource persons, and directory of the Institute's manpower must be developed which will help the administrators and decision makers to use the skilled personnel in the thrust areas to fulfill the needs of the different units of the organisation. This system will also familiarise the individuals as well as new comers about the policies and activities of the organisations. Knowledge is power and it grows when shared, transferred, managed skillfully and harnessed for the benefit of society. Use of ICT tools can create a knowledge network and disseminate information in thrust areas. Further, to find out the area where more knowledge is needed and use collective approach of wisdom of intellectual assets to create and disseminate new knowledge.

9.2.15 Strengthen Knowledge Repository and Its Use

Knowledge repository covers organisational policies, procedures, meeting agendas, minutes, reports and other important published and unpublished documents for the future use of scientists, researchers, research scholars and administrators. Knowledge workers strive to capture the electronic products whether it is published or unpublished from the scientists, researchers and project staff to preserve and make them accessible for sharing on the networks with others round-the-clock. Its storage and retrieval process must be user-friendly. Knowledge repository management presents several challenges for establishing standards for the storage, viewing and retrieval of full-text documents. Web-based search and access of full-text documents stored in the knowledge management pool makes the searches easy and user-friendly. Advent of information technology and software has improved and brought qualitative change in the storage and use of full-text publications. Web browser helps to retrieve and access the documents available in different formats such as Word, Excel, PowerPoint, PDF (portable document format), HTML (hypertext mark-up language) and others. Users can access these files in different formats which they require. Online knowledge management repository in any scientific and technical organisation can make available knowledge sharing through published books, proceedings, reports, policies and unpublished reports, research studies to the research community of the campus as well as extranet users easily and round-the-clock.

9.2.16 Adequate Financial Aid

Last but not the least is the problem of inadequate fund of these libraries. The libraries of these scientific and technical institutions may be provided adequate financial aid in order to build the adequate collection of books, journals as well as electronic material. Otherwise limited allocation of funds in these libraries not only would affect the library resources and services but also the research activities of the parent organization. The present allocation of fund to library resources is not sufficient and new ways and means must be developed to augment more resources to fund the facilities required.

9.3 FURTHER RESEARCH AREAS

The present study "Effectiveness and Use of Library and Information Services of the Laboratories of Council of Scientific and Industrial Research in India" addresses many important aspects of library improvement. However, the study feels that further research work in related areas, will not only be of interest, but also of importance to the users, to the world of science, to the nation and to the mankind. Some of the areas where useful research work can be carried out are:

1. Growth and development of CSIR laboratories and their libraries.
2. Collection development and its impact on the library services.

3. Application of Information and Communication Technology for the development of library services.

Research on topics of interest to the library, library professionals and library users should be encouraged by CSIR. It may consider promoting research by offering fellowships and paid study leave to the existing employees. Building a culture of research will make the libraries another laboratory within a specialised laboratory.

Appendix - I

EFFECTIVENESS AND USE OF LIBRARY AND INFORMATION SERVICES OF THE LABORATORIES OF COUNCIL OF SCIENTIFIC AND INDUSTRIAL RESEARCH IN INDIA

Dear Sir/Madam,

A study on the "EFFECTIVENESS AND USE OF LIBRARY AND INFORMATION SERVICES OF THE LABORATORIES OF COUNCIL OF SCIENTIFIC AND INDUSTRIAL RESEARCH IN INDIA" is being undertaken by me for my Ph.D. work under the supervision of Dr. K. G. Tyagi Director (NASSDOC), New Delhi and Prof. S. M. Tripathi in the Department of Library and Information Science, Jiwaji University, Gwalior (MP).

You have an important contribution to make towards the completion of this study by filling up the attached questionnaire. The same may be returned to me. The information provided will be kept confidential and will be used for research purposes only. I am sure you will extend your co-operation by devoting sometime for this academic endeavour.

Thanking you,

Yours faithfully,

DR. K. G. TYAGI (DIRECTOR) [DAVINDER SINGH THAKUR]
National Social Science Documentation
Centre, ICSSR, 35, Ferozeshah Road
New Delhi - 110001.

Address for Correspondence

Davinder Singh Thakur
National Institute of Adult Education
(Library and Documentation Centre)
10-B, Indraprastha Estate
New Delhi - 110002.

QUESTIONNAIRE FOR USER

Please put [✓] mark or strike off either Yes or No whichever is applicable or fill in the blank/s for the following items :

1. **BACKGROUND INFORMATION**

1.1 Name: Dr./Mr./Ms. : ....

1.2 Sex : Male/Female

1.3 Position : ....

i) Research scholar [ ]

ii) Scientist [ ]

iii) Any other (please specify) ....

1.4 Please indicate your highest level of qualification :

....

....

1.5 Area of specialisation

1.6 Name and address of the institution/organisation with which you are working..

....

....

1.7 Are you a member of local, state, national and international professional association/society?

Yes/No

If yes, please indicate name/s of the association(s)/ society(ies):

i) Local..

ii) State ....

iii) National ....

iv) International ....

1.8 Please indicate the number of Conferences/Seminars/ Workshops/Symposia/Congresses, etc. you have attended during the last five years:

NUMBER	NATIONAL	INTERNATIONAL
0	[ ]	[ ]
1 - 3	[ ]	[ ]
4 - 6	[ ]	[ ]
7 - 9	[ ]	[ ]
10 and above	[ ]	[ ]

1.9 Have you contributed papers/articles, etc. during the last five years. Yes/No

1.9.1 If yes, please indicate the number of your contributions.

....

1.10 Do you use the library? Yes/No

1.10.1 If yes, for what purposes do you use it?

i) Research [ ]

ii) Writing papers/articles [ ]

iii) Book writing [ ]

iv) Preparation of bibliographies [ ]

v) Any other (please specify) ....

1.10.2 If no, indicate the reasons for not using the library.

i) Literature of interest is not available/accessible [ ]

ii) Sufficient material available in personal collection [ ]

iii) Enough literature available from friends/colleagues and others [ ]

iv) Consulting other libraries [ ]

v) Literature directly received from institutions/ publishers/organisations, etc. [ ]

vi) By attending conferences/seminars [ ]

vii) By personal purchase [ ]

viii) Any other (please specify) ....

1.11 How often do you visit your institution's library?

i) Daily [ ]

ii) Twice a week [ ]

iii) Once a week [ ]

iv) Fortnightly [ ]

v) Once a month [ ]

vi) Any other (please specify) ....

1.12 How much time do you usually spend on your each visit to library?

i) 0-1 hour [ ]

ii) 2-3 hours [ ]

iii) 4-5 hours [ ]

iv) 6 hours and above [ ]

1.13 Please indicate the stage at which you consult the library for research purposes.

i) At the time of identifying area for research [ ]

ii) Survey of literature [ ]

iii) At the time of experiment [ ]

iv) At the time of analysis of data [ ]

v) At the time of report writing [ ]

vi) At all the above stages [ ]

vii) Any other (please specify) ....

1.14 How useful do you find your library at different stages in research?

	Very useful	Useful	Not useful
i) At the time of identifying area for research	[ ]	[ ]	[ ]
ii) Survey of literature and studies available in the area for research	[ ]	[ ]	[ ]
iii) At the time of experiment	[ ]	[ ]	[ ]
iv) At the time of analysis of data	[ ]	[ ]	[ ]
v) At the time of report writing	[ ]	[ ]	[ ]

vi) Any other (please specify) ....

2. LIBRARY COLLECTION

2.1 How do you rate the collection of your library?

a. **Books**	Excellent	Good	Poor	N.A.
i) On science in general	[ ]	[ ]	[ ]	[ ]
ii) In the area of your specialisation	[ ]	[ ]	[ ]	[ ]
iii) Reference books	[ ]	[ ]	[ ]	[ ]
b. **Theses/Reports/other Documents**				
i) Theses/Dissertations	[ ]	[ ]	[ ]	[ ]
ii) Research/Project reports	[ ]	[ ]	[ ]	[ ]
iii) Government documents	[ ]	[ ]	[ ]	[ ]
iv) Conference/Seminar/ Workshop papers/reports	[ ]	[ ]	[ ]	[ ]
v) Standards, Specifications and Patents	[ ]	[ ]	[ ]	[ ]
vi) Pamphlets and Reprints	[ ]	[ ]	[ ]	[ ]
vii) Any other (please specify)				
c. **Periodicals**				
i) Science journals and serials	[ ]	[ ]	[ ]	[ ]
ii) Indexing journals	[ ]	[ ]	[ ]	[ ]
iii) Abstracting journals	[ ]	[ ]	[ ]	[ ]
d. **Non-book material**				
i) Micro-film/micro-fiche	[ ]	[ ]	[ ]	[ ]
ii) Audiocassettes	[ ]	[ ]	[ ]	[ ]
iii) Videocassettes	[ ]	[ ]	[ ]	[ ]
iv) Slides	[ ]	[ ]	[ ]	[ ]
v) CD-ROM Databases	[ ]	[ ]	[ ]	[ ]
vi) Online Databases	[ ]	[ ]	[ ]	[ ]
vii) Maps/atlases	[ ]	[ ]	[ ]	[ ]
viii) Picture transparencies/ photos	[ ]	[ ]	[ ]	[ ]
ix) Any other (please specify)				

2.2 What are your suggestions for improving the following collection?

i) Books ....

ii) Theses/reports/other documents ....

iii) Periodicals ....

iv) Non-book material ....

3. LIBRARY-SERVICES

A. DOCUMENT DELIVERY AND RELATED SERVICES

3.1 Please indicate the document delivery and related services available in your library.

i)	Lending of books	Yes/No
ii)	Lending of scientific journals	Yes/No
iii)	Interlibrary loan	Yes/No
iv)	Procuring/acquiring specific material from other countries on request	Yes/No
v)	Help in searching/locating the material	Yes/No
vi)	Guidance regarding using library	Yes/No
vii)	Provision of specific information when required	Yes/No
viii)	Any other (please specify)	Yes/No

3.2 How do you rate the above services?

		Excellent	Good	Poor	N.A.
i)	Lending of books	[ ]	[ ]	[ ]	[ ]
ii)	Lending of scientific journals	[ ]	[ ]	[ ]	[ ]
iii)	Interlibrary loan	[ ]	[ ]	[ ]	[ ]
iv)	Procuring/acquiring specific material from other countries on request	[ ]	[ ]	[ ]	[ ]
v)	Help in searching/ locating the material	[ ]	[ ]	[ ]	[ ]
vi)	Guidance regarding using library	[ ]	[ ]	[ ]	[ ]

vii) Provision of specific information when required [ ] [ ] [ ] [ ]

viii) Any other (please specify) ....

3.3. What are your suggestions for improving document delivery and related services? Please specify.

i) Lending of books ....

ii) Lending of scientific journals ....

iii) Interlibrary loan ....

iv) Procuring/acquiring specific material from other countries on request ....

v) Help in searching/locating the material ....

....

vi) Guidance regarding using library ....

....

vii) Provision of specific information when required

....

viii) Any other (please specify) ....

B. REFERENCE SERVICE

3.4 Indicate the reference services provided by your library.

i)	List of new books acquired	Yes/No
ii)	List of journals subscribed/discontinued	Yes/No
iii)	Preparation of bibliography on demand	Yes/No
iv)	Indexing and abstracting services	Yes/No
v)	Bibliographic services	Yes/No
vi)	Literature search	Yes/No
vii)	Contents of periodicals	Yes/No
viii)	SDI service	Yes/No
ix)	Digest of scientific, technical and industrial information	Yes/No
x)	Any other (please specify)	Yes/No

3.4.1 If yes, how do you rate these services?

		Excellent	Good	Poor
i)	List of new books acquired	[ ]	[ ]	[ ]
ii)	List of journals subscribed/discontinued	[ ]	[ ]	[ ]
iii)	Preparation of bibliography on demand	[ ]	[ ]	[ ]
iv)	Indexing and abstracting services	[ ]	[ ]	[ ]
v)	Bibliographic services	[ ]	[ ]	[ ]
vi)	Literature search	[ ]	[ ]	[ ]
vii)	Contents of periodicals	[ ]	[ ]	[ ]
viii)	SDI Service	[ ]	[ ]	[ ]
ix)	Digest of scientific, technical and industrial information	[ ]	[ ]	[ ]

x) Any other (please specify) ....

3.5 Does your library subscribe to the journals in your area of specialisation?

i) Indexing journals Yes/No

ii) Abstracting journals Yes/No

3.5.1 If yes, how do you rate these journals?

		Excellent	Good	Poor
i)	Indexing journals	[ ]	[ ]	[ ]
ii)	Abstracting journals	[ ]	[ ]	[ ]

3.6 Does your library provide following services?

i) Translation service Yes/No

ii) Reprographic service Yes/No

3.6.1 If yes, how do you rate these services?

		Excellent	Good	Poor
i)	Translation service	[ ]	[ ]	[ ]
ii)	Reprographic service	[ ]	[ ]	[ ]

3.6.2 Please indicate, how do you rate the charges for these services?

	Costly	Reasonable	Cheap
i) Translation service	[ ]	[ ]	[ ]
ii) Reprographic service	[ ]	[ ]	[ ]

3.7 Does the library have any arrangement to obtain the photocopy of material for you from other libraries? Yes/No

3.7.1 If no, do you feel need for the same? Yes/No

C. COMPUTERISED SERVICES

3.8 Does your library provide computerised information services to you? Yes/No

3.8.1 If yes, does your library provide following types of services?

i) Literature search Yes/No

ii) Index of periodicals Yes/No

iii) Bibliography compilation Yes/No

iv) Any other (please specify) Yes/No

3.8.2 If yes, how do you rate these services?

	Excellent	Good	Poor
i) Literature search	[ ]	[ ]	[ ]
ii) Index of periodicals	[ ]	[ ]	[ ]
iii) Bibliography compilation	[ ]	[ ]	[ ]
iv) Any other (please specify)	[ ]	[ ]	[ ]

3.8.3 If no, i.e. if computerised services are absent do you feel the necessity for the same? Yes/No

3.9 Does your library provide online searching of national and international databases? Yes/No

3.9.1 If yes, please specify the name of service(s)/database(s)

....

....

....

4. ORGANISATION OF READING MATERIAL AND READING ROOM FACILITIES

4.1 How do you find the arrangement of books/journals on the shelves?

		Excellent	Good	Poor
i)	Books	[ ]	[ ]	[ ]
ii)	Journals	[ ]	[ ]	[ ]
iii)	Research/Project reports	[ ]	[ ]	[ ]
iv)	Any other (please specify)	[ ]	[ ]	[ ]

4.2 Please offer your suggestions for better arrangement of books/journals/research and project reports, etc.

i) ....

ii) ....

iii) ....

iv) ....

4.3 Please indicate the kind of reading room facilities available in your library.

i)	Individual study carrels	Yes/No
ii)	Comfortable place for reading/study	Yes/No
iii)	Adequate lighting	Yes/No
iv)	Any emergency light during light failure	Yes/No
v)	Seminar/Conference room	Yes/No
vi)	Any other (please specify)	Yes/No

4.3.1 If yes, how do you find these facilities?

		Excellent	Good	Poor
i)	Individual study carrels	[ ]	[ ]	[ ]
ii)	Comfortable place for reading/study	[ ]	[ ]	[ ]
iii)	Adequate lighting	[ ]	[ ]	[ ]
iv)	Any emergency light during light failure	[ ]	[ ]	[ ]
v)	Seminar/Conference room	[ ]	[ ]	[ ]

vi) Any other (please specify) [ ] [ ] [ ]

Please give your suggestions for improvement of the library and information services to meet your information needs more effectively.

....

....

....

....

[Thanks for your cooperation]

Appendix - II

QUESTIONNAIRE FOR INFORMATION SERVICES IN-CHARGE/LIBRARY IN-CHARGE

Please put [✓] mark or strike off either Yes or No whichever is applicable or fill in the blank/s for the following items :

1. BACKGROUND INFORMATION

1.1 Name of the In-charge : ....

1.2 Designation : ....

1.3 Sex : Male/Female

1.4 Age : ....

1.5 Educational qualification : ....

1.6 Name of the institution : ....

1.7 Name of the library : ....

1.8 Please indicate the year of establishment of the following:

i) Your institution : ....

ii) Library and Documentation Centre of the institution : ....

1.9 Please state the details of staff working in the library.

i) Professional Staff : ....

ii) Semi-Professional Staff : ....

iii) Non-Professional Staff : ....

2. LIBRARY FINANCES

2.1 Budget for the institution and the library for 1992-93 and 1993-94.

(in '000 Rupees)

Year	*Institution Budget*	*Library Budget (excluding salaries)*
1992-93	________	________
1993-94	________	________

2.2 Break-up of the library budget (excluding salaries)

(in '000 Rupees)

S.No.	*Category*	*Budget for 1992-93*	*Budget for 1993-94*
i)	Books	______	______
ii)	Journals	______	______
iii)	Computerisation	______	______
iv)	Others (please specify)	______	______

2.3 Please indicate the adequacy of library budget :

Fairly adequate [ ] Adequate [ ] Inadequate [ ]

2.4 In case budget is inadequate, what should be the percentage of the increase on total budget?

____

3. LIBRARY COLLECTION

3.1 Please indicate the number of volumes available in the following categories in your library.

Categories	Number of Volumes
i) Books	________________
ii) Reference books	________________
iii) Bound volumes (Journals)	________________
iv) Non-book material	________________
v) Theses/Dissertations	________________

vi)	Research/Project reports	________
vii)	Government documents	________
viii)	Conference/Seminar/ Workshop papers/reports	________
ix)	Standards, Specifications and Patents	________
x)	Pamphlets and Reprints	________
xi)	Any other (please specify)	________

3.2 How do you rate your library collection in meeting users' needs and requirements?

		Fully	Moderately	Partially
i)	Books	[ ]	[ ]	[ ]
ii)	Reference books	[ ]	[ ]	[ ]
iii)	Bound volumes (Journals)	[ ]	[ ]	[ ]
iv)	Non-book material	[ ]	[ ]	[ ]
v)	Theses/Dissertations	[ ]	[ ]	[ ]
vi)	Research/Project reports	[ ]	[ ]	[ ]
vii)	Government documents	[ ]	[ ]	[ ]
viii)	Conference/Seminar/ Workshop papers/reports	[ ]	[ ]	[ ]
ix)	Standards, Specifications and Patents	[ ]	[ ]	[ ]
x)	Pamphlets and Reprints	[ ]	[ ]	[ ]
xi)	Any other (please specify)	[ ]	[ ]	[ ]

3.3 Number of periodicals being received at present.

		Indian	**Foreign**
i)	By subscription	________	________
ii)	As gifts	________	________
iii)	On exchange	________	________

3.4 To what extent the periodicals subscribed in your library are able to meet the requirement of users?

		Fully	Mod-erately	Parti-ally
i)	Indian	[ ]	[ ]	[ ]
ii)	Foreign	[ ]	[ ]	[ ]

3.5 Please indicate the availability of non-book material in your library.

- i) Micro-film/Micro-fiche [ ]
- ii) Audiocassettes [ ]
- iii) Videocassettes [ ]
- iv) Slides [ ]
- v) CD-ROM Databases [ ]
- vi) Online Databases [ ]
- vii) Maps/atlases [ ]
- viii) Picture transparencies/photos [ ]
- ix) Any other (please specify) [ ]

4. TECHNICAL PROCESSING AND CIRCULATION ACTIVITIES

4.1 Scheme used for the classification: DDC/UDC/CC/Other of documents (specify edition) ________

4.2 Does the library has catalogue Yes/No

4.2.1 If yes, does the catalogue cover

- i) Entire collection [ ]
- ii) Partial collection [ ]

4.3 Type of catalogue

Dictionary/Classified/Other (specify)________

4.4 Catalogue Code used

AACR-1/AACR-2/CCC-5/ALA/No code/Any other (specify)

____

4.5 Methods adopted for issue/return of documents Newark/Browne/Ledger/Other (specify)

____

4.6 Do you provide the following services?

i) Book reservation Yes/No

ii) Interlibrary loan Yes/No

4.7 How often these services are utilized by the library users ?

	Regularly	Occasionally	Not at all
i) Book reservation	[ ]	[ ]	[ ]
ii) Interlibrary loan	[ ]	[ ]	[ ]

5. LIBRARY SERVICES AND FACILITIES

5.1 Is there any arrangement with other organisations for resource sharing? Yes/No

5.1.1 If yes, how useful is this arrangement?

Very useful [ ] Useful [ ] Not useful [ ]

5.1.2 Please specify the organisations with which you share the resources?

i) ....

ii) ....

iii) ....

iv) ....

5.2 Does the library has any arrangement to procure material from other countries on request? Yes/No

5.2.1 If no, do you feel need for the same? Yes/No

5.3 Do you feel the need for conducting orientation programme (user's education) for users? Yes/No

5.4 Does your library provide the following services?

i) Bringing out new additions in the library Yes/No

ii) List of journals subscribed/discontinued Yes/No

iii) Indexing and abstracting services Yes/No

iv) Bibliographic services Yes/No

i) On demand Yes/No

ii) In anticipation Yes/No

v) Literature search Yes/No

vi) Contents of periodicals Yes/No

vii) SDI service Yes/No

viii) Digest of scientific, technical and industrial information Yes/No

ix) Any other (please specify) Yes/No

5.5 Do you provide translation service? Yes/No

5.5.1 If yes, please indicate the languages covered.

English	[ ]	French	[ ]	German	[ ]
Russian	[ ]	Japanese	[ ]	Spanish	[ ]

Others (please specify) ....

5.6 Do you maintain a panel of translators? Yes/No

5.6.1 If no, who does the translation work?

Library staff [ ]

Research staff [ ]

Teachers [ ]

Any other (please specify) [ ]

5.7 Do you provide reprographic services? Yes/No

5.7.1 Type of reprographic services available.

Microfilming	[ ]	Ammonia Printing	[ ]
Microfiche	[ ]	Reader-Printer	[ ]
Photocopying	[ ]	Slide making	[ ]

Any other (please specify) ....

5.8 What are the charges for photocopying per exposer?

Rs.______

5.9 Is your library air-conditioned? Yes/No

6. COMPUTER APPLICATION

6.1 Are the computer facilities available in your library?

Yes/No

6.1.1 If yes, please indicate the type of computer

			Type	Number
i)	Micro	[ ]	______	______
ii)	Mini	[ ]	______	______

iii) Mainframe [ ] ______ ______

6.2 When was the computerisation of Library/Documentation centre started? ______

6.3 Please indicate the computerised activities of your library.

i) Accession list [ ]

ii) Book order list [ ]

iii) Current awareness services [ ]

iv) Circulation [ ]

v) Cataloguing [ ]

vi) Document delivery [ ]

vii) Retrospective literature search [ ]

viii) Serial control [ ]

ix) SDI Services [ ]

x) Other (please specify) [ ]

6.4 Please specify the software being used by you:

....

....

6.5 Whether computerisation had impact on the following?

i) Better utilisation of the library Yes/No

ii) Reducing the pressure on staff Yes/No

iii) Introducing new library services Yes/No

iv) Creation of in-house databases Yes/No

v) Efficiency and accuracy of library works Yes/No

vi) Any other (please specify) Yes/No

6.6 Please indicate the number of computer databases available in your library :

i) In-house databases ....

ii) CD-ROM databases ....

iii) Online databases ....

iv) Any other (please specify) ....

6.7 Does your library provide online searching to national and international databases? Yes/No

6.7.1 If yes, please name the most frequently accessed databases.

Indian	**Foreign**
....	....
....	....
....	....

6.8 Please indicate whether following facilities are available in your library :

i) Telex [ ]

ii) Fax [ ]

iii) E-mail [ ]

6.9 Does the library participate in any National Information Network such as NICNET, SIRNET, etc? Yes/No

6.9.1 If yes, please specify ....

a)	(b)	(c)
d)	(e)	(f)

6.10 Does the library participate in any International Information Network Agency? Yes/No

6.10.1 If yes, please specify ....

6.11 Suggestions, if any:

[Thanks for your cooperation]

Appendix - III

CSIR ESTABLISHMENTS

1. Central Building Research Institute (CBRI), Roorkee - 247667
2. Central Drug Research Institute (CDRI), Lucknow - 226001
3. Central Electrochemical Research Institute (CECRI), Karaikudi - 623006
4. Central Electronics Engineering Research Institute (CEERI), Pilani - 333031
5. Central Food Technological Research Institute (CFTRI), Mysore - 570013
6. Central Fuel Research Institute (CFRI), Dhanbad - 828108
7. Central Glass and Ceramic Research Institute (CGCRI), Kolkata - 700032
8. Central Institute for Medicinal and Aromatic Plants (CIMAP), Lucknow – 226016
9. Central Leather Research Institute (CLRI), Chennai - 600020
10. Central Mechanical Engineering Research Institute (CMERI), Durgapur - 713209
11. Central Mining Research Institute (CMRI), Dhanbad - 826001
12. Central Road Research Institute (CRRI), New Delhi - 110020
13. Central Salt and Marine Chemicals Research Institute (CSMCRI), Bhavnagar - 364002
14. Central Scientific Instruments Organisation (CSIO), Chandigarh - 160020
15. Centre for Cellular and Molecular Biology (CCMB), Hyderabad - 500007
16. Indian Institute of Chemical Biology (IICB), Kolkata - 700032

17. Indian Institute of Chemical Technology (IICT), Hyderabad - 500007
18. Indian Institute of Petroleum (IIP), Dehradun - 248005
19. Industrial Toxicology Research Centre (ITRC), Lucknow - 226001
20. Institute of Genomics and Integrative Biology, Delhi – 110007 (erstwhile CBT)
21. Institute of Himalayan Bioresource Technology, Palampur - 176061
22. Institute of Microbial Technology (IMT), Chandigarh - 160036
23. National Aerospace Laboratories (NAL), Bangalore - 560017
24. National Botanical Research Institute (NBRI), Lucknow - 226001
25. National Chemical Laboratory (NCL), Pune - 411008
26. National Environmental Engineering Research Institute (NEERI), Nagpur - 440020
27. National Geophysical Research Institute (NGRI), Hyderabad - 500007
28. National Institute of Oceanography (NIO), Goa - 403004

29.* National Institute of Science Communication and Information Resources, New Delhi - 110012 (After merger of erstwhile NISCOM and INSDOC)

30. National Institute of Science Technology and Development Studies, (NISTADS), New Delhi - 110012
31. National Metallurgical Laboratory (NML), Jamshedpur - 831007
32. National Physical Laboratory (NPL), New Delhi - 110012
33. Regional Research Laboratory (RRL), Bhopal - 462026
34. Regional Research Laboratory (RRL), Bhubaneshwar - 751013
35. Regional Research Laboratory (RRL), Jammu Tawi - 180001

36. Regional Research Laboratory (RRL), Jorhat - 785006
37. Regional Research Laboratory (RRL), Thiruvananthapuram - 695019
38. Structural Engineering Research Centre (SERC), Chennai - 600113

* NISCAIR was formed by merging the National Institute of Science Communication (NISCOM) and the Indian National Scientific Documentation Centre (INSDOC) on 30 September 2002.

List of Abbreviations

ADINET	Ahmedabad Library Network
AACR-2	Anglo American Cataloguing Rules, 2nd ed.
AEET	Atomic Energy Establishment Trombay
AIS	Associateship in Information Science
ATIRA	Ahmedabad Textile Industry's Research Association
BALNET	Bangalore Library Network
BARC	Bhabha Atomic Research Centre
BLISc	Bachelor of Library and Information Science
BONET	Bombay Library Network
BSIR	Board of Scientific and Industrial Research
CALIBNET	Calcutta Library Network
CAS	Current Awareness Service
CBRI	Central Building Research Institute
CBT	Centre for Biochemical Technology
CC	Colon Classification
CCMB	Centre for Cellular & Molecular Biology
CDRI	Central Drug Research Institute
CD-ROM	Compact Disk-Read Only Memory
CDS/ISIS	Computerised Documentation Service/ Integrated Set of Information Systems
CECRI	Central Electrochemical Research Institute
CEERI	Central Electronics Engineering Research Institute
CFRI	Central Fuel Research Institute
CFTRI	Central Food Technological Research Institute
CGCRI	Central Glass and Ceramic Research Institute

CIMAP	Central Institute of Medicinal and Aromatic Plants
CLISc	Certificate of Library and Information Science
CLRI	Central Leather Research Institute
CMERI	Central Mechanical Engineering Research Institute
CMRS	Central Mining Research Station
CRRI	Central Road Research Institute
CSIO	Central Scientific Instruments Organisation
CSIR	Council of Scientific and Industrial Research
CSMCRI	Central Salt & Marine Chemicals Research Institute
DAE	Department of Atomic Energy
DDC	Dewey Decimal Classification
DELNET	Developing Library Network
DESIDOC	Defence Scientific Information and Documentation Centre
DOD	Department of Ocean Development
DOE	Department of Electronics
DOS	Department of Space
DRDO	Defence Research and Development Organisation
DSIR	Department of Scientific and Industrial Research
ERNET	Education and Research Network
FITT	Foundation for Innovation and Technology Transfer
GSI	Geological Survey of India
IACS	Indian Association for Cultivation of Science
ICAR	Indian Council of Agricultural Research
ICMR	Indian Council of Medical Research
IHBT	Institute of Himalayan Bioresource Technology (Formerly CSIR Complex)

IICB	Indian Institute of Chemical Biology
IICT	Indian Institute of Chemical Technology
IIP	Indian Institute of Petroleum
IIS	Indian Institute of Science
IIT	Indian Institute of Technology
IMTECH	Institute of Microbial Technology
INFLIBNET	Information and Library Network
INSDOC	Indian National Scientific Documentation Centre (Now NISCAIR)
ISC	International Scientific Collaboration
ISI	Indian Statistical Institute
ISRO	Indian Space Research Organisation
IT	Information Technology
ITRC	Industrial Toxicology Research Centre
IVRI	Indian Veterinary Research Institute
KSIDC	Kerala State Industrial Development Corporation
MALIBNET	Madras Library Network
MIS	Management Information System
MLISc	Master of Library and Information Science
MPhil	Master of Philosophy
MRDF	Marine Research and Development Fund
M.Sc.	Master of Science
MYLIBNET	Mysore Library Network
NACIDS	National Access Centres to International Database Services
NAL	National Aerospace Laboratories
NBRI	National Botanical Research Institute
NCB	National Centre on Bibliometrics
NCCC	National Collection Centre for CD-ROMs Published in India and on India
NCL	National Chemical Laboratory

NCST	National Centre for Software Technology
NEERI	National Environmental Engineering Research Institute
NGRI	National Geophysical Research Institute
NIC	National Informatics Centre
NICAC	National Information Centre on Advanced Ceramics
NICDAP	National Information Centre for Drug and Pharmaceuticals
NICDROM	National Information Centre on CD-ROM
NICFOS	National Information Centre for Food Science and Technology
NICHEM	National Information Centre for Chemicals and Chemical Technology
NICLAI	National Information Centre for Leather and Allied Industries
NICMAN	National Information Centre on Management
NICMAP	National Information Centre for Machine Tools and Production Engineering
NICMAS	National Information Centre on Marine Sciences
NICMAT	National Information Centre on Tea Manufacturing and Marketing
NICNET	National Informatics Centre Network
NICRYS	National Information Centre for Crystallography
NICTAS	National Information Centre for Textile and Allied Subjects
NIO	National Institute of Oceanography
NISCAIR	National Institute of Science Communication and Information Resources
NISSAT	National Information System for Science and Technology
NISTADS	National Institute of Science, Technology and Development Studies

NML	National Metallurgical Laboratory
NPL	National Physical Laboratory
OCLC	On-line Computer Library Centre
ONGC	Oil and Natural Gas Commission
OSTA	Ocean Science and Technology Agency
PID	Publications & Information Directorate
PUNENET	Pune Library Network
R&D	Research and Development
RRL	Regional Research Laboratory
SDI	Selective Dissemination of Information
SERC	Structural Engineering Research Centre
SIRNET	Scientific and Industrial Research Network
TDEs	Technical Development Establishments
TIFR	Tata Institute of Fundamental Research
TUD	Technology Utilization Division
UDC	Universal Decimal Classification
VJTI	Victoria Jublee Technical Institute
WHO	World Health Organisation
WIPO	World Intellectual Property Organisation
WRIC	Western Regional Instrumentation Centre

List of Selected Readings

Adeyemi, Nathaniel Motunbade. Co-operation among libraries in Nigeria: A pilot study. Ph. D. Thesis. Univeısity of Pittsburgh, 1975. 163p.

Aggarwal, D. S. Lectures on universe of knowledge. Delhi: Academic Publications, 1985.

Ahlstrom, David and Nair, Anil. The role of know-why in knowledge development within biomedicine: Lessons for organizations. *Asia Pacific Journal of Management,* 17(2), 2000, 331-351.

Ahmed, Rais and Rakesh, Madhulika. Insight into scientific research: In Indian universities and the institutes of technology. New Delhi: Council of Scientific and Industrial Research (CSIR), 1991. 154p.

Ala, Roland Astall. Special libraries and information bureaux. Asia Publishing House, 1966.

Allen, B. Academic information services: A library management perspective. *Library Trends,* 43, 1995, 645-662.

Arnold, K. Virtual transformations: The evolution of publication media. *Library Trends,* 43, 1995, 609-626.

Ashworth, Wilfred. Special librarianship. London: Clive Bingley, 1979.

Atkinson, R. Library functions, scholarly communication, and the foundation of the digital library: laying claim to the control zone. *Library Quarterly,* 66, 1996, 239-265.

Bandyopadhyay, P. K. Information technology: The promise it holds. *Yojana,* 42(1), 1998, 59-61.

Bannerjee, B. N. Rise of science-technology libraries in India. In: Sen, N. B., (ed.). *Development of Libraries in New India.* New Delhi: New Book Society of India, 1965, 205-14.

Barron, T. A. Smarter Frankenstein: The merging of e-learning and knowledge management. Alexandria, VA: American Society for Training and Development (ASTD), 2000.

Bawden, David. User-oriented evaluation of information system and services. Hampshire: Gower Publishing, 1990. 209p.

Beerli, Alfred J., Falk, Svenja and Diemers, Daniel, eds. Knowledge management and networked environments: Leveraging intellectual capital in virtual business communities. New York: AMACOM Books, 2003.

Bernal, J. D. Preliminary analysis of pilot questionnaire on the use of scientific information. (Royal Society Information Conference, 1948).

Berners-Lee, Tim with Fischetti, Mark. Weaving the Web: The original design and ultimate destiny of the World Wide Web. USA: HarperBusiness, 1999. 246p.

Berry, J.W. Digital libraries: New initiatives with worldwide implications. *IFLA Journal*, 22, 1996, 9-17.

Bolef, Doris. The special library. In: Katz, Bill (ed.). *The How-to-do-it Manual for Small Libraries.* New York: Neal-Schuman Publishers, 1988, 54-63.

Bonn, G. S. Evaluation of the collection. *Library Trends*, 22, 1973-1974, 265-304.

Borgman, Christine L. The invisible library: Paradox of the global information infrastructure. *Library Trends*, 51(4), Spring 2003, 652-674.

Borgman, C. L. et al. Rethinking online monitoring methods for information retrieval systems: From search product to search process. *Journal of the American Society for Information Science*, 47, 1996, 568-583.

Borgman, Christine L. et al. Social aspects of digital libraries: Final report to the National Science Foundation, 1996, 35p.

Available:http://www.ifla.org/documents/libraries/net/ ucladl01.pdf

Bosseau, D.L. The formerly virtually neutral library. *Journal of Academic Librarianship*, 21, 1995, 121-122.

Bradford, S. C. Documentation. London: Crosby Lockwood, 1948.

Branse, Y. et al. Libraries on the Web. *Electronic Library,* 14, 1996, 117-121.

Brophy, Peter and Coulling, Kate. Quality management for information and library managers. Mumbai: Jaico Publishing House, 1997. 196p.

Bryson, Jo. Effective library and information centre management. Bombay: Jaico Publishing House, 1996.

Buck, Paul. Libraries and universities: Addresses and reports. Boston: Harvard University Press, 1969. 191p.

Buckholtz, Alison. SPARC: The scholarly publishing and academic resources coalition. *Issues in Science and Technology Librarianship.* Spring 1999.

Available: http://www.library.ucsb.edu/istl/99-spring/article2.html

Budd, John M. and Harloe, Bart M. Collection development and scholarly communication in the 21st century: From collection management to content management. In: Gorman, G. E. and Miller, Ruth H. (eds). *Collection Management for the 21st Century: A Handbook for Librarians.* Westport: Greenwood Press, 1997, 3-25.

Burk, Mike. Knowledge management: Everyone benefits by sharing information, *Public Roads,* 63(3), November/December 1999.

Available: http://www.tfhrc.gov/pubrds/novdec99/km.htm

Burke, Anthony Joseph. An evaluation of a communication support system for the dissemination of scientific and technical information in the development of public policy within the Massachusetts State Legislature and recommendations for future communications applications. Ed. D. Boston University, 1979. 232p.

Burkett, Jack. Library and information networks in the United Kingdom. London: Aslib, 1979.

Cain, M. Periodical access in an era of change: Characteristics and a model. *Journal of Academic Librarianship,* 21, 1995, 365-370.

Carrigan, D. P. Data-guided collection development: A promise unfulfilled. *College & Research Libraries*, 57, 1996, 429-437.

Carter, Jane Robbins and Zweizig, Douglas L. Are we there yet? Evaluating library collections, reference services, programs, and personnel. *American Libraries*, 16(9), 1985, 624-627.

Cawkell, Tony. Electronic books. *Aslib Proceedings*, 51(2), 1999, 54-58.

Chakraborti, A.K. Information use of industrial scientists and engineers. *Library Science with Slant to Documentation*, 15(2), 1978, 89-91.

Chandler, G. Libraries in the modern world. Oxford: Pergamon Press, 1965.

Cheweh, Steven Seokho. User criteria for evaluation of library service. *Journal of Library Administration*, 2(1), 1981, 35-46.

Chhotey, Lal and Bhatia, S. Adoption of information technology by agricultural libraries in India. *Annals of Library Science and Documentation*, 40(1), 1993, 6-11.

Chowdhury, G. G. Introduction to modern information retrieval. London: Library Association Publishing, 1999. 452p.

Clapp, V. W. and Jordan, R. T. Quantitative criteria for adequacy of academic library collection. *College and Research Libraries*, 26(5), 1965, 371-380.

Clausen, H. Online, CD-ROM and Web: is the same difference. *Aslib Proceedings*, 19(7), 1997, 177-183.

Cline, N. M. Local or remote access : Choices and issues. In: Chiang, W. S. S. and Elkington, N. E. (eds.). *Electronic Access to Information: A New Service Paradigm*. Mountain View, CA: Research Libraries Group, 1994, 17-24.

Conway, P. Preservation in the digital world. Washington, DC: Commission on Preservation and Access, 1996.

Creth, S. D. A changing profession: Central roles for academic librarians. *Advances in Librarianship*, 19, 1995, 85-98.

CSIR handbook 1995. New Delhi: Council of Scientific and Industrial Research, 1995.

Cunningham, S. and Rosebush, J. Electronic publishing on CD-ROM. Bonn: O'Reilly, 1996.

Dannelly, G. N. Resource sharing in the electronic era: Potentials and paradoxes. *Library Trends,* 43, 1995, 663-678.

Davenport, Thomas H. and Prusak, Laurence. Working knowledge. Boston: Harvard Business School Press, 1998.

Demas, S. et al. The Internet and collection development: Mainstreaming selection of Internet resources. *Library Resources & Technical Services,* 39, 1995, 275-290.

Deshmukh, C. D. Reflections on finance education and society. Delhi: Motilal Banarsidass, 1972. 238p.

Dickinson, G. K. Selection and evaluation of electronic resources. Englewood, CO: Libraries Unlimited, 1994.

Diwakar, K. K. Knowledge culture. *ERP Journal,* 1(10), 1999, 28-31.

Dongaonkar, Dayanand. Higher education in India: The varied dimensions – convocation address. *University News,* 42(21), 2004, 22-25, 28.

Dood, James B. The gap in standards for special libraries. *Library Trends,* 31(1), 1982, 85-91.

Dougherty, R. M. and Hughes, C. Preferred futures for libraries. Mountain view, CA: Research Libraries Group, 1991.

Doustdar, Yahya. A design for co-operation and networking among academic libraries of Iran. Ph. D. Thesis. Case Western Reserve University, 1980. 419p.

Dow, R. F., Meringolo, S., and St. Clair, G. Academic collections in a changing environment. In: McCable, G. B. and Person, R. J. (eds.). *Academic Libraries: Their Rationale and Role in American Higher Education.* Westport, CT: Greenwood Press, 1995.

Drucker, Peter. Knowledge work. *Executive Excellence,* June 2000, 11-12.

DuMont, Paul F. and DuMont, Rosemary Ruhig. A goal typology and systems model of library effectiveness. *Journal of Library Administration,* 2(1), 1981, 13-23.

DuMont, Rosemary Ruhig, DuMont, Paul F. Assessing the effectiveness of library service. Urbana: Illinois University, Graduate School of Library and Information Science, 1981. 24p. (Occasional Paper No. 152)

Dunkin, Ruth. Motivating knowledge workers: Lessons to and from the corporate sector. *Higher Education Management and Policy,* 15(3), 2003, 41-49.

Edenius, Mats and Borgerson, Janet. To manage knowledge by intranet. *Journal of Knowledge Management,* 7(5), 2003, 124-136.

Ewing, K. and Hauptman, R. Is traditional reference service obsolete? *Journal of Academic Librarianship,* 21, 1995, 3-6.

Foskett, D. J. Information service in libraries. New Delhi: Akashdeep, 1990.

Fox, E. A. et al., eds. Digital libraries. *Communications of the ACM,* 38(4), 1995, 15-110.

Gates, Jean Key. Introduction to librarianship. 3rd ed. New York: Neal-Schuman Publishers, 1990. 198p.

Ghikas, M. W. Collection management for the 21st century. *Journal of Library Administration,* 11(1/2), 1989, 119-135.

Gothberg, Helen M. User satisfaction with a librarian's immediate and nonimmediate verbal-nonverbal communication. Ph. D. Thesis. University of Denver, 1974. 132p.

Goyal, D. P. Management information system: Concept and application. New Delhi: Deep & Deep Publications, 1994. 203p.

Gupta, Anuradha. Growth and development of Government of India libraries in Delhi. Ph. D. Thesis. Delhi: Delhi University, 1991.

Handy, C. The age of paradox. Boston: Harvard Business School Press, 1994.

Hannabus, Stuart. The importance of performance measures. *Library Review,* 36(4), 1987, 248-253.

Hansen, M. T., Nohria, N. and Tierney, T. What's your strategy for managing knowledge? *Harvard Business Review,* 77(2), 1999, 106-116.

Hansen, Morten T. and von Oetinger, Bolko. Introducing T-shaped managers: Knowledge management's next generation. *Harvard Business Review,* 79(3), 2001, 106-116.

Haravu, L. J. et.al. Computer applications to library and information work at the technical information centre, BHEL Corporate R&D Division. *Annuals of Library Science and Documentation,* 32(1-2), 1985, 41-49.

Haravu, L. J. Library automation and networking in India - An overview of recent developments. *Annals of Library Science and Documentation,* 40(1), 1993, 32-40.

Harrison, T. M. and Stephen, T. D. The electronic journal as the heart of an online scholarly community. *Library Trends,* 43, 1995, 592-608.

Hawgood, J. and Morley, R. Project for evaluating the benefits from university libraries. Durham University OSTI. Report 5056, 1969.

Hayes, R. M. and Borko, H. Mathematical model of information system use. *Information Processing and Management,* 19(3), 1983, 173-186.

Henderson, Madeline M. Standards: Developments and impacts. *Special Libraries,* 72(20), 1981, 142-148.

Henkle, H. W. Introduction: What is special? *Library Trends,* 1, 1952, 169-172.

Henry, Chauncey. Regional and national computer networks for resource sharing by colleges and universities. In: Kent, Allen (ed.). *Resource Sharing in Libraries.* New York: Marcel Dekker, Inc., 1974, 268p.

Hitchingham, Eileen. Collection management in light of electronic publishing. *Information Technology and Libraries,* 15, 1996, 38-41.

Holholt, Pat. The nature of information and its influence on libraries. *Special Libraries,* 1984, 247-251.

Hunter, K. Issues and experiments in electronic publishing and dissemination. *Information Technology and Libraries,* 13, 1994, 127-132.

Ifidon, Sam E. The evaluation of performance. *Libri*, 36(3), 1986, 224-239.

Ifidon, S. E. A quantitative assessment of adequacy of Nigerian university library collections in the humanities and the social sciences in relation to postgraduate research. Ph. D. Thesis. University of Ibadan, 1977. 286p.

Inder Vir. Science communication: Problems and prospects with special reference to scientific and technical libraries in India. Ph. D. Thesis. Chandigarh: Punjab University, 1986.

India. Education Commission (1964-66) (Chairman: D. S. Kothari) Report. 275p.

Information sources: Tracking down 'Grey Literature'. *Information Today & Tomorrow*, 14(2/3), 1995, 11.

In service of the nation: CSIR's contributions to national development. New Delhi: Council of Scientific and Industrial Research, 1988.

Jasperse, J. Are we losing a generation of manuscripts? *Online and CD-ROM Review*, 21(2), 1997, 30-32.

Jeffcoate, J. Multimedia in practice: Technology and applications. New York: Prentice-Hall, 1995.

Joffe, Ruth. Determining the effectiveness of the use made of the industrial and management engineering library. Israel: Technion-Israel Institute of technology, 1971.

Johns, Ada Winifred. Special libraries: Development of the concept, their organisations, and their services. Metuchen: The Scarecrow Press, 1968.

Joshi, Navin Chandra. Management information system. *Lok Udyog*, 13(9), 1979, 53-55.

Kaegbein, P. National collection building in the Federal Republic of Germany. *The Journal of Academic Librarianship*, 13, 1987, 81-85.

Kaniki, Andrew M. Meeting the needs of agricultural researchers in Africa: The role of unpublished reports. *Information Development*, 8(2), 1992, 83-89.

Kanwal, D. R. Growth and development of social science

research libraries. Ph. D. Thesis. Delhi: Delhi University, 1990.

Kashyap, B. C., et al., comp. and eds. CSIR handbook. New Delhi: Council of Scientific and Industrial Research, 1989.

Kaul, H. K. DELNET: An Indian model of library resource sharing. In: *Naclin'98 National Annual Convention on Library and Information Networking.* 16th-18th November, 1998. Souvenir. New Delhi: Delhi Library Network, 1998.

Kaul, H. K. Library Networks: An Indian experience. New Delhi: Virgo, 1992.

Kent, Allen and Galvin, Thomas J. eds. Information technology: Critical choices for library decision-makers. New York: Marcel Dekker Inc., 1982. 477p.

Kent, A. and Galvin, Thomas. Library resource sharing proceedings of the 1976 conference on resource sharing in libraries Pitsburg, Pennsylvania. New York: Marcel Dekker, 1977.

Khanna, J. K. Handbook of library information systems and services. New Delhi: Beacon Books, 1996.

Kidwell, Jillinda J. et al. Applying corporate knowledge management practices in higher education. *EDUCAUSE Quarterly,* 4, 2000, 28-33.

King, Donald W. et al. Library economic metrics: Examples of the comparison of electronic and print journal collections and collection services. *Library Trends,* 51(3), 2003, 376-400.

Kohl, David F. Resource sharing in a changing Ohio environment. *Library Trends,* 45(3), Winter 1997, 435-447.

Kong, L. M. Reference service evolved. *Journal of Academic Librarianship,* 21, 1995, 13-14.

Koskinen, Kaj U., Pihlanto, Pekka and Vanharanta, Hannu. Tacit knowledge acquisition and sharing in a project work context. *International Journal of Project Management,* 21(4), 2003, 281-290.

Kovacs, D. K. et al. A model for planning and providing reference services using Internet resources. *Library Trends*, 42, 1994, 638-647.

Kovacs, D. K. et al. Scholarly E-conferences on the academic networks: How library and information science professionals use them. *Journal of the American Society for Information Science*, 46, 1995, 244-253.

Krueger, Ruth. Special libraries in the United States. *IASLIC Bulletin*, 3(1), 1958, 17.

Krusas, Anthony Thomas. Business and industrial libraries in the United States, 1820-1940. New York: Special Libraries Association, 1965. 133p.

Kumar, R. P. and Attri, P. Development of new technologies in India and their impact on the dissemination of information. *International Library Reviews*, 19(4), 1987, 360-387.

Kuruvilla, P. K. Legal aspects of patenting and information support. *Library Science with a slant to Documentation*, 18(1), 1981, 37-53.

INSA. Pursuit and promotion of science: The Indian experience. New Delhi: Indian National Science Academy, 2001, 399p.

IIT Review Committee, 1986. Ministry of Human Resource Development, Government of India.

Ladendorf, Janice. The special librarian in the modern world. *Special Libraries*, 61, December 1970.

Lancaster, F. W. Evaluation of information services: A typology. In: Ingwersen, Peter, Kajberg, Leif and Petersen, Annelise Mark (eds.). *Information Technology and Information Use: Towards a Unified View of Information and Information Technology.* London: Taylor Graham, 1986, 147-155 & 194.

Lancaster, F.W. et al. Evaluation of interactive knowledge-based systems: Overview and design for empirical testing. *Journal of the American Society for Information Science*, 47, 1996, 57-69.

Lancaster, F. W. The evolution of electronic publishing. *Library Trends*, 43(4), Spring 1995, 518-27.

Lancaster, F. W. If you want to evaluate your library...? London: The Library Association, 1988.

Lancaster, F. W. Libraries and librarians in an age of electronics. Arlington, VA: Information Resources Press, 1982.

Lancaster, F. W. The measurement and evaluation of information services. In: Olsgaard, John N. (ed.). *Principles and Applications of Information Science: For Library Professionals.* Chicago: American Library Association, 1989, 120-136.

Lancaster, F. W. The measurement and evaluation of library services. Washington, DC: Information Resources Press, 1977.

Lancaster, F. W. The measurement and evaluation of library services. 2nd ed. Arlington, VA: Information Resources Press, 1991.

Lancaster, F. W. The paperless society revisited. *American Libraries,* 16 September, 1985, 554.

Lancaster, F. W. et al. The relationship between literature scatter and journal accessibility in an academic special library. *Collection Building,* 11(1), 1991, 19-22.

Lancaster, F.W. and Loescher, J. The corporate library and issues management. *Library Trends,* 43, 1994, 159-169.

Lancaster, F. W. and Sandore, Beth. Technology and management in library and information services. London: Library Association, 1997. 322p.

Lang, J. Managerial concerns in knowledge management. *Journal of Knowledge Management,* 5(1), 2001, 43-57.

Laudon, K. and Laudon, J. Management information systems-organisation and technology in the networked enterprise. Englewood Cliffs, N.J.: Prentice Hall, 1999.

Lee, Sul H., ed. Access, ownership and resource sharing. New York: The Haworth Press, 1994.

Leonard-Barton, D. Wellsprings of knowledge. Boston: Harvard Business School Press, 1995.

Leonard, D. and Sensiper, S. The role of tacit knowledge in group innovation. *California Management Review,* 40(3), Spring 1998, 112-132.

Licklider, J. C. R. Libraries of the future. Cambridge: MIT, 1965.

Liu, Lewis G. The economic behavior of academic research libraries: Toward a theory. *Library Trends,* 51(3), Winter 2003, 277-292.

Loring, C. Getting books and journals from other libraries. *Library Line,* 6, March, 1995, 1.

Low, Kathleen, ed. The roles of reference librarians: Today and tomorrow. New York: The Haworth Press, 1996. 173p.

Lowry, C. B. Preparing for the technological future: A journey of discovery. *Library Hi Tech,* 13(3), 1995, 39-53.

Lucas, Henry C. Information technology for management. 7th ed. Boston: McGraw-Hill, 2000.

MacDougall, Alan F. and Prytherch, Ray, eds. Handbook of library co-operation. New Delhi: Jaico Publishing House, 1997.

Mackenzie, Graham and Prytherch, Ray, eds. Librarianship and information work worldwide 1992. London: Bowker Saur, 1993. 273p.

Macrill, Rose Mary. Evaluation by type of library. *Library Trends,* Winter 1985, 267-95.

Malhan, I. Scientific and technical libraries in India. *International Library Review,* 20, 1988, 387.

Malhotra, Y. It's time to cultivate growth. *Leading Views,* March 2001. Available: http://www.youcan.bt.com/youcan/flash/lw/mar2001/cultivate_growth.html

Malinconico, M. Electronic documents and research libraries. *IFLA Journal,* 22, 1996, 211-225.

Mashelkar, R. A. Economics of knowledge. In: *India in the Knowledge Millennium.* ASSOCHAM Summit. December 18-20, 1999, Vigyan Bhawan, New Delhi. ASSOCHAM: New Delhi, 1999, 18-32.

Mashelkar, R. A. Wealth creation through knowledge. *New India Digest,* 4(6), November 1999 - February 2000, 28-33, 144-146.

Masse, Bloomfield. Role of the technical library in support of an information centre. *Special Libraries*, 57(1), 1996, 39-44.

Massil, S. W. The place for automation in libraries in developing countries. *Journal of Library and Information Science*, 11(1), 1986, 38-44.

McClure, Charles R. and Reifsnyder, Betsy. Performance measures for corporate information centers. *Special Libraries*, 75(3), 1984, 193-204.

McGill, Michael J., Brown, Gerhard E. and Siegel, Sidney. Chemical substances information network. National online meeting 1983: Proceedings of the Fourth National Online Meeting New York, April 12-14, 1983/edited by Martha E. Williams and Thomas H. Hogan. Medford, New Jersey: Learned Information, 1983, 367-376.

Mestrovic, Matko. How actual are democratic virtues? *Futures*, 30(1), 1998, 83-90.

Miller, J. and Doyle, B. A. Measuring the effectiveness of computer-based information systems in the financial service sector. *MIS Quarterly*, March 1987, 107-124.

Misra, Jogesh. History of libraries and librarianship in modern India since 1850. Delhi: Atma Ram & Sons, 1993.

Mohan, S. Forty years of research – CSIR overview. *Journal of Scientific and Industrial Research*, 47, 1988, 354-55.

Moll, Peter. Should the third world have information technology? *IFLA Journal*, 9(4), 1983, 296-308.

Mookerjee, S. Special libraries, our problems. *IASLIC Bulletin*, 4(1), 1959, 118.

Morse, Philip M. Library effectiveness: A systems approach. Cambridge: The MIT Press, 1968.

Mount, Ellis, ed. Collection management in sci-tech libraries. New York: The Haworth Press, 1989.

Mount, Ellis. University science and engineering libraries. Westport: Greenwood Press, 1985.

Mountifield, H. M. Electronic current awareness service: A survival tool for the information age? *Electronic Library*, 13, 1995, 317-323.

Mukherjee, A. K. Fundamentals of special librarianship and documentation. Calcutta: IASLIC, 1969.

Mukherjee, A. K. Librarianship: Its philosophy and history. Bombay: Asia Publishing House, 1966.

Mukherjee, B. Role of special libraries in India. *IASLIC Bulletin*, 18(4), 1973, 175-90.

Mukhopadhyay, Marmar. Educating the nation: Need for a dedicated satellite. Ahmedabad: ISRO, 2003. 35p.

Myers, Marcia Jean. The effectiveness of telephone reference/ information services in academic libraries in the Southeast. Ph. D. Thesis. Florida State University, 1979. 393p.

NACID inaugurated at ATIRA, Ahmedabad. *NISSAT Newsletter*, 13(3), 1994, 4.

Neelameghan, A. Use of information in research, invention and innovation studies, DRTC Annual Seminar, 9, 1971, 115-138.

Nehru, Jawaharlal. Convocation address by Jawaharlal Nehru, University of Allahabad, 1947.

Nehru, Jawaharlal. The Discovery of India. New Delhi: Jawaharlal Nehru Memorial Fund, 1981. 582p.

Nisonger, T. E. Collection management issues for electronic journals. *IFLA Journal*, 22, 1996, 233-239.

Nonaka, Ikujiro and Takeuchi, Hirotaka. The knowledge-creating company: How Japanese companies create the dynamics of innovation. Oxford: Oxford University Press, 1995.

Nonaka, I. et *al.* A theory of organisational knowledge creation. *International Journal of Technology Management*, 11(7/ 8), 1996, 833-845.

Norris, Donald M. and others. A revolution in knowledge sharing. *EDUCAUSE Review*, September/October 2003, 14-26.

Odlyzko, Andrew M. Tragic Loss or Good Riddance? The impending demise of traditional scholarly journals. In: Peek, Robin P. and Newby, Gregory B. (eds.). *Scholarly Publishing: The Electronic Frontier*. Cambridge: The MIT

Press, 1996, 91-101

Oldman, Christine M. The value of academic libraries: A methodological investigation. Ph. D. Thesis. Cranefield Institute of Technology, 1978.

Olsgaard, John N., ed. Principles and applications of information science: For library professionals. Chicago: American Library Association, 1989. 142p.

Orne, Jerrold. The place of the library in the evaluation of graduate work. *College & Research Libraries,* January 1969, 28.

Palmer, C. L. Information work at the boundaries of science: Linking library services to research practices. *Library Trends,* 45, 1996, 165-191.

Peek, Robin. European impact of electronic publishing. *Information Today,* :.4(6), 1997, 58

Peek, R. P. and Newby, G. B., eds. Scholarly publishing: The electronic frontier. Cambridge, MA: MIT Press, 1996.

Pickett, Richard A and Hamre, William B. Building portals for higher education. *New Directions for Institutional Research,* no.113, Spring 2002, 37-55.

Poh-Kam, Wong. Knowledge creation management: Issues and challenges. *Asia Pacific Journal of Management,* 17(2), 2000, 193-200.

Polanyi, M. The tacit dimension. Reprinted in L. Prusak (ed.). *Knowledge in organisation.* Boston: Butterworth-Heinemann, 1998, 135-146.

Potter, William Gray. Scholarly publishing, copyright, and the future of resource sharing. In: Baker, Shirley K. and Jackson, Mary E. (eds.). *The Future of Resource Sharing.* New York: The Haworth Press, Inc., 1995, 49-66.

Powell, Ronald R. The relationship of library user studies to performance measures: A review of the literature. Champaign, Illinois, University of Illinois Graduate School of Library and Information Science, 1988. 41p.

Prabhakar, A. S. and others. Higher agricultural education in India: Thoughts for future planning. *University News,* 39(24), June 11-17, 2001, 7-9.

Pritchard, A. and Aukland, M. Library effectiveness. London: City of London Polytechnic, 1974.

Prusak, L. The eleven deadliest sins of knowledge management. Boston: Butterworth-Heinemann, 1998.

Prytherch, Ray. Information management and library science: A guide to the literature. New Delhi: Jaico Publishing House, 1997.

Quinn, F. Roadkill on the electronic highway? The threat to the mathematical literature. *Notices of the American Mathematical Society,* 42(1), 1995, 53-56.

Quinn, F. A role for libraries in electronic publication. *Serials Review,* 21(5), 1995, 27-30.

Rahman, A. Science and technology in India. New Delhi: National Institute of Science, Technology and Development Studies (NISTADS), 1984. 212p.

Rahman, Abdur, ed. Science and technology in India, Pakistan, Bangladesh and Sri Lanka. Essex: Longman, 1990.

Raj, Janak. Effectiveness and efficient library usage under present financial limitations. In: Vashishth, C. P. et al. *New Horizons in Library and Information Science: Dr. Velaga Venkatappaiah Festschrif.* Madras: T. R. Publications, 1994, 449-458.

Rajagopal, N. R., ed. 40 years of research – A CSIR overview. New Delhi: CSIR, 1987.

Rajagopal, N. R., et al. The CSIR SAGA: A concise history of its evolution (Vol.1-upto 1965). New Delhi: Publication and Information Directorate, 1991.

Ramananda, B. S. and Ranjita, Chandran. Developing a computerised SDI service: A case study. *Library Science with a Slant to Documentation,* 24(1), 1987, 29-45.

Ra, M. Technology and resource sharing: Recent developments and future scenarios. *Advances in Library Resource Sharing,* 1, 1990, 141-153.

Rangachar, H. N. Nucleus of special libraries in renascent India: Council of Scientific and Industrial Research and its national laboratories. *Indian Librarian,* 10(4), 1956, 147.

Rangachar, H. N. India and its special libraries. *Indian Librarian,* 7(3), 1952, 72.

Ranganathan, S. R. Reference service. 2nd ed. Bombay: Asia Publishing House, 1961.

Ranganathan, S. R. Research libraries in Madras. *Modern Librarian,* 12(2), 1942, 77.

Rao, C. N. R. and Mohan Ram, H. Y., eds. Science in India: 50 Years of the academy. New Delhi: Indian National Science Academy, 1985. 109p.

Rao, K. Ramakrishna. Library development in India. *The Library Quarterly,* 31(2), 1961, 135-153.

Rao, S. N. Krishna. Mysore Library Network: MYLIBNET (Network with a difference). *Information Today & Tomorrow,* 21(1). 2002, 13-14, 30.

Available: http://www.mylibnet.org/nissat/vol21/mylibnet. html

Rao, Siriginidi Subba. Networking of libraries and information centres: Challenges in India. *Library Hi Tech,* 19(2), 2001, 167-178.

Rash, Wayne. Who's in Charge? *Knowledge Management.*

Available: http://www.destinationcrm.com/km/dcrm_km_article.asp?id=981

Ravindran, Sreedevi. New initiatives of NISSAT in 2000-2001). *Information Today & Tomorrow,* 20(3), 2001.

Available: http://www.mylibnet.org/nissat/vol20/nissr01.htm

Ray, Amulya Chandra. Special library in aid of research. *Indian Librarian,* 17(3), 1962, 151.

Ray, Morgan Roy. A survey and analysis of United Methodist Regional Resource Centers with suggestions for improved services. Ed. D. Indiana University, 1978. 166p.

Razasa, P. V. and Baker, N. R. Measures of effectiveness for a university library. Atlanta: Atlanta School of Industrial and System Engineering, Georgia Institute of Technology, 1971.

Realizing the information future: The Internet and beyond. Washington, D.C.: National Academy Press, 1994.

Reed-Scott, Jutta. Future of resource sharing in research

libraries. In: Baker, Shirley K. and Jackson, Mary E. (eds.). *The Future of Resource Sharing*. New York: The Haworth Press, Inc., 1995, 67-75.

Reid, E.O.F. Exploiting Internet as an enabler for transforming library services. *IFLA Journal*, 22, 1996, 18-26.

Roy, K. K. Future role of special libraries in India. *Special Libraries*, 65(5,6), 1974, 237-239.

Saha, J. Special libraries and information services in India and in the U.S.A. Metuchen, NJ: The Scarecrow Press, 1969.

Sanders, Donald H. Computers today. 3rd edition. New York: McGraw-Hill Book Company, 1988.

Saracevic, Tefco. Perception of the needs for scientific and technical information in less developed countries. *Journal of Documentation*, 36(3), 1980, 214-267.

Sasikala, C. Industrial library systems. New Delhi: Reliance Publishing House, 1994. 278p.

Seetharaman, M. N. Introducing online search services in India: Case study of experiment project in NAL, Bangalore. *Library Science with a Slant to Documantation*, 24(2), 1987, 98-107.

Sell, Betty Marie. Toward a general open system model for effective management and research of the academic library in its setting. Ph. D. Thesis. Florida State University, 1981.

Serban, Andreea M. and Luan, Jing. Knowledge management: Building a competitive advantage in higher education. *New Directions for Institutional Research*, no.113, Spring 2002, 5-16.

Shankar, P. S. and others. Status report on science and technology in India. New Delhi: Publications and Information Directorate, 1986. 83p.

Sharma, B. C. et al. comp. & ed. CSIR handbook. New Delhi: Council of Scientific and Industrial Research, 1993.

Sharma, C. D. Use of libraries: A guide to better use of libraries and their resources. New Delhi: Metropolitan Book, 1978.

Sharma, Pandey S. K. Libraries and society. 2nd revised and enlarged ed. New Delhi: Ess Ess Publications, 1992.

Sharp, Harold S. A survey of electronic libraries. *Special Libraries,* 49(4), 1958, 63-67.

Shera, Jesse H. Research and development in documentation. *Library Trends,* 10, October 1961, 224-242.

Sikka, Pawan. Management of scientific institutions in India a new model. *University News,* 31(51), December 20, 1993, 29-32.

Singh, Dev Raj. University library professionals: Some sociological aspects. *Journal of Library and Information Science,* 17(2), 1992, 2.

Singh, S. P. Impact of library services of the Indian Institute of Technology. Ph. D. Thesis. Delhi: Delhi University, 1994.

Sirkin, Arlene Farber. Marketing planning for maximum effectiveness. *Special Libraries,* 82(1), 1991, 1-6.

Skyrme, David J. Knowledge networking: Creating the collaborative enterprise. Oxford: Butterworth Heinemann, 1999. 311p.

Slater, Margaret, ed. Research methods in library and information science. London: The Library Association, 1990.

Sohan Lal and Singh, Prem. Growth and development of Agricultural University Libraries in India: A case study of Haryana Agricultural University Library. *Library Science with a slant to Documentation,* 32(1), 1995, 41-55.

Special Libraries Association. Objectives and standards for special libraries. *Special Libraries,* 55(10), 1964, 671-680.

Speh, Marcus. Knowledge management. In: Scammell, Alison (ed.). *Handbook of Special Librarianship and Information Work.* 7th ed. London: Aslib, 1997, 145-157.

Srinivasan, R. March towards digital economy. *CSI Communications,* 23(4), 1999, 5-8.

Star, S. L. and Ruhleder, K. Steps toward an ecology of infrastructure: Design and access for large information spaces. *Information Systems Research,* 7(1), 1996, 111-134.

Status report on science and technology in India: 1994. New Delhi: Council ofScientific and Industrial Research, 1994. 191p.

Steele, Colin. Netscope: The future for libraries in a networking environment. In: Dempsey, Lorcan, Law, Derek and Mowat, Ian (eds.). *Networking and the Future of Libraries 2: Managing the Intellectual Record: An International Conference.* University of Bath, 19-21 April 1995. London: Library Association Publishing, 1995.

Steinke, Cynthia, A. Sci-tech libraries of the future. New York: The Haworth Press, 1992. 238p.

Stenmark, Dick. Leveraging tacit organisational knowledge. *Journal of Management Information Systems,* 17(3), Winter 2000-2001, 9-24.

Stoffle, C. J. et al. Choosing our futures. *College & Research Libraries,* 57, 1996, 213-225.

Strable, Edward G. Special libraries: A guide for management. New York: Special Library Association, 1996.

Strauss, Lucille J., Shreve, Irene M. and Brown, Alberta L. Scientific and technical libraries: Their organisation and administration. 2nd ed. New York: Becker & Hayes, 1972.

Sutcliffe, Glyn. Slide collection management in libraries and information units. New Delhi: Jaico Publishing House, 1997. 219p.

Sweeney, G. P. The use of national resources to encourage the more effective use of information by industry. *Aslib Proceedings,* 29(2), 1977, 91-103.

Tandon, J. C. Measuring library effectiveness. *Lucknow Librarian,* 16(2), 1984, 65-75.

Tedd, L. A. An introduction to sharing resources via the Internet in academic libraries and information centres in Europe. *Program: news of computers in libraries,* 29, 1995, 43.

Tenopir, C. and King, D. W. Setting the record straight on journal publishing: Myth vs reality. *Library Journal,* 121, 1996, 32.

Thakur, D. S. and Thakur, K. S. Approaches to knowledge management in higher education. *Annals of Library and Information Studies,* 52(4), 2005, 115-118.

Thakur, D. S. and Thakur, K. S. Electronic publishing and its future. In: Mujoo-Munshi, Usha (ed.). *Information Management in New Millennium.* 19th Annual Convention and Conference of Society for Information Science, Indian National Science Academy (INSA), New Delhi, 27-29 January 2000. New Delhi: Allied Publishers, 2002, 354-366.

Thakur, D. S. and Thakur, K. S. Knowledge acquisition, management and sharing in higher education. In: Kamalavijayan, D. et al. (eds). *International Conference on Information Management in a Knowledge Society.* Vol.2. IASLIC, Mumbai, February 21-25, 2005. New Delhi: Allied, 2005, 703-709.

Thakur, D. S. and Thakur, K. S. Knowledge management: A growing discipline. *Library Herald,* 41(4), 2003, 259-274.

Thakur, D. S. Knowledge management system and its role in higher education. In: *Knowledge Creation, Preservation, Access and Management.* International Conference on Digital Libraries (ICDL), The Energy and Resources Institute (TERI), New Delhi, February 24-27, 2004, 18p.

Thakur, D. S. and Thakur, K. S. Online information resources and intranet: A case study of NIEPA Library. In: Shokeen, Ashu, Madhusudhan, Margam and Singh, D. V. (eds). *Knowledge Organisation in Digital Environment in Libraries (KODEL): Introspect and Prospects.* Seminar papers of 50th All India Conference, M. S. University of Baroda, Vadodara, 1-4 December 2004. Delhi: Indian Library Association, 2004, 438-455.

Thakur, D. S. and Thakur, K. S. Resource sharing and its necessity in the changing environment. *Indian Journal of Information, Library and Society,* 13 (3&4), 2000, 197-207.

Thakur, D. S. Effectiveness and use of library and information services of the laboratories of Council of Scientific and Industrial Research in India. Ph. D. Thesis. Gwalior: Jiwaji University, 1997. 540p.

Thakur, D. S. Growth and development of the library at National Institute of Financial Management - A case study. *Annals of Library and Information Studies,* 50(4), 2003, 163-174.

Thakur, D. S. Knowledge sharing in higher education. In: *Information Services in Business and Management Libraries: Recent Trends: Proceeding.* 6th National MANLIBNET Convention, ICSSR Western Regional Centre, Mumbai, 12-14 May 2004, 19p.

Thakur, D. S. Value of information and online information resources. In: *Emerging Digital Library Initiatives and Future of Business and Management Information in India: Proceeding.* 5th National MANLIBNET Convention, XLRI, Jamshedpur, March 6-8, 2003, 303-310.

Thorburn, Lyndal. Knowledge management, research spinoffs and commercialisation of R&D in Australia. *Asia Pacific Journal of Management,* 17(2), 2000, 257-275.

Tilak, Jandhyala B. G. Knowledge society, education and aid. *Compare,* 32(2), 2002, 297-310.

Turner, Anne M. Overdue reminder notices: A study of their effectiveness in medium-sized public libraries. D.A. Simmons College, 1979.

Tuttle, Marcia and Darling, Karen D. Advances in serials management. Vol.5. Greenwich, Connecticut: Jai Press, 1995. 138p.

25 years of CSIR. New Delhi: Council of Scientific and Industrial Research, 1968.

UNESCO. National science policy and organisation of scientific research in India. Paris: Unesco, 1972.

Walker, G. and Janes, J. Online retrieval: A dialogue of theory and practice. Englewood, CO: Libraries Unlimited, 1993.

Wallace, Burma Morgan. Analysis, usefulness and effectiveness of academic library consortia in the Southeastern States. Ph. D. Thesis. University of Alabama, 1975. 83p.

Ward, Gareth. Publishing in the digital age. London: Bowerdean Publishing Company Limited, 1998.

Waters, D. The distributed national collection, conspectus, resource sharing and co-operative collection development. *Australian Academic and Research Libraries,* 23, 1992, 20-24.

Watson, Ian. Internet, Intranet and extranet: Managing the information bazaar. *Aslib Proceedings,* 51(4), 1999, 109-114.

Weibel, S. L. The World Wide Web and emerging Internet resource discovery standards for scholarly literature. *Library Trends,* 43, 1995, 627-644.

Wesley, Cecile. Human resources for information development in Sudan. *Information Development,* 8(3), 1992, 159-163.

Wessel, C. J., et al. Criteria for evaluating the effectiveness of library and services. John Thompson, 1967.

White, H. S. Growing user information dependence and its impact on the libraryfield. *Aslib Proceedings,* 31(2), 1979, 74-87.

White, Robert L. Evaluating library services and programs. *Journal of Educational Media and Library Sciences,* 24(1), 1986, 53-65.

White, Virginia P. Handbook of research laboratory management. Philadelphia: ISI Press, 1988. 240p.

Whittakar, Kenneth. The basics of library based user services. London: Library Association Publishing, 1993. 133p.

Wilson, Tom. Electronic publishing and the future of the book. A paper delivered at the International Conference on Book Science to Commemorate the 450th anniversary of the first Lithuanian book, Vilnius University Lithuania, 24-28 September, 1997.

World Bank. Constructing knowledge societies: New challenges for tertiary education. Washington, DC: World Bank, 2001.

Valluri, S. R. CSIR and technological self-reliance. *Economic and Political Weekly,* 28(14), April 3, 1993.

Varnado, Kay Lorrell Ford. An analysis of library services at the University of the District of Columbia as perceived by administrators, faculty members and students. Ed. D. George Washington University, 1981. 229p.

von Krogh, G. and Roos, J. Five claims of knowing. *European Management Journal,* 14, 1996, 423-426.

Zaidi, J. A. et al. Emergence of new technologies in Biomedical information: A CDRI perspective. In: Kaul, H. K. and Das, B. B. (eds). *Library and Information Networking: NACLIN 2003.* New Delhi: DELNET, 2004, 421-431.

Ziman, John M. Public knowledge: An essay concerning the social dimension of science. Cambridge: Cambridge University Press, 1968.

Index